People, Jobs and Mobility in the New Europe

The **European Science Foundation** is an association of its 56 member research councils, academies, and institutions devoted to basic scientific research in 20 countries. The ESF assists its Member Organisations in two main ways: by bringing scientists together in its Scientific Programmes, Networks and European Research Conferences, to work on topics of common concern; and through the joint study of issues of strategic importance in European science policy.

The scientific work sponsored by ESF includes basic research in the natural and technical sciences, the medical and biosciences, the humanities and social sciences.

The ESF maintains close relations with other scientific institutions within and outside Europe. By its activities, ESF adds value by cooperation and coordination across national frontiers, offers expert scientific advice on strategic issues, and provides the European forum for fundamental science.

This volume arises from the work of the ESF Scientific Programme on Regional and Urban Restructuring in Europe (RURE).

Further information on ESF activities can be obtained from:

European Science Foundation
1, quai Lezay-Marnésia
F–67080 Strasbourg Cedex
France

Tel. (+33) 88 76 71 00
Fax (+33) 88 37 05 32

People, Jobs and Mobility in the New Europe

Edited by

Hans H. Blotevogel
University of Duisburg, Germany

and

Anthony J. Fielding
University of Sussex, Brighton, UK

JOHN WILEY & SONS
Chichester · New York · Weinheim · Brisbane · Singapore · Toronto

Published in 1997 by John Wiley & Sons Ltd,
　　　　　　　　Baffins Lane, Chichester,
　　　　　　　　West Sussex PO19 1UD, England

　　　　　　　　National　　01243 779777
　　　　　　　　International (+44) 1243 779777
　　　　　　　　e-mail (for orders and customer service enquiries): cs-books@wiley.co.uk
　　　　　　　　Visit our Home Page on http://www.wiley.co.uk
　　　　　　　　　　　　　or http://www.wiley.com

Other Wiley Editorial Offices

John Wiley & Sons, Inc., 605 Third Avenue,
New York, NY 10158–0012, USA

VCH Verlagsgesellschaft mbH, Pappelallee 3,
D–69469 Weinheim, Germany

Jacaranda Wiley Ltd, 33 Park Road, Milton,
Queensland 4064, Australia

John Wiley & Sons (Asia) Pte Ltd, 2 Clementi Loop #02–01,
Jin Xing Distripark, Singapore 129809

John Wiley & Sons (Canada) Ltd, 22 Worcester Road,
Rexdale, Ontario M9W IL1, Canada

Library of Congress Cataloging-in-Publication Data

People, jobs and mobility in the new Europe / edited by Hans H. Blotevogel and Anthony J. Fielding.
　　p. cm.
　Includes bibliographical references and index.
　ISBN 0–471–94901–9
　1. Labor mobility–Europe. 2. Labor market–Europe. 3. Alien labor–Europe. 4. Europe–
Emigration and immigration. 5. Population geography–Europe. 6. Europe–Economic
conditions–1945–Regional disparities. I. Blotevogel, Hans Heinrich. II. Fielding, A. J.
HD5717.5.E78P46 1997
331.12'794–dc20　　　　　　　　　　　　　　　　　　　　　　　　　　　　96–38721
　　　　　　　　　　　　　　　　　　　　　　　　　　　　　　　　　　　CIP

British Library Cataloguing in Publication Data

A catalogue record for this book is available from the British Library

ISBN 0–471–94901–9

Typeset in 10/12pt Sabon by Vision Typesetting, Manchester
Printed and bound in Great Britain by Biddles Ltd, Guildford and King's Lynn
This book is printed on acid-free paper responsibly manufactured from sustainable forestation, for which at least two trees are planted for each one used for paper production.

Contents

Contributors

Prefessor Hans H. Blotevogel
Department of Geography, University of Duisburg, D–4100 Duisberg, Germany

Professor Carminda Cavaco
Centro de Estudos Geograficos, Alameda da Universidade, 1699 Lisboa Codex, Portugal

Professor Tony Champion
Department of Geography, University of Newcastle upon Tyne, Newcastle upon Tyne NE1 7RU, United Kingdom

Professor Frans Dieleman
Faculty of Geographical Sciences, University of Utrecht, PO Box 80 115, 3508 TC Utrecht, The Netherlands

Professor Michael F. Dunford
School of European Studies, University of Sussex, Brighton BN1 9QN, United Kingdom

Dr Heinz Fassmann
Institute for Urban and Regional Research, Austrian Academy of Sciences, Postgasse 7, A–1010 Wien, Austria (now Professor at University of Munich)

Professor Anthony J. Fielding
School of Social Sciences, University of Sussex, Brighton BN1 9QN, United Kingdom

Dr M. Lucinda Fonseca
Centro de Estudos Geograficos, Alameda da Universidade, 1699 Lisboa Codex, Portugal

Dr Rein B. Jobse
Faculty of Georgraphical Sciences, University of Utrecht, PO Box 80 115, 3508 TC Utrecht, The Netherlands

Professor Franz-Josef Kemper
Geographisches Institut, Humboldt-Universität, D–10099 Berlin, Germany

Professor Russell L. King
School of European Studies, University of Sussex, Brighton BN1 9QN, United Kingdom

Dr Jan Mønnesland
Norwegian Institute for Urban and Regional Research, PO Box 1031 Blindern, N–0313 Oslo 3, Norway

Professor Sture Öberg
Department of Social and Economic Geography, Uppsala University, S–752 36 Uppsala, Sweden

Dr Franco Salvatori
Societa Geografica Italiana, via della Navicella 12, 00184 Roma, Italy

Dr Peter Shirlow
School of Geosciences, Queen's University, Belfast BT7 1NN, United Kingdom

Dr Ian Shuttleworth
School of Geosciences, Queen's University, Belfast BT7 1NN, United Kingdom

Professor Christian Vandermotten
CP 246 Department of Geography, Université Libre de Bruxelles, B–1050 Bruxelles, Belgium

Dr Gerald Wood
Department of Geography, University of Duisburg, D–4100 Duisburg, Germany

Preface

This volume represents the third of four publications emerging from the work of the 'Population' subgroup of the European Science Foundation's research programme on 'Regional and Urban Restructuring in Europe' (RURE). Most of the chapters included here started life as presentations to this study group at their various meetings around Europe; the others have been specially commissioned for this volume. At the lively discussions we had during these meetings, it became obvious that, although there were common trends and tendencies in the patterns and processes of urban and regional restructuring and population change in contemporary Europe, there were also lasting differences between countries and a degree of complexity of local situations that could not be ignored. We hope that this volume achieves a balanced picture, one which identifies the important common elements and yet does justice to the complexity of particular instances.

Hans Blotevogel
Tony Fielding

Part I
CONCEPTS AND CONTEXT

1 Introduction: Population and Economic Restructuring

University of Duisburg, Germany

INTRODUCTION: THE FOCUS

The central focus of this book is the mutual relationship between socio-spatial mobility of the population on the one hand, and the ongoing process of economic restructuring on the other. This perspective will be unfolded through a set of theoretical as well as empirical contributions with reference to different European countries and regions.

The two domains of society, the production system and the population system, are usually regarded separately or even held to be largely independent of each other. Demographers tend to look at population as an aggregate of groups or individuals with respect to the most basic features of births, deaths, marriages, cohabitation behaviour, fertility, migration etc., while the economy is mainly seen as a kind of background variable which is not ignored but seldom considered in its complex interdependencies. Economists, on the other hand, tend to conceive of the economy as a distinct system with population as an exogenous variable. People are essentially seen as economic actors: as members of the labour force, as consumers, as entrepreneurs etc.

Our object, however, is to combine both sides in one perspective and to tackle the complex mutual relationships between population and economy with special regard to the emergence of the New Europe. The main arguments behind this object can be outlined as following:

(i)   In recent years Europe has witnessed a dynamic socio-spatial restructuring without historical precedent. The completion of the Single Market, the enlarged European Union, the socio-economic transformation of the eastern half of Europe and the re-emergence of nationalism in East Central Europe are just a few elements of this far-reaching process. The traditional political map of Europe showed a mosaic of equivalent nation-states, grouped into two political blocs divided by the Iron Curtain. This map has been superseded by a new one, the contours of which, however, are at best barely perceptible.

(ii)   Demographic issues are back on the political agenda. The observed and expected demographic trends and their political assessment are, however,

People, Jobs and Mobility in the New Europe. Edited by Hans H. Blotevogel and Anthony J. Fielding.
© 1997 European Science Foundation. Published in 1997 by John Wiley & Sons Ltd.

strikingly contradictory. On the one hand, an alarming fertility decline, a threatening future labour shortage and an ongoing ageing of the population are noticeable – at least in most countries of the western half of Europe. On the other hand, sustained unemployment, increased immigration rates and persistent immigration pressure from Eastern Europe, Asia and Africa seem to evoke just the opposite impression.

(iii)   Economic restructuring is occurring and even seems to be accelerating. As the main driving force the globalization of economic relations (especially flows of goods and capital) can be identified, increasing competition between firms, cities and countries and reinforcing the speed of production reorganization. The many spatial outcomes, however, are hard to generalize. Agricultural and old industrial areas are losing employment and population; new industrial spaces are emerging; large cities are substituting their economic base through a shift from manufacturing to service industries with variable success.

Although a great deal of literature exists on European integration, on demographic patterns and developments as well as on regional economic restructuring, systematic work on the mutual relationships between economy and population is still rare.

On the one hand there is a continuous process of economic integration of European countries. The Single European Market has become one of the main poles of the global economy. Strategies of firms and transnational corporations (TNCs) are no longer national, but continental and global. The emerging new economic geography of Europe implies a rearrangement of countries and regions within a new system of cores and peripheries, of metropolitan nodes, old industrial areas, newly prospering areas and backward rural regions. European integration and the increasing global competition of the economy cause a 'restructuring shock' to local and regional economies all over Europe. On the other hand, demographic processes still seem to be a national matter. Although (nearly) all European countries belong to the group of demographically 'advanced' countries, demographic figures of fertility, mortality, migration, urbanization, occupation, unemployment etc. still vary considerably from one country to another. Demographic processes are largely a result of national traditions, values, social conditions and politics. Two reasons can be offered for this: (i) the inertia of demographic processes compared to economic processes; and (ii) the importance of national population policy and national migration policy.

THEORETICAL APPROACHES

Our consideration of the general interplay between population and economy starts with a schematic representation of some contrasting characteristics (Table 1.1).

Putting some characteristics of the economy and population subsystems side by side may offer a first impression of the subject but hardly any deeper

Table 1.1. Some characteristics of the economy and population system in Europe

Economy	Population
Functional integration of national economies into the Single European Market	Declining international migration flows
Distinct inter-regional disparities of GDP	Assimilation of national demographic patterns
Rapid restructuring	Slow evolution
Long and short cycles	Long-term transition
Direct political control	Indirect political control
System behaviour influenced by large organizations (oligarchic decision pattern)	System behaviour influenced by individual decisions (atomistic decision pattern)

analytical understanding of the mutual relationships. What we need are theoretical concepts that enable us to look more closly at the interplay between economic restructuring and population change. Unfortunately, a well developed and empirically grounded theory is not available. Although an enormous bulk of literature on both economic restructuring and population development and a number of studies on both economic aspects of population and demographic aspects of the economy exist, little work has been undertaken on a systematic examination of the complex inter-relations.

It is impossible here to give a complete overview of all relevant theoretical attempts. But if we try to summarize and classify the varied spectrum of theoretical approaches in a very approximate way, two main threads of theories or strands of thinking can be distinguished: (i) neoclassical theory; and (ii) regulation theory.

The neoclassical tradition of thinking and theory building has been dominant for the last few decades and is still the main paradigm in economics and economic policy, although it is increasingly criticized in the other social sciences. The basic conceptualization is rather simple: economy and population are conceived as (at least analytically) distinct systems interacting through *markets*. The core connection is performed by the labour market where the supply of labour enables the economy to use labour as a main factor input (Figure 1.1). The availability of labour – in quantitative (number, shortage etc.), qualitative (skills) and monetary (wages) terms – can be seen as the main demographic factor on the input side of the production system.

A second important link is constituted by the markets for commodities and services. The earnings of the work force are the decisive monetary source of demand for consumer goods and household services. Although there are several other monetary circuits (social transfers, investments by firms, real estate etc.) which are not considered here, the main links between economy and population are performed by these markets where population is mainly seen in its roles of both labour force and consumers.

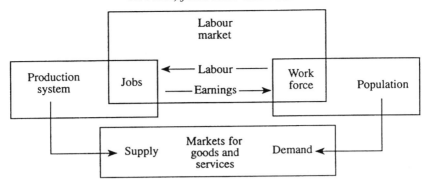

Figure 1.1. Production system and population in a neoclassical framework

According to neoclassical theory the nature of relations between the production system and population is essentially market driven: regulated by prices for labour and commodities as a result of the relationship between supply and demand. The market-price mechanism may also be applied to explain the spatial mobility of households and firms in so far as wage differentials (labour cost differentials) are taken to be the main factor triggering household migration and firm mobility. This principle is even applied to explain demographic behaviour, especially the temporal and spatial variability of fertility rates (cost–benefit decision to have a child).

Although these basic assertions may give a preliminary idea of the main inter-relations, this way of neoclassical thinking has increasingly been called into question. In the last one or two decades the French school of regulation theory has drawn much attention as a complement or even as a possible alternative mode of explanation. The main critical arguments against the neoclassical model from this perspective are threefold:

(i)   A close inter-relation between economy and society is claimed and the autonomy of either system is denied. According to regulation theory a full understanding of economic restructuring requires an adequate consideration of its political, social and cultural character and implications, whereas pure economic and demographic approaches are likely to become overly reductionistic.

(ii)   The nature of inter-relations is claimed to be inadequately conceptualized by the neoclassical market-price model alone, and to require a wide range of different modes such as asymmetrical power control or trusting cooperation. As empirical research has shown, labour markets do not usually meet the assumptions of the market model according to neoclassical theory. Although labour markets have been subject to significant deregulation measures in most western countries since the 1970s in order to improve their functioning as markets, they have become increasingly unstable, polarized and multi-segmented.

(iii)   The ahistorical (and ageographical) nature of neoclassical theory is criticized, whereas regulation theory tries to develop empirically grounded

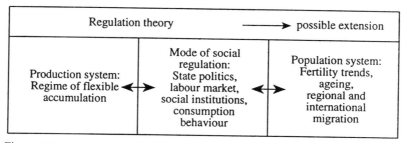

Figure 1.2. Production system and population in a regulationist framework

knowledge about societies in concrete historical and geographical situations. A considerable degree of consent has evolved over the transition from a former rigid 'Fordist' regime of accumulation to a recent type of flexible accumulation that is typical of certain characteristics of the present production system, at least in the advanced economies (Figure 1.2).

A crucial point is the nexus between the type of economic accumulation on the one hand and the mode of social 'regulation' on the other. Included here is a broad set of state policies, behavioural norms and social institutions that regulates social life on both the systemic and the life-world level. On this side of the nexus many links to the population system exist (Figure 1.2). Population is somewhat like a background variable of the interplay between the production system and the mode of regulation, although usually not explicitly considered in the regulationist literature.

The similarities between this theoretical concept and the neoclassical model mentioned above are obvious, but here an economistic reductionism is avoided and the social nature of the inter-relations between both the production and the population systems is stressed. Both models agree on the central position which the labour market holds as the main institution of connection.

Our theoretical models stress the idea that changes in the production system are mutually interconnected with the population system and cannot simply be seen as an independent variable affecting the socio-demographic side of the model. The widely held assumption of a one-sided impact is presumably partly caused by the remarkable mismatch of:

(i) rapid and turbulent structural changes of the production system (acceleration of innovation cycles, growth of new industries, decline of old industries); and

(ii) the relative inertia of population distribution (calm population system, levelling off of regional migration rates). The different time scales of change give the misleading impression of an active economic system and a passive population system.

This partial incompatibility of scales causes adjustment friction in both systems, mainly mediated through the labour market. An important example is the growing and continuing unemployment and loss of employment in depressed areas. Nevertheless, adjustment processes are alleviated by social subsidies from the state and the social security system. Fiscal transfers and social services have maintained income and jobs where otherwise an economic downward spiral would have set in.

With regard to the future, this compensating mechanism seems rather unstable. Inter-regional fiscal redistribution is mainly a matter of the increasingly jeopardized welfare state and the redistributive fiscal effects of the EU are so far rather small and partly counter-balance each other. The European Agricultural Policy, for example, favours the core countries, whereas European Regional Policy favours the peripheral regions. Inter-regional fiscal transfers have hitherto not been very effective and a powerful European system of fiscal transfers would require political unity and solidarity, which up to now has been exclusively a sentiment of national identity. In the longer term the EU will probably lack independent sources of finance and democratic institutions to legitimize the necessary taxes and redistribution (Mackay 1993).

PRESENT TRENDS OF ECONOMIC RESTRUCTURING

In this section some significant processes of the present economic restructuring are sketched extremely briefly in order to provide a basis for the following sections which will deal with the demographic responses and feedback.

As a starting point, there is a continuing contraction in mining, traditional 'smokestack industries' and other 'old' manufacturing industries. The main reasons for this decline are the lack of international competitiveness in traditional manufacturing branches and the shrinking demand for obsolete products. As most affected regions have failed to modernize their production structure, the declining demand for labour leads to stagnating or decreasing population, increasing unemployment, a declining demand for immigrant workers who originally staffed these industries and regions, decreasing employment rates and early retirement. In most countries, however, the decline of the industrial base in those areas is cushioned by public subsidies and transfer payments so that the effects on the population are weakened.

Another more recent type of decline affects the Fordist industries producing mass products for mass consumption. The following can be identified as the main reasons: declining international competitiveness of mass production, declining importance of scale economies and a growing differentiation of consumption styles. The demographic effects are similar to those mentioned above, but unlike the old industrial regions this experience of a shrinking manufacturing base is rather new for the affected regions: shrinking labour force, decreasing employment rate and increasing unemployment, reduced demand for traditional labour skills, a declining demand for traditional immigrant workers of the type recruited in the 1960s and early 1970s, early retirement and partly return migration.

Opposite to the decline of traditional manufacturing stands the growth of high-tech industries and producer services in (i) modern metropolitan centres (mainly producer services) and (ii) new industrial regions (mainly modern manufacturing industries). Economic globalization favours highly competitive industries with high research and development (R&D) input and high innovation intensity. These are mainly located in modern metropolitan areas and attractive rural areas with a good R&D infrastructure and a qualified labour force, but without manufacturing traditions, influential trade unions and environmental handicaps. In those regions a growing demand for skilled labour and increasing immigration of skilled international labour can be observed. Unlike old industrial cities, modern metropolitan areas usually experience sustained, although moderate, population growth.

Fourthly, the internal structure of cities is changing fundamentally. In contrast to the socio-spatial integration of the 'welfare city' of the Fordist era, increasing socio-economic cleavages are emerging according to the model of a threefold split of the city:

(i)   the shrinking segment of the 'Fordist city' with traditional industries, lower-middle classes, skilled workers, municipal infrastructure of libraries, public baths etc.;

(ii)   the modern business city with office buildings, hotels, shopping and convention centres, gentrified housing areas, predominantly professionals and other white-collar workers;

(iii)   the growing marginalized segment of the poor and unemployed, with a high proportion of new poverty immigrants and a growing expansion of the informal economy of the secondary labour market and increasing possibilities for ethnic entrepreneurship. The main effect is a growing economic, social and ethnic heterogeneity of the urban population, resulting in a volatile balance between increasing social and ethnic tensions on the one hand a multi-cultural diversity with a possible creative milieu on the other.

The fifth point refers to the ongoing internationalization and globalization of the economy, not only the completion of the European Single Market but also the increasingly global nature of markets for commodities and services and the rising amount of foreign direct investment by transnational corporations (TNCs). The resulting growth effects are by no means evenly distributed over Europe but are concentrated in a few cities and regions, mainly semi-urban areas in the UK and the Benelux countries. Investors from East Asia, for example, prefer greenfield sites, an international cultural climate and young, well-educated labour. One direct demographic effect is increasing international mobility of managers, whereas unskilled labour migration remains rather moderate.

The sixth point covers structural changes in labour markets. Whereas labour markets in the Fordist era were characterized by a predominant manufacturing sector, stable labour conditions, institutionalized wage bargaining, important internal markets between large firms and a dual segmentation with a large upper segment of skilled workers, post-Fordist labour markets have become dominated by service industries, increasing instability, multiple segmentation and persistent high unemployment. Greater flexibility of labour markets has led to increasing diversity and instability in employment conditions, the weakening of trade unions and a growing polarization between a highly skilled and well-paid upper group and a growing vulnerable lower group of unskilled and poorly paid workers with insecure jobs (Boje 1991).

The demographic effects of these restructuring trends in labour markets are poorly researched and not easy to assess. Little attention has been paid to the demographic effects of greater employment uncertainty on both younger people still in education and training and employees in insecure working conditions. Both groups are affected by fundamental unpredictability in their working and living conditions and by unsteadiness in their life perspective. Demographic results are late marriages or avoidance of marriage, more single-person households and extremely low birth rates. Although one might expect the opposite, another effect of this situation is decreasing migration rates, as jobseekers are increasingly oriented to local and regional labour markets, trying to substitute commuting for migration, whereas the large-scale job-oriented inter-regional and international migrations of the Fordist era are much less common. This trend, however, seems to oppose the neoclassical hypothesis, such claims that inter-regional economic imbalances induce migration to compensate.

This point leads to the question of whether the present processes of economic restructuring aggravate or mitigate the social and demographic cleavages in Europe. Looking at the literature the answer does not seem to be clear, as it depends at least partly on the theoretical perspective adopted (which discloses the implicit normative character of these theories).

A first type of rather inductive generalization suggests a general increase in international and inter-regional disparities and a deepening core–periphery divide. Much attention has been paid to the hypothesis that the spatial integration of the European economy will lead to a transformation of the former pattern of both international and intra-national core–periphery disparities into a single European system of central and peripheral regions, consisting of a 'European backbone' (the extended Rhine axis from London to Milan) and other large metropolitan areas (like Paris) on the one hand and the extensive peripheries of the southern, western, northern and eastern European fringes on the other.

Further empirical research has shown, however, that the European map of regional economic growth and decline cannot be condensed into a single large-scale spatial divide. In contrast to the Fordist pattern of the 1960s and early 1970s, no clearcut spatial pattern of growth and decline has yet emerged in the 1980s and early 1990s (Champion and Illeris 1990). Rather, the new map of European economic restructuring resembles a patchwork of regions and places fluctuating between expansion and contraction of production and employment.

It is not yet clear, however, whether this pattern is to be understood as an essentially new, post-Fordist type or just as a temporary transitional stage from former concentration to a new large-scale deconcentration.

In fact, there are at least some theoretical arguments for assuming a general balancing of European regional disparities. The removal of barriers to the mobility of capital, commodities and labour within the EU is supposed to reinforce balancing growth by enabling firms to use differentials between countries and regions more efficiently. Thus a spread of manufacturing production from the European core countries to peripheral countries with cheap labour is expected.

Actual data, however, do not confirm this simple neoclassical conjecture. On the contrary, it was the Fordist period of the 1960s and early 1970s when high mobility rates of capital and labour led to a convergence of regional disparities within the EC, whereas the trend seems to have reversed in the late 1970s and the 1980s. A possible explanation refers to the acceleration of economic restructuring which cannot be compensated for by an equivalent and generally decreasing rate of inter-regional and international labour mobility.

Thus, which 'new map' of European economic restructuring is emerging? New manufacturing industries are merely spatially scattered and do not lead to new large urban agglomerations, as did the traditional large plant industries of the former Kondratieff cycles (pre-Fordist and Fordist industries). Rather they are scattered in small and medium-sized towns in semi-rural environments. New industries are locally and regionally *embedded*, they are based on endogenous resources, especially traditions, qualifications, values and informal personal networks. Thus they do not induce large-scale migration flows but stability and slow growth *in situ*.

DEMOGRAPHIC RESPONSES TO ECONOMIC RESTRUCTURING

Compared to the short-term fluctuations of inter-regional and international migration, natural demographic development seems to be extremely inert. Changes of national or regional fertility rates, age and household structure etc. are usually fairly slow compared to economic and other social variables.

In the following section some basic features of recent demographic development and its interplay with the restructuring processes of the production system are discussed. Obviously a complete treatment of all demographic aspects cannot be attempted.

Fertility decline

First and foremost, the ongoing decline of fertility has to be emphasized. This 'megatrend', which started in the second half of the 1960s and has not yet stopped, has affected all European countries, although from different starting points and with different speeds and results.

Up to the early 1990s nearly all European countries have witnessed a slipping of their net reproduction rate below 1.0 (a rate which indicates a stationary population) and are thus confronted with a negative natural balance. In the 1970s Germany experienced the lowest birth rate in the world, but in the 1980s the most distinct decline affected the Mediterranean countries where the net reproduction rate fell to 0.64–0.69 in 1990 (Hof 1993, p. 97). Currently the lowest fertility rates are observed in Italy, Spain and Germany (around 0.5–0.6), whereas France, the United Kingdom and the Scandinavian countries are holding a mid position (around 0.7–0.8) and Ireland's net reproduction rate has only recently, in the early 1990s, slipped below 1.0.

This dramatic decline has quite convincingly been interpreted as Europe's 'second demographic transition' (van de Kaa 1987). According to this interpretation a set of combined social and economic factors can be identified: fundamental shifts of values and norms have led to a far-reaching switch from altruism to individualism, from family orientation to an emphasis on individual rights and self-fulfilment. The former norm of a child-centred family and family-oriented life options is being replaced by a trend towards single households, unmarried cohabitation and dinkies (double income, no kids). Avoiding having a child corresponds with growing divorce rates and a general instability in cohabitation (which is not caused, but is facilitated by secularization).

Shifts in basic socio-cultural norms and behaviour are connected with economic causes. When traditional altruistic norms are waning the explanatory power of the economic calculus of maximizing individual benefit grows.

Our first economic hypothesis argues that the decision to have a child is heavily influenced by an (at least partly monetary) cost–benefit calculation. In addition to direct expenditure on food, housing etc., the crucial question is whether motherhood regularly requires loss of a professional career or even of employment. This difficult balancing problem of mainly female life options can partly be solved, however, by extensive facilities for child care and legal provisions for motherhood protection and generous maternity leave.

This last point explains the surprisingly low negative correlation between female employment and fertility rates in European countries. Whereas Scandinavian countries are characterized by the highest female employment rates and a moderate decline in their birth rates, the lowest birth rates are observed in the Mediterranean countries where female employment has traditionally been extremely low.

Our second hypothesis argues that an adequate explanation for changes and breaks in fertility rates requires consideration of the economic conditions and expectations of the respective time-specific parental cohorts. The baby boom of the 1950s and 1960s, for example, coincided with the post-war economic upswing and – probably more importantly – with widespread economic optimism and steadily growing wealth and welfare. The same correlation working in the other direction, also holds true when the general decline of fertility in the 1970s and 1980s, and especially the dramatic decline of births in the former Communist countries of Eastern Europe around 1990, is considered.

In Western European countries the growing economic instability of the post-Fordist era, with the prolongation of education and training, the shortage of stable employment and the increase of insecure jobs in the secondary labour market, leads to widespread pessimism or at least scepticism with regard to life options. A significant trend to 'delayed adulthood' and 'delayed parentage', observed to some degree in all countries of Western Europe, most notably in Germany, Italy and Spain, may be interpreted as a demographic response to post-Fordist economic turbulence, with its strong competition for qualified training and the few well-paid stable jobs. Even more important than the actual chances on the labour market is the perception of a significant deterioration in life chances.

As regards the socio-economic transition of the former Communist countries to market economies, the Eastern European countries experienced a swift fertility decline without any historical precedent. The economic and political transformation starting at the end of the 1980s resulted in deep uncertainty and a widespread feeling of insecurity, due to the unfamiliar risks of unemployment and the loss of housing through dramatically rising rents. In Eastern Germany, for example, the number of births tumbled from 199 000 in 1989 to 80 500 in 1993, pushing the net reproduction rate down to a historically unique figure of 0.32!

A similar demographic shock took place in Russia where the figure fell to 0.56 (1993), thus declining to a level similar to that of Italy and Spain. It is as yet unclear whether this trend is just a temporary postponement of births or whether it is a permanent phenomenon according to the theory of the second demographic transition (choice between material wealth and children, shift of values and life options of couples and especially of young women).

The economic results of the long-time decline and low level of fertility rates can only be dealt with very briefly. In the first instance, improvements in child-care facilities and the education system have to be mentioned, followed by a boost to the labour market and thus a moderation of the widespread problem of youth unemployment. In the second instance, however, the lack of young demographic cohorts will reduce the ratio of economically active to inactive people and thus cause severe budget bottlenecks in the social security system. In some regions where low birth rates and out-migration coincide (mainly East Germany and rural peripheries of Mediterranean countries) a kind of demographic 'implosion' will occur, leading to severe capacity problems of public and private infrastructure and cumulative socio-economic erosion.

In the long run a general shortage of labour and a growing need for 'replacement' labour will occur. After the conflicting experiences of the immigration waves of the last few decades, it should be clear that a sound immigration policy has to be put on the EU's political agenda in order to establish long-term reliable conditions for both the potential migrants and the target countries. These considerations are, however, merely academic, as immigration policy still seems to be an 'anathema' in these times of rising xenophobia and persistent unemployment.

The changing European map of employment and unemployment

As mentioned above, the labour market can be seen as the main field of direct interplay between the systems of economy and population, and thus a closer look has to be taken at some important features of recent changes in the European labour market. These changes reflect different aspects of the transition from the Fordist to the post-Fordist regime of flexible accumulation which has transformed the European 'landscape' of employment and joblessness.

There are still striking national differences between the educational and vocational training systems in European countries. Figures on participation in tertiary education, for example, show a clear centre–periphery disparity. Whereas the European average for male students has reached around 20% (of a year's cohort), the figure is 27% in Denmark, around 23–25% in Germany, the Netherlands and Italy, but only 12–14% in the UK, Ireland and Portugal (Renard 1993, p. 130). Engineering and related studies attract more than 17% of students in Germany and the Netherlands, but less than 10% in France, Italy and Spain.

These striking differences can be interpreted in three ways. First, they reflect national traditions in cultural values, attitudes and behaviour which still seem to be effective regardless of cultural globalization via mass media and tourism. A second point has regard to the still important institutional differences in national educational and vocational training systems. Lastly, these differences reflect different ways and capabilities of reacting and adapting to the challenges of economic restructuring.

The Latin countries of the European South, for example, seem to value higher education in the arts higher than do the countries of Central and Northern Europe, where vocational training and higher education in practical and technical subjects rank higher. It seems somewhat bold to infer different capabilities of adjustment to the new economic challenges from those disparitites, but the contribution of the educational and vocational training system to an improvement in international and global technical and economic competitiveness is increasingly discussed in all European countries.

Our second point refers to a fundamental change in labour markets which have, step by step, worsened in all European countries with every economic downswing over the last two decades. Although international official unemployment figures are not strictly comparable, the European map of unemployment currently shows a clear mix of three patterns: a large European centre–periphery divide; national peculiarities; and intra-national regional disparities (Vandermotten 1993).

Exceedingly high unemployment rates can be observed in Spain, Southern

Italy, Ireland, northern UK and parts of Portugal. In addition, some pockets of persistent unemployment exist in countries of the European core: in Wallonia (Belgium), parts of northern France (Nord, Lorraine), the Ruhr (Germany) and the whole of Eastern Germany. Although there are some remarkable exceptions such as the relatively favourable employment situation in Greece, a distinct correlation between unemployment and the degree of continental centrality/peripherality exists favouring the most central countries (Vandermotten 1993, pp. 145f).

Superimposed on this European pattern are national differences caused by specific strengths and weaknesses of national economic situations and differing results of national labour market policies. The third pattern, reflecting intra-national inter-regional disparities, is created by structural deficiencies of regional adjustment capability, mainly observed in rural areas with high agricultural employment and in old industrialized areas.

A closer look at the most affected demographic groups reveals that the large-scale European centre–periphery pattern is accentuated by international differences between the European core and fringe of both youth unemployment and female unemployment. The highest youth unemployment rates, for example, are observed in Spain, Ireland, the Italian Mezzogiorno and in Southern Belgium (Wallonia) (Ballesteros 1993, p. 157).

In a similar way, the increasing supply of female labour meets an insufficiently expanding or even shrinking demand for labour. A relatively favourable situation has been achieved in countries with a high share of part-time employment, such as the Netherlands (30.8% in 1990) and Denmark (24.2% in 1990, cf. Hof 1993, p. 111). Adequate female participation in employment only seems to be achievable through a considerable expansion of part-time employ-ment and a transformation of full-time into part-time jobs. Although the growth of the service sector generally favours an extension of part-time employment, the striking differences and disappointingly low participation rates in many coun-tries emphasize the efficacy of national institutional impediments such as rigid wage agreements, wage discrimination and shortcomings in social legislation.

The causes of the European 'chronic disease' of obstinately high base unemployment can only be dealt with briefly without considering intra-European differences. Compared to the USA and Japan, the European situation is remarkably unfavourable and provokes the conclusion of a general failure of the traditional Keynesian mode of labour market regulation oriented to the goal of full employment. Whereas Japan succeeded in keeping nearly full employ-ment by improving international economic and technical competitiveness through speed of innovation and productivity increases, the USA expanded employment via real wage reduction, acceptance of high income differentials and low welfare expenditure. Western Europe, in contrast, witnessed distinctly lower innovation and productivity rates than Japan, but maintained on the whole the traditional welfare system with expensive social subsidies and rigid wage agreements. The incapacity of European labour market policy to solve the problem of high basic unemployment can thus be interpreted as a combination of two factors: the weakness of growth and the lack of political consensus over a far-reaching deregulation policy. There is still a widespread delusion in the European trade unions and the public generally that full employment of the Fordist type is attainable.

An even more difficult situation has occurred in the former Communist countries of East Central Europe and the former Soviet Union. Rapid socio-economic transformation resulted in a collapse of the formerly over-large public sector, which cannot be compensated for by the still weak private sector. A sharp increase in unemployment, which had been virtually unknown, was an unavoidable result, which seriously threatens the necessary basic consensus on the political transformation process.

There are many demographic implications of the generally deteriorating labour market situations in all European countries. The shortage of secure jobs and paid work and the multiple segmentation of labour markets have put into question the Fordist norm of a stable and reliable life-long employment career (which has never been the norm of female employment).

The delay in first employment, caused by both prolonged and improved education and training as well as by the lack of demand for youth labour, resulted in the emergence of a new life-cycle period of economically dependent 'post-adolescence' and an increasing delay in marriage and parenthood. The bottlenecks in entering the labour market, leading to unreliability in life courses and a restriction of life options, form one of the main reasons for the increasing proportion of single households and the postponement or even total avoidance of parenthood.

The increasing imbalances in the labour markets evoke demographically relevant reactions on both individual and political levels. Wage agreements and political measures to alleviate the labour market led to a reduction of weekly and annual as well as life-long working periods. The result was not only a reduction in individual work loads and a distinct increase in leisure time, but also a better distribution of paid work within the labour force. Due to delayed entrance and improved opportunities for early retirement, the working life span has shrunk from 45–50 years on average in the 1960s to around 40 years or even down to 30 years after long academic training. The Fordist type of typical employment biography, starting at the age of 15–18 and ending at the retirement age of 65, has virtually become the exception rather than the norm (Hof 1993, p. 30).

Early retirement is not only a measure of labour market policy but also an important factor influencing the living conditions of the older population. With regard to the expected future labour shortages and the increasing imbalance between economically active and inactive parts of the population, the strategy of early retirement seems to be rather risky and is increasingly becoming a subject of political discussion. Older employees are thus assigned a 'buffer' function in order to alleviate cyclic demographic effects on the labour market similar to that of the 'guest-workers' in the 1960s and 1970s.

A positive effect of labour redistribution via the reduction of working periods was the, at least partial, success of increasing female participation in the labour market. Female activity rates, however still vary considerably between European countries, showing high figures in Scandinavia and the UK, but still very low figures in the Mediterranean South, thereby indicating a distinct European North–South divide. Whereas the age-specific activity rates of the male and female population are nearly the same in Denmark, many other European countries are still lagging behind. Germany, the Benelux countries and France hold a mid position, but gender-specific differences are still strikingly high in the Mediterranean countries as well as in Ireland (Hof 1993, pp. 105f).

Ageing

In remarkable contrast to the turbulent economic development, there is a stable and persistent trend of increasing life expectancy in all European countries. This genuine demographic process, combined with the ongoing fertility decline, leads to a fundamental change of the age structure which is usually referred to as *ageing* in the literature. This term includes both an absolute aspect of increasing life expectancy and a relative aspect of a growing share of the elderly population (usually defined by the age of 55+).

According to Eurostat the life expectancy of the EU male population (12 countries) will increase from 71.7 (1990) to around 76 (2019) and the respective figure for the female population from 78.2 to around 81, thus reaching a similarly high level to the one which Japan and Iceland are witnessing at present. Hof (1993, pp. 160ff) estimates an increase of the average age of the EU population (12 countries) from 37.9 (1990) to around 43–44 in 2020. According to him, national differences will persist or even increase. Whereas in 1990 the range was 6.6 years between the 'oldest' population (Germany: average age 39.3 years) and the 'youngest' population (Ireland: 32.7 years), the range will be around 5–8 years in 2020 (according to different migratory assumptions). In all countries the average age will increase, most remarkably in Italy, Spain, Portugal, the Netherlands and Ireland (+6–8 years). In 2020 the 'oldest' population will be that of Germany and Italy with an average age of around 45–46, due to both increased life expectancy and extremely low birth rates.

The secular process of ageing will have far-reaching social, economic, cultural and political effects which go far beyond the scope of this chapter. A short look at the interplay with economic restructuring can only touch on a few points.

First, a significant general improvement of the economic situation of the elderly can be observed. There are, however, still considerable differences both between the European countries as a whole and between different groups of the elderly within each country. Distinctly unfavourable is the economic situation of a large group of old, single women without former employment who mainly draw very small pensions. On the other hand, however, several decades of peace and economic prosperity permitted a historically unique accumulation of savings and wealth (at least in the western half of Europe). Generally speaking, the income situation of retired people has roughly become similar to households with salaries from active employment.

The greater number and spending power of the elderly led to the emergence of large new 'grey markets' of consumer goods and services. As income from pensions and rents is largely independent of business cycles and of the economic success and failure of the respective regions, these expenditures are generally very stable and thus have a balancing effect on regional economic disparities.

Part of these 'grey markets' are the elderly-specific services of health care and old-age assistance. Not only has the growing number of old-age people led to a rapid increase in demand for care services, but also the growing substitution of care by professional organizations for home care by mainly female relatives in all modern urbanized societies. Care services have thus largely changed their nature from intra-family and charity to help to economically regulated *markets* offering new employment opportunities for both skilled and unskilled, mainly female labour. These jobs are, however, often poorly paid, part-time and insecure, but they do offer new employment opportunities for unskilled females, including immigrant women with otherwise very poor chances on the labour market.

The worsening balance of economically active and inactive people as a result of the growing share of retired or elderly people has already been mentioned, but will be looked at more closely in this section. According to a projection of the European age structure calculated by Hof (1993, 12 countries) the share of the elderly population (65+) will increase from 14.4% in 1990 to 20.2% in 2020. Including the age group of 55–64, the figure will increase from 25.3% to 34.1%. In Germany, for example, the relation between the number of employees and the number of pensioners will worsen from 2:1 in 1990 to around 1:1 in 2020, if present trends of delayed entrance into the labour market and early retirement continue.

It is as yet rather uncertain how the resulting budgetary bottlenecks of the social security system can be resolved. As pensions are largely financed not from existing assets, but from premiums paid by the economically active population, it seems rather questionable if the underlying inter-generation consensus will hold. More feasible are struggles between the generations for public funds when either pensions or other social provisions have to be cut or the premium load of the economically active population escalates drastically. According to this scenario the emergence of age-specific political parties does not seem particularly unrealistic. Although the existing 'grey parties' have had only limited success so far, for example in the Netherlands, their voting potential will grow considerably in relation to both the evolving age structure and the strength of inter-generational political issues.

CONCLUSION

The analysis has revealed a broad set of complex inter-relations between economic and demographic systems. Population can neither be taken as a simple independent nor as a simple dependent variable, but as a kind of 'background system', reacting rather inertly compared to the economic system and therefore often underestimated in its medium- and long-term feedback effects.

If the production system and population are inter-related in this way, the question that emerges is whether or not the model of a socio-economic transition from Fordism to post-Fordism can be transferred to the population system. Does it make sense to speak of an emerging 'post-Fordist demographic regime' that replaces the former demographic system corresponding to the Fordist era?

There are some signs which support this interpretation:

– the new inter-regional and international migration regime which has superseded the Fordist mass migrations of the 'guest-worker' type;
– the 'second demographic transition' leading to a persistent fertility decline and an 'anti-birth culture' stressing individual self-fulfilment via private consumption, social competition and professional career instead of an orientation towards family and children as an aim in life;
– the new household and marriage pattern with increasing temporary cohabitation and divorce rates instead of lifetime partnerships, with delayed or even abandoned marriages and births and a dominance of single-person households;
– the shortage of stable employment and replacement of full employment by an obstinately high base unemployment and an increase in the second labour market and in poorly paid insecure jobs, leading to widespread existential uncertainty and an unpredictability and restriction of life options.

But we have to be careful not to come to hasty conclusions. Three arguments against a simple extension of regulation theory to current demographic processes can be pointed out.

First, regulation theory may permit a rather satisfying understanding of the past Fordist era, but its interpretations of the present situation are confusingly divergent and agree only in a negative demarcation from the past, as is indicated by the prefix 'post-'. This main weakness of regulation theory confines its explanatory power if applied to demographic processes, as it seems rather presumptuous to subordinate a heterogeneous set of phenomena ranging from industrial production to fertility and ageing to a single, all-purpose theory.

Secondly, the at least partial autonomy of the demographic system has to be stressed. Prolonged life expectancy is a genuine demographic factor, virtually independent from the socio-economic system. Also, the 'second demographic transition', including the significant fertility decline, is only partially interconnected with the process of economic restructuring. Just as important are processes of cultural change including altered attitudes, values and norms.

And last one has to be careful not to generalize demographic patterns and simply to correlate these with socio-economic variables. Demographic phenomena are basically time and space specific. They depend largely on specific historical experiences of different age cohorts as well as on different national and regional conditions, e.g. housing policy, social subsidies, labour market policy etc. Hence it is hardly adequate to infer from the process of European economic integration a correspondingly simple demographic assimilation.

REFERENCES AND FURTHER READING

Ahnström, L. (1990) Economic Growth, Stagnation and the Working Population in Western Europe. London: Belhaven.
Bade, F.-J. and Kunzmann, K.R. (1991) Deindustrialisation and regional development in the Federal Republic of Germany, in Rodwin, L. and Sazanami, H. (eds) Industrial Change and Regional Economic Transformation. London: HarperCollins, pp. 69–104.
Ballesteros, A.G. (1993) Unemployment: regional variations in age- and sex-specific rates, in Noin, D. and Woods, R. The Changing Population of Europe. Oxford: Blackwell, pp. 151–60.
Boje, T.P. (1991) Flexibility and fragmentation in the labour market, in Amin, A. and Dietrich, M. (eds) Towards a New Europe? Structural Change in the European Economy. Aldershot: Edward Elgar, pp. 137–65.
Camagni, R. (ed.) (1991) Innovation Networks: Spatial Perspectives. London: Belhaven.
Champion, T. and Illeris, S. (1990) Population redistribution trends in Western Europe: mosaic of dynamics and crisis, in Hebbert, M. and Hansen, J.C. (eds) Unfamiliar Territory: the Reshaping of European Geography. Aldershot: Avebury, pp. 236–53.
Cribier, F. and Dieleman, F. (1993) La mobilité résidentielle des retraités en Europe occidentale. Espace-Populations-Sociétés, 10: 445–9.
Fielding, A.J. (1994) Industrial change and regional development in Western Europe. Urban Studies 31:679–704.
Heilig, G., Büttner, T. and Lutz, W. (1990) Germany's population: turbulent past, uncertain future. Population Bulletin 45 (4): 1–45.
Hof, Bernd (1993) Europa im Zeichen der Migration. Köln: Deutscher Instituts-Verlag.
Illeris, S. (1991) Counter-urbanization revisited: the new map of population in central and north-western Europe, in Bannon, M.J., Bourne, L.S. and Sinclair, R. (eds) Urbanization and Urban Development: Recent Trends in a Global Context. Dublin: University College, pp. 1–16.
Lesthaeghe, R. (1992) Der zweite demographische Übergang in den westlichen Ländern: eine Deutung. Zeitschrift für Bevolkerungswissenschaft 18:313–54.
Mackay, R.R. (1993) A Europe of the regions: a role for nonmarket forces? Regional Studies 27:419–31.
Morris, J.L. (1991) Japanese manufacturing investment in the EEC, in Morris, JL. (ed.) Japan and the Global Economy. London: Routledge, pp. 195–212.
Naschold, F. (1994) Beschäftigung und Arbeitslosigkeit im OECD-Vergleich, in Schönbohm, W. (ed.) Deutschland-Perspektiven, München: Olzog, pp. 142–50.
Noin, D. and Woods, R. (eds) (1993) The Changing Population of Europe. Oxford: Blackwell.
Renard, J. (1993) Education, in Noin, D. and Woods, R. (eds) The Changing Population of Europe. Oxford: Blackwell, pp. 127–34.
Rogers, A., Frey, W.H., Rees, P., Speare, A. and Warnes, A. (eds) (1992) Elderly Migration and Population Redistribution: a Comparative Study. London: Belhaven.

Tickell, A. and Peck, J.A. (1992) Accumulation, regulation and the geographies of post-fordism: missing links in regulation research. *Progress in Human Geography* 16:190–218.

van de Kaa, D.J. (1987) Europe's second demographic transition. *Population Bulletin* 42(1):3–57.

Vandermotten, Ch. (1993) The geography of employment, in Noin, D. and Woods, R. (eds) *The Changing Population of Europe*. Oxford: Blackewell, pp. 135–50.

Wendt, H. (1994) Von der Massenflucht zur Binnenwanderung. Die deutsch-deutschen Wanderungen vor und nach der Vereinigung. *Geographische Rundschau* 46:136–40.

2 Theories on Inter-Regional Migration: An Overview

STURE ÖBERG

Uppsala University, Sweden

INTRODUCTION

Migration between local labour markets is usually seen as either the result of individual decisions or as a response to structural forces. This chapter will deal with both ideas, but will concentrate on the latter, especially on how changes in the production system will influence migration. The ideas put forward will deal with contemporary Western European societies. Most ideas can be found in the literature – only a few originate from lesser-known research.

The approach in the first part of the chapter will be mainly *economic*, since theories from economic disciplines, including regional economics and economic geography, will be emphasized. It usually means that people are defined as rational in the sense that they are loyal to their preferences and maximize place utility functions in well-known market economies, in order to speculate in the outcome of decision processes. Several alternative approaches are possible based on, for example, microsociology (Rossi 1955; Holm and Öberg 1984), time-geography (Hägerstrand 1970; Öberg 1979a) or empirical generalizations. These will be studied in the second part of the chapter.

ECONOMIC APPROACHES

Wage differences

The following discussion on economic restructuring and migration is based on regional economics. Individuals use migration as a means to increase their standard of living or utility function. According to theory (and some empirical evidence) people migrate (net) to areas with a higher wage level. This is the basic 'law' of migration in regional economics.

The macro interpretation of this law is that a state of equilibrium tends to emerge. Migration is one of the processes to reach this equilibrium. There can be either a push effect in areas with low wages, a pull effect in areas with high wages, or a combined effect due to the difference. The larger the difference, the

People, Jobs and Mobility in the New Europe. Edited by Hans H. Blotevogel and Anthony J. Fielding.
© 1997 European Science Foundation. Published in 1997 by John Wiley & Sons Ltd.

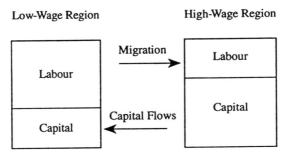

Figure 2.1.   The basic law of migration in regional economics tells us that different wage levels, due to, for example, different labour/capital ratios, cause inter-regional migration flows. In the long run, if mobility of capital and labour is allowed, market forces tend to create a new equilibrium where wages have the same levels in all regions

more wage earners will migrate. When regional economists model migration, the choice of model will reveal how much they believe in push or pull factors (Alonso 1976).

The distinction between push and pull factors is usually unclear from a scientific point of view (Öberg 1994). High income in one region can be a pull factor attracting migrants from a less wealthy region, but the same phenomenon – lack of high income – could also be described as a push factor in the sending region. A researcher's choice to label a wage gap, or any other regional difference, as a push or pull factor is a matter of taste, not a choice based in theory or differentiating against the alternative.

Also, when efforts are made to define a push factor in a region in relation only to internal changes over time, such as a period of specific high demand for labour, it is difficult to distinguish between push and pull factors. A larger flow of migrants to a region during a period of high demand for labour in the receiving region is not necessarily an effect of that demand. It could also be the result of an earlier low demand for labour in the sending region. From a technical point of view, delayed effects are difficult to sort out. Depending on how researchers treat the time lags, they can conclude that either push or pull factors are more important, basing their conclusions on the same time series of data. There are examples of this in the literature on international migration. For example, Thomas (1941) says that the migration flows between Sweden and the US were mainly determined by the economic conditions in Sweden, while Wilkinson (1967) says that the labour demand in the US was more important. Quigley (1972) shows that conditions both in the sending and the receiving country were important.

On the micro scale the decision to migrate will depend on the size of the wage increase and how long it will last. With a neoclassical approach (Becker 1993), the expected difference over time will be discounted to a present value and compared with the costs involved. Since young people can gain a higher salary during a longer time than people closer to retirement age, this will 'explain' why young people migrate more often. This theory can be extended from individuals to households, where the man and the woman can have different wage functions over space and time, and the decision to migrate is a joint process on the household level.

How do these wage differences between regions emerge? According to conventional theory, they may be seen as disturbances in the equilibrium due to changes in, for example, technology or demand functions. Restructuring in the production system will cause imbalance between supply and demand for labour on different local labour markets and thus to different wage levels.

A disruption to an equilibrium would, according to theory, normally lead to some adjustments and then a new equilibrium. If, for example, a large factory closes down in a local labour market, the first effects will be a surplus of labour which in turn will lower wages and thus create some net out-migration and attract some new firms. A new equilibrium will soon emerge. The disruption could also have very different consequences. If the closure of the factory leads to lower demand for services in the region, perhaps this part of the labour market will have bankruptcies and closed firms. Still more people will have to out-migrate. Still more units will have to close down, until the whole region is empty. This spiral effect (Myrdal 1968) will emerge when a large proportion of the local production is dependent on local demand, and when there are many threshold effects due to indivisibilities and economies of scale in the service production.

An interesting question is how large a salary increase a person needs in order to migrate. As indicated above, theory tells us that this increase could be smaller for younger persons, since they can benefit from the increase during a larger number of years. A Swedish study on men in the age group 30–39 (Springfeldt et al. 1977) showed that a wage increase of at least 20% was needed to attract inter-regional migrants.

International differences in wages (for an overview see Greenwood and McDowell 1992) is not a direct concern for inter-regional migration within countries, but of course it has impacts on regional in- or out-migration. The very large international variations in wage levels as a driving force is one of the indirect explanations behind the regional redistribution of population within countries, since international flows often end up in larger cities.

Using wage differences to stimulate regional development

Usually market forces will transform economies into new types of production. A question for governments in both centrally planned and market-oriented economies is whether governmental actions can make restructuring processes more efficient for the actors on the market. Should governmental policies encourage labour movement between sectors and regions in order to promote economic growth? Let us here use the discussion on movement of labour between production sectors of the economy (Scitowsky 1976) as an example, and draw some parallels to ideas on movement of labour between geographical areas. As discussed above, micro theory tell us that a wage difference will stimulate individuals to move. One could argue that the actual wage differences are too small for an efficient spatial relocation of labour between regions. Larger wage differences between regions would create the right structural environment for a sensible wage earner to migrate – a rational act for both the migrant and the society as a whole. Governments should then support investments in, for example, public infrastructure in successful regions in order to increase their competitiveness so that they would attract more migrants. The idea behind this measure is to influence the behaviour of people, to encourage them to migrate through increased regional production of service facilities in successful regions.

Of course, this policy aimed at economic growth is the opposite of the traditional regional policy mainly concerned with transfers of wealth from rich to poor regions. Distributional aspects can only partly be motivated by efficiency and welfare concerns for people. In the public debate welfare for regions is wrongly considered to be equal to welfare for individuals.

A totally different measure to create higher geographical mobility, compared with the above-described method to stimulate individuals to move, could be developed if we base our ideas on macro theory. It could be argued that the actual wage differences are too large for an efficient spatial relocation of labour (Öberg 1989). A more equal wage level in expanding and contracting regions would speed up the restructuring process. If the firms in expanding regions paid less for labour than they were actually able to, they would make higher profits, increase their ability to invest and expand faster. If the firms in contracting regions paid more than they were able to, bankruptcy would come about faster and then, of course, they would not able to pay any employees at all. Following this idea, governments should then try to raise minimum wage levels and force local authorities in poor regions to increase their public sector to the same standard as the rich regions. The idea behind this measure is to influence the behaviour of firms, which would have indirect effects on inter-regional migration.

The same idea can be carried through by demanding a too-expensive service level in poor regions – a service level that has to meet national standards but as to be paid for by the local population. This would increase local taxes and force more people to migrate to rich regions where there are more occupational opportunities and where they could contribute better to economic growth.

Unemployment and migration

Unemployment due to an uneven regional slowdown in business cycles will cause migration. Available jobs in one region and few opportunities of employment in another could be seen as a special case of wage differences with zero wage in one region and a wage in the other. As indicated earlier, the growth of cities during recent history is a physical expression of a decline in rural-based agriculture, and a growth in urban-based industry and service.

This force still exists in Western Europe, but it is weaker than on free markets due to social security programmes for unemployed, large subsidies to agricultural production and heavy restrictions on imports of foods from countries in Eastern Europe or outside Europe. Another factor slowing down the migration effect of economic restructuring is higher daily geographical mobility. Cars and public transportation make the urbanization process slower because a growing number of alternative jobs can be reached within a reasonable commuting time, even from remote places in the countryside. Inter-regional commuting as a substitute for inter-regional migration is also becoming more common.

Wage differences in subsectors

If wages on average are the same in two regions, we can still explain inter-regional migration with a neoclassical micro-economic approach. One way to do this is to include occupational markets with different wages, adding up to the same average, and individuals grouped in families (Stark 1991). It is then possible to 'explain' not only migration in one direction, but also return migration. We can see some relation between, on the one hand, the aggregated wage levels for the total labour markets and the disaggregated levels for occupations and, on the other, the famous idea of the *ecological fallacy* (Robinson 1950), developed in more detail by Alker (1969). Over the last few decades there has been a debate in the literature between neoclassical economics, where individuals maximizing their utilities are matched against a production system based on marginal productivity theories, and new economic theories regarding dual or segmented labour markets (for an overview, see Cain 1976). The neoclassical approach is, however, still dominant in studies of migration.

Occupational restructuring

Unemployment due to an uneven regional occupational restructuring will also cause migration. This is probably one of the more important causes behind inter-regional gross flows in Western Europe. Contemporary structural changes in the production system results in new stages which have been given many names, such as post-Fordism, flexible production systems, economics of scope, the post-modern era and the information society. Most of these concepts are used as ideas or as theoretical support for case studies. Here, empirical figures from a more traditional division of occupational statistics will be used in order to compare one of the old divisions of the production system with one of the most recent ones.

The old division has its roots in the 1930s, became popular in the 1950s and is still used in modified versions in statistical offices all over the world. Divided

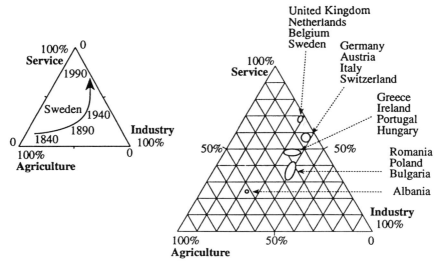

Figure 2.2.   Sectoral employment structure in some European countries in 1990 (right), and restructuring of employment between these sectors in Sweden 1840–1990 (left)

into three groups, all production activities could be labelled agriculture, industry or service. We all know how the number of people employed in agriculture has decreased from a large majority 100 years ago to a small minority today. This 'primary' sector usually also includes fishing and forestry. Industry reached its peak some years or decades ago in most developed countries. Today we are living in service economies. The general pattern in several Western European countries and the development during the twentieth century in one country are shown in Figure 2.2.

A Swedish geographer (Holm 1988) has developed a classification system which determines how many working hours are devoted to the production and transportation of physical goods, personal services and handling of information. All occupational groups can be classified individually with respect to the proportion of their time that is devoted to practical work with these three tasks. The results, applied to occupations in Italy, show that 50% of all working hours are still devoted to the handling of goods, agricultural products, building materials, industrial products etc. The rest is distributed between the two new growth sectors of the economy – information and personal services.

We know that the demand for labour varies according to the economic structure of the region and the rate at which different economic sectors expand or contract. Changes in economic sectors will then affect the occupational structure and thus the demand for people with different skills. National averages on an aggregated level, such as the ones shown for Italy in Figure 2.2, give us information about general changes in the production system. Specific occupations change even more drastically over time. Further structural changes within

Table 2.1. Restructuring of the labour market in Italy between traditional sectors 1935–85 and divisions of labour in 1985 according to a division of labour built on working hours in three types of activities

	1935	1985	1985	
Agriculture	28	10	58	Goods handling
Industry	29	21	23	Personal service
Service	43	69	19	Information
Total	100	100	100	

Demand for Labour

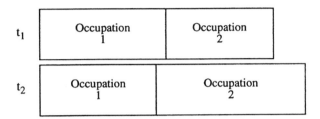

Figure 2.3. Structural changes in the production system will influence the total demand for labour in a region and also the demand within occupational sectors. In this case the local demand is growing between time t_1 and t_2, but the demand for occupation 1 is decreasing at the same time

and between regions are necessary and constantly occurring, and they will always lead to migration.

These imbalances within regions in labour markets demarcated by occupations create two types of gaps – occupational gaps within each occupation and a gap between total supply and demand for labour (see Figure 2.3). The latter, unbalanced regional development is discussed above. The former, where occupations are included in the theory, influences migration by the same mechanism but enlarges the flows. As indicated earlier, it will also create flows between regions, with a balance between supply and demand on the aggregated level.

Balance in occupational submarkets but still migration

So far, we have discussed geographical and occupational imbalances. With a perfect long-term balance in these two dimensions and the same wage level for each occupation, migration can be a necessity. If we consider that there are barriers between occupations and small labour markets – observe the word 'markets' – and that there is a time dimension, we will still get migration with a conventional neoclassical regional economic approach. First, there are costs involved when people change occupations and many of us thus have to change

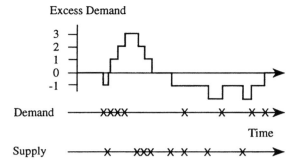

Figure 2.4. Long-term balance and short-term imbalance in local labour markets. With the same number of vacancies and job seekers on local labour markets in long-term balance, short-term imbalances will cause inter-regional migration

jobs within the same occupations. Secondly, local labour markets – the word 'local' indicating that you only can reach jobs located close to your dwelling – are often small. Thirdly, there is a time dimension which complicates the allocation process between supply and demand.

A seldom-discussed mechanism behind migration is the unplanned occurrence of new jobs and newly educated job seekers in all Western European market economies. The problem can be shown by means of a straightforward example. If 100 people apply for jobs as teachers of mathematics in a small local labour market during a period of ten years, and 100 vacancies of this kind occur in the same period, one's first inclination might be to suppose that none of the applicants would fail to obtain employment as a teacher. But the odds are that the vacancies will occur at irregular intervals throughout the period, and the people concerned may apply for jobs more or less randomly during the period. As a result of these random variations, there will sometimes be a queue of teachers looking for employment, while at other times there will be a shortage. Sometimes the line of applicants will be so long that a person looking for employment as a teacher will not be able to expect such a job to be available until quite a long time has passed.

Added to these actual imbalances is lack of information, seldom considered or modelled in migration theory. People searching for jobs cannot possibly judge how long it will be before a vacancy occurs, and therefore they cannot wait for one. The teacher in our example can thus choose between staying unemployed for a while, getting a different kind of job in the locality, or moving to another locality where there is an available job in the occupation they are trained for.

How important are these random variations as an explanatory factor behind migration flows? They are perhaps not as important as structural imbalances or business cycle variations, but in advanced economies, and especially in submarkets with a large degree of specialization, they are substantial. They are, for example, important for most readers of this text. Well-educated people living in

Table 2.2. The proportion of job applicants not obtaining employment in their home region in differently sized labour markets in a long-term state of equilibrium between supply and demand within the various occupational sectors; calculated examples

Size of local labour market= average number of persons employed in a certain occupation sector	Proportion of job applicants		
	obtaining work at once	obtaining work after a waiting period (less than six months	not obtaining work (potential migrants)
1000 (in average 50 vacancies and job applicants per year)	47	51	2
100 (in average five vacancies and job applicants per years)	40	40	20

Note: The calculated example rests on the following presuppositions. The average period of employment in the labour market is here supposed to be 20 years. If the anticipated period of unemployment exceeds six months the person concerned migrates from the local labour market. A vacancy will be filled by an in-migrant if the anticipated waiting period for an applicant from the local labour market will exceed six months. The local labour market is in equilibrium in the long-term perspective (supply equals demand).

Table 2.3. Number of employed in some occupations in some local labour markets in Sweden in 1990

Local labour market*	Gainfully employed	Drivers	Assistant nurses	Police	Dental nurses	Firefighters	Opticians
Vindeln	7000	344	341	12	20	2	0
Mora	15000	549	427	55	45	9	8
Oscarshamn	18000	561	529	48	39	25	7
Hässleholm	54000	1779	2030	194	162	48	25
Örebro	68000	2212	2635	284	238	79	34

*A local labour market is defined as a commuting area (within 30 km from the local centre)

small local labour markets with few employed in their occupation are those most likely to be affected.

It is theoretically possible to determine the importance of random variations with some calculations (Öberg 1974; Öberg and Oscarsson 1979). They are based on ideas from time-geography and on a model which will calculate the emigration from local labour markets assuming a turnover of vacancies and a flow of people wanting employment within different occupational specialties. An example will be given of the scale of migration due to matching problems among new entrants into different labour markets of different sizes.

One of the presuppositions of these calculations is that the supply and demand for labour remain constant over a longer period. However, owing to random variations over time, there will be temporary waiting lists or shortages. If anticipated unemployment exceeds six months, it is presumed in the model that a person wishing to obtain gainful employment will leave the area. And if the employer believes that he or she has to wait more than six months for 'local labour', people from other local labour markets will be employed. Some results are shown in Table 2.2. As indicated earlier, a large proportion of all migratory moves to and from minor local labour markets can be explained by the need for exact planning in time, concerning the junctures when jobs need to be filled and when people wish to enter the labour market.

As shown in Table 2.3, the occupations do not have to be esoteric to be rather small in number, and therefore – probably – they are showing rather a high incidence of randomly caused migration. The number of gainfully employed persons in a prominent occupation in the largest local labour market in Table 2.3 is not more than 2600. This number of workplaces corresponds to the theoretical limit where, according to the conditions of the example, allowance no longer needs to be made for random variations in the supply of labour as a factor influencing the situation of the individual in the labour market and thus influencing migration. Since the number is not significantly exceeded by any occupation in the areas, random variations do have a certain bearing on the situation of the individual and on migration and occupational changes in the majority of local labour markets in sparsely populated countries in Northern Europe.

To strengthen the theoretical argument, it is possible to compare empirical data. The actual scale of gross migrations in differently sized local labour markets in Sweden will support our argument. Larger labour markets have lower migration frequencies for married couples who moved more than 50 km in 1971. A figure on immigration figures would have the same characteristics.

More jobs in the service sector – more inter-regional stability

Agricultural employment is slowly disappearing in Western Europe. The same is true for industrial employment. Increasing productivity in these sectors makes them produce more with less people involved. The more we invest in modern industry the more machines, computers and robots we buy, the fewer workers are needed. It is the information and service sectors that are growing.

Much has been written on the role of the new information industry (Goddard et al. 1985) and of knowledge in general in the production system (Törnqvist 1990; Öbert 1990). We know that this industry is more common in rich countries (see Figure 2.6). Thus it is either a driving force in economic development or something only rich countries can afford.

The importance of the traditional sector – personal services – cannot be overemphasized. We often forget this sector because we take it for granted. This sector and its size are similar to the information sector, also depending on economic performance. In rich countries there are more people working directly in personal services. One of the results of economic growth is that we can afford

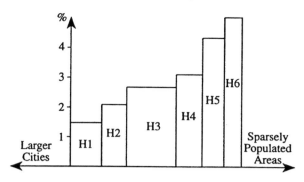

Figure 2.5. Out-migration frequencies for married couples who moved more than 50km in 1971. The husband's age is 30–39 years. The husband's income is higher than the median income for men in the same age group. The wife's income is higher than the upper quartile for corresponding women. The width of each bar is proportional to the number of inhabitants. Note: the H-regions are based on a classification of municipalities according to, among other things, the local labour market. (H1: Stockholm; H2: Goteborg and Malmo; H3: larger cities; H4: remaining parts of southern Sweden; H5: densely populated areas of northern Sweden; H6: sparsely populated areas of northern Sweden.)

more personal services and thus growth will create more employment in this sector. We also know that it is not possible to increase productivity within this sector in the same way as in a sector where goods are produced. The standard joke is that a symphony cannot be played faster in order to increase productivity. Today, a large part of the economy in Western Europe is targeted towards personal services, consumed locally.

According to theory, when a larger part of local production depends on local demand, this will stabilize regional development.

Human capital theory

Human capital is a much more valuable asset in our society than physical capital. According to one idea, this capital will increase for individuals with the length of their education and experience in working life. This process could continue for individuals in most occupations until the age of 45–65. This is the essence of the human capital theory.

If we believe in this theory and in this age group being more valuable on the labour market, then it would be possible to deduce several ideas from that. One is that one part of the changes in economic growth over time has to do with demography and age structure. Changing proportions of older and experienced persons in the labour force will partly explain changes in economic growth. This could also be shown for Japan (Klein 1992) and OECD countries (Malmberg 1992). Indirectly, this will also influence the speed of economic restructuring and thus inter-regional migration.

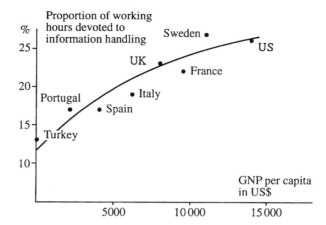

Figure 2.6. Proportion of working hours devoted to information handling, and GNP per capita in some European countries and the USA in 1985 (Source: Öberg 1989)

Another deduced idea is that if employers believe in the human capital theory, they are prepared to pay more for older workers and their knowledge. This will also lower their willingness to lose experienced workers, especially in the dominant white-collar sector. At the same time they are hesitant to employ new workers and train them for high productivity. Both attitudes will lower the mobility of older workers and thus also their migration rates. As the population in Western Europe becomes older, there will be a tendency toward lower mobility because of this effect of the human capital theory.

The human capital theory is not self-evident. Many would argue that older people are less attractive in the labour market because their knowledge has not kept up with modern technology. In physical hard work, older workers produce much less on average. However, more and more occupations are white-collar ones, where experience has an increasing value over time.

As seen in Figure 2.7, a growing proportion of the population in Western Europe will be in the age group 45–65 during the coming decade. The effect should be a tendency towards fewer inter-regional migrants.

Physical capital theory

One interesting characteristic of rapid population changes due to inter-regional migration is that, in the short and medium term, the new demand for physical infrastructure must be satisfied within a given amount of supply. In most countries the building sector will only add to the existing housing stock by around 1% per year, for example. This figure, 1% is a practical rule for possible changes in the physical infrastructure in a large region or a nation. There are not many exceptions from this rule. Based on this knowledge we can draw some conclusions.

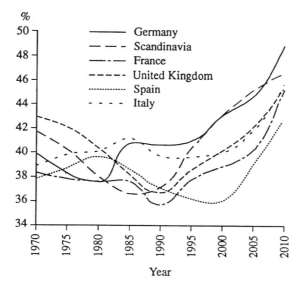

Figure 2.7. Population in the 'most productive' age groups (45–64) as a percentage of total population 20–64 in some European countries 1970–2010 (Source: UN statistics)

Most of our physical infrastructure has thus been developed for a population with another production system, another lifestyle and another demographic composition. The physical infrastructure is 'always' unmodern and not suitable for present lifestyles and demand. It is also located in regions which do not always fit into a modern production structure.

Also, the changes we try to implement today, often based on present need or demand, will imprison future generations in a physical structure, limiting their choice of location.

It is possible to somewhat exceed the 1% rule if we compare the number of new dwellings with the existing stock. However, when we look at the value of all physical capital, it is a very strong restriction on the geograhical mobility of capital. Very large housing programmes have to rely on and adapt to existing infrastructure to be economical. This is why the 1% rule limits the inter-regional reallocation process, making regional development time consuming.

The welfare state is accumulating physical capital and therefore its value becomes greater for each decade. It was easy to desert a wooden mining town in the USA 100 years ago, but it is impossible to empty a modern European mining town when the mine closes down. There are two reasons for this. First, too much value is invested in the physical infrastructure; and second, it would be too costly to build this infrastructure in another place. It is impossible to move Manchester to London.

The conclusion is simple: the higher the value of the physical infrastructure, the lower the net migration. This is probably one of the most important new factors behind the contemporary diminishing net migration figures in Western European economies.

APPROACHES IN SOCIAL GEOGRAPHY

On average, geography is a more applied science than economics. It is less theoretical in the sense that it is not a coherent set of findings founded in axioms concerning individual behaviour and systems rules. Theories in geography are more founded in empirical observations. While (political) economy is very much concerned with changes of national economic indicators over time, geography is concerned with social and economic processes in space.

As human geography is a young and small discipline, it is natural that geographers use several ideas and methods from economics as well as from other social science traditions when they study spatial and contextual determinants of behaviour. When economists work with migration studies, they usually use theory and apply it to net flows between two regions. When geographers work with migration studies, they usually also work with many regions and gross flows.

The following overview will start with some general macro ideas on migration commonly used in geography, and end in an overview of micro-geography, including the way it is understood in the time-geography tradition. It is mainly this latter part which distinguishes the overview from others (Öberg and Wils 1992 or Öberg 1994).

Development phases

A common way to understand changes and restructuring processes in a society is to compare them with corresponding contemporary or historical changes in other societies. Applied to population changes, we are familiar with the demographic transition where relations between demographic factors are arranged in time sequences and historical phases. The same approach applied to inter-regional migration is called the *mobility transition* (see Figure 2.8). According to Zelinsky (1971) it is possible to hypothesize relationships between different types of migration flows and general processes, such as urbanization, industrialization and modernization. Five stages of change are recognized in the transition of a society from one depending on traditional agriculture to the super-advanced (post-industrial) one where migration flows are absorbed by modern telecommunications systems.

Like the demographic transition, the mobility transition with its development phases is a descriptive model with little explanatory power. It is based on vague empirical generalizations said to reflect processes in most countries. It is thus a deterministic and universal model and, as one can guess, it is regarded both as a brilliant summary of ongoing processes by some researchers, and as an uninteresting combination of intuitively defined concepts by others.

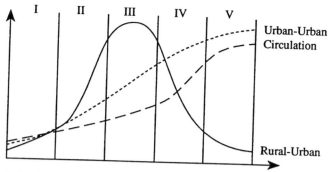

Figure 2.8. Zelinski's hypothesis of the mobility transition and its five phases: a simplified version (after Zelinski 1971)

Empirical generalization

In many studies on migration, the main effort is to find empirical numbers on historical or contemporary flows. In most countries there is a shortage of information on migration flows and thus there are many indirect ways of trying to estimate the numbers. In some countries, researchers work more with these estimates than with other matters related to inter-regional migration. When they are found, the next step is to put them in a theoretical framework. This is not easy. For example, if there is in-migration to larger cities, then many causal links compete to give the best explanation for this. Many geographers would discuss the type of urbanization in public debate. This type of discussion is of course more popular than the scientific. It reminds us of the ongoing discussion among economists where many skilful ideas are put forward to explain why a business cycle is changing direction. Similarly, geographers are seldom able to apply their ideas to real-world situations when they do not know the actual figures. Our theories can seldom explain real-world processes in advance, since the macro processes are results of an unlimited number of (chaotic) complex micro processes. It could be quite embarrassing to explain why there is an ongoing movement into cities if suddenly new statistics show that there has been a turnaround for many years.

In geography, as in other social sciences, a common approach to studying stable relations between data is to make empirical generalizations. As an example of correlated data, Figure 2.9 shows how inter-regional migration co-varies with the number of available jobs. Models based on empirical and quantitative data can be formulated more or less closely to theory. In the latter case, social sciences can still learn much from natural sciences where so-called data mining has been used with success in many research fields. Prognoses of future migratory flows most often use historical data treated with some kind of model. An example of a relatively recent approach is a dynamic migratory model connecting the micro level of individual decisions with the macro level of

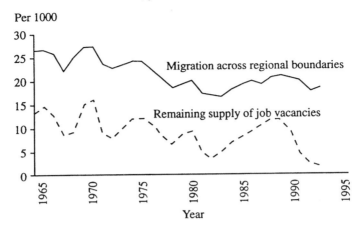

Figure 2.9.   Some inter-regional migration is due to the supply of job vacancies; data for Sweden 1965–94 (Source: Statistics Sweden and the Swedish Labour Market Board)

the migratory process, making use of master equations (Weidlich and Haag 1988). Many new theories and large fields of knowledge have been introduced after successful data mining. With more scientists and better computing facilities, data mining will probably be more common during the coming decades. Already, its efficiency in predicting and in pattern recognition, e.g. with the help of computer-based neural networks, has shown interesting results.

A few persons have tried to generalize empirical findings into migration 'laws'. If one researcher from each century should be mentioned, Kryger (1764), Ravenstein (1885, 1889) and Lee (1966) are good examples. The latter two work with ideas of how aggregated behaviour follows a general pattern. For example, a primary migration flow from region *a* to region *b* will later be followed by a flow of return migrants.

Forecasting inter-regional migration due to restructuring processes on local labour markets with econometric methods can be done in many ways, but for geographers it is common to use gravitation ideas when the models are specified.

Gravitation models

One of the strongest theories in applied geography is the spatial gravitation model. It has its roots in Newtonian physics. The idea that the volume of migration is inversely related to distance was stated more than a century ago by a German geographer working in London, Ravenstein (1885, 1889). This idea became known in geography through the works of Zipf (1941). It was transformed and developed by Stouffer (1940), who stated that the number of persons going a given distance is directly proportional to the number of intervening opportunities; by Hägerstrand (1957), who modelled migration with gravitation principles and Monte Carlo principles; by Lee (1966), who broadened the theory from the notion that migration is determined only by distance and (economic) opportunities; and finally by Wilson (1974), who generalized and developed the mathematics of these ideas.

According to estimates in several countries, a large proportion of inter-regional moves can be 'explained' by the basic gravitation formula. In France, the explanatory power of the model, measured by R^2, is 0.85 for inter-regional migration flows (Pumain 1988). Few theories in other social sciences can be applied with the same accuracy on empirical figures.

It is always possible to debate whether spatial gravitation is a theory, a law, a model, an empirical generalization or some type of idea. For some, it is only the aggregated outcome of micro rules for behaviour. Andersson and Persson (1993) showed how the idea corresponds to neoclassical micro theory.

Systems approaches

In geography, as in other disciplines, systems approach has a tradition. An early, well-known migration study on rural–urban flows using a systems approach is carried through by Mabogunje (1972). The basic idea behind a systems approach is that it does not see migration in 'oversimplified' terms of cause and effect. Feedback effects and circular effects, together with interdependent and self-modifying processes, guarantee that changes in one part of a system may have a ripple effect in other parts and thus in the whole. Mabogunje's studies of migration in Africa have resulted in a theory/model/system made up of three elements. The potential migrant is encouraged to leave the village by stimuli from the environment. Institutional forces and adjustment mechanisms then influence the outcome of the process. The way people are informed, or misinformed, also plays an important role for the outcome.

Vacancy chains also show how systems work. Vacancy chain analysis was developed by White (1970). He used empirical data from an organization as a base for the development of more general algorithms. The same ideas have been used to quantify aggregated effects of occupational changes (Öberg 1979b). This study was based on empirical studies of indirect effects of job recruitment. When a person is recruited, he or she often leaves a job that in turn must be filled by a new person. Furthermore, jobs are sometimes taken by workers employed in another local labour market. If this migrant has a spouse also leaving a job, still more people are involved in both job mobility and geographical mobility. The result of the study was that the relocation of 11 000 public jobs from the Swedish capital to other cities, in spite of the fact that only a minority of the civil servants moved with their jobs, caused 10 000 moves between local labour markets and 30 000 job changes in total.

Systems approaches can deal with both macro and micro theory. A micro approach – where individuals are always treated as persons related to two other persons and a physical environment, and where the location in time and space is important for an understanding of all ongoing parallel processes – has a special label in geography: time-geography.

Time-geography

Time-geography is a set of ideas developed by Hägerstrand (1954, 1970). They have been applied to migration (Hägerstrand 1947, 1969), see Figure 2.10, as well as to other areas. Since most of the literature is in Swedish, some space will now be used to explain a time-geographical approach to migration. When a person migrates, this is seen as one of a whole set of actions carried through by interaction with other individuals and depending on structural conditions. Time-geography is a way of thinking, but it can also be used in a modelling context. In fact, computer facilities and object-oriented languages are prerequisites for an applied time-geographic approach on larger systems, as well as for other versions of applied social sciences, where theory and descriptions use complex interactions and work with parallel processes.

Techniques to model time-geographic approaches were used by Hägerstrand (1957) in his Monte Carlo approach to spatial innovation processes. Three decades passed before the technique to model dynamic interactive parallel processes was developed to fit the theoretical approach, see e.g. Öberg (1979a) or Holm et al. (1989). Ideas from Hägerstrand (1947, 1970), Simmons (1968), Rossi (1955) and others can now be used in dynamic models working with parallel processes. The difference between the representation chosen in time-geographic approaches and the more traditional mobility literature is the emphasis on a life-path perspective and cultural/demographic causes of moves, as opposed to the emphasis on conditions in the local labour markets as the most important cause of moves.

Let us start the introduction to a time-geographic modelling approach by reading a short description of the life of Siv Petterson (Holm et al. 1989). The following quoted text was created by a computer. The language is poor and contains some expressions which depend on some specific conditions of the model aimed at keeping track of modalities, such as *prefer* and *ought to*, but it is easy to see that the text outlines the story of a human life. For the computer to be able to write a text of this kind, it has to be given instructions. In this case it has been fed about a thousand general rules which state – in extraordinarily simplified terms – how the lives of different people are interconnected. The computer was thus not instructed by means of rules pertaining to the particular life of Siv Petterson. Her life history is the result of general rules of behaviour and interaction. All events are dependent on unique contexts but are determined by the system as a whole. The rules are general. The same rules, with some variations, also apply to other individuals. With these rules, the model will describe aspects of our lives. The emphasis is given to the ways in which people educate themselves, work, move from one place to another and change their household status.

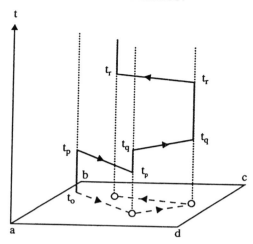

Figure 2.10. A time-geographic approach to migration from 1969. Part of the time-space path of an individual. Dotted vertical lines represent stations. Movements take place between stations at times t_p, t_q and t_r. Dashed lines project movements on the landscape. (Source: Hägerstrand 1969)

In August, 1952, Siv Petterson was born in Stockholm. Her parents were Johan Petterson and Kerstin Svensson. In January, 1968, Siv Petterson and Artur Nilsson formed a couple, which they absolutely wanted to and ought to. They were then 15 and 18 years old, respectively. Siv Petterson left elementary school in June, 1968. During August, 1969, Siv Petterson moved to Malmö in order to start education. 1969, in August Siv Petterson began an education, which she absolutely wanted to and perhaps ought to. It belonged within the educational sector. In February, 1971, Siv Petterson separated from Artur Nilsson. In February, 1971, Siv Petterson and Ivar Larson formed a couple, which they preferred and ought to. They were then 18 and 19 years old, respectively. In 1971 (in August) Siv Petterson formed a new household together with Ivar Larson, which she wanted to and perhaps ought not to. In August, 1975, Siv Petterson finished her education. She was then 23 years old, a cohabitee, and had a completed education within the educational sector. In November, 1976, Siv Petterson had a daughter called Barbro by Ivar Larson, which she preferred and ought to. In April, 1978, Siv Petterson did not find a single vacant job. In September, 1980, Siv Petterson had a daughter called Maria by Ivar Larson, which she preferred not to but ought to. Siv Petterson began a new job during August, 1981, which she preferred and perhaps ought to. It was within the educational sector at the college level. In January (1983) Siv Petterson moved away from Ivar Larson. Siv Petterson left her job in February, 1987. She was then 34 years old. Siv Petterson began a new job in February, 1987, which she preferred and ought to. It was at the college level within the manufacturing sector. She then changed jobs four more times before her retirement in 2018. In August, 2033, Petterson finally died aged 81 years.

This particular time-geographic approach is different from other models developed within the social sciences in that it handles a considerably greater number of rules. From a technical point of view it is more advanced than its predecessors, as it is able to work with a complex system of parallel processes.

Although the model is governed by general knowledge of human behaviour, it is able to cope with an accommodate all persons as individuals. Hence, the life histories of different people become interdependent. It is possible to write life stories for all other persons in the model and they would be internally consistant. For example in the life story of Ivar Larsson, he was born in 1951, moved in with Siv Petterson in 1971 and had two daughters with Siv before they separated in 1983. Even rules for admissions to schools, or for recruitment to workplaces, affect the way in which lives are developed and described in the model. We might say that it is concerned with people who cooperate and compete for various resources in a temporal space.

When time-geographers and other social scientists resort to advanced techniques, this has the advantage of facilitating detailed accounts of what happens, or might happen, in a society. One drawback, however, is that outsiders find it difficult to understand, and therefore to accept, all those rules that are built into the model. In complex interactive models, masses of knowledge – experiential as well as theoretical – are brought together to form pictures of matters we want to learn more about (Holm et al. 1988). Like many technical systems, the model that gave rise to the computer-written text above clearly produces an intelligible result. It does so despite the fact that it would take a skilled social analyst several working days just to peruse and comprehend the interaction between the thousand or so rules that govern the model. This effort would, however, be easier than analysing a complex model with macro variables, since the rules in our time-geographic model often apply to human actions in situation which we have experienced ourselves, or with which we are at least thoroughly familiar.

As it is hard to gain an insight into more than parts of the model in a short time, one may well ask whether it can properly be said to express a theory for a discipline within the social sciences. After all, the purpose of a theory is to simplify and to provide a helpful perspective. However, everybody who wants to render the intricate interaction of human beings in one or a few rules can seldom use this simplification in applied research. Nor does the time-geographic approach live up to such ambitions. It is too complex in several dimensions. Since life histories of people can hardly be based on a small number of principles, we have to accept an understanding of more complex processes.

CONTEMPORARY PROGRESS IN RESEARCH

Regional restructuring of local labour markets is one of the causes of inter-regional migration flows. Other causes are lifestyle changes and/or household changes. Economic restructuring of the production system and occupations is more important as a cause of net flows than of gross flows. As a theory, the idea of links between labour market performance and migration is stronger on the macro level than on the micro level.

Restructuring in the production system is mirrored in salaries and in the demand for different skills. In this chapter we have indicated that two regions

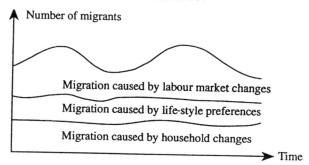

Figure 2.11. Inter-regional migration is caused by processes in the local labour market as well as by other causes

with the same average wage level could still theoretically have inter-regional migration flows. Occupational imbalances or salary differences can exist within the aggregated figures. Furthermore, short-term imbalances over time can exist in labour markets in long-term balance.

In economic theory, a higher wage is better for an individual than a lower, *ceteris paribus*. In the real world, decisions are made as a response to several, only partly understood, complex and heterogeneous processes. If we only consider migration as a household-decision process and different types of physical movement to a new context, it is hard to apply our theory on actual situations. The basic theory can only be used to indicate the directions of net flows if we have a general understanding of other conditions in the interacting regions. With this in mind, the basic 'law' of migration is still a strong theory.

The only possible candidate for an even stronger theory is the fact that we have preferences for lifestyle, such as urban lifestyle or rural lifestyle, available only in some regions. If lifestyles values are incorporated in the 'wage' concept, it is still our old theory. However, if all utilities are included in the wage concept, it becomes a tautology to say that people move because they believe that they can increase their wages. No information will remain in the concept. If wage/income and lifestyle/quality of life are regarded as different dimensions of life, then the latter pair become strong theoretical concepts. They could compete with economic measures as strong driving forces behind inter-regional migration. We already know that they are strong forces behind intra-regional migration: some prefer suburban life, others city centres when choosing where to live within regions. Furthermore, a proportion of inter-regional moves are always caused by household changes, e.g. marriages between people from different regions (see Figure 2.11).

Two other economic theories have also been discussed. According to the human capital theory, less inter-regional migration will occur when a larger proportion of the labour force is in the age group 45–65. This is an idea which, of course, is more important in a post-modern service society where blue-collar workers are rare. According to the physical capital theory, net flows between regions seldom exceed 1% per year. This value of physical capital in regions in welfare states is so large compared to the production capacity that inter-regional net flows can only be larger than 1% in extreme situations. We will return to this idea.

Developing parts of social science theory is not the sole purpose of this chapter. It is also intended to introduce new forms of description in time-geography – forms that belong somewhere between the symbols of rigid mathematics and imprecise verbal presentation. This idea will be developed further.

New languages merging theory and reality

Time-geography as an idea can be used as a base for the development of scientific tools, or a 'scientific language' to describe the mobility of individual actors and artifacts, their actions and physical movements in time and space according to a set of rules. If economic theory describes how actors would behave in a 'hypothetical' world, e.g. in markets if they were rational, time-geography describes how actors behave in the 'real' world. The description in time-geography is ideally made with a language which is not restricted to the verbal language, but uses graphics or better high-level computer languages. This time-geographic language enables us to model parallel processes.

A precondition for the development of time-geography from an idea or a way of thinking to a scientific language, to describe how actors behave in a dynamic system, is the present development in computer technology. At least during the last decade, the software tools have been sufficient. The time-geographic migration models described earlier in this chapter were developed more than a decade ago. Now the hardware seems to be sufficient for larger population systems. Contemporary development with parallel, fast processors will make it possible to develop the idea of a detailed geographic language further. Large-scale models, with very large numbers of individuals acting as individuals normally do and a quite detailed physical environment, will be the future social science version of virtual reality.

Net migration stability in welfare states

Some societal changes tend to increase inter-regional migration, while others have the opposite effect. Better education and more experience with non-native regions makes us mobile, while access to better transportation and higher female participation in the labour force make us stable. In addition to these trends, we can think of two new tendencies for structuring forces. They will probably be discussed more during the coming decade because they will, to a large extent, stabilize future inter-regional migration flows.

The first is that inhabitants in welfare societies have become so rich and have accumulated so much real capital that we now live in a physical structure which

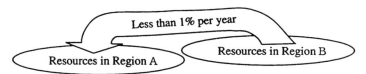

Figure 2.12. The 1% rule indicates the maximum yearly transfer of physical resources between regions in welfare societies

cannot be changed in its spatial distribution on a macro scale in a short- or medium-term perspective. In this chapter, the 1% rule (see Figure 2.12) is a contemporary empirical expression of this more general stability condition for net migration. Any valuable, long-lasting, geographic, immobile, physical capital will stabilize inter-regional migration.

The second new structuring force is not fully recognized in the public debate. There is no return to a society where many people would work in industry. Already in the USA, the 500 largest service companies have as many employees as the 500 largest industrial companies. More investments in industries would mainly result in robots, computers and other equipment, not in employment. The growing employment sector is service activities targeted at individuals and households. A large number of people will not be employed, but they will still have an income through child allowances, public and/or private pensions, unemployment insurances, unemployment benefits, social insurances, assistance allowances and other money transfers. These money transfers will create a steady basic demand for personal services in all regions in welfare societies.

Furthermore, public consumption, such as day nurseries, schools, hospitals, road maintenance etc., will also create a large number of jobs in the service sector in all Western European societies, thus adding to a basic demand for labour in local labour markets. Financial problems in the public sector will force production processes into efficiency improvements, and some of it will be privatized, but it will still be more reliable than industry when it comes to employment in local labour markets. Together with money transfers directly to individuals, public consumption of personal services will create spatially decentralized employment in the service sector.

The two new structural conditions discussed here – a more valuable physical capital and larger substantial demand services – can partly explain changes in the net migration pattern during the last few decades. In only one generation, the migration pattern in most welfare states has changed dramatically. The quite strong urbanization process during the 1960s, and the migration turnaround during the 1970s with net migration out from the larger cities, have been transformed into a more stable phase with low figures for inter-regional net migration.

REFERENCES

Alker, H.S. (1969) A typology of ecological fallacies, in Dogan, M. and Rokkan, S. (eds) *Quantitative Ecological Analysis in the Social Sciences*. Cambridge, Massachusetts: MIT Press, pp. 69–86.

Alonso, W. (1976) *A Theory of Movements*. Cambridge, Massachusetts: Center for Population Studies, Harvard University.

Andersson, Å.E. and Persson, O. (1993) Networking scientists. *The Annals of Regional Science* 27:11–21. Berlin: Springer Verlag.

Becker, G. (1993) *Human Capital, A Theoretical and Empirical Analysis, with Special Reference to Education*. Third edition. Chicago: Chicago University Press.

Cain, G.G. (1976) The challenge of segmented labor markets theories to orthodox theory. A survey. *Journal of Economic Literature* 14:1215–57.

Goddard, J.B., Gillespie, A.E., Robinson, J.F. and Thwaites, A.T. (1985) The impact of new information technology on urban and regional structure in Europe, in Thwaites, A.T. and Oakey, R.P. (eds) *The Regional Economic Impact of Technological Change*. London: Frances Pinter, pp. 215–41.

Greenwood, M.J. and McDowell, J.M. (1992) The Macrodeterminants of International Migration. Paper presented at the IIASA Conference on Mass Migration in Europe, Laxenburg, Austria, March 5–7.

Hägerstrand, T. (1947) En landsbygdsbefolknings flyttningsrörelser. *Svensk Geografisk Årsbok* 23:114–42. Lund, Sweden: South-Swedish Geographical Society.

Hägerstrand, T. (1954) *Innovationsförloppet ur korologisk synvinkel*. Lund, Sweden: Gleerups.

Hägerstrand, T. (1957) Migration and area, in Hannerberg, D. (ed.) *Migration in Sweden*. Lund, Sweden: Gleerup Studies in Geography, Ser. B., No. 13, pp. 27–158.

Hägerstrand, T. (1969) On the definition of migration. *Scandinavian Population Studies* 1:63–72. Helsinki.

Hägerstrand, T. (1970) Tidsanvändning och omgivningsstruktur. *SOU* 1970:14. Stockholm.

Holm, E. (1988) Regional Production Systems. Working Paper. Umeå, Sweden: Department of Geography, University of Umeå.

Holm, E. and Öberg, S. (1984) Hushållsförändringar som förklaring til flyttningar. Sociala aspekter på regional planering. *SOU* 1984: 1. Stockholm.

Holm, E., Mäkilä, K. and Öberg, S. (1988) Population systems as interacting individuals. *Scandinavian Population Studies* 8. Copenhagen, pp. 163–84.

Holm, E., Mäkilä, K. and Öberg, S. (1989) Tidsgeografisk handlingsteori, Att bilda betingade biografier. *GERUM* 8. Umeå, Sweden: Department of Geography, University of Umeå.

Klein, L.R. (1992) A linear model for environment and development. *Science and Sustainability – Selected Papers on IIASA's 20th Anniversary*. Laxenburg, Austria: International Institute for Applied Systems Analysis, pp. 213–42.

Kryger, J.F. (1764) *Svar på den af Kongl VetenskapsAkademien, För sistledit år 1763, framställde Frågan: Hvad kan vara orsaken, att sådan myckenhet svensk folk årligen flytter ur landet?* Stockholm: KVA, Royal Swedish Academy of Sciences.

Lee, E.S. (1966) A theory of migration. *Demography* 3(1):47–57.

Mabogunje, A. (1972) *Regional Mobility and Resource Development in West Africa*. Montreal: McGill-Queens University Press.

Malmberg, B. (1992) Economic Growth and Life-cycle Accumulation of Human Capital. Working Paper. Uppsala, Sweden: Department of Social and Economic Geography, Uppsala University.

Myrdal, G. (1968) *Asian Drama*. London: Allen Lane.

Öberg, C.S. (1974) Arbetslöshet orsakad av tillfälliga jämviktsbrister. *SOU* 1974:2, bilaga 4, kap 2. Stockholm.

Öberg, S. (1979a) Matchningsprocessor på och mellan lokala arbetsmarknader – En individbaserad simulering av bla flyttningar i samband med arbetsbyte. *ERU, F12.* Stockholm: Ministry of Labor.

Öberg, S. (1979b) Offentlig sysselsättning – Expansionens konsekvenser för omflyttningen. *ERU, F14.* Stockholm: Ministry of Labor.

Öberg, S. (1989) Lavoro e pianificazione regionale nel futuro. *L'ufficio in via di estinzione?* Milano: Il Sole 24 Ore Libri, pp. 41–8.

Öberg, S. (1990) An historical background to the geography of creativity – The case of Europe, in Shachar, A. and Öberg, S. (eds) *The World Economy and the Spatial Organization of Power.* Aldershot: Avebury, pp. 128–48.

Öberg, S. (1994) Spatial and economic factors in future south–north migration, in Lutz, W. (ed.) *The Future Population of the World. What Can We Assume Today?* London: Earthscan, pp. 361–85.

Öberg, S. and Oscarsson, G. (1979) Regional policy and interregional migration – Matching jobs and individuals on local labor markets. *Regional Studies* 13(1):1–14.

Öberg, S. and Wils, A.B. (1992) East–west migration in Europe. *POPNET*, 22 (winter). Laxenburg, Austria: International Institute for Applied Systems Analysis.

Pumain, D. (1988) France, in Weidlich, W. and Haag, G. (eds) *Interregional Migration, Dynamic Theory and Comparative Analysis.* Berlin: Spring Verlag, pp. 131–54.

Quigley, J.M. (1972) An economic model of Swedish emigration. *Quarterly Journal of Economics* 86(1):111–26 (February).

Ravenstein, E.G. (1885) The laws of migration. *Journal of the Statistical Society* 48 (June): 167–227.

Ravenstein, E.G. (1889) The laws of migration. *Journal of the Statistical Society* 52 (June): 241–301.

Robinson, W.S. (1950) Ecological correlations and the behavior of individuals. *American Sociological Review* 15(3):351–7.

Rossi, P. (1955) *Why Families Move: A Study of the Social Psychology of Urban Residential Mobility.* London: Sage Publications (Revised Edition 1980).

Scitowsky, T. (1976) *The Joyless Economy: An Inquiry into Human Satisfaction and Consumer Dissatisfaction.* New York: Oxford University Press.

Simmons, J. (1968) Changing residence in the city. *Geographical Review* 58:622–51.

Springfeldt, P., Tegsjö, B. and Öberg, S. (1977) Inkomstutveckling i samband med flyttning. *ERU, F6.* Stockholm: Ministry of Labor.

Stark, O. (1991) *The Migration of Labor.* Oxford: Blackwell.

Stouffer, S. (1940) Intervening opportunities. A theory relating mobility and distance. *American Sociological Review* 5:845–67.

Thomas, D.S. (1941) *Social and Economic Aspects of Swedish Population Movements.* New York: Macmillan.

Törnqvist, G. (1990) Towards a geography of creativity, in Shachar, A. and Öberg, S. (eds) *The World Economy and the Spatial Organization of Power.* Aldershot: Avebury, pp. 103–27.

Weidlich, W. and Haag, G. (eds) (1988) *Interregional Migration, Dynamic Theory and Comparative Analysis.* Berlin: Springer Verlag.

White, H.C. (1970) *Chains of Opportunity.* Cambridge, Massachusetts: Harvard University Press.

Wilkinson, M. (1967) Evidence of long swings in the growth of Swedish population and related economic variables, 1860–1965. *Journal of Economic History* 27:17–38 (March).

Wilson, A.G. (1974) *Urban and Regional Models in Geography and Planning.* New

York: John Wiley.

Zelinsky, W. (1971) The hypothesis of the mobility transition. *Geographical Review* 61:219–59.

Zipf, G.K. (1941) *National Unity and Disunity: The Nation as a Bio-Social Organism.* Bloomington, Indiana: The Principia Press.

Part II

EMPIRICAL OVERVIEWS

3 The Economic Framework of Migrations in Europe, 1960–90

CHRISTIAN VANDERMOTTEN
Université Libre de Bruxelles, Belgium

INTRODUCTION

The main migratory trends, especially those linked with labour markets, occur within the framework of the spatial patterns of the economy. It is therefore important to show what these patterns were during the period we are considering.

Expressed in terms of gross domestic product (GDP) per head, the gaps between western European states, from Scandinavian countries to Greece, are appreciably higher than the inter-state differences in the United States. If one takes the regional economic structures into account, the level of GDP and the population weights, one may summarize European structures on the country scale (except for Italy, which will systematically be divided into two parts, the north and the centre on the one hand, the south on the other hand) as an asymmetrical centre–periphery pattern (Table 3.1, Figure 3.1):

— the central countries (United Kingdom, western Germany, the Benelux, France, Alpine countries and northern and central Italy) contain 71% of the European population, with GDP per inhabitant 11% higher than the European average (in purchasing power standard–PPS);
— the rich but sparsely inhabited periphery of the Scandinavian countries, with 6% of the population (including Denmark) and a GDP per inhabitant 5% higher than the European average;
— the poor periphery, from Greece to Ireland, containing 23% of the population and a GDP at a level of just two-thirds of the average.

Today one may add to these two peripheries the former German Democratic Republic, with its obsolete industrial structure, where GDP per inhabitant has fallen to a little more than one-third of the European average after reunification, i.e. at the level of the poorest regions of Greece. Neither the former GDR nor, further away, Central and Eastern Europe will be studied here. Let us note though, the potential tensions as regard to mass migrations engendered by German reunification and the opening up of the East; while the highest GDP per

People, Jobs and Mobility in the New Europe. Edited by Hans H. Blotevogel and Anthony J. Fielding.
© 1997 European Science Foundation. Published in 1997 by John Wiley & Sons Ltd.

Table 3.1. GDP per inhabitant, by comparison with West European average

	Population 1990 (millions)	GDP per inhabitant (PPS, Western Europe=100)					
		1960	1966	1973	1982	1987	1990
United Kingdom	57.3	121	110	103	96	102	99
Netherlands	15.0	114	109	109	103	100	100
Belgium	10.0	96	97	102	105	101	104
Luxembourg	0.4	134	121	121	111	119	123
Germany (west)	62.7	123	119	115	116	116	116
Switzerland	6.8	175	165	155	138	136	134
Austria	7.7	94	94	97	105	103	106
France	56.6	106	109	112	115	111	111
Italy (north and central)	37.8	102	104	106	116	117	119
Central countries	**254.2**	**115**	**112**	**110**	**111**	**110**	**111**
Ireland	3.5	56	54	55	62	61	68
Portugal	9.8	38	42	54	53	51	55
Spain	39.0	58	70	76	71	72	74
Italy (south)	19.9	53	60	63	70	70	66
Greece	10.2	34	41	50	51	48	46
Western and Mediterranean periphery	**82.3**	**51**	**60**	**66**	**66**	**65**	**66**
Denmark	5.1	115	116	110	108	112	107
Norway	4.2	90	89	84	100	110	101
Sweden	8.6	120	121	114	111	112	107
Finland	5.0	86	87	94	100	103	104
Iceland	0.3	91	99	91	113	116	100
Scandinavian periphery	**23.2**	**106**	**106**	**103**	**106**	**110**	**105**
East Germany	16.0	–	–	–	–	–	36
Western Europe	**375.7**	**100**	**100**	**100**	**100**	**100**	**(a)100**
Central metropolitan	69.0	(b)136	(b)131	(b)130	127	129	131
Secondary central metropolitan	15.2	126	126	119	124	121	115
Early heavy manufacturing	28.2	115	109	104	101	100	99

Other central regions	66.1	(b)118	(b)113	(b)111	107	107	106
Peri-central-Parisian Basin type	17.3	89	93	95	98	94	96
Peri-central-German type	15.0	91	90	90	93	94	97
Peri-central-Scandinavian type	7.4	105	106	103	104	107	104
Peri-central-Third Italy type	30.0	(b)76	(b)85	89	92	91	96
Intermediate and Alpine regions	46.5	(b)100	(b)99	(b)96	97	98	96
Peripheral metropolitan	13.5	(b)55	(b)59	65	67	63	61
Southern and western periphery	45.4	(b)43	(b)50	57	60	61	61
Scandinavian periphery	6.1	81	79	80	82	83	79

Sources: OECD, Eurostat, National Statistics
(a) East Germany excluded.
(b) Including our own estimations for Swiss regions in 1973, for Swiss, Portuguese and Greek regions in 1960 and 1966.
The evolutions by types of regions could be influenced by a compound of 'national' and 'regional' effects, but in fact the trends are quite similar if the data are calculated inside each country by comparison to each national average.

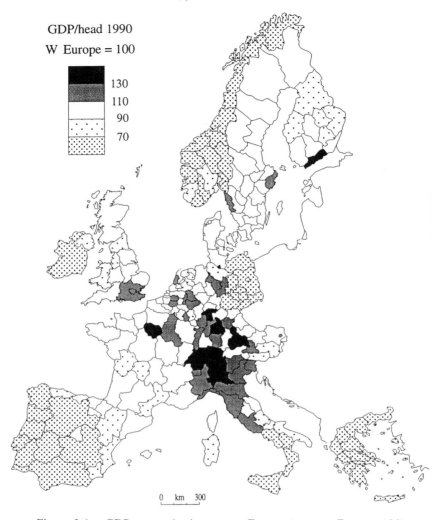

Figure 3.1.　GDP per capita in western Europe (western Europe=100)

head gaps in Italy, between Lombardy and Calabria, are 2.4 to 1, they are 5.9 to 1 between Hamburg and regions less than 100 kilometres away.

A STATIC ANALYSIS AND A DYNAMIC ANALYSIS

The economic structures of western Europe (in its wide sense, i.e. the European OECD countries, excluding the former Yugoslavia and Turkey) will be analysed in two steps.

First, the description of the structures will be based on the subdivision of GDP in 1980 into 21 sectors, 3 for the primary sector, 12 for mining, manufacturing and building industries, 6 for the tertiary sector (Sortia et al. 1986; Vandermotten 1993).

Secondly, the analysis of trends between 1960 and 1990 will be based on the evolution of GDP per head, in parity of purchasing power, taking into account differences in the prices of goods and services in the various countries and so reducing slightly the gap between the centre and the periphery in comparison with data on the exchange rate, and on the evolution of the main sectorial proportions, but here only at the level of the countries (always with a north–south division in Italy).

Within the national frameworks, an analysis in terms of GDP increases the disparities in comparison with an analysis in terms of income per inhabitant; transfers of various incomes, especially due to social security mechanisms, reduce the inter-regional gaps. Also, in cases where large cities constitute territorial units in themselves (for example Brussels or Hamburg), a high percentage of their active population, contributing to the creation of GDP, is living in neighbouring regions where the incomes will be accounted for. It is thus important to take into account the geographical scale of the analysis. In some countries, the structures have been analysed on a finer geographical scale than the evolutions (Figure 3.2).

THE REGIONAL STRUCTURES

The 516 territorial units covering the whole of western Europe have been merged together step by step, on the basis of the most similar economic structures, by using an ascendent typological analysis. This takes into account the respective economic weight of the various units and their territorial contiguities, to form wider units, until the level of a 25% loss of total variance of the initial matrix. Then these units have been drawn together, this time without taking into account the territorial contiguities, to define major structural types, numbering a dozen (Figure 3.2).

Table 3.2 shows the main characteristics of these major structural types, allowing one to model the structure in concentric layers:

— central metropolitan regions;
— the remaining parts of the centre;
— peri-central regions;
— intermediate regions;
— peripheral regions, richer ones (in Scandinavia), poorer ones (in Ireland and in the Mediterranean periphery).

The central metropolitan regions

Here GDP per inhabitant is the highest, on the whole more or less 30% higher than the European average. The constituent areas are the main capital regions of

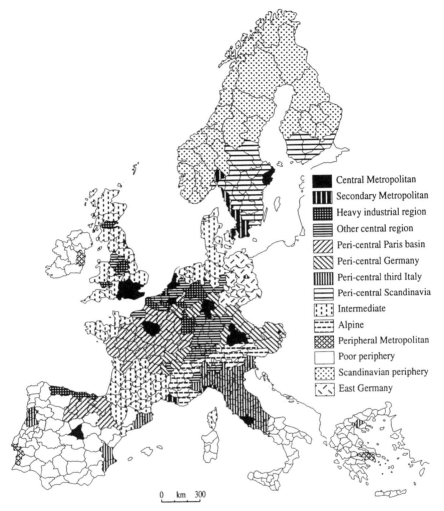

Central Metropolitan
Secondary Metropolitan
Heavy industrial region
Other central region
Peri-central Paris basin
Peri-central Germany
Peri-central third Italy
Peri-central Scandinavia
Intermediate
Alpine
Peripheral Metropolitan
Poor periphery
Scandinavian periphery
East Germany

0   km   300

Figure 3.2. A classification of the economic regions of western Europe

the European centre (London, Paris, Amsterdam, Brussels), but also Stockholm, Rome, Madrid and major business cities such as Hamburg, Frankfurt, Munich Zurich, Geneva and Milan).

These multifunctional regions are highly tertiarised (nearly 70% of their GDP since 1980), with a high concentration in banking, insurance and market services (more in the UK and France, less in the FRG and Italy). Here there are the major headquarters of the top businesses of the big countries of the European centre, strongly linked with the worldwide networks of management.

The manufacturing industries which survive after the deindustrialization

Table 3.2.   Structure of GDP 1980

1	2	3	4	5	6	7	8	9	10	11	12	13	14	15	16	17	18
1980	% of total area	% of total population	% of total GDP	Mining and manufacturing (%)	Tertiary (%)	Agriculture, forestry, fishing (%)	Food, beverages (%)	Energy, basic metal, non-metal products (%)	Chemicals, metal products (%)	Textile and other manufacturing (%)	Building (%)	Trade, transports (%)	Banking, market services (%)	Non-market services (%)	9+10 +11 (%)	10/(8 +11)	14/15
Central metropolitan	2.8	16.7	21.5	24.6	68.2	1.1	2.2	4.4	12.8	5.2	6.1	24.3	29.0	14.9	17.8	1.72	1.95
Secondary metropolitan	1.2	3.5	4.9	24.2	67.7	1.3	3.4	5.3	11.2	4.3	6.5	26.5	21.5	19.7	22.0	1.44	1.09
Heavy early manufacturing	2.5	8.5	9.2	31.8	53.5	1.7	3.0	14.7	15.0	5.1	7.0	19.5	20.0	14.0	39.0	1.85	1.43
Other central	4.9	17.1	20.6	36.9	53.9	2.3	3.6	6.0	18.9	8.4	6.9	20.9	20.0	13.0	16.3	1.59	1.54
Parisian Basin type peri-central	8.0	5.5	5.5	23.8	51.2	7.9	5.2	6.1	14.8	7.7	7.2	18.1	20.2	12.9	18.0	1.14	1.57
German type peri-central	4.5	4.7	4.9	36.2	50.0	5.1	4.0	8.1	15.3	8.8	8.7	17.8	18.5	13.7	22.4	1.20	1.35
Scandinavian type peri-central	6.4	2.1	2.7	32.1	55.6	5.1	2.6	6.6	12.5	10.4	7.2	18.4	16.6	20.6	20.7	0.96	0.81
Third Italy type peri-central	5.2	10.0	7.3	34.9	51.4	6.9	3.8	6.4	10.9	13.8	6.8	23.4	17.2	10.8	18.3	0.62	1.60
Intermediate	14.2	12.0	11.8	28.3	57.2	6.6	4.7	8.2	10.2	5.2	7.8	19.8	20.4	17.0	28.8	1.03	1.20
Alpine	3.5	2.3	2.5	26.6	59.9	4.5	3.3	6.9	10.3	6.1	9.2	24.6	21.1	14.2	26.0	1.10	1.48
Peripheral metropolitan	0.7	3.0	1.4	24.6	64.9	3.6	3.3	5.4	8.3	7.6	7.0	27.8	19.2	17.9	21.9	0.76	1.07
Southern & western peripheral	21.0	12.9	5.9	20.5	54.6	15.1	4.1	6.4	4.6	5.4	9.8	23.1	16.2	15.3	31.1	0.48	1.06
Scandinavian peripheral	25.3	1.7	1.9	24.3	54.5	10.5	3.0	7.9	7.6	7.8	8.8	21.5	14.6	18.4	30.2	0.70	0.79
Western Europe (without seas)	100.0	100.0	100.0	30.7	57.9	4.3	3.5	6.9	13.3	7.0	7.2	21.8	21.4	14.7	22.6	1.27	1.46
North Sea		100.0						100.0							0.0	0.0	0.0

Sources: Sortia et al. 1986; *Atlas Economic de L'Europe*.

sustained by these regions since the beginning of the 1960s is concentrated within the sectors with a high added value, more and more often limited to design, management and marketing rather than to production in itself. Basic heavy industry is clearly not strongly represented. These regions are the privileged places for the concentration of highly qualified manpower and of research and development.

One may now add in secondary metropolitan centres, in general less central ones and also less within the international management networks (Oslo, Göteborg-Malmö-Copenhagen, Bremen, Berlin, Vienna, Genoa, Marseilles). Market services, banking and insurance are here proportionally less developed, in contrast with the non-market and the transport sectors, most of those cities being ports.

Together the major and secondary central metropolitan regions supply more than a quarter of the added value in western Europe (Table 3.3).

Early heavy manufacturing and other central manufacturing regions

The central European belt with high densities of population stretching from north-western England to northern Italy, through the Benelux and the Rhine axis, is mainly part of the two central manufacturing types in our classification, when it is not inserted within the central metropolitan regions. As in the central metropolitan regions, manufacturing industries with high technological content and high asset intensity are widely represented here.

Today the less prosperous of these central manufacturing regions are the nineteenth-century early industrial basins, and especially those where mining and basic metallurgy were strongest, still supplying them with more or less 15% of their GDP and nearly a quarter of the gross manufacturing product in 1980: Glasgow, Midlands, South Wales, the Nord-Pas-de-Calais mining basin, the Walloon industrial axis, Lorraine-Luxembourg-Sarre, Ruhr, as well as Asturias, Cantabria and parts of the Basque Country. Today the GDP per inhabitant is slightly lower than the Western European average. The rigid social structures, derelict landscapes, and the deficiencies and weaknesses of local entrepreneurship are rendering their reconversion difficult. The Rhine–Ruhr region is probably one of the best off among these regions: it possesses major head offices on its fringes (Düsseldorf, Cologne), even in its centre (Essen). One finds here the virtues of the strong integration of manufacturing and financial systems in Germany.

GDP per head is higher in the remaining part of the central manufacturing regions. Here the manufacturing structures are more diversified, declining heavy sectors having less weight. Chemicals and mechanical engineering are better represented. Often local capital and entrepreneurship have also remained stronger, for example in regions marked by a textile tradition and smaller enterprises (for instance Flanders, Alsace, Franconia).

Table 3.3.. Repartition of the population and GDP (East Germany excluded, in PPS)

Regions	Population						GDP					
	1960	1966	1973	1982	1987	1990	1960	1966	1973	1982	1987	1990
Central metropolitan	18.3	18.8	19.1	19.1	19.1	19.2	24.8	24.6	24.8	24.4	24.6	25.2
Secondary central metropolitan	4.3	4.3	4.3	4.2	4.2	4.2	5.5	5.4	5.1	5.2	5.0	4.9
Early heavy manufacturing	8.5	8.5	8.3	8.0	7.9	7.8	9.7	9.2	8.6	8.1	7.9	7.8
Other central regions	18.4	18.6	18.7	18.4	18.3	18.4	21.8	21.0	20.7	19.7	19.6	19.5
Peri-central Parisian Basin type	4.7	4.7	4.8	4.8	4.9	4.8	4.2	4.4	4.5	4.7	4.6	4.6
Peri-central German type	4.5	4.4	4.4	4.2	4.1	4.2	4.0	4.0	3.9	3.9	3.9	4.0
Peri-central Scandinavian type	2.1	2.1	2.1	2.1	2.0	2.1	2.2	2.1	2.1	2.1	2.2	2.1
Peri-central Third Italy type	8.0	8.0	8.1	8.5	8.5	8.3	6.0	6.7	7.2	7.8	7.7	8.0
Intermediate and Alpine regions	12.7	12.7	12.8	12.9	12.9	12.9	12.7	12.6	12.3	12.5	12.7	12.4
Peripheral metropolitan	3.0	3.2	3.3	3.7	3.8	3.8	1.6	1.9	2.2	2.5	2.4	2.3
Southern and western periphery	13.8	13.1	12.4	12.5	12.7	12.6	5.9	6.6	7.1	7.5	7.7	7.6
Scandinavian periphery	1.8	1.7	1.7	1.7	1.7	1.7	1.4	1.4	1.4	1.4	1.4	1.3
Western Europe	100.0	100.0	100.0	100.0	100.0	100.0	100.0	100.0	100.0	100.0	100.0	100.0

Sources: OECD, Eurostat, national statistics (including some own estimations for 1960, 1966 and 1973)

The peri-central regions

Located on the fringes of the central regions, even sometimes penetrating within them, the peri-central regions have a GDP per inhabitant around or slightly less than the European average, but are less densely populated than the central regions. Here, in percentage of product, manufacturing is a little less important. We will distinguish four types of such regions.

(i) The 'Parisian basin' type, to which one may add north-eastern Belgium and some parts of northern Spain, is characterized by the importance of Fordist manufacturing relocation during the 1960s and at the beginning of the 1970s, in areas where manufacturing traditions and local entrepreneurship were weak. The search for reserves of unqualified manpower for assembly lines, especially in the mechanical engineering and automobile sectors, has led to the industrialization process. Apart from this recent industrialization, those regions have often kept an important agricultural base, at least where large-scale farming is practised, doubled downstream by a significant food industry.

(ii) The peri-central regions of the German type are occupying the eastern fringes of the Rhineland central belt and are insinuated within it in the old Hercynian massifs. Similar structures are continuing in northern Austria. In these regions, the weight of the agro-food channels is less important. On the contrary, textile and mechanical engineering register themselves as the prolongation of an ancient craftsman's tradition and are profiting from local entrepreneurship, ensuring stability of the industrial fabric.

(iii) In southern Sweden and southern Finland, the peri-central regions occupy vast areas, where low population densities are one of the main characteristics. The economic structures are related to those of the German peri-central regions, except for the very high weight of the non-market tertiary sector, generally characteristic of the Scandinavian welfare economies.

(iv) The fourth and last variant of the peri-central regions covers the 'Third Italy'. Catalonia, Valencia and the Porto region are related to it. Manufacturing, where textile and clothing are very highly represented, is relying on strong manpower resources, sometimes still cheap and, more than anywhere else, on a dense network of local entrepreneurship, on small strongly performing and innovative enterprises, and even on the hidden dynamics of an informal sector. These regions have inherited from ancient times a craftsmanship and merchant capitalist tradition, but had been forgotten by the early phases of the industrial revolution. Growing flexibilization of the economy over three decades is restoring the value of their flexible and consenting social structures.

The intermediate and Alpine regions

As in the 'Parisian basin' variant of the peri-central regions, the agro-food channels weigh rather heavily in the economy of the intermediate regions (peripheric UK and Denmark, northern Germany, western and southern

France). For the remaining part, the economic structures are rather less typical. Here manufacturing is less developed than in the peri-central regions: further away from the European centre, they have benefited less from Fordist decentralisations, thus they often keep small and medium-sized enterprises or raw materials and local resource-based manufacturing. Population densities are often low.

On a more detailed scale, the intermediate regions include insulated areas appearing as projections from the centre. Qualifying in this way are some new manufacturing poles cultivating their environmental advantages, some towns exploiting their cultural and university potentials, developing specializations in research and development within specific sectors, high-quality industries and leisure activities. Many of those poles are spread in the intermediate areas of southern England and southern France.

In the Alpine variant, the agro-food channels are less developed. On the contrary, the percentage of the product supplied by transport, trade and hotels but also building industry is very high, due to the importance of tourism and transit, but also, as far as building is concerned, of a rather high population growth and demand for second homes.

The poor periphery

The outer crescent stretching from Ireland to Greece corresponds not only to the poorest part of western Europe, with a product per inhabitant not exceeding 60% of the average, but also to the less industrialized part. Moreover, manufacturing industries with a high added value are especially poorly represented. The high percentage of agriculture, still more or less 15% of GDP in 1980, is characterized by low agricultural productivity and is not accompanied by significant agro-food developments downstream.

Some peripheral metropolitan regions, such as Lisbon, Naples and Athens, are spread through this belt, but their influence does not exceed their national or regional frameworks. Even if these centres are as well tertiarized as the central metropolitan regions, here the percentage of banking, insurance and market services remains low. Only trade and transport sectors show a relatively high development.

On the whole, in this western and southern periphery of western Europe, the market tertiary sector is badly developed in comparison with the non-market one. This general assessment hides very different situations according to the various countries; the market sector, especially banking, is more developed in Spain than in Southern Italy, where the relative importance of the non-market tertiary sector is reflecting an economy strongly marked by public transfers and clientelist practices.

The Scandinavian periphery

Here remoteness is the main characteristic, but it is not reflected in as low a level of GDP per head as one finds in the western and Mediterranean periphery. However, the product per inhabitant falls to around 80% of the European average, in spite of an important non-market tertiary sector. The standard of life is widely supported by income transfers, within the framework of a welfare economy. Fishing and forestry were still supplying nearly 10% of production in 1980. Manufacturing is relatively little developed, except in some isolated poles, often dominated by mining or the initial transformation of raw materials.

CHANGES BETWEEN 1960 AND 1990

The disparities between European regions and countries have not changed radically between 1960 and 1990 (Table 3.3). However, one may distinguish two periods, separated by the oil crisis, the first one corresponding to an A phase of a Kondratieff's cycle (yearly average growth of GDP of 4.7% from 1960 to 1973) and the second one to a B phase (growth rate of only 1.9% from 1973 to 1982 and 2.7% from 1982 to 1990).

Phase A up to 1973: reduction of inter-regional and international gaps

During phase A, spatial restructuring is stronger; in particular, the gap between rich countries in the centre and poor peripheral countries is perceptibly narrowing. From an index of 115 for the first ones to 51 for the second ones in 1960, it went down to the range 110 to 66 in 1973. Thus inter-regional disparities were reducing.

 Within a context of full employment in the rich regions, there is a tendency for capital and manpower to migrate in opposite directions. Income transfers towards poorer populations and regions increase, leading to a growth of income, which in turn generates some growth of the local productive sector.

 Important investments in the periphery, as well as in the peri-central regions of the Fordist type, are supported by a strong Keynesian policy of public aid to industrial investments and to infrastructure. Strong investments and public policy interventions also support the dynamics of 'Third Italy' peri-central regions, but here in the framework of a high local initiative.

 In the meantime, the relative position of the central regions slightly deteriorates. This is due to:

— first, the effects of industrial deconcentration in the central metropolitan regions, linked to a lack of space and to the weakness of their manpower reserves during a full employment period, in spite of immigration; but this industrial deconcentration, mainly felt in the production activities themselves, is well compensated for by the growth of the management tertiary sector;

— secondly, the coal crisis and restructuring problems in many regions of early industrialization; there is a low general manufacturing dynamism in many of the other central regions, again this is especially a problem at times of full employment and tensions in the labour market.

The structure of the regional economies is strongly modified during this period (Table 3.4):

— The importance of the primary sector is decreasing, especially where it had remained strong, in the western and Mediterranean peripheries, but also in Scandinavia.
— The relative weight of industry is slowly weakening in the central countries (from 49.1% in 1960 to 42.5% in 1973), for the benefit of the tertiary sector, mainly since the end of the 1960s. At this time, the percentage of the tertiary sector becomes higher than the secondary one.
— On the contrary, the percentage of industry is growing in the western and Mediterranean periphery (from 32.8 to 36.9%), simultaneously with the growth of the tertiary sector. A major manufacturing weakness persists in southern Italy, faced with excessive non-market tertiary activities linked to clientelist practices, and in Greece, where the archaic agriculture continues to weigh heavily. This relative industrialization pertains not only to the rural areas but also to the metropolitan areas of the poor periphery, which, unlike the metropolitan zones of the centre, are becoming relatively industrialized during this period. The manpower reserves are rather abundant there and remain a major focus for the rural exodus; the infrastructural deficiencies and the remoteness of large parts of the rural areas are still often serious handicaps acting against manufacturing investments.

During phase B, after 1973: the gaps remain or are even growing again

During phase B unemployment increases. Investments are more often defensive rationalization processes and thus modify the spatial patterns less radically, even if recent development regions are often facing the crisis better than the regions of older development. Social transfers are relatively reduced and (linked with budgetary constraints) the means granted for regional policies and territorial planning are weakened. Capital enjoys a growing percentage share of income in comparison with labour; there is a reduction in progressive taxation and a rise in neoliberalism. Furthermore, European unification begins to limit the protection which weak regions benefited from within their national frameworks. More-over, the accelerated globalization of the economy increasingly directs manufac-turing transfers towards the rest of the world.

These developments have strengthened financial concentration, benefiting central metropolitan regions and top-level management centres. At the same time, the industrial crisis has resulted in the closing of whole sections of the manufacturing infrastructure in the central regions, and new industrial invest-ments have occurred less frequently in the poor European periphery, becoming

Table 3.4. Structure of GDP (primary=only fishing, agriculture and forestry; mining included in secondary)

	1960			1966			1973			1982			1990		
	I	II	III	I	II	III	I	II	III	I	II	III	I	II	III
Europe	9.7	46.9	43.5	7.7	46.0	46.3	5.8	41.5	52.7	4.3	37.2	58.5	3.1	34.7	62.2
Italy	13.3	41.8	44.9	11.1	38.6	50.3	7.7	41.9	50.4	5.2	37.3	57.5	3.2	33.4	63.4
United Kingdom	4.4	47.3	48.3	3.0	46.0	51.0	2.5	37.3	60.2	2.2	39.8	58.0	1.8	34.8	63.4
Netherlands	9.1	45.5	45.4	8.3	49.6	42.1	5.7	40.1	54.2	4.5	34.3	61.2	4.5	33.4	62.1
Belgium	6.3	42.7	51.0	5.8	41.2	53.0	3.9	41.0	55.0	2.5	33.8	63.8	1.9	31.9	66.2
Luxembourg	8.0	52.2	39.8	6.1	52.1	41.8	3.5	46.3	50.1	2.8	33.3	63.9	2.0	34.4	63.6
Germany (West)	6.0	54.0	40.0	4.2	51.6	44.2	3.0	48.1	48.9	2.4	42.1	55.6	1.7	40.6	57.8
Switzerland	–	–	–	–	–	–	4.6	36.0	59.4	4.4	36.7	58.9	3.0	33.6	64.4
Austria	11.0	49.0	40.0	8.9	52.5	38.6	6.5	48.4	45.1	4.0	40.1	55.9	3.3	37.5	59.3
France	9.2	49.0	41.8	9.3	50.3	40.4	7.1	40.5	52.4	4.8	33.3	61.8	3.5	29.6	66.9
Italy (north and central)	10.5	45.5	43.9	8.8	42.0	49.2	6.0	45.1	48.9	4.6	42.9	52.5	2.5	35.8	61.7
Central countries	7.2	49.1	43.8	6.1	48.1	45.8	4.6	42.5	52.9	3.5	38.8	57.7	2.5	35.2	62.4
Ireland	25.3	29.9	44.8	20.0	33.0	47.0	17.9	35.4	46.7	11.2	35.2	53.6	10.5	44.0	45.5
Portugal	25.0	37.0	38.0	20.0	42.0	38.0	16.3	44.6	39.1	8.5	37.8	53.8	6.3	38.9	54.7
Spain	23.7	35.5	40.8	18.0	35.0	47.0	11.6	39.0	49.4	6.4	34.5	59.1	4.5	37.0	58.6
Italy (south)	22.5	29.1	48.5	18.8	26.9	54.3	13.8	30.7	55.4	10.2	32.6	57.2	5.6	25.0	69.4
Greece	25.8	24.7	49.5	24.0	26.0	50.0	20.4	33.2	46.4	18.4	19.1	52.5	15.7	27.3	57.0
Western and Mediterranean periphery	23.7	32.8	43.5	19.0	32.7	48.3	13.6	36.9	49.5	8.9	33.8	57.3	6.1	33.7	60.1
Denmark	14.6	39.6	45.8	10.0	40.0	50.0	6.8	31.8	61.4	6.4	27.1	66.5	4.4	27.5	68.1
Norway	9.1	37.4	53.5	7.1	38.4	54.5	6.3	35.8	57.9	4.0	42.2	53.9	3.1	37.8	59.1
Sweden	7.9	44.9	47.2	6.5	50.0	43.5	4.5	42.0	53.5	3.7	32.3	64.0	2.8	32.3	64.9
Finland	20.0	38.9	41.1	16.0	39.0	45.0	12.5	44.3	43.2	8.6	37.1	54.3	6.0	32.9	61.1
Iceland	–	–	–	–	–	–	–	–	–	10.1	33.9	56.0	11.9	30.4	57.6
Scandinavian periphery	11.9	41.4	46.7	9.2	43.8	47.0	6.9	39.0	54.1	5.5	33.8	60.8	4.0	32.3	63.7

Sources: UN Statstical Yearbooks, Eurostat and national statistics

too integrated to offer salary advantages comparable with those offered by some Third World countries and now also by nearby central Europe (Hungary, Czech Republic, Poland and Slovenia in the first instance).

In these circumstances, the relative levels of GDP in the various types of countries and regions are modified a great deal less than during the preceding period. Central countries remain at a relative level of 110 to 111 during the whole period, the countries of the western and Mediterranean periphery at the level of 66, those of Scandinavia oscillate from 103 to 110.

In the central regions, metropolitan areas are showing a tendency to maintain their relative position during the 1980s. This shows a radical reinforcement of their tertiarization and their management power. The modifications in the transport networks, high-speed railways and airport hubs are improving their competitive position for top-level services. At the same time, their deindustrialization is proceeding. This relative reinforcement of the central metropolitan regions is encompassed on a scale where it may hide decentralization for the benefit of peri-urban areas and growing socio-geographical inequalities inside those regions.

The decline of early heavy industrialized regions is also proceeding, even if it seems to slow down at the end of the period. The serious concern about the future of this type of regions lies in the fact that a decline in manufacturing is accompanied by a decline in services (by comparison with the European average), unlike that which can be observed for the rest of the central industrial regions, now clearly richer than the areas of early heavy industrialization.

The central manufacturing regions with the best performance are those where dynamic and policy-supported restructuring is taking place and those which have the best links with the international communication networks. The worst performances are in regions with a high percentage of big manufacturing sectors now hit by the crisis, such as the automobile industry or some parts of the chemical industry undergoing defensive restructuring processes, located in regions where the environment is not taken sufficiently into account.

Among the peri-central regions, those possessing the most interconnected industrial fabrics and where the local management system is the most powerful are improving their relative position in a crisis situation more quickly: notably peri-central German and Scandinavian regions and the 'Third Italy' type. The developments are less favourable where the developments were based more on Fordist decentralization with little local management ('Parisian basin' type).

The 'catching-up', which were very significant in the wider periphery during phase A, now cease in phase B. This is true for both the poor peripheries and the Scandinavian peripheries.

Regarding structures, the various European economies are more and more homogenizing, through a radical reduction of the percentage of the product coming from agriculture in the remote regions, and through an increase of the percentage of the tertiary sector around a European standard which is today 60% or more of total GDP. Among the central countries, the percentage of the tertiary sector is weaker where the industrial priorities have been stronger, but also where manufacturing internalizes most of its services (Germany and Austria). In the poor periphery, it is stronger where the tertiary sector is the most parasitical (southern Italy). In the Scandinavian countries, the weaker percentage of the tertiary sector in Norway and in Iceland can be explained by the importance of the primary sector (fishing), or by the importance of the secondary sector (crude oil).

A shift of the centre of gravity of the European economy from the north towards the centre, along the Rhine axis

All the changes described above mean an overall upholding of the weight of the central countries in the European economy: 81.8% of total gross product in 1960, 79.1% in 1973, 78.1% in 1990. For the total period, the western and Mediterranean peripheral countries (including southern Italy) increased from 11.2% to 15.1% (14.2% in 1973); Scandinavia remains just under 7% (Table 3.3). Nevertheless, inside the central countries one witnesses a clear shift of the centre of gravity in the European economy towards the south: this is linked to the weakening of the northern flank of the central regions, where the main part of the early industrial basins are concentrated, especially those of the Hercynian coal fields, and to the relative reinforcement of the economy in northern and central Italy (Figure 3.3). The centre of gravity of the European economy is thus moving from the vicinity of northern Rhineland to southern Germany.

CONCLUSION

Looking at the most recent trends, the slight reduction in the gap between western European regions and countries between 1960 and 1973, and probably since the end of the second World War, may have been only a temporous step. Moreover, it should also be stated that lessening spatial gaps as measured by quantitative indicators can mask growing qualitative gaps, in terms of ability to manage innovation or to master economic decisions, inside the framework of a deepening functional division of labour at the worldwide scale. In fact, recombining disparities continue to favour the central metropolitan regions (if one excludes their derelict central areas) and some very strongly linked specialized poles and areas welcoming research and development activities, sometimes owing to environmental advantages (including even some privileged parts of the periphery, often centred on Mediterranean cities with strong cultural and urban politics). They also disadvantage other parts of the periphery, more and more in competition with some Third World and some central and eastern European countries, but also the central early manufacturing regions.

Budget constraints and more liberalism risk weakening regional and territorial planning policies and the economic developments induced by income

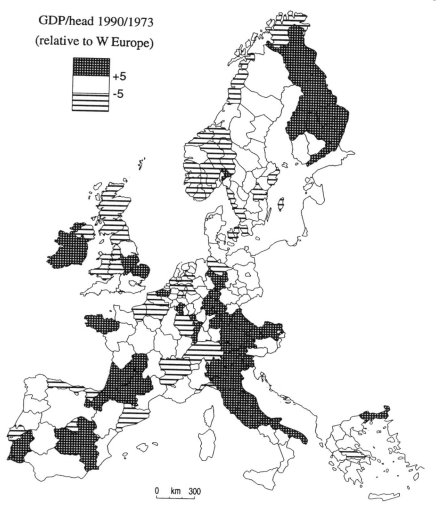

GDP/head 1990/1973
(relative to W Europe)

+5
-5

0   km   300

Figure 3.3.   Regional patterns of GDP growth

transfers. In general, the large Fordist peripheral manufacturing developments either pertain to the past, or are forming outside the European Union.

REFERENCES

Sortia, J.R., Vandermotten, Ch. and Vanlaer, J. (1986) *Atlas Economique de l'Europe.* Bruxelles: Société Royale Belge de Géographie, Université Libre de Bruxelles.
Vandermotten, Ch. (1993) *Les Régions de la Communauté Européenne: Convergence, Divergence ou Recomposition de Disparités?* Lille: Hommes et Terres du Nord, pp. 3–14.

4 Migration, Counterurbanization and Regional Restructuring in Europe

TONY CHAMPION AND CHRISTIAN VANDERMOTTEN
University of Newcastle upon Tyne, UK and Université Libre de Bruxelles, Belgium

INTRODUCTION

The central theme of this chapter is that during the past three decades the scale and patterning of migration and associated population redistribution in Europe have undergone some marked changes. The underlying aim is to discover the factors which have helped to bring about these changes and thereby to provide a basis for assessing their implications for the future map of population change. In particular, since the 1960s the importance of changes in the economy in producing population shifts has been challenged in the light of evidence that social and 'quality of life' factors were becoming increasingly important in inter-regional migration, notably those involving movement away from major urban centres and more heavily populated regions.

Within the context of this book, the main purpose of this chapter is therefore to document the changes which have taken place in regional patterns of net migration across Europe and to examine the extent to which they conform to expectations arising from the wider literature on recent population change. It takes its lead from research on the changing situation in the USA which has attempted to distinguish the relative importance of counterurbanization and economic restructuring in producing the new patterns of migratory change (see, for instance, Frey 1987, 1989). In doing this, the chapter provides an empirical framework within which the more localized studies appearing later in the book can be situated.

The chapter begins with a description of the regional patterns of net migratory change for the 18 countries of the European Economic Area, comparing the experiences of 1960–70, 1970–80 and 1980–89. It then examines the extent to which the patterns of each decade can be explained statistically, first in terms of population movement between regional economic types, and secondly in terms of shifts from more heavily populated areas to more rural regions. This is

People, Jobs and Mobility in the New Europe. Edited by Hans H. Blotevogel and Anthony J. Fielding.
© 1997 European Science Foundation. Published in 1997 by John Wiley & Sons Ltd.

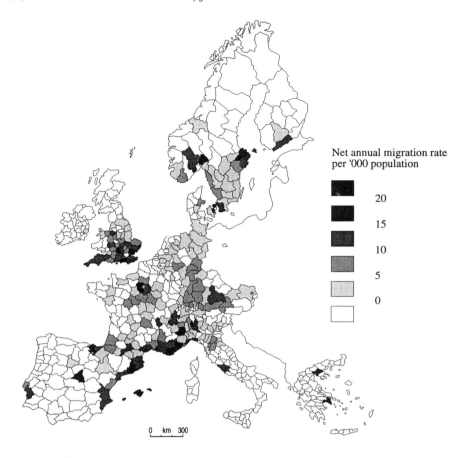

(a) Net migration gains 1960–70

Figure 4.1   Annual average rate of net migration by region in the 1960s

followed by a case study of the relationship between population and employment change in Britain, which in its turn leads on to a discussion of the factors which can distort this relationship.

REGIONAL PATTERNS OF NET MIGRATION IN EUROPE, 1960–89

This essentially descriptive part of the chapter covers all 12 member states of the then European Community, excluding the former German Democratic Republic. It also includes Austria, Switzerland, Iceland, Norway, Sweden and Finland. The regional units are a combination of NUTS 2 and 3 for the European

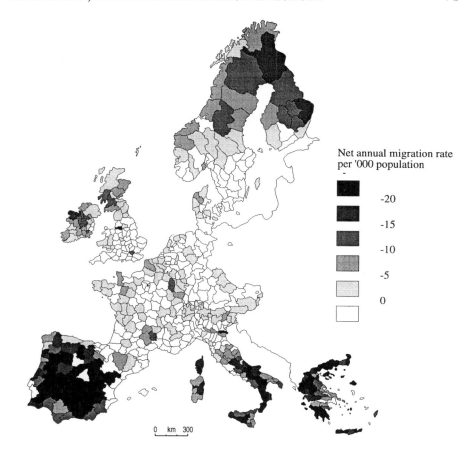

Net annual migration rate per '000 population

- -20
- -15
- -10
- -5
- 0

(b) Net migration losses 1960–70

Community, together with broadly equivalent statistical areas for the other countries, except that Iceland is treated as a single unit.

The regional patterns of net migration for the three separate decades are presented in Figures 4.1, 4.2 and 4.3. These are based mainly on data provided by National Statistical Offices and Eurostat. It should be stressed that the basic migration data are estimates rather than direct counts and have been calculated as a residual by subtracting estimated natural change from total population change. The estimated levels of net migration change are related to mean regional populations for the respective periods and expressed in terms of annual rates per thousand people.

Even a cursory glance at these maps reveals significant differences between the three periods, with the most radical changes occurring between the 1960s and 1970s. The most conspicuous feature of the 1960–70 patterns (Figure 4.1) is the

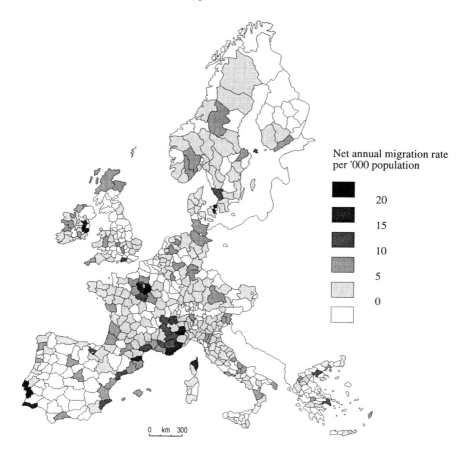

Net annual migration rate
per '000 population

20

15

10

5

0

0   km   300

(a) Net migration gains 1970–80

Figure 4.2.   Annual average rate of net migration by region in the 1970s

high level of net migratory losses sustained by the more peripheral parts of
Europe, notably the large number of more rural regions across southern Europe
from Portugal to Greece, but also the Atlantic fringe of the UK and all but the
more accessible parts of Scandinavia. Across the remainder of Europe, the
dominant pattern of the 1960s is one of net migratory gains, with particularly
strong growth in or around major metropolitan centres, most notably in
southern England, the Paris region and Provence in France, northern Italy,
southern Germany and the Scandinavian capital cities. The main exceptions are
found in some of the remoter rural areas, for instance in France and Germany,
but in most cases the levels of population loss are very much lower than in the
more peripheral parts of Europe.

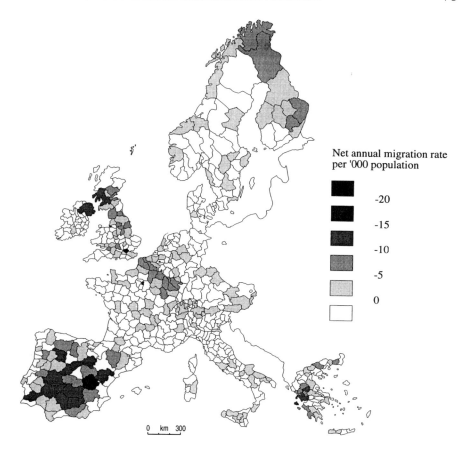

(b) Net migration losses 1970–80

In the following decade (Figure 4.2), virtually all the more peripheral parts of Europe experienced much lower rates of migratory loss than in the 1960s, with the few remaining regions that were still registering net out-migration of 10 per thousand or more being largely concentrated in Iberia. Indeed, for many of the more rural regions of southern Italy, Greece, Ireland and Scandinavia (apart from Finland), net in-migration had replaced net out-migration. In parallel, the level of migratory gains by the core regions was generally much lower in the 1970s than previously or had switched to a net loss, as is the case for southern England, Stockholm, Madrid and Rome. As a particular example, France exhibits both stability and change in the 1970s, with strong net in-migration continuing in the Paris region and a wide area based on Rhône-Alpes but with a number of rural *départements* in the west and south-west moving from losses to

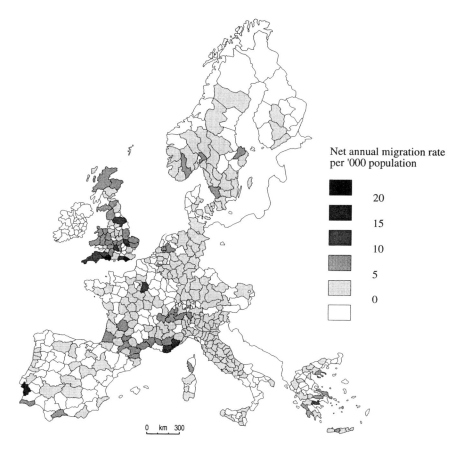

(a) Net migration gains 1980–89

Figure 4.3.   Annual average rate of net migration by region in the 1980s

gains and with losses becoming more entrenched along the northern border.
    Turning to the patterns for 1980–89 (Figure 4.3), a further shift away from
large-scale net migration losses in southern Europe can be seen, with hardly any
losses of 5 per thousand or over, even in Iberia. Elsewhere in Europe, the number
of regions experiencing migration loss has increased somewhat since the 1970s,
but apart from Ireland, northern Norway and north-east France the rates of net
out-migration are low. Similarly, the number of regions recording higher rates of
migratory gain are also much smaller than for the 1970s. Indeed, the general
picture conveyed by Figure 4.3 is one of remarkably low net migration
exchanges compared with the two previous decades, with both the removal of
the broad core–periphery contrast observed for the 1960s and a marked

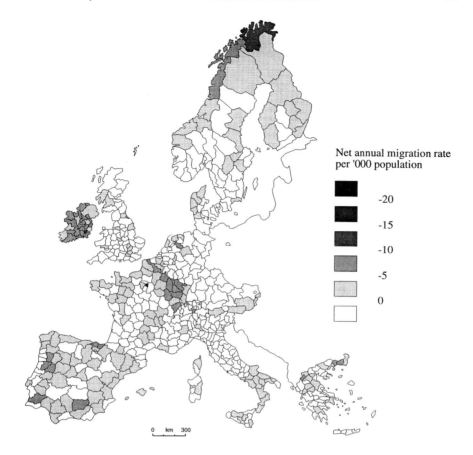

Net annual migration rate per '000 population

- -20
- -15
- -10
- -5
- 0

(b) Net migration losses 1980–89

reduction in the more localised within-country variations in migration rate which were still evident in the 1970s.

Given all the attention which has been paid in the last few years to the population exodus from Eastern Europe and the increasing pressure from refugees, asylum seekers and illegal migrants, the comparatively static picture for the 1980s might seem rather surprising. In fact, this slowdown in migration since the 1960s – and, more particularly, since the economic recession of 1974–5 – is corroborated by other data sources which measure migration directly and results both from lower levels of both net migration between Europe as a whole and the rest of the world and from a reduction in net movements between European countries. At the same time, it should be pointed out that the period under study, terminating in 1989, misses the main period of population upheaval in the former USSR satellite countries, and it should be acknowledged that the data may not represent very accurately the impact of illegal movements into and within southern Europe, though these too are believed to have been taking place at a relatively low level before the late 1980s.

In any case, the potential effect of any data problems pales into insignificance beside the scale of the changes in estimated levels of migration since the 1960s. According to the results of analysis of variance, applied to the net migration rates of the 557 regions shown in Figures 4.1–4.3, the level of inter-regional variance fell from 113.3 to 42.2 between the 1960s and the 1970s and had contracted by a similar factor by the 1980s when it stood at only 15.2. This development raises major questions in its own right, but these are best addressed after a fuller examination of the migration patterns of the two earlier decades.

ANALYSIS OF NET MIGRATION RATES BY REGIONAL ECONOMIC TYPES

Given that a strong association is normally held to exist between migration attractiveness and economic growth, this section examines the degree to which the regional variation in net migration rates observed in the previous section corresponds with the role of the regions within the European economy. The following analysis makes use of a 13-fold typology of regions developed by Vandermotten (see Chapter 3) and calculates the weighted average net migration rate of the regions making up each type. The results are presented in two ways: first the full list of migration rates for the 13 regions in Table 4.1, and secondly in diagrammatic form in Figure 4.4, with regional types arranged in a broadly geographical pattern and with regional types joined together in cases where the performance of one is not significantly different from another (as measured at the 1% level by the Student t-test).

This analysis reveals a marked degree of variation between regional types for the period 1960–70. It confirms the massive exodus from the more peripheral parts of Europe noted in Figure 4.1, with net out-migration averaging 6.4 per thousand in the Scandinavian periphery (Iceland, most of Norway and the northern halves of Sweden and Finland) and as much as 15.4 per thousand a year in the 'poor Periphery' (most of southern Europe and Ireland). At the other extreme, metropolitan regions were proving very attractive on average, and not just the central and secondary metropolitan regions but also those in the southern and western periphery (a small group comprising the regions dominated by Athens, Naples, Lisbon and Dublin). Most of the central core of Europe was characterized by fairly strong net in-migration, including 'other central regions', the 'Alpine zone', the 'Third Italy', 'pericentral Scandinavia' (essentially southern Finland and the non-metropolitan parts of southern Sweden), and the 'intermediate regions'. The only region type in the core that experienced net out-migration was the 'early heavy manufacturing' category, though two peri-central categories (the German and Paris Basin types) averaged only 0.5 per thousand – the European average at this time.

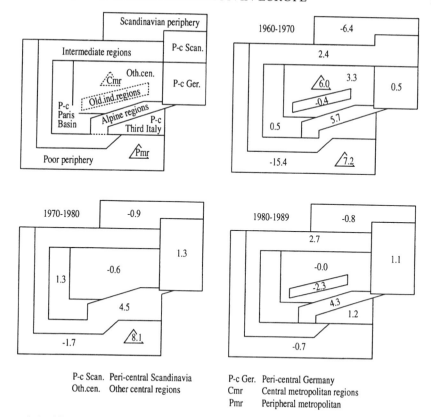

P-c Scan. Peri-central Scandinavia
Oth.cen. Other central regions

P-c Ger. Peri-central Germany
Cmr   Central metropolitan regions
Pmr   Peripheral metropolitan

Figure 4.4 Net migration rates by regional economic types (for details on the typology see Chapter 3)

The equivalent regional analysis for the 1970s and 1980s is much less discriminating in terms of migration differentials. The absolute range of migration rates is much lower than for the 1960s, more of the regional types are not significantly different from each other and there is no clear geographical dimension to the patterns. The main elements of both core and periphery share remarkably similar net migration balances in both decades, with much lower rates of net loss experienced by the poor and Scandinavian peripheries than in the 1960s and with a significant reduction in the net gains of the 'core' regional types – indeed involving a switch into net loss for the central metropolitan regions and other central regions. In the 1970s the fastest gaining type comprises the peripheral metropolitan category, but even this had slipped into net out-migration in the 1980s, leaving the Alpine, intermediate, secondary metropolitan and three peri-central types as the only ones averaging migration gain.

At the same time, however, Table 4.1 also shows that very few of the 13 regional types followed a consistent trajectory in net migration rates between

Table 4.1. Net migration rate, 1960–89, by type of region

Type of region (number of regions)	1960–70	1970–80	1980–89
Central regions			
Central metropolitan (35)	6.0	–0.3	–0.1
Secondary metropolitan (18)	6.2	1.0	3.8
Early heavy manufacturing (25)	–0.4	–1.6	–2.3
Other central (44)	3.3	–0.8	–0.4
Peri-central regions			
Paris Basin type (43)	0.1	1.7	–0.9
Germanic type (19)	0.9	0.6	1.0
Scandinavian type (21)	2.5	1.8	1.4
Third Italy type (58)	2.1	4.3	1.2
Alpine/intermediate			
Alpine (29)	5.7	6.0	4.3
Intermediate (84)	2.6	4.3	2.7
Peripheral regions			
Peripheral metropolitan (6)	7.2	8.1	–0.7
Poor periphery (147)	–15.4	–1.7	–0.7
Scandinavian periphery (28)	–6.4	–0.9	–0.8
All types (557)	0.5	0.9	0.4

Note: annual rate per thousand people, weighted averages

the three decades. The only clear case is that of the early heavy manufacturing type, with the steady increase in net out-migration rate from 0.4 in the 1960s to 1.6 in the 1970s and 2.3 in the 1980s. In some other cases, the 1980s can be viewed as essentially a consolidation of the rates reached in the 1970s, such as for the Scandinavian and poor periphery types, the other central regions and the central metropolitan type, even if the latter two involve a small rebound from their 1960s to 1970s trajectory in the final decade. By contrast, relatively marked departures from a consistent trend appear to have affected the secondary metropolitan type, with its pronounced dip in net in-migration in the 1970s, and some of the semi-peripheral regional types, notably the Paris Basin, Third Italy and intermediate types.

In this context, particular attention should be paid to the experience of the metropolitan regions because of the debate which is currently raging over the future of deconcentration trends (see below) together with signs of 'reurbanization' in the 1980s. The estimated average net migration rates for the three separate metropolitan types are presented by country in Table 4.2, usually comprising only one metropolitan concentration per country though any one may involve the aggregation of several statistical regions (for instance, metropolitan London comprises 12 countries in south-east England). These data confirm that for the central and secondary metropolitan types the reduction in net in-migration rate was universal between the 1960s and 1970s, with a significant number switching to net migration loss. In the 1980s a reversal of this

Table 4.2. Net migration rate, 1960–89, by metropolitan type and country

Type/country	1960–70	1970–80	1980–89	Regions based on
Central metropolitan regions				
Belgium	6.3	1.6	0.2	Brussels
France	4.6	-2.3	-2.1	Paris
Germany (FRG)	8.1	4.9	1.4	Frankfurt/Hamburg/Munich
Italy	14.3	-1.4	0.0	Milan/Rome
Netherlands	0.0	-1.6	1.3	Randstad
Spain	22.9	9.4	-2.8	Madrid
Sweden	10.2	-0.3	3.8	Stockholm
Switzerland	10.8	-1.6	2.4	Geneva/Zurich
UK	0.3	-3.7	-0.3	London
Secondary metropolitan regions				
Austria	5.2	1.2	1.4	Vienna
Denmark	4.8	-1.7	-0.5	Copenhagen
France	13.3	9.4	-1.4	Marseilles
Germany (FRG)	3.3	-1.9	13.0	Berlin (West)/Bremen
Italy	5.6	0.8	1.8	Genoa
Norway	7.2	-1.3	4.8	Oslo
Sweden	7.8	1.4	3.0	Malmö/Göteborg
Peripheral metropolitan regions				
Greece	21.0	10.1	-0.7	Athens
Ireland	2.5	2.7	-9.3	Dublin
Italy	-4.9	-4.0	-2.1	Naples
Portugal	7.3	22.3	4.1	Lisbon

Note: annual rate per thousand people, weighted averages of regions in each type and country

trend is evident for three-quarters of the places, though this has generally involved only a small upward shift in rate rather than a resumption of 1960s' levels of migration attractiveness. Table 4.2 also reveals that a sizeable proportion of the faster growth of the secondary metropolitan type shown in Table 4.1 can be attributed to the special case of West Berlin; otherwise, the experience of the secondary category in the 1980s is not markedly different from the central metropolitan type. Table 4.2 also disaggregates the peripheral metropolitan type, revealing that all but Naples contributed substantially to the negative shift in this type's migration balance between the 1970s and the 1980s.

The main conclusion to be drawn from this analysis of regional migration rates by regional economic type is that, while the latter provides a relatively good description of the patterns of regional differentiation in the 1960s, subsequently it is much less satisfactory. This reduction in discriminatory power can be summarized statistically in terms of the amount of inter-regional variance that is accounted for by the 13-fold typology. In the 1960s, it takes up a sizeable share of the overall inter-regional variance in migration rate, with between-group variance amounting to almost 40% of the total (45.6 out of 113.3). By the 1970s, however, this proportion was down to a sixth of the very much smaller total variance (6.9 out of 42.2) and by the 1980s it had contracted further (2.2 out of 15.2).

THE ROLE OF COUNTERURBANIZATION

The results of the analysis based on the economic typology of regions raise the question as to whether there are other factors with a stronger relationship to population redistribution patterns. Perhaps the most obvious candidate is the 'counterurbanization' phenomenon, involving net migration away from larger, more metropolitan centres and more heavily urbanized regions and down the urban hierarchy into more rural and remote areas, hence the often-used alternative labels of 'population deconcentration' and 'urban–rural shift'. International comparative studies and a wide range of case studies have shown that this phenomenon became particularly strongly developed in the 1970s (see Champion 1989 for a review), while clear signs of this process have also been seen from the analysis in the previous section, most notably the switch of metropolitan-type regions from migratory gain to loss in many European countries.

This section therefore explores the role of the urban–rural dimension in providing a framework for making sense of the regional variation in net migration rates shown in Figures 4.1–4.3. Following the approach of Fielding's (1982) seminal work on counterurbanization, population density is used as a surrogate measure of a region's urban status and allows the 557 regions to be grouped into eight density classes spanning the rural–urban continuum from heavily built-up (averaging at least 1200 inhabitants per square kilometre) to very sparsely populated (under 18.75). The relationship between regional migration rates and population density is examined here in three ways: first, by analysis of variance; secondly through the calculation of average migration rates for the eight density classes; and thirdly by correlation and regression analysis on the 557 regions and subsets of these.

Analysis of variance

The results of the analysis of variance for eight density classes are displayed in Table 4.3, alongside those for regional economic types and for countries. It can be seen that for the 1970s the density classes account for a significantly higher share of the inter-regional variance than does the regional economic typology in that decade (11.4 as opposed to 6.9). Even so, the share of the variance captured then is very little more than a quarter (11.4 out of 42.2), markedly lower than that of the economic types in the previous decade and indeed very similar to its own share then (28.3 out of 113.3). It is also clear that the emergence of density as a key dimension in regional patterns of net migration is relatively short-lived, for in the 1980s the eight density classes account for less than one-tenth of the total variance, lower than the regional typology and indeed lower than the

Table 4.3. Analysis of between-region variance in net migration rates, for alternative classifications of 557 regions

Classification/ source of variance	1960–70	1970–80	1980–89
Total variance (557 regions)	113.3	42.2	15.2
Regional types (13 groups)			
Between groups	45.6	6.9	2.2
Within groups	67.7	35.3	13.0
Density (8 groups)			
Between groups	28.3	11.4	1.4
Within groups	85.0	30.8	13.8
Countries (18 groups)			
Between groups	11.4	3.1	1.6
Within groups	101.9	39.1	13.6

grouping by country (although admittedly the latter involves considerably more groups, 18 as opposed to 8).

Mean migration rate for density classes

An indication of the overall relationship between net migration rate and population density can be obtained by calculating the average migratory change rate for each of the eight density classes. The results are plotted for each of the three decades in Figure 4.5. This immediately shows the reason for the decrease in variance explained by the density grouping, because the range between group means drops markedly between the 1960s and 1970s and the line drawn between group means flattens out even more in the 1980s.

As regards the nature of the relationship, the 1960s presents the clearest pattern, with the majority of density classes fitting closely to a straight line denoting a positive link between the two variables (Figure 4.5). This pattern of net in-migration for higher-density areas and net out-migration for lower-density areas is interpreted as 'urbanization' by Fielding (1982), as the population is shifting into the more heavily populated (i.e. more urbanized and built-up) areas and is becoming more concentrated in its distribution. This relationship, however, is not found across the whole range of densities. In particular, the most heavily populated regions (with densities of at least 1200 persons per square kilometre) were not sharing in the rapid migratory gains of the next two highest groups, but instead averaged net out-migration of almost 3 per thousand annually. At the other end of the urban–rural scale, the lowest-density category has a significantly lower rate of net out-migration than the adjacent category (significant at the 5% level according to the Student t-test), suggesting that the attractive force of the larger urban centres had not penetrated so deeply into these most rural regions by this stage, or that these areas had

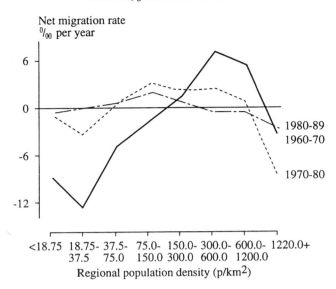

Figure 4.5 Annual average net migration rate 1960–89 for regions grouped by population density

already passed through their main phase of economic adjustment and associated depopulation.

By themselves, the relationships for the 1970s and 1980s appear much less dramatic, but nevertheless they exhibit several important features both individually and in comparison with each other (Figure 4.5). First, they retain a fair degree of regularity despite their flatter shapes. As in the 1960s, the lines follow an inverted U-shape, denoting net out-migration at the density extremes and net in-migration in between. Second, and especially impressive, is the relatively consistency of the shift in the relationship between decades. Particularly noteworthy is the major change in the migration experience of the density groups between the 1960s and 1970s, with the marked decrease in net out-migration for the next two classes, and the substantial downward shift in migration for the two lowest-density classes, the switch from net out- to net in-migratory balance for the three highest-density classes.

But it is also apparent that the 1980s, rather than seeing a reversal of this development, actually represent a consolidation and extension of it. This is shown by the continuation of the 'clockwise' rotation of the relationship, with the upward shift of the two lowest-density classes between the 1970s and the 1980s and the downward shift of most of the higher-density classes (Figure 4.5). The one exception to this generalization is provided by the highest-density class, which in the 1980s experienced a substantial recovery from the very high rate of migratory loss to which it had plummeted in the 1970s. This largely reflects the widespread migration-rate upswing of metropolitan regions observed in Table 4.2, but within the context of this density-based analysis it should still be noted that the highest-density category retains its 1970s position as the least attractive of the eight classes in terms of net migration rate.

Correlation and regression analysis

Two considerations suggest that the findings from the analysis of mean migration rates need to be explored more fully. First, as has been indicated by the analysis of variance reported above, within each density class there must be a considerable spread of cases around the mean figure. Secondly, not all parts of Europe will have been affected at the same time or to the same extent by the processes which underlie the relationships being examined here, notably because of the legacy of the stage of development reached by the beginning of the study period. A related factor is that, with this period predating the latest progress made towards the removal of migration barriers between many European countries, there are significant national variations in rates of migratory change resulting from differences in their openness to immigration both from other European countries and from the rest of the world. This section therefore examines the relationship between net migration rate and population density at the level of the individual region, first at the Europe-wide scale but then for individual countries and finally for broad zones of Europe.

The results of correlation and regression analysis for Europe as a whole are shown in the top data row of Table 4.4. (It should be noted that the logarithm of population density has been used throughout so as to transform this variable into an approximately normal distribution.) Correlation applied to the 557 regions for the 1960s data yields a positive relationship that is significant at the 1% level, indicating that the higher the regional population density, the higher the rate of net in-migration or – at the lower density end of the scale – the lower the rate of net out-migration, leading to the greater concentration of population in the already more congested regions. For the two subsequent decades, by contrast, the level of correlation is virtually zero across Europe, with relationships that are not significant even at the 10% level. This constitutes a major change from the concentration trend of the 1960s, but reveals that across Europe as a whole there was no discernible tendency towards either further regional population concentration or dispersal.

The national-scale picture provided by the main panels of Table 4.4, however, shows a much more important urban–rural dimension to migratory change in the 1970s and 1980s for a number of countries. In both these decades 7 out of the 16 countries register relationships of at least a 5% level of significance, only one fewer than in the 1960s. The analysis also confirms the big swing between the 1960s and the 1970s in the general direction of the relationship, for whereas all the significant ones in the first decade were positive (indicating population concentration), by the 1970s four of the seven were negative (indicating deconcentration or 'counterurbanization') – a pattern which holds up fairly well in the 1980s when three were negative. In terms of the countries involved, it was the UK, Germany, France and the Netherlands that had the most significant tendency towards deconcentration in the 1970s, and the UK, France and Belgium/Luxembourg in the 1980s. Those experiencing the most significant concentration (or 'urbanization') in the 1970s were Finland, Greece and Spain, and in the 1980s Norway, Sweden, Finland and Germany.

Evidently, there have been some remarkable changes since the 1960s at the individual country level, some of which have been more sustained than others. In particular, the UK and France moved into strong deconcentration in the 1970s and appear to have continued in this manner into the 1980s, whereas Germany and the Netherlands switched to concentration after the 1970s, as did Denmark and Sweden. The three largest Scandinavian countries have generally been dominated by strong concentration tendencies, but the experience of Mediterranean countries and Ireland has altered substantially across the three decades, from one of strong concentration to much weaker relationships with (albeit non-significant) deconcentration tendencies for some.

These patterns are captured to some extent in the analysis for three broad European regions shown in the bottom panel of Table 4.4. This indicates continuous concentration in Scandinavia, a progressive reduction in the role of concentration in the group containing Mediterranean Europe and Ireland, and for the rest of Europe a swing into a strong deconcentration relationship in the 1970s followed by a weakening of this tendency.

THE RELATIONSHIP BETWEEN MIGRATION AND ECONOMIC PERFORMANCE

Thus far this chapter has examined the significance of two potentially important dimensions of population redistribution over the last three decades. These analyses provide some insight into the relationship between migration and economic factors, but only indirectly and to a limited extent. The next step is to explore the degree to which migration patterns appear to form a response to regional variations in economic performance. Unfortunately, this is by no means an easy task in the European context, not least because many of the basic economic indicators are normally produced for less disaggregated regional frameworks than those used for population statistics. For present purposes, therefore, recourse is made to a case study of the UK, where data on population and employment change have been assembled for a rigorously defined set of labour-market areas.

A CASE STUDY OF GREAT BRITAIN

This case study draws on data collected and processed during the course of the 'Booming Towns' research of Champion and Green (1985, 1988, 1990). This involved the calculation of key diagnostic variables relating to the economic standing and performance of places in Britain and the derivation from these of

Table 4.4. Relationship between net migration rate and population density, by individual country and country groupings

Country (number of regions)	1960–70 r	R²	S	1970–80 r	R²	S	1980–89 r	R²	S
Europe (557)	0.35	0.12	***	-0.01	0.00		0.06	0.00	
Individual countries									
Finland (12)	0.87	0.76	***	0.73	0.54	***	0.64	0.41	**
Norway (19)	0.34	0.12	***	0.01	0.00		0.62	0.39	***
Sweden (24)	0.80	0.64	***	-0.24	0.06		0.43	0.19	**
Austria (9)	0.24	0.06		0.24	0.06		0.25	0.06	
Belgium/Luxembourg (12)	0.21	0.04		-0.42	0.18		-0.58	0.34	**
Denmark (15)	-0.08	0.01		-0.47	0.22	*	0.09	0.01	
France (96)	0.23	0.05	*	-0.25	0.06	**	-0.29	0.09	***
Germany (FRG) (30)	-0.01	0.00		-0.38	0.14	**	0.44	0.19	**
Netherlands (11)	-0.03	0.00		-0.69	0.47	**	0.23	0.05	
Switzerland (24)	0.36	0.13	**	-0.14	0.02		-0.19	0.04	
UK (65)	-0.07	0.01		-0.65	0.42	***	-0.39	0.15	***
Greece (51)	0.68	0.46	***	0.33	0.11	**	0.09	0.01	
Ireland (26)	0.60	0.36	***	0.09	0.01		-0.32	0.10	
Italy (92)	0.43	0.18	***	-0.09	0.01		-0.15	0.02	
Spain (50)	0.75	0.56	***	0.72	0.52	***	-0.22	0.05	
Portugal (20)	0.62	0.38	***	0.34	0.12		0.33	0.11	
Country groupings									
Scandinavia (excl. Denmark) (56)	0.57	0.32	***	0.09	0.01		0.58	0.33	***
Central & northwest Europe (262)	0.12	0.02		-0.36	0.13	***	-0.17	0.03	*
Mediterranean and Ireland (239)	0.56	0.31	***	0.35	0.12	***	0.17	0.03	*

Note: data represent the correlation coefficient (r) and coefficient of determination (R^2) between regional net migration rate and the logarithm of regional population density. S denotes significance level: * 10%, ** 5%, *** 1%.

Table 4.5. Correlation between population change, employment change and selected indicator variables for the UK's 280 Local Labour Market Areas

Indicator variable	Population change 1981–5	Employment change 1981–4
Amalgamated Index of Local Economic Performance	0.503	0.596
Change in total employment, 1981–4	0.525	(1.000)
Unemployment rate, July 1987	−0.461	−0.545
Population change, 1981–5	(1.000)	0.525
Mean house price, 1986	0.404	0.390
Mean duration of completed unemployment spells	−0.346	−0.413
Change in the price of housing, 1982–6	0.337	0.336
Proportion of employment in producer services and high-technology (PSHT) industries, 1984	0.150	0.151
Change in unemployment rate, 1984–7 (July)	0.136	0.047
Change in employment in PSHT industries, 1981–4	0.082	0.250
Economic activity rate for working age, 1981	−0.034	−0.049

Note: date are correlation coefficients calculated across 280 LLMAs. See the source for more detailed specification of the variables.
Source: derived from work presented by Champion and Green (1988).

an amalgamated index on which the places could be ranked in terms of overall economic strength. The 'places' comprised the 280 Local Labour Market Areas (LLMAs) developed by the Centre for Urban and Regional Development Studies at the University of Newcastle upon Tyne and defined on the basis of urban centres and surrounding commuting hinterlands so as to be relatively self-contained in journey-to-work terms.

The results presented here draw on the 1988 study in which one of the key variables was population change 1981–5. This can be correlated across the 280 LLMAs with the other nine variables used in producing the amalgamated index, one of which was employment change for the roughly corresponding period 1981–4, as well as with the amalgamated index itself. From this it is possible to gauge the degree of correspondence between population change and local economic performance. (It should be noted that, unfortunately, population change data must be used here as a surrogate for migratory change, because migration data are not available for the ward-level units which serve as building blocks for these non-standard statistical areas.)

Table 4.5 shows the correlation coefficient of the relationship between population change and the amalgamated index, together with those with the other nine key variables. It can be seen that there is a relatively strong correspondence between population change and the amalgamated index (r=0.503) and also that the relationship between population change and employment change is marginally higher than this (r=0.525), these two being the highest correlations with population change. The same form of analysis applied to employment change (in the final column of Table 4.5) confirms the salience of population change, in that it is second only to unemployment rate in its level of correlation with employment change.

At the same time, however, these levels of correlation indicate that local economic performance and change in employment opportunities account for only a relatively small proportion of the variation between places in population growth rates. The variance in amalgamated index 'explains' (in statistical terms) barely a quarter of the variance in population change rate ($r^2=0.253$), the variance in employment change only marginally more (0.276). Three-quarters of the variation in population growth rates between the 280 LLMAs remains to be explained by other factors.

It has to be admitted that the above constitutes a rather demanding test of the relationship between aspects of population and employment change, given that it involves a relatively short period and a considerable degree of geographical disaggregation, as well as using a surrogate for migratory change. An analysis by Cross (1990) of net migration rates for the 10-year period 1971–81 for the broader geographical scale of the 54 counties of England and Wales revealed substantially higher correlations with measures of employment change, that with total employment change producing a 61% level of explanation ($r^2=61.2$). Similarly, using regression analysis to measure relationships at county level in south-east England for 1971–81, Champion and Congdon (1989) discovered a 59% level of explanation between population change and employment change, with the best-fit line indicating that a 1% change in employment is matched by a 0.6% change in population.

These tests of the relationship between measures of population and economic performance yield some clear results. There exists a highly significant positive relationship between the two, although the precise extent of the correspondence varies between studies. On the other hand, this appears to fall a long way short of a one-to-one correspondence, with the level of explanation ranging from a quarter to three-fifths depending principally on the geographical scale of analysis and with an indication that the regression coefficient is considerably less than unity.

FACTORS AFFECTING THE RELATIONSHIP BETWEEN MIGRATION AND EMPLOYMENT CHANGE

How far are these results to have been expected? There are at least three well-known factors that can account for the positive relationship between the two. First, the growth of jobs in a relatively self-contained labour market area will put pressure on labour supply, which raises wages and encourages net in-migration of workers and their families. Secondly, population growth in an area, whether by net in-migration or natural increase, generates extra jobs through the service multiplier. Thirdly, both these types of changes will increase the economic size of the place and the confidence of entrepreneurs about its future potential, making it attractive for further investment, particularly for the location of activities which have a size threshold for viability in terms of infrastructure, labour supply or local market.

At the same time, there are at least as many factors which can be brought to bear to explain why the relationship between migration and employment change can fall far short of a perfect fit. One concerns the level of self-containment of individual places. In the context of job growth, this relates to the extent to which commuting from surrounding areas can increase labour supply as an alternative to in-migration. In relation to the service multiplier, it depends on the extent to which the extra goods and services are imported from other areas rather than being supplied locally. The smaller the regional unit for analysis, the greater this distortion is likely to be, helping to account for the lower level of explanation found above for the more disaggregated LLMA framework than for the county scale.

Secondly, there is the possible effect of at least two other local labour-supply responses besides commuting. Shortage of workers resulting from employment growth can lead to a reduction in the number of unemployed people in the local labour force. It can also induce people who have not sought jobs previously to enter the labour market, thus increasing the rate of labour-force participation by working-age people. These two responses can also work in reverse in a situation of declining job opportunities, where unemployment rises and participation rates fall, the latter being most commonly found for married women because, more than other groups, they tend to move into and out of the labour market without recourse to 'official' unemployment status. Green and Owen (1991) have shown, through the medium of labour-market accounts applied to local labour-market change in early 1980s Britain, that these two factors can play a significant role and also that their role can vary significantly across the country; for instance, with higher unemployment and withdrawal from the labour market being the dominant response to job losses in some areas (e.g. south Wales) but with net out-migration being dominant in others (e.g. north-east England).

Third is the time factor. It can be expected that in the context of job growth the importing of commuters or goods and services, or the reduction in numbers unemployed, is more likely in the short term, with migration and service functions responding to the extra demand in due course as new housing, infrastructure and so on are developed. The shorter the period under study, the more serious this distortion is likely to be, this perhaps also helping to explain the lower correlations found above for the 1981–5 analysis compared to those for 1971–81. But the success of an approach which allows for the time factor will depend very much on whether it is employment growth that is the key factor in local growth or whether it is population growth arising, for instance, from retirement migration or the influx of commuters. In theory, if it is the former, then the migration response can be expected to lag behind the increase in jobs, and vice versa if the latter, with the appropriate lag effects needing to be incorporated in any statistical test.

These aspects relating to the time factor take us to the heart of one of the principal issues in the counterurbanization debate and our discussion about the extent to which economic restructuring can be considered responsible for the recent developments in European migration. There is a line of argument which maintains that migration is being increasingly influenced by non-job considerations, most notably by 'quality of life' factors including environment and cost of living, and that this is becoming as much a feature of long-distance moves as in its traditional milieu of local suburbanization. Such work (e.g. Findlay and Rogerson 1993) refers to the consistent results produced by surveys which ask people to rank the features which they feel lead to a good 'quality of life', results which place a premium on low pollution, low crime, good health care and low cost of living. These studies also show how an increasing proportion of the population is able to realize their aspirations: through such factors as the increasing proportion of (wealthy) retired people, the growth of self-employment, easier long-distance communications, and the greater sensitivity of employers to the needs of their highly qualified staff.

CONCLUSION

From the evidence examined in this chapter, it would seem that the scale of net migration movement between the regions of Europe contracted markedly between the 1960s and 1980s. This does not, however, mean that its relative importance in influencing geographical patterns of overall population change has diminished, nor does it make any easier the task of analysing regional variations in rates of migratory change or anticipating future trends. Indeed, as regional variations in rates of natural increase have narrowed, migration has grown in its significance for population forecasting, but conventional approaches to explaining regional migration differentials have lost much of their power.

In particular, there would seem to be considerable uncertainty over the extent to which the changes in net migration patterns since the 1960s are a response to changes which are taking place in the economy. As has been shown clearly above, the regional typology based on economic structure – which was such a powerful discriminator of regional migration differentials in the 1960s – has subsequently lost most of its explanatory power. Given the massive economic restructuring which has affected many parts of Europe in recent years, however, the question arises as to whether an improved level of explanation could be achieved by reference to other explanatory frameworks.

One leading alternative has been examined in this chapter, namely that of population deconcentration or 'counterurbanization'. The results are by no means conclusive and raise more questions. While there were significant changes between the 1960s and 1970s in the relationship between net migration patterns and the urban–rural dimension, generally towards deconcentration or at least slower concentration, this tendency weakened again in the 1980s, except in one or two countries. Moreover, there has been much debate over the extent to which any net migration down the urban–rural gradient can be attributed to the changing geography of employment opportunities as opposed to residential preferences linked to 'quality of life' considerations.

This is the reason for taking a closer look at the relationship between migration and economic performance. The case study of Britain showed that there is a relatively strong relationship between the two, but that substantial proportions of regional variation in population growth rates cannot be explained by basic measures of economic change such as total employment growth. Moreover, even where a strong relationship has been found to exist between the two, it has not been possible to tell whether this arises because of migration following job growth or the other way round. Techniques more sophisticated than correlation are required, as well as in-depth case studies of the processes involved. Hence the later chapters in this book are important for exploring these relationships in more detail.

REFERENCES

Champion, A.G. (ed.) (1989) *Counterurbanization: The Changing Pace and Nature of Population Deconcentration*. London: Edward Arnold.

Champion, A.G. and Congdon, P.D. (1989) Trends and structure in London's migration and their relationship to employment and housing markets, in Congdon, P. and Batey, P. (eds) *Advances in Regional Demography*. London: Belhaven, pp. 180–204.

Champion, A.G. and Green, A.E. (1985) *In Search of Britain's Booming Towns*. Discussion Paper 72, Centre for Urban and Regional Development Studies, University of Newcastle upon Tyne.

Champion, A.G. and Green, A.E. (1988) *Local Prosperity and the North–South Divide*. Coventry/Newcastle upon Tyne: Booming Towns.

Champion, A.G. and Green, A.E. (1990) *The Spread of Prosperity and the North–South Divide*. Kenilworth/Gosforth: Booming Towns.

Cross, D.F.W. (1990) *Counterurbanization in England and Wales*. Aldershot: Avebury.

Fielding, A.J. (1982) Counterurbanization in Western Europe, *Progress in Planning* 17:1–52.

Findlay, A. and Rogerson, R. (1993) Migration, places and quality of life: voting with their feet? in Champion, A.G. (ed.) *Population Matters: The Local Dimension*. London: Paul Chapman Publishing, pp. 32–49.

Frey, W.H. (1987) Migration and depopulation of the metropolis: regional restructuring or rural renaissance? *American Sociological Review* 52:240–57.

Frey, W.H. (1989) United States: counterurbanization and metropolis depopulation, in Champion, A.G. (ed.), *Counteurbanization: The Changing Pace and Nature of Population Deconcentration*. London: Edward Arnold, pp. 34–61.

Green, A.E. and Owen, D.W. (1991) Local labour supply and demand interactions in Britain during the 1980s, *Regional Studies* 25:295–314.

5 Restructuring and Socio-Spatial Mobility in Europe: The Role of International Migrants

RUSSELL KING

University of Sussex, UK

INTRODUCTION

While other chapters in this volume focus on the mutual relationship between economic restructuring and the internal socio-spatial mobility of European populations within various national and regional settings, this chapter examines the dialectic between restructuring and international migration. It looks both at the impact of economic change on established immigrant groups, most of whom entered as 'guestworkers' during the 1950s and 1960s but ended up by staying permanently or semi-permanently in their new countries of residence, and at the implications of economic restructuring for present and future waves of immigration. It is important to realize at the outset, however, that immigrants are not merely the passive recipients of the impact of economic restructuring; they can also be active components in changing and reshaping the production system, and this line of causation will be analysed too.

The chapter is in five main parts. The first looks at the question of how the socio-occupational profile of established immigrant communities is affected by economic restructuring. In the second part skilled international migration will be analysed as an expression of the restructuring and internationalization of the European and world economies. In the third section, instead of treating immigrant workers as the dependent variable, we will examine immigrants as a positive factor in economic restructuring. This section of the chapter will pay particular attention to the theme of ethnic entrepreneurship. The fourth section looks at the extent to which ethnic minorities have been geographically mobile within their countries of settlement, migrating internally in response to economic opportunities or imperatives, or perhaps because of other factors. Finally, we look at ways in which the restructuring of the European economy creates demands and opportunities for the newer waves of immigrants who have been entering Europe, mainly from developing countries, during the 1980s and 1990s. The conclusion will look briefly to the future.

People, Jobs and Mobility in the New Europe. Edited by Hans H. Blotevogel and Anthony J. Fielding.
© 1997 European Science Foundation. Published in 1997 by John Wiley & Sons Ltd.

Table 5.1.   Socio-economic restructuring and immigration: some hypothesized links

Socio-economic restructuring system changes	Possible impact on immigrants and immigration trends
Changes in the production system	
Further contraction in mining and in traditional 'smokestack' industries	Shrinking demand for immigrant workers who originally staffed these industries in the early post-war period
Decline in 'Fordist' factories mass producing goods for mass consumption	Reduced demand for traditional immigrant workers of the type recruited in the 1950s, 1960s and early 1970s
Rise in high-tech industries and advanced producer services	Increase in demand for skilled international immigrants
Expansion in small and medium-sized enterprises and in the informal economy	New opportunities for international migrants, particularly those willing to work in the 'secondary' labour market; possibilities for ethnic entrepreneurship
Changes in the demographic system	
Ageing of European populations	Increase in demand for labour in the 'care' sector, especially female immigrants
Fertility decline	Eventual decline in new labour market entrants: need for 'replacement' labour
Changes in the social and educational system	
'Embourgeoisement' of native workforce through traditional association of previous waves of immigrants with lower-status jobs	Rejection by native workers of lowest-status jobs creates further demand for immigrants
Increasing length of full-time education boosts employment aspirations of new labour market entrants	Increased demand for immigrant labour to fill low-status jobs

Economic restructuring is a complex process, multi-faceted and multi-layered, and it is not the only process affecting the socio-economic position of immigrants in Europe. Table 5.1 is an attempt to summarize, in a very crude way, the three clusters of system changes which may be identified as having an influence over the changing status of immigrants in the core economies of Europe. Further reference to this table will be made at various points throughout the rest of this chapter.

THE IMPACT OF ECONOMIC RESTRUCTURING ON ESTABLISHED IMMIGRANT COMMUNITIES

The European experience of mass immigration between the end of the Second World War and the 1970s displays many common elements between the main countries receiving migrants. Heavy inflows of labour from southern Europe and from former colonies occurred in the period between the late 1950s and early 1970s, this labour being mainly directed to low-status jobs in factories, mines, building sites and menial services. Although it was anticipated in some countries (notably Germany and Switzerland) that the migrant workers would return home after a few years, most ended up by staying for good (Castles et al. 1984). These structural characteristics of timing, labour market position and transition to permanent settlement hold true for a remarkable diversity of nationalities in the different receiving countries.

Kindleberger (1967), among others, stressed the positive, indeed crucial, role that elastic supplies of low-cost immigrant workers played in fuelling fast industrial growth without inflation. The workers were 'cheap' not only because of the comparatively low wages they received (low in comparison to the norm for the receiving country but high in relation to what they could have earned had they stayed at home – hence the attractiveness of migration), but also because the host country had been spared the costs of reproduction of labour. Subsequently the stereotyping of ethnic groups with certain kinds of jobs (West Indian bus conductors in London, Turkish refuse collectors in Germany etc.) made these 'dead-end' jobs even more unattractive to indigenous workers and probably led to enhanced ethnic discrimination practices.

Over the past 10–15 years, economic restructuring in the core of Europe[1] has changed the geography of opportunity for immigrants. A new range of opportunities has been offered to certain regions and certain groups of people, while simultaneously opportunities previously available have been withdrawn in other regions and from other groups.

The basic features of economic restructuring in western Europe are summarized in the top section of Table 5.1. The further decline in mining and heavy industries such as iron and steel and shipbuilding continues a process in train throughout much of the post-war era, and the 1980s and 1990s have seen the virtual disappearance of these sectors of economic activity in many regions where they were once the very lifeblood of the economy. The presence of immigrant labour in these industries was highly variable from one country to another and between industries: in many British industrial regions, mining, steelworking and other old, heavy industries were bastions of the native working class; whereas in France and Belgium, Poles and Italians were recruited *en masse* both before and shortly after the Second World War to work in the mines. The closing down of these industries therefore had some deleterious impacts on immigrant employment, but in many cases the workers were elderly and close to retirement.

The contraction of Fordist production methods since the 1970s, however, has had a much more dramatic effect on the immigrant workforce, since in many cases foreign labour had been specifically recruited in the 1960s to staff these plants. The penetration of foreign labour into these industries of mass production varies from country to country and can be usefully interpreted with reference to the dualistic concept of a primary and secondary labour market (Piore 1979), which is also central to the later analysis of this chapter.[2] In (West)

Germany manufacturing industry was the main recruiter and employer of foreign labour, *Gastarbeiter* or 'guestworkers' being especially concentrated in the more unpleasant factory jobs (for instance in noxious or noisy environments) and in the declining textile sector. Construction was also an important employer of foreign workers in Germany, but until recently relatively few were employed in the service sector. Although most of the migrants occupied rather low-level manual jobs on the factory floor, and were recruited initially on short-term contracts, they became members of the primary labour market with fixed hours, fixed rates of pay and some measure of protection by collective bargaining. In France, on the other hand, the pattern of immigrant employment has been skewed more towards construction and services. When immigration was at its peak in the late 1960s and early 1970s some 30% of new migrants into France were going into building and public works. This sector, together with health services, had by far the greatest reliance on foreign workers – over 30%, double the proportion of foreign workers in those sectors in Germany (Gordon 1991, p. 13). Overall, a substantially greater share of immigration into France has been directed towards the secondary labour market of unprotected, often part-time jobs. As we shall see later, the French model of immigrant employment has been the one followed, and extended, by recent immigration into southern Europe from Africa and Asia.

Gordon (1991) has shown that economic restructuring not only involves an overall sharp decline in traditional manufacturing industry, but that deindustrialization and the loss of manual jobs in restructured transport and distribution activities induces a growing polarization of employment opportunities within the service sector, especially within the most advanced regions. On the one hand the stable employment opportunities of the primary labour submarket are increasingly concentrated in tertiary and quarternary sector activities such as business services and professional occupations. These posts tend to require formal educational qualifications, which makes traditional labour migrants manifestly ineligible. Such jobs are therefore taken by highly qualified natives, together with a certain quota of skilled international migrants from within the advanced countries of Europe. Some movements of highly trained migrants – for example in the legal and teaching fields and in the civil service – are limited by the incompatibility of qualifications, by security concerns, and by barriers erected by professional associations. Within the European Union, these imperfections in the Single Market for labour have yet to be resolved.

On the other hand, service sector jobs which do not require authorized training are increasingly found in the expanding private consumer services, often in small establishments operating within highly competitive industries or in individual-scale petty trading activities, both served mainly by the secondary labour market. Sassen-Koob (1984) has shown that there *can* be a growing demand for immigrant labour in these small-scale service industries, especially in big cities, but the channels of recruitment are quite different from those which supplied the large-scale Fordist industries with part of their primary labour

Table 5.2.   France: employment of foreign workers in firms with 10 or more employees, 1973–9

Branch	1973	1979	Change No.	Change %
Food industries	31200	25600	−5600	−17.9
Oil and gas production	1300	1000	−300	−23.1
Capital and consumer goods	570400	463000	−107400	−18.8
Building, civil engineering	407500	310000	−97500	−23.9
Distribution	70000	71000	+1000	+1.4
Hotels and catering	23100	26000	+2900	+12.6
Transport (excluding SNCF)	25500	29100	+3600	+14.1
Industrial services	91600	128800	+36400	+39.7
Financial services, real estate	6000	7600	+1600	+26.7
Total foreign wage earners	1226600	1061300	−165300	−13.5
Foreign employment as % of total	11.8	10.1		

Source: *SOPEMI Report 1982*, p. 59.

demand during the earlier period. The restructuring thesis thus suggests that, in at least partial compensation for the loss of foreign workers' jobs in Fordist factories, there have been expanding opportunities for less organized migration into jobs drawing on the secondary labour market, where there is still a strong demand for flexible, cheap labour.

The rather scattered data on the impact of economic restructuring on ethnic employment patterns lack cross-country comparability because of the way different categories of employment are used in each country. Generally, however, the available information supports the existence of the processes outlined above and summarized in the top part of Table 5.1. Gordon's (1991) digest of Eurostat data for the 1980s for an aggregate of four countries (Belgium, France, Germany and the Netherlands) reveals a major shift in the balance of foreign worker employment from mining, manufacturing and construction, which accounted for almost two-thirds of jobs in 1980, to services, which comprised 41% of total foreign employment in 1986. The services' share in 1986 was approximately half in Belgium, France and the Netherlands; it was a third in West Germany where a majority (albeit reduced) of foreign employment remained in manufacturing.

There is evidence from France that the shift of migrant employment away from industry and into services pre-dates the 'restructuring decade' of the 1980s and can be traced at least to the first oil crisis of the mid-1970s (Table 5.2). Mass recruitment of foreign workers into industry ceased abruptly in 1974 and there was, in any case, a natural tendency among many migrant groups to seek self-improvement away from the factory production-line. Table 5.2 shows that between October 1973 and October 1979 there was a loss of 210 800 industrial and construction jobs held by foreigners, and this was only partially compensated by an increase of 45 500 service-sector jobs. Note, however, that these figures refer only to firms with at least 10 employees.

The annual reports of SOPEMI, the OECD's international migration monitoring unit,[3] also refer – repeatedly – to the fact that industrial redundancies have had disproportionate impacts on western Europe's immigrant populations. For instance, the 1988 report, commenting on national statistics from Austria, France, Germany, Sweden and Switzerland, analysed the situation in the following terms:

> In declining industries, notably the basic industries, motor vehicles, engineering and building, the employment of foreigners has fallen relatively more than that of natives. The concentration of foreigners, however, varies in these industries from one country to another. The relative gap is all the wider the lower the skills and training of the foreign labour and the older its age. In manufacturing, exposed to competition from developing countries, foreign workers have borne the full brunt of the redundancies prompted by reductions of activity and relocation of all or part of production. But, at the same time, immigrants are moving into the ever-changing tertiary sector. For example, the growth of foreign employment in domestic service, which makes extensive use of foreign female labour, is accompanying the rising participation rate of native women and the resulting increase in the need for labour for household chores. Maintenance work and caretaking for industry, shops and government departments are increasingly subcontracted to service firms, which recruit foreign workers of both sexes. (OECD 1989).

Unemployment data for foreigners also shed light on the differential impact of restructuring, although the data must be examined carefully to understand what lies behind the figures. While it is true that unemployment statistics provide the best available evidence on the relative vulnerability of ethnic minorities to economic slump, the figures are recorded on different criteria in different countries, and unemployment may be hidden if migrants return home.[4] Age and educational factors also need to be taken into account. Nevertheless, even when these complications are borne in mind, the vast majority of the evidence suggests that, ever since the first oil crisis (although possibly not before), foreign workers have suffered disproportionately from the passing of full employment in Europe and as a result are about twice as likely to experience unemployment as their native counterparts. Naturally the precise figures vary between countries, between migrant groups and through time. In general non-European migrants (e.g. those from North Africa or the Caribbean) have tended to post higher unemployment rates than southern European immigrant groups such as the Portuguese or Greeks. Gordon (1991, p. 20) notes a general tendency for the largest migrant groups in each country to suffer the highest rates of unemployment (e.g. Turks in Germany, Algerians in France, Turks and Moroccans in the Netherlands); he attributes this, somewhat speculatively, to the more supportive environment which large communities can provide for their temporarily unemployed members. Time-series data indicate that the gap between the minority unemployment rate and the national average tends to widen when the employment market is slack. Over the longer period, the change in unemploy-

Table 5.3.   Unemployed foreigners as a percentage of total unemployment in selected European countries, 1986–90

Country (foreigners as % of total workforce, 1988)		1986	1987	1988	1989	1990
Austria	(5.2)	5.9	6.3	6.3	7.1	11.0
Belgium	(9.8)	14.4	14.4	15.3	15.6	16.1
France	(6.6)	11.5	11.4	11.7	12.5	12.8
Germany	(6.5)	11.1	11.8	12.0	11.4	10.8
Netherlands	(2.9)	10.1	10.8	11.2	12.2	13.0

Source: *SOPEMI Report 1990*, pp. 28–9

ment (and sectoral employment) patterns between the 1960s and the 1980s has also corresponded to a generational contrast; many of the ethnic minority job seekers in the 1980s and 1990s are second-generation entrants to the labour market who have been job hunting during the period of recession and restructuring. Although there are some exceptions (for example the Indian population of Britain, which will be described presently), the educational qualifications of the members of the second generation are often poor and by no means guarantee them better job opportunities than their parents.

Table 5.3 shows the share of total national unemployment contributed by foreigners during the second half of the 1980s for five European countries. In all cases, foreign workers recorded higher shares of national unemployment than national employment in the respective countries. The situation in Austria worsened appreciably in 1989–90 owing to the chaotic influx of asylum seekers from Eastern Europe. In Germany, on the other hand, foreign unemployment appeared to contract during 1988–90, but the German figures are complicated by unification and by the mass arrival of ethnic Germans from Eastern Europe. Further contrasts appear when the various immigrant nationalities are compared. For example in the Netherlands the Turks and the Moroccans, who make up respectively 19% and 13% of the total foreign labour force, contribute respectively 37% and 25% of total foreign unemployment (average figures for the late 1980s). Naturally these two groups experience very high crude unemployment rates: 33% for the Turks and 37% for the Moroccans. In both Belgium and the Netherlands, Turks and Moroccans have been disproportionately affected by rising unemployment in the 1980s because they were concentrated more than other groups in recession-hit manufacturing. Moreover, technological change and robotization have removed the jobs of many of these workers who were originally recruited to perform repetitive, low-skill jobs. In the Netherlands, Turkish and Moroccan unemployment has continued to rise even when the national figure has been falling. Overall, the high, and increasing, rates of foreigner unemployment revealed in Table 5.3 appear to be spurred by a double age squeeze – older migrants laid off by industrial closures lack the skills or language abilities to retrain for alternative branches of employment, while younger and second-generation job seekers lack the educational qualifications to compete effectively in a tighter job market.

ECONOMIC RESTRUCTURING AND THE EXPANSION OF SKILLED INTERNATIONAL MIGRATION

While the 'down side' of European economic restructuring – industrial closures – has negative impacts on established immigrant communities, the more 'upbeat' side of the process – the internationalization of capital, the growth of high-tech industries and the remarkable expansion of advanced producer services – favours the development of a newer kind of international migration, the highly skilled. Although less visible racially and culturally than most labour migrants, skilled international migrants contribute their own distinct patterns to the social geography of many European cities, especially those such as Brussels and Geneva where several international organizations are headquartered (White 1984). Statistically the increased importance of these highly mobile, almost nomadic high-status migrants employed by multinational companies and international agencies is not easy to demonstrate. However, their expensive education, training and relocation packages and their economic and managerial power give them a strategic importance beyond their unknown numbers in the shifting typology of European migration in the 1980s and 1990s.

The essential economic and geographical features of skilled international migration can be outlined as follows (Findlay 1993; Salt 1984, 1992a). The spatial patterns have been mainly two-way 'brain exchanges' between highly developed countries within Europe (or involving global powers like the United States and Japan) rather than the earlier periphery-to-core flows of low-skill labour migrants. Nevertheless, some European metropolitan powers have encouraged brain drains from Third World countries in order to save on training costs and plug particular gaps in the skilled labour market (e.g. for doctors or certain kinds of teachers). Even this brain drain has not been wholly one way, however, as significant flows of technically highly skilled workers have left the more developed countries to manage and provide technical expertise at production sites in less-developed countries. In very recent years there has been much debate about the development of post-1989 brain-drain flows from Eastern to Western Europe. While it is true that there has been a considerable migration of scientists and academics, continuing both the more dramatic exoduses of the past (Hungary 1956, Czechoslovakia 1968) as well as officially tolerated 'leakages' (e.g. Poland since 1959), migration barriers thrown up by the countries of the West have meant that most East–West movement has been clandestine and short term. Such movements have often involved de-skilling or 'brain waste', tolerated by the migrants because any job in the West is better paid than intellectual employment (or unemployment) at home (Okolski 1992; Rhode 1993).

An understanding of the economic significance of skilled migration within the mature capitalist countries of Western Europe takes as its starting point the fact that labour markets have become increasingly differentiated. Educational qualifications, training schemes and job experience are the key determinants of this differentiation, particularly as regards the upper echelons of the labour hierarchy. As technological levels have advanced and the scale of organization increased, growing specialization in the production system has led to ever more refined divisions of labour. Global production patterns with numerous and diverse branch plants have resulted in the spatial separation of control functions from production: the former are concentrated in major metropolitan centres which attract large numbers of graduates and others with professional, managerial and financial expertise; the factories are often relegated to more peripheral locations where labour is cheap and plentiful and regional incentives may be on offer. This hierarchical spatial division of labour can be related to international migration both between and within different levels in the hierarchy. Such migration often takes place within the internal labour markets of large multinational firms. At this point, conventional concepts of international migration responding to regional or national income differentials become inappropriate. Instead, the advantages of international transfers within the internal labour markets of multinational companies take on a different form. For the organization, international transfers of employees save money on recruiting and training, ensure knowledge of the employees' calibre and track record, and reinforce loyalty to the company. From the employee's point of view the move is less risky and time consuming than changing company and provides a ready-made environment for career advancement.

The Netherlands is one of the few countries furnishing some data on the scale and trends of skilled international migration. Here the stock of skilled immigrants (defined as the employed foreign workers who are scientific personnel, artists, administrative workers, managers and executives) increased from 43000 in 1983 to 60000 in 1989 (an increase of nearly 40%), whereas other (mainly low-skilled) foreign workers remained practically stationary (131000 in 1983, 133000 in 1989). German data indicate similar trends. These show, that while total foreign employment decreased from 1.89 million in 1977 to 1.69 million in 1989 (a reduction of 10.6%), the trends for low qualification, middle-level qualification and graduate employees were −18.8%, −1.1% and +23.3% respectively (Salt 1992a). For the United Kingdom too, various sources of data such as the International Passenger Survey, the Labour Force Survey and work permit records (none of them very satisfactory, however) show a steady increase in the migration (both in and out) of professional, managerial and technical workers. The UK has used the work permit system to control carefully the inflow of economically desirable skilled labour. In the mid- and late 1980s 60–85% of work permits issued by the UK government were to professional and managerial workers, and about 60% of long-term permits were to intra-company transfers, reflecting the increasing importance of transnational corporate labour markets in the new global economy. By 1990 one quarter of the 933000 foreign nationals working in the UK were professional employees and managers, a higher proportion than for the national workforce, 21.6% (Salt and Ford 1993).

What of the future for skilled international migration? There are perhaps two aspects to an answer to this question. At an aggregate level, the European demand for scientists, technicians and the highly skilled in general is predicted to rise until at least the early decades of the twenty-first century. With falling birth rates in many countries and with a marked preference on the part of many young people for a humanities or social science training rather than a scientific or technological education, the supply of locally trained, high-level labour may fall well below demand. This sets the scene for further immigration of educated labour from peripheral regions of Europe where the supply of highly trained persons outstrips the capacity of the local economy to absorb it (e.g. Ireland, Eastern Europe, Greece), and perhaps too from Third Worth countries suffering high levels of intellectual unemployment (e.g. Egypt, India, Sri Lanka). Such flows might be expected to be targeted at those specific subsectors of the labour market where there is a marked shortfall. For instance Salt (1992a, p. 484) predicts that East–West skilled migration will grow in those areas such as the 'caring' professions (especially nursing) where salaries in the West are low and where there is an endemic and growing demand (because of ageing), and in sectors where there is an univeral 'language', such as computer technology.

The second aspect of the future trend of skilled migration relates to its organizational structure and its dependence on the continued evolution of corporate business structures and the consequent internationalization of the labour markets of large employers. Within Europe the scale of 'brain exchange' between highly developed countries will probably continue to grow as companies continue to evolve international business structures. However, such expansion is by no means guaranteed and there are already signs that it is slowing down. Some employers are now 'localizing' their recruitment and use of labour instead of moving their established staff around the various branches of their corporate empire. Joint ventures and the greater use of subcontracted specialist business services are tending to reduce international transfers of staff. Other companies are modifying the pattern of movement of their key staff from relocation to shorter-term business travel and trouble-shooting visits (Salt and Ford 1993). While one can hardly envisage a collapse of skilled international migration comparable with the 'recruitment stop' of low-skill labour migration in the 1970s, the period of rapid expansion of skilled international migration may be coming to an end.

THE CONTRIBUTION OF IMMIGRANTS TO ECONOMIC RESTRUCTURING, WITH SPECIAL REFERENCE TO ETHNIC ENTERPRISE

The discussion so far has moved from an analysis of how established immigrant groups are, by and large, negatively affected by economic restructuring to a consideration of the new demand and opportunities for a specialized cadre of internationally mobile high-flyers. Between these two poles of low skill and high skill is another group whose role in the economic restructuring process is rather different. These are the 'ethnic entrepreneurs' whose numbers appear to be increasing all over Europe and among virtually all groups of immigrants.

As Ward and Jenkins (1985) show, the ethnic community creates a parallel system of channels of upward mobility, including professional opportunities, within the evolving structure and needs of the immigrant group. Considerable socio-spatial mobility can occur for certain members of the group, although the extent to which these emerging stratifications build on previous status differences within the group (e.g. based on caste or rural/urban origin) undoubtedly varies, even if this question has hardly been investigated by researchers. Generally there has been a tendency to assume that all immigrants coming from a single country such as Turkey or Bangladesh originate from the same class and educational background. This is not necessarily the case – differences among the immigrants may be inherent right from the start, or social differences may develop as the character of the migration stream from a given country changes over time. Then, of course, there are complex social hierarchies which develop between different nationality groups: these relate to such factors as length of time settled in the host country, language, religion, education, colour of skin, and differential racism imposed both by the host society and among the immigrant communities themselves.

Our main concern in this section, however, is to document the socio-economic mobility which occurs within the 'enclave' economies and social systems of immigrant communities based on self-employment in such businesses as restaurants, shops, travel agents, accountancy firms etc. Most of these concerns originally grew up to service the ethnic community, but some (notably shops and restaurants) may also serve 'outsiders'. A closely related phenomenon is that of the formation of immigrant socio-economic niches, whereby a specific sector or service is opened up, taken over and perhaps eventually monopolized by an immigrant group who may even trade on their ethnicity – Italian hairdressers or ice-cream parlours would be a case in point (Palmer 1985). Sometimes this 'niching' may provoke agglomeration tendencies leading to the creation of a specialized industrial district profiting from external economies and social or kinship contacts (e.g. Asian textile firms in Bradford and Leicester); in other cases dispersion, in order to spread competition, may be the rule (e.g. Chinese take-aways).

The increase in the proportion of ethnic minority populations engaged in independent activities reflects the progressive tertiarization of the foreign workforce. Particularly in the 1980s, changes in labour management and in the production system (more flexibility, development of subcontracting, retreat of trade union power etc.) set the scene for the creation of small enterprises by foreign workers. A surprising number of these businesses have been set up by younger foreigners (including second-generation immigrants) who seek faster

Table 5.4. Economic status of working males aged 16+ in Greater London by ethnic group, 1991 (%)

Ethnic group	Employees		Self-employed	Work scheme	Unemployed
	Full time	Part time			
White	67.4	3.2	16.7	0.8	11.9
Black	57.9	4.5	7.9	2.8	26.9
Indian	62.0	2.6	22.0	1.4	12.0
Pakistani	52.9	3.4	17.3	2.1	24.3
Bangladeshi	48.4	3.5	10.1	2.0	36.0
Other	62.9	3.2	13.9	1.4	18.6

Source: after Cross 1993, p. 126.

social mobility than their parents and predecessors who have mainly occupied dead-end jobs.

The spread of foreign workers into non-dependent employment has been affected by institutional barriers and a history of restrictive national legislation in some countries such as Germany, Switzerland and the Netherlands. By contrast, the more liberal business environments in France and the UK regarding foreigners have allowed the multiplication of ethnic enterprises – for example building concerns owned by Italians, Portuguese and North Africans in France and shopkeeping by Indians and Pakistanis in the UK. Now, very clear signs of independent employment are emerging in Germany where the Turks, in particular, have made a significant impact on the retailing of food and electronic equipment. A study carried out by the Centre for Turkish Studies in Bonn (Aksöyek 1991) found that in 1990 there were 33 000 independent enterprises among Turkish immigrants in Germany: 30% of these entrepreneurs are under 35 years of age and 10% are women. A similar penetration is taking place in vocational areas of employment, so that Germany now has 4000 Turkish teachers, 950 doctors, 500 social workers, 150 artists and 130 journalists. Entry into the elite professions is still very limited, however.

Probably the most significant recent instance of ethnic success in self-employment in Europe is the Indian business community in the UK. Table 5.4, based on the 1991 census, demonstrates the progress that the Indian population has made as regards self-employment compared to other ethnic groups. Their rate of self-employment is now significantly above that of the native white population and nearly three times that of the Afro-Caribbean population. The Pakistanis also have a higher than average rate of self-employment; but their unemployment figure is more than twice the national average, although not as high as the Bangladeshi or West Indian rates.[5]

There have been many attempts to interpret the reasons for the success of South Asian business in Britain and to collect relevant empirical data.[6] Although ethnic minorities as a whole were among the worst losers under Thatcherism (Owen and Green 1992), specific subgroups benefited from the new opportunities offered by 'shopkeeper' capitalism and by dint of incredibly hard work and long hours were able to access wealth and status which had previously been denied them. Both the economic and political climates were supportive of small business development during the 1980s, in tune with the growing flexibility and specialization of demand for goods and services.

On the other hand, the rather limited time-series data from the Labour Force Survey and from the Longitudinal Study suggest that the real breakthrough for the South Asian business community in Britain came in the 1970s, not the 1980s, i.e. ahead of the general revival and restructuring period. According to the Longitudinal Study there was marked upward socio-economic mobility of South Asians (especially Indians) during 1971–81, with particularly significant shifts from semi-skilled and unskilled manual employment into self-employment and white-collar jobs (Robinson 1990b). The Labour Force Survey showed that, over the same period, self-employment rates for men born in India and Pakistan rose from 3 percentage points below to 7 percentage points above the national average. The fact that this remarkable change took place during a time of rapidly rising unemployment suggests that the growth of ethnic self-employment may have been at least partly a defensive response to general economic decline (Gordon 1991). This line of reasoning is supported by the fact that most of the Asian businesses opened up at this time were in retailing and distribution which were nationally in decline; typically Asians moved into inner-city shop and factory premises vacated by the out-migration of the majority white population (Cross 1993). Although for many of these businesses survival has only been possible by working long hours for minimal rewards, such ethnic entrepreneur-ship has made a positive contribution to the urban economy and in many districts has arrested inner-city decay and abandonment. Thus ethnic businesses contribute to both economic restructuring and urban rejuvenation.

The socio-professional success of Asian immigrants in Britain seems likely to continue through the educational achievements of the second generation. Numerous studies have shown that Indian children attain higher educational qualifications than the white population (see the review in Cross 1993). On the face of it, the Asian (and especially Indian) experience in Britain shows how successfully this major immigrant group has been able to exploit the two traditional routes out of economic marginality – independent business activity and educational success. Second-generation Indians are increasingly entering white-collar employment on the back of educational qualifications, notably success at A-level and an impressively rising rate of entry to university.

The above discussion has shown, however, that there is a darker side to the Asian success story. For every wealthy Asian business person there are dozens if not hundreds of marginal enterprises: corner shops with half-stocked shelves and few customers, tiny factories in dingy premises, taxi drivers who work 16 hours a day to make a living, and a high rate of business failure. It seems that, even within the apparently privileged world of the self-employed, economic restructuring has created an increasing polarization between the successful and the upwardly mobile on the one hand, and the failures and the barely surviving on the other.

Self-employment among ethnic minorities is widely regarded by European governments as a desirable trend to foster as an antidote to unemployment and economic marginalization and as an expression of the currently popular free-market ideology. It needs to be stressed, however, that many such businesses are themselves precarious and survive on extremely low marginal productivities. They are often less a driving force for strutural change and more an adaptive strategy against general economic difficulty. Because many migrant businesses in manufacturing and contruction are effectively subcontractors, they can hardly be regarded as independent enterprises; instead they are at the mercy of their employers and are hence vulnerable to wider economic trends beyond their control. The business success of some members of some immigrant groups such as the Indians and the Chinese often reflects the specific circumstances of their migration. Governments could probably do more to foster ethnic business initiatives, but they must be careful to resolve the conflict between formal bureaucratic structures and the informal social structures on which ethnic enterprise depends (Gordon 1991, pp. 28–9).

SPATIAL MOBILITY OF ETHNIC MINORITIES

How have ethnic minority workers responded to some of the changes and opportunities referred to above in terms of their willingness and ability to be geographically mobile within their chosen country of residence? This is one of the major missing links in the evolving migration map of Europe. Few researchers have tried to answer this question, largely because of the paucity of relevant data.

Much of the information which exists on the 'secondary migration' of immigrant groups merely refers to local-scale intra-urban mobility, tracing migrants' residential relocation patterns with reference to variables such as family size, income and housing tenure. A comprehensive overview of the literature up to the early 1980s enabled White (1984, p. 123) to state that suburbanization of foreign migrants is a feature common to many European cities. For long-established migrants who remain in employment, the accumulation of savings and family reunion and enlargement are the main factors which enable or encourage them to move out of their cramped inner-city flats and hostels and into larger apartments or even (especially in the case of the UK) separate houses located in more spacious surroundings. Housing policy may also facilitate this suburbanization. Throughout France, for instance, large numbers of migrants have been moved into the peripheral *grands ensembles* as a result of city-centre slum clearance, the removal of the notorious *bidonvilles* (shanty-towns which had sprung up on vacant land near industrial zones, road intersections etc.) or qualification for public housing. However, such peripheral housing, with its lack of community facilities and of easy access to the main centres of employment, has generally proved unpopular with immigrants, as recent outbursts of unrest have shown.

More recent reviews by White (1993a, 1993b, 1993c) tend to reveal a more complex picture. While segregation indices for ethnic minority populations in many European cities have continued to fall in the 1980s (although Germany appears to be an exception), the economic restructuring of many large cities currently underway may restrict opportunities for further residential assimilation; the reconquest of city centres by the wealthy leading to inner-city gentrification does trigger ethnic minority dispersion, but to new segregated locations around the city edge. The phasing out of major urban renewal programmes and the slowing down of the construction of new social housing have tended to stabilize ethnic residential patterns within a tighter overall housing market. Social factors have also played a role: over the past decade the strengthening of in-group orientations has reduced the speed of residential change for many groups, leading sometimes to a consolidation around certain favoured districts with a strongly ethnic character, as well as to high degrees of segregation between ethnic groups.

In the UK, too, there is widespread evidence of both suburbanization and concentration of ethnic minority populations. Here the suburbanization process has been influenced less by public housing policy than by immigrants' progression up the hierarchically differentiated British housing ladder towards large owner-occupied houses situated in the outer suburbs. Only relatively small proportions of the various immigrant groups have made this transition; moreover, there are rather clear inter-ethnic contrasts to be observed. Studies of non-black groups such as the Irish, the Italians and the Cypriots reveal them to have become progressively suburbanized in their various urban settings (King and Bridal 1982; King and King 1977; King et al. 1989; Walter 1986). The West Indians, on the other hand, remain highly concentrated in 'undesirable' innter-city boroughs, particularly in London where well over half of the British Afro-Caribbean population lives. Peach (1982) has shown that the population of Caribbean origin is locked by the housing market (and by the discriminatory policies of local authorities who assign them the least desirable social housing) into an allocative system that is concentrating them in areas that the white population is abandoning; therefore it seems inevitable that an increasing degree of socio-spatial polarization between blacks and whites will occur. At the same time the economic depressions of recent decades, and the more general process of economic restructuring, have had a disproportionately negative impact on the British Caribbean population, especially young second-generation blacks. Loss of jobs has been high in the inner cities where they remain concentrated. Most lack the qualifications for alternative jobs; those who are qualified are probably discriminated against in a highly competitive job market. But cultural factors operating from the country of origin should not be overlooked. According to Hollis (1982) the West Indian community does not have a strong tradition of property ownership in the Caribbean and this may help to explain why they have mostly settled in parts of cities where owner occupation is either rare or expensive and the dominant tenure is social housing, reached by way of the privately rented sector. A different set of experiences surrounds the Asian groups. Many of these immigrants have backgrounds as peasants, traders and entrepreneurs and this tends to make property ownership important to them. As we have seen, their higher level of involvement in business in the UK has often given them the means to move up the housing ladder, so that they now have higher levels of house ownership than the population at large. Asians also tend to buy property in multi-generation and extended family groups, sometimes pooling financial resources to buy up several adjacent properties. In some cities, notably Leicester which acts as a kind of central place for a large part of the Asian business community, Asians are the owners of the most luxurious houses in the best suburbs.

All of the above says little about inter-regional mobility and the reaction of immigrants to the changing geography of occupational opportunity within their countries of destination. This question has been tackled by Robinson (1991, 1992a, 1992b) in a series of papers which examine the Indian, Pakistani and West Indian populations in Britain. Robinson's data source is the Longitudinal Study (LS), a 1% sample of individuals linked across the censuses (in simple cross-census comparison of the spatial distribution of immigrants it is impossible to separate out internal migration from natural increase and international arrivals and departures). The analysis can only be made for the 1971–81 inter-censal interval, pending the release of the 1991 data. It was based on a four-category sample of 371000 people of UK origin, 4600 Indians, 3600 West Indians and 1500 Pakistanis. Small sample size meant that the analysis had to be limited to the nine standard regions. However, on the positive side, since the samples were defined by father's place of birth (not the individual's birthplace), 'black British' are included and not left out as in the census.

The patterns observed by Robinson may be summarized as follows. Propensity to migrate inter-regionally was three times higher among Pakistanis (15.0 per thousand per year) than among West Indians (4.9); Indians (11.2) and the UK-origin population (8.1) occupied intermediate positions. Patterns of inter-regional migration were dominated by the influence of the South-east region which, as well as being the key region economically, also had the major concentrations of ethnic minorities, especially of West Indians. Three-quarters of this group's (limited) gross migration starts or ends in the South-east region, as do their six biggest inter-regional flows. For Indians, two-thirds of inter-regional mobility is with the South-east, and six of their seven biggest flows involve the region. However, Indians are also mobile between the West and East Midlands, an inter-regional flow which has no parallel in the West Indian pattern of migration. Pakistanis have half their gross inter-regional flows linked to the South-east but, reflecting their more widespread distribution in northern industrial towns such as Bradford and Blackburn, they also have high levels of gross circulation in other regions such as the West Midlands, Yorkshire and

Humberside, and the North-west. When net migration figures are analysed within the context of the UK's North–South divide, the results show that the net migration rates out of the North were higher for ethnic minority populations than for the UK population; whereas the native population only saw a 0.5% net transfer from North to South, the figures for the minorities were Pakistanis 2.4%, West Indians 1.3% and Indians 1.2%.

Robinsons's tabulated and mapped data on individual inter-regional transfers are probably too small in sample scale to be fully reliable, but the indications are that ethnic minorities – especially Asians – have been especially sensitive to economic decline in the centres of contracting industry, such as the textile districts in Yorkshire and the North-west. When regional gains are examined, the East Midlands emerges as the second most attractive region for ethnic minorities after the South-east. Indian inter-regional migration also exhibits elements of counterurbanization, with significant transfers from the South-east to adjacent regions (South-west, East Midlands and East Anglia but not to the industrially troubled West Midlands). The West Indians have a higher propensity to remain in the same region and to be less mobile overall: this can be interpreted partly because of their class and tenure characteristics – engaged in manual occupations and living mainly in public housing – and partly because they are more concentrated in the South-east (the main destination region for inter-regional ethnic migration) than the other groups. Asians, on the other hand, are less tied to council house tenure, have a more scattered distribution within the UK and (Indians especially) are more diverse occupationally. For Indians there is a strong link between educational and spatial mobility: their predilection for academic qualifications predisposes them to be geographically mobile. Moreover, their entrepreneurial instincts also encourage them to move to better their business prospects, in spite of certain risks involved. Pakistanis have a rather different set of contexts for their inter-regional mobility. With them it is often the unemployed, uneducated and unskilled who migrate in order to escape collapsing regional industries. Unlike West Indians, Pakistanis are not locked into social housing but (like some Indian groups) move along kinship networks; unlike Indians, however, their migrations are generally dictated by economic survival, not social or business enhancement.

Space does not allow a detailed comparison of Robinson's findings on the UK with other European situations, but parallels undoubtedly exist. To conclude this section by citing just one example, data on Moroccan and Turkish migrants' geographical mobility within the Netherlands during the 1970s and early 1980s reveal a progressive concentration in the largest cities such as Amsterdam, The Hague and Utrecht, and a relative retreat from smaller towns, rural areas and industrial cities such as Rotterdam and Twente (Atzema and Buursink 1985). The same authors reveal that, while Turkish and Moroccan mobility was high during the 1970s, it dipped below that of the Dutch population in the 1980s when work opportunities became tighter and the rewards of moving diminished.

ECONOMIC RESTRUCTURING AND THE NEW IMMIGRANTS

A recurrent and central theme in this chapter has been the differential impact of economic restructuring on groups of migrants. This differentiation has been shown to operate according to nationality of the immigrants, their socio-occupational characteristics, and the economic and policy context of the destination country. It also needs to be stressed that the character and context of the immigration flows themsleves have changed, particularly since the early 1980s. As many recent studies have pointed out (see e.g. Champion and King 1993; King 1993a; Salt 1992b; van de Kaa 1993), the 'new waves' of immigrants entering Europe over the past decade are very different from the great *Gastarbeiter* migrations of the 1960s and early 1970s. Recent migrations have comprised increasing numbers of asylum seekers. 'Push pressures' for migration have assumed greater importance *vis-à-vis* the 'pull' of labour demand. New destination countries have replaced some of the earlier major destination countries; particularly important here are Spain, Italy and Greece, which in a surprisingly short time have been transformed from countries of mass emigration to countries of mass immigration (King and Rybaczuk 1993).

Flows into southern Europe are partly redirections or resurgent flows from established sources such as the Maghreb states or West Africa, but new origins have also come 'on stream' – the Philippines, Cape Verde, Ethiopia/Eritrea, Poland, Albania and many other countries. The multiplicity and diversity of ethnic groups among these 'new' immigrants makes it hard to generalize about their experience.[7] Yet in one sense their very diversity of form and origin has a common explanation: migration has become an increasingly global phenomenon prompted by economic, political and demographic processes which are expressing themselves at ever wider scales and greater intensities. War, environmental crisis, the end of the Cold War and the sharpening of both the economic divide and the demographic gradient between Europe and the 'south' are just some of the significant elements which set the scene for an increasingly complex matrix of migration paths for Europe's newest immigrants. Nor should the technological component be overlooked; now, through modern communications networks, informal yet well-organized channels operate in recruiting workers and directing flows on a worldwide scale.

Reference back to Table 5.1 reminds us of the key importance of economic restructuring in altering the nature of the labour requirements of European employers in the post-Fordist era. The most significant change as regards recent immigrants is the shift from the primary labour market of unionized, secure, high-wage workers to the secondary labour market of low-wage, unprotected, casual jobs in which immigrant workers are regarded by employers as more appropriate (because they are more exploitable). Some of the employers themselves will be immigrants and they will have a greater likelihood of employing other immigrants, reinforcing the ethnic enclave nature of some sectors of the secondary labour market. On a wider scale, within the increasingly segmented European labour market where, at the lower end, the main demand is for low-cost casual and seasonal workers, the new waves of immigrants have been able to underbid most categories of local labour, especially for work in the tourist, hotel and catering sector, in seasonal farm labour, in casual construction work and as domestic servants, office cleaners etc.

Underbidding implies a direct labour market competition which is not always the case. In southern Europe, increasing levels of education and social aspiration among the indigenous workers make them unwilling to offer themselves for many categories of menial work, so they prefer to remain voluntarily unemployed (often as semi-permanent university students) and rely on family and state welfare support. The immigrants, for their part, are willing to accept low wages and poor working and housing conditions, since their chances of work and of a cash income are even less in their home countries. Thus they play into the hands of employers who are the chief actors in capitalism's historic tendency to seek out and exploit cheap and malleable labour.

Despite recent attempts to regularize the situation of many of these migrant workers (e.g. in Spain in 1985 and 1991 and Italy in 1986 and 1990), a considerable proportion of them are illegal immigrants. Some of them entered clandestinely as part of the growing trade in human smuggling; others arrived legally on tourist or student visas but then stayed on illegally to work.

There is a complex and subtle set of inter-relationships between illegality, immigration policy, labour demand and the willingness of the migrants to suffer 'self-exploitation'. For instance, the administrative halt to further non-EU immigration into Italy was made without appropriate labour-market adjustment, with the result that the continuing expansion of the informal economy and the secondary labour market led to an increase in illegal entry and work to satisfy a rising demand for flexible labour (Calvanese and Pugliese 1988). Morever, the immigrant workers' illegal status and propensity for self-exploitation boost the demand for their services, particularly in the underground economy that makes up around 25–30% of the GNP in southern European countries. In Italy Dell'Aringa and Neri (1987, p. 122) have advanced the thesis that the influx of illegal immigrants has inflated the informal economy causing 'a type of displacement wage effect with respect to the local workforce. Such an effect . . . operates through the mobility of capital that illegal immigrants attract towards the hidden economy . . . transferred towards this sector along with part of the legally employed workforce.' This is another way in which recent immigration has contributed in an active sense to the restructuring of European economies. The evidence for this is clearest for Italy, but the process can be inferred for Greece, Spain and Portugal, and probably also for France as well. Moreover, the linked phenomena of illegal immigration and the informal economy are unlikely to be a temporary, marginal occurrence; authors have noted their persistence and even their growth into areas, such as agriculture, where they were previously unimportant (King and Rybaczuk 1993; Venturini 1988). Many immigrants do not take up opportunities to legalize their status because to do so would make them less attractive for employers. In Italy one of the conditions for a migrant to become legalized is a certificate of work from an employer – but some employers are unwilling to grant this, since they prefer illegal workers who are cheaper in terms of both wages and social insurance payments.

A detailed discussion on the numbers of new immigrants in southern Europe is pointless because of the large number of illegals and the fact that the immigrant population is in a constant state of flux (although tending always to increase). Estimates from various sources vary widely. Those from the respective labour ministries indicate about 1 million in Italy, 600 000 in Spain, 400 000 in Greece and 150 000 in Portugal. But the real total figure may be nearer 3 million than 2 million (King and Rybaczuk 1993). In Italy, for example, the estimate of the national statistical agency ISTAT is 1 144 000 for 1990, more than twice the number of foreigners recorded by the 1991 census, 502 000 (King 1993b).

Most of the immigrants in southern Europe work in a range of marginal, mainly service-sector jobs which are quite different from those performed by Italian, Spanish, Portuguese and Greek emigrants in northern Europe in the 1950s and 1960s. The heterogeneity of occupational roles performed by the new immigrants within the secondary labour market is noteworthy. For instance, North Africans (mainly Moroccans) are highly mobile and have unstable jobs; they are overwhelmingly young, single men who work in large towns and cities in low-grade service jobs, although some are travelling salesmen working in rural regions and others are seasonal agricultural workers. Tunisians have virtually taken over the fishing industry of western Sicily. In Spain and Italy the sub-Saharan group, originating from many different countries, is engaged in a range of fringe tertiary activities, notably peddling in the main towns and tourist resorts. This group is also predominantly male. By contrast, migrants from the Philippines are mainly female and work especially as domestic helpers, often on a live-in basis, to middle-class families in major cities such as Madrid, Barcelona, Rome and Milan.

Differences in occupational structure between the old and the new immigrants are replicated by differences in social relations and social integration. In the 1950s and 1960s the mainly intra-European migrant workers entered the industrial working class of the host countries and eventually became part of it, although with many subtle variations in different countries. For these groups factory life, trade union membership, industrial conflict, stable housing, family reunion and permanent settlement were the main features of their social relations. These elements represented a fundamental break with their previous life as peasants, rural labourers and village artisans – except of course for those who returned home.[8]

The new immigrants have a different set of experiences. Their less stable work situation, mainly in the tertiary sector, corresponds to a more marginal social position and to more provisional housing conditions. Forms of horizontal solidarity expressed in trade unions, workers' organizations and the large-scale takeover of chunks of urban space are not present in the new migrations, where jobs are fragmented, access to housing tenuous, and ethnic community facilities undeveloped. The large number of immigrant nationalities represented in the new migrations is an obvious factor which limits ethnic social solidarity when compared to the mass, homogenous migrations of Turks, Algerians, Portuguese, West Indians etc. Migrants' illegal status and their occupational concentration in the informal economy naturally tend to preserve their marginal social position and block progress towards integration in mainstream society. Solidarity tends to be confined to small-scale kinship or community ties. The social situation of the post-industrial migrants is made more difficult by increasingly restrictive immigration legislation. Uncertainties over rights to continued residence and employment not only weaken the immigrants' bargaining power and increase their chances of being exploited, they also diminish their commitment to integration and their incentives to make investments in physical or cultural capital (buying a flat, learning the language etc.) which might set them on the road to assimilation (Gordon 1991, p. 16).

It must also be acknowledged that immigrants' cultural backgrounds as members of (for want of a better term) traditional Third World societies make it less likely that the process of integration will start quickly. The migrants' own propensities may be very far from wanting integration and permanent settlement. For individuals who are part of a family unit or extended kinship network in their own country, migration to Europe may be one part of a family-based strategy for economic survival or advancement. As Stark (1992) has suggested, families in poor regions allocate their labour assets over geographically dispersed and structurally different markets. This is done both to maximize returns and to minimize risks while maintaining the family unit intact in its original setting. After migration, family members pool and share their incomes. This pooling, or co-insurance, covers the risks of losing income in any one place and is akin to a portfolio investment of labour. Seen in this light, a street-hawking migrant from Senegal or a Filipino domestic servant working in Rome are not to be narrowly conceptualized as random individuals whose chances of full integration into Italian society are slim; rather, their migration behaviour and remittances are an integral part of the family's economic and social strategy which has its base in their home countries.

CONCLUSION: THE FUTURE OF INTERNATIONAL MIGRATION AND IMMIGRANTS' SOCIO-SPATIAL MOBILITY IN EUROPE

Few socio-geographic phenomena are as difficult to forecast as international migration, since many migration flows are the product of unforeseen circumstances such as political conflict and arise quite suddenly. Predicting the trajectories of immigrants' socio-spatial mobility patterns is also difficult; although these processes are likely to be more gradual, they are subject to a wide range of often conflicting contextual circumstances such as national and EU policies, numbers of 'new' versus 'old' migrants, socio-occupational and educational factors, racism, housing policy and many more.

Future trends in the occupational structure of the European labour market will continue to have a key role in conditioning the migrations of the future and the social integration of new immigrants. Tertiarization and casualization of the job market will probably continue. Labour market theory has its limitations, however. On the one hand, the reliance on unemployment data as a proof that immigrants are not needed and will not find employment is a myth, since the labour market is so differentiated that the immigrants offer themselves to do jobs that the indigenous labour force, driven by rising educational achievements and occupational aspirations, would not be willing to do. On the other hand, the presence of a recently arrived labour force cannot be taken as undisputed proof of unsatisfied labour demand, even in the secondary labour market. This is because the expulsive pressure of the push effect from Third World countries is so strong; and because the immigrants have shown themselves to be very inventive at creating their own labour market niches (street peddling, washing windscreens at traffic lights etc.) where none existed before.

Thus labour demand theory cannot by itself explain contemporary migrations to Europe, for which cultural factors and home-country poverty are more relevant variables. Several studies have shown that, in the countries which currently send migrants to Europe, an unimaginably high level of economic growth and employment creation would be required to reduce the migration potential (see e.g. Golini et al. 1993; Montanari and Cortese 1993; Venturini 1988). Even maintaining the unemployment level in these countries at its present (high) rate appears impossible given the escalating number of new labour market entrants due to high birth rates. Add to this powerful socio-cultural factors (the lure of Western lifestyles etc.) and a wage differential of maybe 10 or 20 times, and the scene is set for irresistible pressures for further migration.

Reference back to Table 5.1 shows that demographic variables can influence both the future course of international migration and the socio-economic roles that future immigrants will play in the host country. Many European countries now have rates of natural increase which are close to zero. During the 1980s West Germany and Denmark had declining indigenous populations. Although Swedish fertility has recently taken an upturn, in aggregate terms 'developed' Europe will continue to experience very low rates of population increase during the 1990s. By contrast, the southern and eastern Mediterranean rim states (Turkey round to Morocco) will increase by 23.6%, or by 58 million people (Golini et al. 1991). Longer-term growth is assured since these countries have, on average, about 42% of their populations under 15 years of age.

Not only are European populations stagnating, they are also changing their structures. As low birth rates and extended education choke the supply of new entrants to the labour market and as increasing longevity reinforces the age–dependency ratio, many demographers predict a shortage of working-age people early in the twenty-first century, coupled with a welfare and pensions crisis for the increasing retired populations. According to Lutz et al. (1991) immigration must play a significant role in the demographic future of Europe. Lutz et al. estimate that, on the basis of calculations of deviations from a desired dependency ratio, mass immigration could resume quite soon and involve around 1–2.5 million people entering western Europe per year. Considering the demographic push from the many developing countries with crowded popula-tions and stagnating economies, there will be little problem to find these migrants if the West lets them in. Already Europe is confronted by a rising tide of asylum seekers, whose numbers rose from 75 000 in 1983 to 537 000 applicants in 1991 (Hovy 1993). However to view renewed immigration as a 'quick fix' to the problem of sustaining pension funds is a flawed policy in both practical and moral terms. Most obviously, it ignores the fact that the immigrants will themselves eventually become old and require pension support. In Europe now there is a marked ageing of the labour migrant cohorts who entered in the 1950s and 1960s. Secondly, if it is thought that new migration can be fashioned as temporary movements, like the initial German *Gastarbeiter* policy, then at least a portion of the taxes paid by immigrants should be repatriated to their home countries to support their welfare needs when they return there.

Although some demographers, such as Lutz et al. (1991), seem to believe that renewed mass immigration into western Europe is almost inevitable, others argue the opposite. Foremost among those who espouse an anti-immigration view is Coleman (1992), who amasses a wealth of age structure and labour force data to try to demonstrate that western Europe 'does not need immi-grants'. It is true that, aside from Germany's privileged treatment of *Aussiedler* or ethnic Germans from the former Soviet Union and Eastern Europe who are encouraged to enter the 'fatherland', no European country seems to be planning for significantly increased levels of immigration. Even countries like Germany, Switzerland and the Netherlands, whose population projections do incorporate a positive migration component, are well aware of the limitations of 'acceptable' levels of immigration in having anything but a marginal impact on altering sustained low fertility and therefore overall population decline (Zlotnik 1991).

Behind these issues is the more fundamental but delicate problem of the socio-political acceptability of new waves of immigrants in countries where public opinion is weighted against such inflows. The rise in anti-immigrant terrorism has been notable in some countries, and although such action is condemned by all official political parties, extreme right parties such as the Belgian *Vlaams Blok* and Jean-Marie Le Pen's *Front National* in France make a great deal of political capital out of massaging public concern over the immigration issue (Vandermotten and Vanlaer 1993). Recent survey data show that about a third of German and Dutch citizens feel that foreigners should ultimately return home, and in Italy 65% and in the Netherlands 85% agreed with the statement that the government should restrict immigration (van de Kaa 1993). Positive attitudes towards migrants and further immigration are mainly

found among the better educated and those with a left-wing political orientation. Such groups are very far from being in the majority at the present time.

Ultimately the future of international migrants in Europe, both quantitatively
in terms of new inflows and qualitatively in terms of progress towards social
integration and social mobility, will depend less on demography and the
perceived needs of the labour market and more on political criteria and the way
in which these feed through to migration policy. Although a common policy on
immigration into the EU has yet to be finalized, all the signs are that western
European countries are introducing increasing barriers to immigration from
'third' countries outside the European Economic Area. Van de Kaa's conclusion
is that European countries will 'individually and jointly use all the means at their
disposal to stem the tide'. In this way, 'the cultural homogeneity of Europeans is
stressed while the perceived differences with non-Europeans are accentuated'
(van de Kaa 1993, pp. 89, 94).

Such a general policy of exclusion will have several outcomes (see Brochmann
1993; Manfrass 1992; van de Kaa 1993). First, it will create (or enhance) a dual
social system among immigrants in Europe. This polarization will result from,
on the one hand, the integration of existing, legally resident groups either on an
assimilationist model as in France or a multicultural one as in Sweden, and on
the other, the marginalization of illegal and semi-legal groups such as clandestine immigrants and asylum seekers awaiting resolution of their cases. Secondly,
the asylum procedure will be speeded up, with quick deportation of those who
fail to satisfy the stricter criteria. Thirdly, selective use of work permits will
allow in those with special skills – soccer and basketball players, computer
software specialists, academics etc. Fourthly, movement within the EU countries
will be encouraged, though not for third-country nationals whose rights of free
movement within the 'Schengen space' have yet to be determined.[9] The ending
of the seven-year transitional period for free movement for Greece (in 1988) and
Spain and Portugal (in 1993) has removed the final barriers to mobility for EU
citizens; given rising levels of welfare and income in these countries, resurgence
of 1960s-style labour migrations to the north has not occurred. Student mobility
throughout Europe, boosted by the Erasmus and Tempus schemes, will
probably continue to increase. This form of movement is particularly significant
because it lays the foundations for easy mobility among graduates in their
subsequent working life, reinforcing the phenomenon of skilled international
migration.

Less easy to predict are the future scale and social roles of illegal immigrants.
Clandestine migration is likely to continue even if anti-immigration controls are
in place. Any set of border controls short of full-scale militarization of frontiers
is likely to leak; and desperate migrants will go to almost any lengths to enter
Europe. As we have seen, immigrants' attractiveness to employers is bolstered by
their clandestine status and tendency to self-exploitation. The lack of interest on
the part of many immigrants in regularization procedures is reinforced by slack
checks on illegality and light penalties for employers employing illegals. This

suggests that tightening internal controls might be more effective than a more intense policing of external borders (van de Kaa 1993, p. 96). Meanwhile, the continued availability of cheap immigrant labour tends to perpetuate highly labour-intensive production processes and to slow their modernization; this can be seen in the diverse fields of small-scale industrial production, seasonal agricultural work done by hand and domestic service. Naturally, the spatial dispersal of the new immigrants in the twilight zones of inner cities, in farming regions, tourist resorts and in small scattered industries in regions like the Third Italy renders them more invisible (and therefore less easy to 'control') than the Fordist 'mass migrants' of earlier decades who concentrated in major industrial cities. It remains to be seen whether the social situation of the recent arrivals, which of course is closely influenced by their economic roles and by national policies towards them, will remain as essentially different from the earlier generation of guestworkers-turned-settlers, or will start to evolve along the same pathways towards integration – family reunion, birth of the second generation, movement up the occupational ladder etc. At present the signs are far from clear. If European nations cannot agree on a common immigration policy, a second-best status quo will result (Martin et al. 1990). In this scenario employers obtain access to cheap foreign labour at minimum risks, migrants enter the country and find employment, and governments can assert that illegal migrants are not establishing equity rights to stay in the country as guestworkers did a generation ago.

NOTES

1. Of course, economic restructuring has also changed the nature and spatial expression of the core itself. Geographically it has extended southwards from its Rhine–Ruhr axis to embrace areas such as Catalonia, the south of France and north–central Italy.
2. Piore's thesis did not go unchallenged; see for instance Böhning 1980, pp. 16–19.
3. These reports were issued in mimeographed form from 1973 to 1990 and were largely for informal circulation only. A new series, formally published, started in 1992 under the title *Trends in International Migration* (SOPEMI 1992).
4. This, of course, was precisely the idea behind the German *Konjunkturpuffer* philosophy – to use migrants as a buffer against conjunctural trends (Salt 1985).
5. These figures for 1991 are more or less confirmed by sample data from the Labour Force Survey for 1987–9. The LFS figures show that ethnic minority self-employment (all groups) is higher than that for native whites (16% as against 12%), and that the figures for South Asians (21%) and Afro-Caribbeans (7%) are very different from each other.
6. For some examples see Modood 1991; Rafiq 1992; Robinson 1988, 1990a, 1990b.
7. In Italy, for instance, no fewer than 11 nationality groups must be summed to reach 50% of the total number of immigrants, and 28 to reach 75%, according to Ministry of Interior data (King 1993b). Data on foreign residents in

southern Europe also reveal two other categories present in significant numbers. The first are returned emigrants (and their foreign-born offspring) who have taken the nationality of their country of migration. Clearly these are not immigrants in the true sense of the term. Secondly there are foreign nationals from other European countries and the United States. Some of these may be the foreign spouses of returned emigrants. Others are free-standing immigrant groups who have settled in southern Europe for work, environmental or retirement reasons.

8. Those who returned home often achieved some social mobility by being able to resettle in their village communities as a *nouveau riche* class, bringing back savings to buy land, build new houses and invest in small business. For more details on the social impact of return migration in Europe see King 1986.

9. The Schengen Agreement for the planned removal of internal barriers to movement was signed in 1985 by France, Germany and the Benelux countries; later Italy, Spain and Portugal joined. For details see Callovi 1992; and Brochmann 1993, Collinson 1993 and Fielding 1993 for discussion of the wider issues.

REFERENCES

Aksöyek, A. (1991) Federal Republic of Turkey: thirty years of Turkish immigration, *The Courier*, 129:60–3.

Atzema, O. and Buursink, J. (1985) The regional distribution of Mediterraneans in the Netherlands, in White, P.E. and Van der Knaap, B. (eds) *Contemporary Studies of Migration*. Norwich: Geo Books, pp. 27–44.

Böhning, W.R. (1980) *Guestworker Employment, with Special Reference to the Federal Republic of Germany, France and Switzerland – Lessons for the United States?* World Employment Programme Working Paper 47. Geneva: International Labour Office.

Brochmann, G. (1993) Control in immigration policies: a closed Europe in the making, in King, R. (ed.) *The New Geography of European Migrations*. London: Belhaven, pp. 100–15.

Callovi, G. (1992) Regulation of immigration in 1993: pieces of the European Community jig-saw puzzle, *International Migration Review*, 26(2):353–72.

Calvanese, F. and Pugliese, E. (1988) Emigration and immigration in Italy: recent trends, *Labour*, 2(3):181–99.

Castles, S., Booth, H. and Wallace, T. (1984) *Here for Good: Western Europe's New Ethnic Minorities*. London: Pluto Press.

Champion, A. and King, R. (1993) New trends in international migration in Europe, *Geographical Viewpoint*, 21:45–56.

Coleman, D.A. (1992) Does Europe need immigrants? Population and workforce projections, *International Migration Review*, 26(2):413–61.

Collinson, S. (1993) *Beyond Borders: West European Migration Policy Towards the 21st Century*. London: Royal Institute of International Affairs and the Wyndham Place Trust.

Cross, M. (1993) Migration, employment and social change in the new Europe, in King, R. (ed.) *The New Geography of European Migrations*. London: Belhaven, pp. 116–34.

Dell'Aringa, C. and Neri, F. (1987) Illegal immigrants and the informal economy, *Labour*, 1(2):107–26.

Fielding, A.J. (1993) Migrations, institutions and politics: the evolution of European migration policies, in King, R. (ed.) *Mass Migrations in Europe: the Legacy and the Future*. London: Belhaven, pp. 40–60.

Findlay, A.M. (1993) New technology, high-level labour movements and the concept of brain drain, in *The Changing Course of International Migration*. Paris: OECD, pp. 149–59.

Golini, A., Bonifazi, C. and Righi, A. (1993) A general framework for the European migration system in the 1990s, in King, R. (ed.) *The New Geography of European Migrations*. London: Belhaven, pp. 67–82.

Golini, A., Gesano, G. and Heins, F. (1991) South–North migration with special reference to Europe, *International Migration*, 29(2):253–79.

Gordon, I. (1991) *The Impact of Economic Change on Minorities and Migrants in Western Europe*. University of Reading, Department of Geography, Discussion Paper 2.

Hollis, J. (1982) New Commonwealth ethnic group populations in Greater London, in Coleman, D.A. (ed.) *Demography of Immigrants and Minorities in the United Kingdom*. London: Academic Press, pp. 119–41.

Hovy, B. (1993) Asylum migration in Europe: patterns, determinants and the role of East–West movements, in King, R. (ed.) *The New Geography of European Migrations*. London: Belhaven, pp. 207–27.

Kindleberger, C.P. (1967) *Europe's Postwar Growth: the Role of Labor Supply*. New York: Oxford University Press.

King, R. (ed.) (1986) *Return Migration and Regional Economic Problems*. London: Croom Helm.

King, R. (ed.) (1993a) *The New Geography of European Migrations*. London: Belhaven.

King, R. (1993b) Recent immigration to Italy: character, causes and consequences, *GeoJournal*, 30(3):283–92.

King, R. and Bridal, J. (1982) The changing distribution of Cypriots in London, *Studi Emigrazione*, 65:93–120.

King, R. and King, P.D. (1977) The spatial evolution of the Italian community in Bedford, *East Midland Geographer*, 6(7):337–45.

King, R. and Rybaczuk, K. (1993) Southern Europe and the international division of labour, in King, R. (ed.) *The New Geography of European Migrations*. London: Belhaven, pp. 175–206.

King, R., Shuttleworth, I. and Strachan, A. (1989) The Irish in Coventry: the social geography of a relict community, *Irish Geography*, 22(2):64–78.

Lutz, W., Prinz, C., Wils, A.B., Büttner, T. and Heilig, G. (1991) Alternative demographic scenarios for Europe and North America, in Lutz, W. (ed.) *Future Demographic Trends in Europe and North America*. London: Academic Press, pp. 523–60.

Manfrass, K. (1992) Europe: South–North or East–West migration? *International Migration Review*, 26(2):388–400.

Martin, P., Hönekopp, E. and Ullman, H. (1990) Europe 1992: effects on labor migration, *International Migration Review*, 24(3):591–603.

Modood, T. (1991) The Indian economic success: a challenge to some race relations assumptions, *Policy and Politics*, 19(3):177–89.

Montanari, A. and Cortese, A. (1993) South to North migration in a Mediterranean perspective, in King, R. (ed.) *Mass Migrations in Europe: the Legacy and the Future*. London: Belhaven, pp. 212–33.

OECD (1989) *SOPEMI Report 1988*, Paris: OECD.

Okolski, M. (1992) Migratory movements from countries of central and eastern Europe, in *People on the Move: New Migration Flows in Europe*. Strasbourg: Council of Europe Press, pp. 83–116.

Owen, D. and Green, A. (1992) Labour market experience and change amongst ethnic groups in Great Britain, *New Community*, 19(1):7–30.

Palmer, R. (1985) The rise of the Britalian cultural entrepreneur, in Ward, R. and Jenkins,

R. (eds) *Ethnic Communities in Business: Strategies for Economic Survival.* Cambridge University Press, Cambridge: pp. 89–104.

Peach, C. (1982) The growth and distribution of the black population in Britain 1945–1980, in Coleman, D.A. (ed.) *Demography of Immigrants and Minorities in the United Kingdom.* London: Academic Press, pp. 23–42.

Piore, M.J. (1979) *Birds of Passage: Migrant Labour in Industrial Societies.* Cambridge: Cambridge University Press.

Rafiq, M. (1992) A comparison of Muslim and non-Muslim businesses in Britain, *New Community*, 19(1):43–60.

Rhode, B. (1993) Brain drain, brain gain, brain waste: reflections on the emigration of highly educated and scientific personnel from Eastern Europe, in King, R. (ed.) *The New Geography of European Migrations.* London: Belhaven, pp. 228–45.

Robinson, V. (1988) The new Indian middle class in Britain, *Ethnic and Racial Studies*, 11(4):456–73.

Robinson, V. (1990a) Roots to mobility: the social mobility of Britain's black population, *Ethnic and Racial Studies*, 13(2):274–86.

Robinson, V. (1990b) Boom and gloom: the success and failure of South Asians in Britain, in Clarke, C., Peach, C. and Vertovec, S. (eds) *South Asians Overseas.* Cambridge: Cambridge University Press, pp. 269–96.

Robinson, V. (1991) Goodbye yellow brick road: the spatial mobility and immobility of Britain's black and Asian populations, *New Community*, 17(4):313–31.

Robinson, V. (1992a) The internal migration of Britain's ethnic population, in Champion, A. and Fielding, A. (eds) *Migration Processes and Patterns Vol. 1: Research Progress and Prospects.* London: Belhaven, pp. 188–200.

Robinson, V. (1992b) Move on upthe mobility of Britain's Afro-Caribbean and Asian populations, in Stilwell, J., Rees, P. and Boden, P. (eds) *Migration Processes and Patterns Vol. 2: Population Redistribution in the 1980s.* London: Belhaven, pp. 271–91.

Salt, J. (1984) High level manpower movements in Northwest Europe and the role of careers, *International Migration Review*, 17(4):633–52.

Salt, J. (1985) Europe's foreign labour migrants in transition, *Geography*, 70(2):151–8.

Salt, J. (1992a) Migration processes amongst the highly skilled in Europe, *International Migration Review*, 26(2):484–505.

Salt, J. (1992b) Current and future international migration trends affecting Europe, in *People on the Move: New Migration Flows in Europe.* Strasbourg: Council of Europe Press, pp. 41–81.

Salt, J. and Ford, R. (1993) Skilled international migration in Europethe shape of things to come? in King, R. (ed.) *Mass Migrations in Europe: the Legacy and the Future.* London: Belhaven, pp. 293–309.

Sassen-Koob, S. (1984) The new labor demand in global cities, in Smith, M.P. (ed.) *Cities in Transformation.* Newbury Park, CA: Sage, pp. 139–71.

SOPEMI (1992) *Trends in International Migration.* Paris: OECD.

Stark, O. (1992) Migration in developing countries: risk, remittances, and the family, in *Two Essays on Migration.* Geneva: International Labour Office, World Employment Programme Working Paper 58.

van de Kaa, D. (1993) European migration at the end of history, *European Review*, 1(1):87–108.

Vandermotten, C. and Vanlaer, J. (1993) Immigrants and the extreme-right vote in Europe and in Belgium, in King, R. (ed.) *Mass Migrations in Europe: the Legacy and the Future.* London: Belhaven, pp. 136–55.

Venturini, A. (1988) An interpretation of Mediterranean migrations, *Labour*, 2(1):125–54.

Walter, B. (1986) Ethnicity and Irish residential distribution, *Transactions of the Institute of British Geographers*, 11(2):131–46.

Ward, R. and Jenkins, R. (eds) (1985) *Ethnic Communities in Business: Strategies for Economic Survival*, Cambridge: Cambridge University Press.

White, P.E. (1984) *The West European City: a Social Geography*. London: Longman.

White, P.E. (1993a) Immigrants and the social geography of European cities, in King, R. (ed.) *Mass Migrations in Europe: the Legacy and the Future*. London: Belhaven, pp. 65–82.

White, P.E. (1993b) Ethnic minority communities in Europe, in Noin, D. and Woods, R. (eds) *The Changing Population of Europe*. Oxford: Blackwell, pp. 206–25.

White, P.E. (1993c) The social geography of immigrants in European cities: the geography of arrival, in King, R. (ed.) *The New Geography of European Migrations*. London: Belhaven, pp. 47–66.

Zlotnik, H. (1991) Official population projections in OECD countries: what they reveal about international migration prospects, in *Migration: the Demographic Aspects*. Paris: OECD, pp. 43–55.

Part III

PEOPLE, JOBS AND RESTRUCTURING IN EUROPEAN PERIPHERAL REGIONS

6 Portugal in the 1980s and 1990s: Economic Restructuring and Population Mobility

MARIA LUCINDA FONSECA AND CARMINDA CAVACO
Alameda da Universidade, Lisboa, Portugal

INTRODUCTION

The 1980s were a time of important changes in the demographic, social and economic structures of Portugal. Production systems underwent reorganization and the country's economy was internationalized even further.

Demographically speaking, the 1980s were characterized by great stability. Between 1981 and 1991 the population of mainland Portugal registered an increase of only 26 508 inhabitants which represented an annual average growth of 0.03%. Nevertheless, a steep drop in birth and fertility rates during the last few years has introduced serious changes in demographic patterns in both the regions and the country as a whole, and it has caused a pronounced ageing in the population (Table 6.1)

These changes were followed by an increasing trend of people to settle along the coast and in the large urban centres. Even the family unit was affected by this trend.

With regard to the family unit, there was a growing tendency to define the family as a less settled, smaller unit with a higher number of single parents and single-parent families. Together with many more women taking their place in the labour market – with all the implications this has for the family's social function, the division of domestic chores and the relationships between the different generations – these changes have also made an impact on the housing market. This is because they have not only led to more frequent moves, but caused a significant increase in the demand for small-family housing, often for single dwellers.

With regard to the economic situation, during the first few years of the 1980s, Portugal suffered the effects of a serious crisis. However, from the mid-1980s onwards, the second financial stability plan which was agreed with the International Monetary Fund[1] started to produce results, and on 1 January 1986 Portugal became one of the 12 members of the EEC.

People, Jobs and Mobility in the New Europe. Edited by Hans H. Blotevogel and Anthony J. Fielding.
© 1997 European Science Foundation. Published in 1997 by John Wiley & Sons Ltd.

Table 6.1.   Population by age group, mainland Portugal 1981–91

Age groups	1981 %	1991 %
0–14	25.3	19.9
15–64	63.2	66.5
65 and more	11.5	13.6

Source: (INE) National Statistical Institute

Portugal's new Community membership, taking place at a time when the international situation favoured Portugal's economy (a drop in oil prices, the devaluation of the dollar, lower international interest rates and renewed economic growth in the main countries receiving Portuguese exports), marked the beginning of a new phase. There was a boom in economic activity and a start was made to modernize and develop industry.

In the 1990s, however, it is not likely that the international economic situation will continue to favour the Portuguese economy as it did during the 1980s. Moreover, the Single Market and Economic and Monetary Union will certainly lead to higher wages. As a result, sectors handling traditional exports (textiles and footwear), which have only managed to compete internationally because of low labour costs, will be forced to modernize and increase productivity – sacking many workers as a consequence.

To counterbalance the negative effects the Single Market will have on the Portuguese economy, and in order to satisfy the principles of economic and social cohesion, between 1 January 1989 and 31 December 1993 the EC Programme for Community Aid transferred to Portugal from the non-reimbursable loan fund ECU 7368 million (1989 prices) or about 3.3% of the country's GNP. These funds helped to finance investments to the sum of ECU 18469 million which are being made by both the public sector (ECU 6665 million) and the private sector (ECU 4443 million).

These funds were mainly used for setting up economic infrastructures and for providing aid to investments made in production as well as to the infrastructures directly connected with such investments. This would include: occupational training and providing skilled manpower, making farming more competitive and encouraging progress in the countryside, reconverting and reorganizing depressed regional economies and industries, and improving local development potential.

The industrial sector has been the main beneficiary of this investment and we believe that it will continue to benefit due to the fact that the process for modernizing and diversifying industry is now underway and is attracting important sums of foreign direct investment (FDI). Nevertheless, the country's industry is still largely based on low-technology goods and cheap labour and, as a result, the productivity rate for traditional exports (foodstuffs, textiles, clothing, footwear, timber and paper) is lagging behind average European rates.

Changes observed in the Portuguese economy and society – as described above – have been unevenly reflected in the different regions of the country. They have given rise to and, in turn, suffered the effects of notable alterations in the volume, composition and origin/destination of international, inter- and intra-regional migratory movements which have led to marked changes in employment and the way local and regional labour markets work. Changes have also been witnessed in the rising socio-professional mobility of the population.

Although there is a dearth of statistical data available allowing us to characterize and analyse the magnitude of these changes, we shall try to outline some of their most significant features. Furthermore, we shall be looking at the way in which they interact with the economic foundations which are currently being reorganized, and the social fabric of both the country as a whole and each of its various regions.

Owing to the fact that there is a continuing drop in farming activity, which is one of the main factors behind the active Portuguese population's geographical and sector-to-sector mobility, we shall be dedicating more time to this particular question. We shall be analysing the rural exodus and decline, and discussing the farm-worker's growing need to become multi-active.

POPULATION MOBILITY: NEW DESTINATIONS AND TYPES OF EMIGRATION, IMMIGRATION AND MIGRATION

Components of demographic evolution

In the 1960s and 1970s, the demographic nature of Portugal was largely determined by notable domestic and international migration. In the 1980s, however, the drastic reduction in the birth rate and the fall in emigration and inter-regional migration caused the natural growth component to rise quite considerably in importance where regional demographic evolution was concerned.

The Portuguese regions continue to be extremely asymmetrical; the population is largely concentrated along the coast north of Setúbal and in the Algarve, while the hinterlands are being increasingly drained of their inhabitants (Figures 6.1 and 6.2).

The greatest poles of demographic attraction have occurred in the Setúbal Peninsula and in the Algarve. Nevertheless, whereas growth in the former region has been mainly due to the internal rearrangement of metropolitan Lisbon (intra-metropolitan residential mobility), in the Algarve the numbers of migrants reflect its true nature as a centre of attraction for inhabitants coming from other areas in the country.

Apart from the Setúbal Peninsula and the Algarve, only the Baixo Vouga and the Oeste registered net gains in population (457 and 2600 people respectively). As a result, the demographic growth witnessed in Cávado, Ave, Grande Porto. Tâmega, Entre Douro e Vouga as well as the Pinhal Litoral can only be

Figure 6.1.   Portugal: (a) districts and (b) NUTS 3 regions

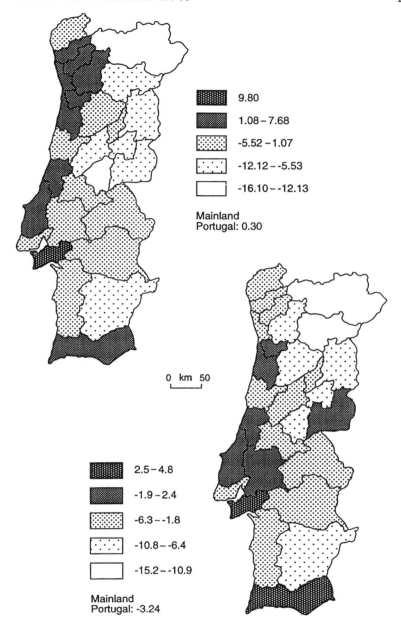

Figure 6.2. Portugal: population change and net migration 1981–91

explained by a birth rate which exceeded the country's average rate by quite a large margin.

In the rest of mainland Portugal, and particularly in the Pinhal Interior and Alto Trás-os-Montes, the serious drop in population witnessed during the period in question was the twofold consequence of people leaving the area and a negative natural growth.

Comparative analysis of migration and natural growth rates also allows us to see that in the 1980s far-reaching changes occurred in the spatial patterns pertaining to emigration and domestic migration.

Grande Lisboa Norte registered a negative migratory balance to the extent of 56 661 people. Even if we take into account the fact that about half of this population settled on the Península de Setúbal, it shows that around 28 000 people emigrated to other countries or moved to other regions in Portugal. As a result, in the 1980s, metropolitan Lisbon (Grande Lisboa Norte and the Península de Setúbal) only managed to absorb 36.3% of its natural growth (births minus deaths).

Grande Porto also witnessed negative migratory growth. However, the region's demographic retention capacity was substantially higher than Lisbon's due to the fact that between 1981 and 1990 it absorbed 52% of its natural growth.

Apart from the Setúbal Peninsula and the Algarve which were mentioned earlier, the Oeste and the Baixo Vouga are the only areas in the country possessing an economic dynamic that has not only allowed them to accommodate extra numbers of their own population, but attracted people from the outside. As a continuation of the metropolitan areas, these coastal zones would therefore appear to offer excellent perspectives for economic growth as they would take advantage of the close proximity of the domestic economy's nerve centres and benefit from the reasonable standards of available infrastructures as well as the high potential with regard to human resources.

Despite the fact that the Pinhal Litoral only managed to retain 76% of its natural growth, there was a sizable increase in both the population and in economic growth that was founded on a growth in industry and the urbanized agglomerations. Contrary to the Pinhal Litoral, the Baixo Mondego continued to lose population. Accentuated demographic drainage affected the rural areas, and neither Coimbra nor Figueira da Foz had the capacity to make those who had abandoned the countryside stay in the area.

A survey covering wider ground shows that, apart from the fact that people are continuing to leave the interior regions, there is a tendency towards increasingly more serious disparities within each of the regions themselves. This is due to a more dense concentration of the population in the most important centres while there are fewer and fewer inhabitants living isolated from one another or in small localities. With the exclusion of the Lisbon and Oporto metropolitan areas,[2] therefore, a higher percentage of people reside in the most important centres in all the regions. Nevertheless, it must be pointed out that this phenomenon has very different characteristics along the coast, in the northern interior and in the Alentejo, not only because they have their own distinctive demographic structures but more importantly because the interior and the Alentejo are continuing to lose a significant amount of people. This means that, instead of growing numbers of inhabitants in the most important centres, we find that their population has either stayed the same or dropped slightly.

International migration – from emigration to immigration

Similar to the events taking place in southern Europe as a result of the 1970s, crisis, emigration from Portugal continued to slow down in the 1980s.[3] Between 1981 and 1990, 58201 permanent, lawfully registered emigrants left the country as compared with the 251667 emigrants between 1971 and 1980. At the same time, the socio-professional standing of the emigrants as well as their host countries changed quite considerably.

As from 1974, predominantly European emigration gave way to overseas emigration: to the USA, Canada, Australia and Venezuela. Former migratory routes were therefore revived and newcomers were helped along by reception networks and local solidarity that was extended to them by older generations of emigrants.

On a par with this, however, temporary emigration above all to France and Switzerland, and to a lesser degree the Middle East, climbed to such an extent that in the 1980s the number of permanent registered emigrants was lower than the number which had only left the country temporarily (58201 and 65598 respectively).

With regard to their geographical origins, it can be seen that the most important temporary emigration currents flowed outwards from the interior districts while permanent emigration derived mainly from the industrial-urban belts along the coast.

The socio-professional composition of the emigrants also changed; now most are semi-skilled workers coming from northern Portugal as well as from the central coastal areas and the Lisbon region. They have thus replaced the unskilled farm labourers who emigrated to France and Germany in the 1960s and the beginning of the 1970s. Nevertheless, it is worth pointing out that temporary emigrants to the rest of Europe, mainly to France and Switzerland, are basically engaged in seasonal work which does not demand higher professional training: farming, the building trade and tourism.

Lower emigration to Europe has been accompanied by a tendency for denser migratory return flows to Portugal; it has been calculated that 290000 emigrants came back home during the 1980s, and most of them settled down once again in their birth places.[4]

Predictable trends for the 1990s and mainly with regard to Europe in essence depend on economic development and the repercussions which the Single Market has on the labour market. If the job market grows in the EU countries, then it is likely that Portuguese emigration to these countries would increase owing to the differences in wages and working conditions between Portugal and the developed countries of nothern and central Europe.

Overseas emigration to the USA and Canada would probably not change to any great extent, although it could come from a wider range of origins. Emigration to Venezuela and South Africa would largely depend on these countries' social and economic progress; as a result it would also depend on whether the Portuguese communities which have already established themselves there feel confident enough to stay on and invest their savings. If this progress turns out to be unfavourable, we could very well see a noticeable flow of returning emigrants, particularly from South Africa.

With regard to emigration to Brazil, unless the economic situation in the country improves, fewer emigrants will be interested in leaving Portugal whereas there could be a rising number of Brazilian immigrants coming into Portugal.

If looked at from the point of view of volume, emigration to the Portuguese-speaking African countries is fairly low. Nevertheless, it has its own distinct characteristics due to the fact that most emigrants are trained personnel who are working within the scope of Portuguese and international cooperation. Whether emigration will increase or not, particularly where Angola and Mozambique are concerned, primarily depends on political and military developments in these countries.

In addition to the changes witnessed in the volume, composition, places of origin and destination of Portuguese emigration during the 1980s and described above, an increasing number of foreign citizens also migrated to Portugal. As a result and despite the fact that Portugal is still basically a country given to emigration, it is receiving more and more foreigners (see Esteves 1991 and Malheiros 1992.)

According to information supplied by the Department for Foreigners and Frontiers at the Ministry of Internal Affairs, there were 102017 registered foreigners residing in Portugal on 31 December 1990. Of these, 64.7% had settled in the Lisbon and Setúbal districts.

Most of the foreigners come from the Cape Verde Islands and represent 30% of all registered immigrants in Portugal. Out of this number, 37.8% settled in Lisbon and Setúbal. After the former Africa colonies, the next most numerous groups of foreigners registered in Portugal come from the EU countries and Brazil. More recently, however, two oriental groups have also expanded in Portugal, although they cannot be compared with the numbers of foreigners mentioned above. One of these comes from India and Pakistan while the other, which is more recent and much smaller, comes from China.

With regard to the economically active foreign population that was legally registered in Portugal on 31 December 1990, the employment rate was higher than it was for the active Portuguese population. The large number of active foreigners exercising a profession (50.5%) would suggest that many came to

Portugal for economic reasons, looking for jobs and better living conditions. After working foreigners, the next most numerous group is composed of housewives and students who make up 22.1% and 23.2% respectively of the total. However, there is only a small number of retired foreigners and immigrants living off their own incomes – 4.9%.

The professional profile of the active population reveals that the most numerous group is composed of industrial workers (45.5%). Next come professionals and scientific workers (24.6%). Among the remaining active foreign population are managers and technical staff, and also administrative and trade personnel, all of whom make up between 5 and 8% of the total. There are 3.5% people employed in security, personal and domestic services, while farming, which offers the least attractive conditions, provides only 1.8% of jobs.

Notwithstanding the fact that this socio-professional data could be somewhat biased because it has failed to take into consideration the illegal immigrants who would swell the ranks of the less-skilled workers, we can discern two major contrasting groups on the labour market into which foreigners in Portugal are divided. The larger group is composed of workers who do the sort of work in Portugal that the Portuguese emigrants did when they went to France and Germany in the 1960s and the early 1970s. These workers possess very little schooling and hardly any job skills, because of which they provide a source of cheap labour, doing only the most menial jobs with the hardest work and the lowest pay (the building trade, industry, cleaning services, transport etc.).

In contrast to these industrial workers and service employees, who mostly come from the Cape Verde Islands, are managers, technical staff, professionals and scientific workers. The majority come from Europe and are connected with transnational corporations increasingly operating in Portugal as a result of the progressive internationalization of the Portuguese economy and the deindustrialization processes occurring in northern and central Europe whereby industry is being relocated in southern Europe.

ECONOMIC RESTRUCTURING AND CHANGES IN THE LABOUR MARKET

The early 1980s were characterized by the effects of a serious economic slump and consequently the mean annual variation in the rate of employment growth was negative. From the mid-1980s, as was mentioned above, Portugal began to recover economically and for this reason the employment rate during the years between 1985 and 1990 witnessed an annual rise of 1.4%.

The favourable upward swing in employment was accompanied by a decrease in unemployment rates, particularly among young people. Nevertheless, unemployment among school leavers continued to stand at double the rate of the overall unemployment figures throughout the period under discussion. In 1991, the number of young people under the age of 25 who were unemployed still represented 40% of the total number of unemployed, despite the fact that this

Table 6.2.   Unemployment rate, mainland Portugal, 1981–91

	1981 %	1986 %	1991 %
Total	8.3	10.2	4.8
Men	4.3	7.9	3.1
Women	13.6	14.1	6.9

Source: (INE) National Statistical Institute

age group constituted a mere 18.4% of the country's active population.

In addition to the young, women were also seriously affected by unemployment. In 1991 the unemployment rate among women was more than twice the rate for men. Although the number of women working accounted only for 44.2% of the total active population, women represented 63.7% of the total number of unemployed people living in the country (Table 6.2).

The gap between the overall employment rate of the Portuguese population and the EU average grew narrower, mostly because of the increasing role which women played in the job market. Jobs for women increased at a much higher rate than they did for men, representing 63.6% of the net growth of jobs between 1981 and 1991.

Where development in the different labour sectors is concerned, there was a sharp fall in absolute and relative terms in the number of farm workers, and an enormous increase in the tertiary sector, mainly to do with personal and collective services, banks, insurance companies, real estate, business services and also services rendered in commerce, restaurants and hotels.

Despite the fact that farming suffered a loss in the domestic job market in relative and absolute terms, there is still a large gap between Portugal and the mean EU rates. Furthermore, as a result of the discrepancy in jobs between men and women – particularly in the least economically dynamic regions – the drop in the number of farm labourers was caused by the male population. It was easier for male farm workers to leave and go to work in other activities in the same region or in other areas of the country or even abroad.

The secondary sector fell in importance with regard to the overall active population, dropping from 36% in 1981 to 34.1% in 1986 and to 33.8% in 1991. Nevertheless, economic growth during the second half of the 1980s witnessed a higher number of workers moving into this sector and the net losses experienced between 1981 and 1986 were easily overturned.

Growth in the tertiary sector was accompanied by a rise in the number of women now being employed. The growth rate for women who were engaged in economic activity was higher than the rate for men. Therefore, while women represented only 44.2% of the labour force in 1981 in the tertiary sector, this number had climbed to 48.3% in 1991.

Apart from the changes already referred to, the reorganization of the country's economy in the 1980s also caused a rise in the number of people working in small and medium-sized companies, mostly in firms employing less than 50 workers. At the same time, and owing to a rise in the number of small companies being set up, there was also an increase in the percentage of self-employed workers with or without their own personnel, as well as workers being employed by others. However, there was a drop in the number of non-paid family workers.

This overall progress hides important differences between the various sectors and in some cases it fails to show development in the opposite direction. In farming, workers are mostly self-employed and employ no one themselves, but between 1983 and 1991 there was a substantial rise in these workers' share of the total volume of employment in the farming sector (55.7% in 1983 and 68.2% in 1991).

Industry has the largest slice of wage earners and it kept to a consistent employment rate of 86% throughout the 1980s. In trade and services the tendency was for most workers to be hired by others and they represented 77% of the population employed in this sector in 1991. However, between 1983 and 1991 they fell by 2.6% in favour of independent workers.

Although the labour market indicators which we have just discussed reveal progress, it is important to stress that at the same time employment became more and more precarious; this could be due to an increase in both part-time work that largely affected female workers and temporary contracts/piece work. As a result, the labour force has become much more mobile owing to alternating periods of work and unemployment. Moreover, this situation has not only possibly been accompanied by changes in professional activity or situations, but also by growing professional mobility within a particular company's staff. This latter phenomenon has been helped along by professional training programmes in an attempt to keep up with demands made by technological innovation, new manufacturing processes and changes in consumer patterns (see Comissao das Comunidades Europeias 1991; OECD 1986, 1992a, 1992b).

In Portugal, greater manpower mobility has been clearly revealed by the rise in turnover rates[5] between 1986 and 1991 which registered 39% for 1991 and only 28% for 1986 in non-farming activities.

RURAL EXODUS: THE DECLINING NUMBER AND MULTI-ACTIVITY OF FARMWORKERS

As we have seen, and not withstanding the difficulties in employment in Europe and the ever-growing competition occurring in recession-hit markets of emigrant workers coming from numerous countries, the decade covering 1980–90 failed to put a stop to people leaving the Portuguese countryside (which is now demographically aged and increasingly less populated) in order to go abroad or live in other areas of Portugal.

On the domestic front, despite the enormous sums being invested in measures and activities promoting regional development, inter- and intra-regional disparities continued to exist and indeed became even worse. This was because the mid-Atlantic strip was much more dynamic and economic activity, infrastructures and equipment were all concentrated in the main centres and their suburban and rural-urban surroundings.

The negative development of the active farming population confirmed the rural exodus because this decline could not be due only to the death rate of elderly people.

In fact, according to the 1979 Agricultural Census, the percentage of individual producers over the age of 65 was fairly high: about 25% on the mainland, although this went up to 34.7% in the district of Faro and 33.6% in Castelo Branco and Guarda.

On the other hand, there were 62.7% farmers of, or over, 50 years of age in the country. However, this percentage was higher in Beja (66.1%), Bragança (68.4%), Castelo Branco (72.1%), Évora (66.9%), Faro (73.9%), Guarda (71.7%), Portalegre (70.4%), Viana do Castelo (65.3%), Vila Real (64.1%) and Viseu (63.0%).

The farming sector lost 157300 active workers between 1981 and 1986 and 114000 between 1986 and 1990. In conformity with these conditions, jobs in agriculture decreased from 25.7% of overall employment in 1981 to 23.3% in 1986 and 19.7% in 1990.

Outward flows leaving agriculture came from the north, the Alentejo and the centre of the country. In other words, it meant leaving the land, whether it was divided up and densely populated, or whether it was the property of only a few and lacking in inhabitants except for the very aged, as happened in the Alentejo and Beira Interior. It is for this reason that different regions lent different weights to the drop in regional farm jobs: while the centre lost a little more than a tenth of its farmers, the Algarve lost almost half and the Alentejo more than half. On the other hand, it also became evident that increased regional investment in farming did not stop workers from leaving agriculture; in some cases development even accentuated the reduction (machinery and equipment as well as farming in the restricted sense of the word being replaced by forestry).

The Lisbon region and the Tagus river valley as well as the Alentejo were where 76% of the loss of active farm workers was concentrated and these areas absorbed 46.6% of the investments coming from the Specific Programme for Developing Portuguese Agriculture (PEDAP), as well as 55.3% of incoming investments on the application of EC Regulation 797 between 1986 and 1991.

We could question the degree of accuracy when dealing with statistics on farm jobs. Nevertheless, we are able to appreciate their true significance when we analyse data supplied by the 1989 Agricultural Census. In the first place, let us take the family population which declared that it was working its own land: vast numbers of these farming families were spread all over the country; however, only a part of them spent more than half their time on their own land. These new statistics come a lot closer to the data we have for 1991 overall if we add numbers corresponding to workers permanently employed by others, particularly in the regions where the owners of the large estates are located (the river Douro valley, the Ribatejo and the Alentejo). Only in the Algarve did the number of farmers who declared in 1989 that they spent more than half their time working their own farms exceed the number of farm jobs indicated by the National Statistics Institute for 1991.

These differences are basically a result of the family's importance among the farming population, and mainly the role of women in the family (wives and female members living with the farmer) because they work the land themselves. They are not recorded as doing so in the Population census, however. Nevertheless the data show that there is a high number of working women in the farmer's household, particularly where spouses are concerned. The percentage of these workers in the country's total farming population, mainly in the north and the central coastal region, indicates a strong feminine component in the farm work undertaken by factory worker/peasant families.

With regard to the different regions, there are serious asymmetries in the incidence of multi-activity and the role which women have in farming. The smallest farms (the north and central coast) have the highest numbers of women working in agriculture, whether they are the producers themselves or whether they are other members of the family, and they spend more time running the farms. The number of female farm workers is also high in the Algarve, whether refering to female producers or wives and other family members who work the land.

There are three main reasons which have given rise to the changes we have described above, although they act in various sorts of combinations and intensities: emigration, the rural exodus to other parts of the country and the farm workers' exodus involving some members of the peasant family without actually causing a rural exodus (here, it means mobility from sector to sector of activity).

Given the evolution of the 1980s, it is likely that the 1990s will continue to see a drop in farming activity, although the seriousness of this fall will vary from region to region, not only because of the differences noted from the outset, but also because of the dynamics and incidence of regional development policies and the EU's agricultural policy.

Indeed, the 1990s have changed the context within which the Portuguese rural and farming world developed. The fact that we have now progressed into the second and last stage of phased integration into the market and pricing system of farming produce has taken on new meaning. It is also significant that we have come to the end of the transition period for many branches of activity, and the near end of the Specific Programme for Developing Portuguese Agriculture (due to finish in 1996). Moreover, the Single Market started operating in 1993 and, as a result, the domestic market will not only have to deal with competition coming from many imported goods but also the reforms made to the Union's agricultural policy. The Maastricht Agreements will most definitely have to be confronted and the Economic and Social Cohesion Fund has to start operating in order to assist member countries suffering from serious development problems, particularly in many of their rural regions.

It has been within the framework of the Common Agricultural Policy and its subsequent measures that we have witnessed a proliferation of political talk about rural development. Development, it is claimed, must be diversified, integrated and aware not only of human beings but also of their quality of life, the social fabric, the environment and the landscape – no longer to concern itself wholly with farming. Hopes blossom (and utopias, too) about rural tourism (rest, pleasure, recreation, culture, tradition, history, ecology . . .) in synergy with handicrafts, particularly in the most outlying farm areas or in the mountains – in other words, in regions which have always been disadvantaged and have traditionally stayed as farm and pasture lands with a strong rural basis.

It is a fact that when speaking about diversification at the local level, which affects the rural and farming population's activity, tourism is often regarded as a solution: selective tourism, not mass tourism, catering for the demands of certain social groups. However, it is important to be aware of environmental and social factors when considering this demand and to weigh up the effects implied by satisfying them: what sort of occupation, employment and income would such tourism involve and, consequently, what kind of local and regional economic development would result and to what extent would the population levels remain stable?

As an example, let us take the lesson given by the Austrian Tyrol, a high alpine range where its peasant farmers were engaged in raising cattle and working in the coniferous forests (both activities suffered in the inter-war depression and became non-competitive). The area's economy has become increasingly more connected with tourism and advantage has been taken of prevalent conditions to turn it into a winter-sports resort where there are cultural attractions, good roads and beautiful scenery.

Given this setting, nature conservation and the landscape gained great importance and the farmers have been called on to act in their defence. However, both the subsidies paid out to sustain the price of farm produce and the subsidies supporting certain techniques and methods of farming, as well as the conservation of the land, have been insufficient to make farming families want to stay. The relatively stable number of farms has been mainly due to non-farming incomes derived from activity connected with tourism.

Despite efforts to protect and improve the quality of the tourist market, tourism decreases during the summer because of non-competitive prices and because there are cheaper airfares to more distant places and new types of interest among young people.

Under conditions such as these, having a peasant world at hand is essential for the recreational value of the landscape. Tourism in general, and especially rural tourism, should therefore not be viewed as replacements for agricultural activity. Rather, farming should act as a complement to tourism, particularly in the deep countryside where there are few economic alternatives. Accordingly and despite the jobs and incomes generated by rural tourism and the renewed image of the once-abandoned regions that have now become attractive again, and in spite of the numerous effects which tourism has had on other activities such as handicraft, the building trade, commerce and services, it will be extremely difficult to restrain, except at the local level and in small areas, a tendency leading to an exodus from and abandonment of farm lands in the interior – reaching from Trás-os-Montes to the Algarve.

NOTES

1. The second financial stabilization plan lasted for 18 months (from mid-1983 to the end of 1984). It allowed both public and external accounts to reach finance-generating standards at the end of the period. However, success in this field has caused enormous social burdens. Real wages during this period decreased 12.5% between 1982 and 1984, unemployment went up and investment fell by 25%.
2. Owing to the persistent demographic decline in the central areas of the cities and the build-up of the urban areas.
3. With regard to recent changes in international migration in Europe, see King 1993.
4. For returning Portuguese emigrants, see: Paiva 1985; Ferreira 1984 and Silva 1984.
5. Turnover rate (incoming and out-going workers)/average number of people employed.

REFERENCES

Comissão das Comunidades Europeias (ed.) (1991) *Emprego na Europa*. Luxembourg. Comissão das Comunidades Europeias.

Esteves, M. do Céu (ed.) (1991) *Portugal, País de Imigração*. Lisboa: Instituto de Estudos para o Desenvolimento, Caderno 22.

Ferreira, E. de Sousa (1984) *Reintegração dos Emigrates Portugueses*. Integração na CEE e Desenvolvimento Económico. Lisboa: EDEP.

King, R. (ed.) (1993) *Mass Migration in Europe: the Lagacy and the Future*. London: Belhaven.

Malheiros, J.M. (1992) *Comunidades Indianas na Área Metropolitana de Lisboa – Geografia de um Reencontro*. Lisboa: Faculdade de Letras.

OECD (1986) *Flexibilité et marché du travail – le débat aujourd'hui*. Paris. OECD.

OECD (1992a) *Perspectives de l'emploi*. Paris: OECD.

OECD (1992b) *High-quality Education and Training for All*. Paris: OECD.

Paiva, A. (ed.) (1985) *Portugal e a Europa: o fim de um ciclo migratório*. Lisboa: Instituto de Estudas para o Desenvolvimento.

Silva, M.A. et al. (1984) *Retorno, Emigração e Desenvolviments Regional em Portugal*. Lisboa: Instituto de Estudos para o Desenvolvimento, Caderno 8.

7 Youth Migration, Labour Market Restructuring and Locality in the West of Ireland

IAN SHUTTLEWORTH AND PETER SHIRLOW
Queen's University, Belfast, UK

INTRODUCTION

Recent Irish migration differs from that of the past. It is now popularly perceived as a 'brain drain' of highly skilled and highly trained young people who have qualified themselves beyond the declining demands of the Irish labour market. This skills exodus has been explained as a result of individual choice and the working of an Irish 'enterprise culture' that leads young people to seek work abroad. We dissent from this simplistic view and suggest that a more structured approach to the understanding of Irish migration is necessary. We agree with MacLaughlin (1991) that a locality-based analysis is necessary. However, we also suggest that the analysis should take some account of the forces of global economic restructuring and their locality-specific impacts.

Economic explanations of Irish migration generally fall into two categories. First, some take the framework of the business cycle as a starting point and conceptualize migration as a response to the conjunctural forces of change in the relative levels of unemployment and wages between Ireland and the rest of the world (Walsh 1974). An influential example of this type of analysis correlates net out-migration from Ireland with the condition of the regional economy of the south-east of England (the destination of some 70% of emigrants from Ireland). The second broad framework for interpreting the causes of Irish migration looks at economic restructuring in terms of deeper changes within the global economy. In this context the Irish experience of migration has been explained as a result of Ireland's position within the international division of labour, whether within the 'old' international division of labour as a reserve army or within the 'new' international division of labour (NIDL) where corporate hierarchies (and the legacy of past peripherality) restrict both the number and types of employment available (Breathnach 1988; Breathnach and Jackson 1991).

Despite different emphases and analyses, both of these analytical approaches

People, Jobs and Mobility in the New Europe. Edited by Hans H. Blotevogel and Anthony J. Fielding.
© 1997 European Science Foundation. Published in 1997 by John Wiley & Sons Ltd.

largely offer only national-level explanations of migration. We argue, on two counts, that such an overt emphasis on the national scale is inappropriate and that further insights into the processes underlying migration can be gained through examination of the local context of migration. The failure to provide detailed locality-based studies has removed the possibility of examining the functional relationships between Irish and global labour markets in structuring migration.

We adopt a locality-based perspective which, we argue, provides a valid empirical base from which to examine the context and consequences of emigration. The example we take is of the Shannon Town local labour market (STLLM), which depends on the Shannon Industrial Estate (SIE), to explore the relationship between economic restructuring and migration through the mediating effects of the regulation of education and training. Although this is a case study it is significant because of the locality's history of industrialization, and the roles (sometimes contradictory) played by the state in providing training and education. In recent years high levels of economic restructuring among foreign companies have produced new labour market relationships which have fundamentally altered access to employment and the nature and extent of emigration.

In order to maintain foreign investment the Irish state has pursued a policy of upgrading the technical and managerial capability of the Irish workforce. The traditional policy of using state apprenticeship training schemes sponsored by Foras Aiseanna Saothair (FAS), the government training board, has gradually been superseded by an emphasis on university-based third-level education. In relation to our case study this has conferred a specific and distinctive role on the University of Limerick. The development of a technically trained workforce and the fostering of technological innovation have become the major objectives of education policy. Within Limerick University the importance of creating a highly skilled workforce is now regarded as an integral part of labour market policy and labour market management in the mid-west of Ireland (Sklair 1988). These policies have been successful in that opportunities in manufacturing employment have increased for those who have gained with higher technical qualifications. But this has been of little benefit for those with technical/craft qualifications who have found traditional routes into the labour market blocked by a technical elite on the one hand, and unskilled workers on the other.

Conventional wisdom that the attraction of foreign capital to Ireland has reduced unemployment and migration needs to be challenged. Between 1980 and 1993, for example, manufacturing employment in the foreign-owned sector fell by 12.1%; indigenous companies shed some 20% of their workforce. This emphasizes the failure of both foreign and Irish capital to create a buoyant demand for labour in manufacturing. Combined with a high rate of natural population increase, this has made the task of creating enough jobs in Ireland more difficult.

The ideology of development, based on the attraction of foreign capital, is questioned because of its failure to comprehend fully the effects of capital restructuring on social and migratory characteristics. The stereotype of brain-drain migration is also critically examined, as is the impact of the investment decisions of large foreign-owned companies on local labour-market structures. This mechanism relates local labour-market disequilibria to national and global developments in the productive system.

The nature of global economic restructuring is highly significant for small peripheral economies whose labour markets are dependent on foreign invest-ment for employment growth, especially because of the weakness of the indigenous sector. Assertions that traditional training policies can correct imbalances in these local labour markets, together with assumptions that better training invariably leads to better employment prospects (Breen 1991), are therefore discussed. The crux of the analytical approach is the ideological importance given by the Irish state to education, training and migration.

INDUSTRIAL RESTRUCTURING: THE IDEOLOGY OF EDUCATION AND TRAINING

In developing this theme of analysing both global and domestic issues, we pay specific attention to the nature and form of the productive base and its effect on the construction of social relations and labour process change. Each of these relationships is set in turn within the context of institutional relationships which are evident in contemporary Ireland.

External relations have generally been determined by the nature of global capitalism and Ireland's geographical and historical transformation within this system. However, it must be stressed that the negative aspects of Ireland's integration into the global economy should not be overemphasized at the expense of examining a whole range of domestic socio-political impediments and institutional relationships which have also retarded Ireland's developmental potential. As noted by McAuley:

> The role of the capitalist state in the process of accumulation and social reproduction is crucial. Patterns of development and underdevelopment of the economy are shaped by state policy and state institutions. Variations in state policy, including regional policy, must be situated in the context of the accumula-tion process and take account of variations in class structures. (1994, p. 36)

Increased global competition, with a premium on price, quality and respon-siveness to customer needs, has promoted rapidly changing technologies which have emphasized the need for flexible and adaptable governance and workforce structures. There has been a general trend to increase productivity and reduce unit costs through introducing more flexible responses. Traditional Taylorist and Fordist approaches to work organization which were evident among transnational corporations (TNCs) in the 1960s and 1970s have been deemed incapable of producing significant productivity gains and reduced unit costs. Similarly, TNCs have come under continuous pressure from their customers to maintain or reduce the price of their product (ICTU 1993; Sweeney 1995).

TNCs have in turn introduced high levels of numerical and functional flexibility within their Irish plants in an attempt to raise productivity and competitiveness (Munck 1993; O'Hehir and O'Mahony 1993). The introduction of flexible labour practices and the promotion of a distinct service class have altered social class structures throughout Ireland. Male domination of labour markets is being eroded due to increased feminization, extended part-time employment and a growth in home working. Male manual employment has also been eroded by the expansion of graduate employment opportunities. The decline in male manual employment opportunities has been constructed around a shrinking rigid sector of full-time workers, and a sizeable growth in peripheral part-time labour and in graduate opportunities. The segmented nature of emerging labour-market structures highlights not only a polarization in employment conditions but also a growing gap in social status, socio-economic opportunity and migration patterns.

Mjoset (1993) argues that less stable global economic conditions and the consequent need for global (and national) capital to reduce labour costs have further destabilized the Irish labour market. Increased capital intensity, based on improving competitiveness, has been accompanied by the modification and replacement of existing technologies (Barry and Bradley 1991). In the context of global recession, TNCs have redefined their recruitment policies in Ireland. Employment of graduates has grown, as has that of semi-skilled/unskilled, mainly female workers (O'Hehir and O'Mahoney 1993) as a result of this increasing capital intensity.

New productive techniques which require technical expertise are generally based on possessing university-based third-level qualifications. Traditional means of access to the labour market for those without university-based third-level qualifications are destroyed as jobs, formerly the preserve of industrial apprentices, have been taken by graduates. As a result, previously well-functioning and dynamic local labour markets have become areas of low opportunity and socio-economic decline due to the incompatibility between local labour demand and the skills of the majority of local people.

The nature of economic restructuring and the need to provide an attractive range of recruits for foreign and indigenous industry have meant that education and training have become central themes in industrial policy. In effect, policy relating to training and education promotes the notion that present policies either support the entrepreneurial 'seedcorn' for indigenous development or a form of 'human capital' which is attractive to foreign direct investors. Recent publications, such as the Culliton Report on Industrial Policy (1992) and the latest Green Paper on education, have both made clear that there is a direct need to 'de-emphasise the bias towards the liberal arts and traditional professions' (Sheehan 1992, p. 36).

This affiliation between education and industry is illustrated by the transformations within university-based third-level education. Third-level education policy is now centred on the development of management, marketing, design, research and development skills which are recognized as an essential prerequisite for the stability and expansion of foreign-owned industry and the development of indigenous industry (NESC 1988). As such, principal developments have been aimed at expanding technologically based education. This functional and highly pragmatic conception of higher education has been ardently endorsed by both the state and its development agencies in order to tie together higher education provisions and labour-market needs.

It is now evident that education and training act as 'social regulatory' mechanisms, in as much as they are promoted as a precondition for industrial activity. Furthermore, there is an indirect implication that education and training are necessary in order to provide those who are unable to enter the domestic labour market with emigration opportunities. Nowhere is this more true than in the STTLM in the West of Ireland, due to the establishment of the technologically biased University of Limerick and the emphasis on training under the auspices of the training organization, FAS, and the local state development body, the Shannon Free Airport Development Company (SFADCO). As noted above, increases in demand for graduates from the TNC sector has run in parallel with a reduction in the need for skilled apprentices.

Restructuring in the foreign sector and the desire to find recruitment alternatives has conferred a specific and distinctive role on the university. The relationship between the university and foreign-based industry is the key to understanding the role of third-level education in the mid-west of Ireland (Shirlow and Shuttleworth 1994). The ideological importance of promoting third-level-based recruitment alternatives has been centred on close links between industry and the university. The main linkage is based on the university's production of technical and managerial staff. A sizeable number of undergraduates spend at least one year of their degree working with companies located in Shannon. The nature of this relationship provides industry not only with a suitable workforce but also with regulated access to a source of tested and amenable workers. This in itself may seem a healthy relationship in that the technical needs of industry are provided for by the university. However, it must be stressed that the growth in technical employment opportunities has been accompanied by significant reductions in manual-based employment. This situation prompted Sklair to state that the link between the university and industry operated 'in the interest of foreign corporations, whether or not these coincided with the goals of national development' (1988, p. 174).

In effect, technical upgrading produces social problems due to the nature of contemporary recruitment policies. As one manager noted about his company's relationship with the university:

> We had to replace many of our previous manual workers since they were incompatible to our goal of technological advance. In the graduate we are looking not just towards their technical background but to their attitudes. Put it this way, we have changed a lot of our technology base of the last ten years and we need results as quickly as possible. The only way to do this is to have a technical

workforce that is prepared to work with management, and that workforce comes from the university. If they work with us we can fully utilize our resources and that is vital in a competitive market. We need to increase productivity and function at 100%. SFADCO and the university have promised a workforce that satisfies our goals and that is why we are in Shannon. (interview 12 May 1990)

Despite the recession and major cutbacks in employment, the number of graduates finding employment has continued to increase, which in turn has augmented the potential skill level of certain sections of the workforce. Limerick University has been successful in providing a suitable workforce, a situation which means that any understanding of productive restructuring is set against the ideological significance of Limerick University. As one manager noted:

Employing university graduates has saved us thousands of dollars. Firstly we have convinced HQ that the university can supply us with production managers which has meant that staff have not needed to go to the US to be trained. You must also consider that the use of graduates means we get the best labour at the cheapest prices. Ireland is unique. They don't have the industry to employ graduates amongst their indigenous stock so that means a surplus exists for the foreign companies to choose from. The last situation we need is a tight labour market and competition for staff. (interview 17 August 1990)

Since 1983, 321 undergraduates have undertaken their placement within the SIE and of these it has been estimated that 40% have been offered full-time posts by their training company (Limerick University 1990). The University of Limerick produced 617 graduates in 1990 of which 87% found employment within their first year of leaving university and 5% entered post-doctoral or Master's programmes (Co-operative Education and External Affairs Division, Limerick University).

There is considerable demand in the local labour market for graduates. But, as we suggested, this is likely to have taken place at the expense of other groups of workers. In the next section we therefore examine how the STLLM has become segmented and male manual employment has decreased as graduate and unskilled employment have grown.

LABOUR MARKET RESTRUCTURING AND MIGRATION

Shannon 'export industrial zone' was established in 1958. At the time it was an influential innovation due to the emphasis placed on the attraction of manufacturing operations. Shannon attracted much attention as it was only one of two non-Dublin based organizations (the other being Udaras na Gaeltacht) with policy-making autonomy (Callanan 1984). Moreover, the distinctiveness of Shannon, with 81% of employees employed by foreign capital (SFADCO 1992), has been recognized on many occasions. As Sklair comments:

Shannon is internationally recognised as the first and probably the most successful of the modern industrial zones, which were deliberately established to provide an environment in which foreign companies feel comfortable to do business and confident that a high level of profit could be sustained. (1988, p. 156)

It has been argued that SFADCO's autonomy and regionally defined role has produced significant socio-economic benefits due to the creation of close institutional links between themselves and foreign and indigenous capital. However, this expectation of labour-market stability is without foundation because of the effect of economic restructuring on local labour markets. Restructuring has directly altered the nature of demand for labour and this process has led to significant growth in unemployment and out-migration. The past dominance of skilled male manual employment in the STLLM has declined because of the recruitment of unskilled and graduate labour. This increase in labour recruitment segmentation has directly affected employment prospects within the STLLM because of the mismatch of labour supply and employer needs. Economic restructuring and changes in the labour process have led to altered demands for labour in both sectoral and occupational terms. These changes in recruitment policies reflect foreign capital's desire to produce a workforce which is both technically competent and flexible in wage demands and task orientation. Therefore the introduction of new technology and the need for productivity gains mean that the skilled male manual labour force of the STLLM has become incompatible with recruitment needs.

In relation to youth training, which is manufacturing based, the number of trainees produced between 1987 and 1992 far outstripped demand. For example, in 1992, 54% of all those trained between 1989 and 1991 by FAS were unemployed. In principle, state training is part of the state-sponsored modernization process. This programme has attempted to foster industrialization but has not addressed social imbalances within Ireland. In conceptual terms, Ireland's socio-economic peripherality within Europe has not been altered by investment in education, training or the attraction of foreign industry, a situation which reflects the incompatibility between national economic goals and social needs.

The process of restructuring in the STLLM presents several contrasting aspects. Global economic forces, experienced by TNCs and transmitted through them to the locality, have combined to alter the structure of labour demand in a way that is specific to the SIE given its distinct history and structure of labour relations. Simultaneously, state intervention via the education and training systems sought to manipulate local labour supply, either as a reaction to these global economic forces or as an attempt to manage them in a construtive way. But contradictions between the labour supply policies, and those policies encouraging foreign investment, have created a social environment ripe for out-migration. Between 1980 and 1991, for example, total manufacturing employment in the STLLM fell by 43% and within the manufacturing sector there were particularly rapid job losses for skilled manual workers. The results of these developments and their impact on the out-migration of young people are investigated in the next section by means of a small survey.

RESULTS

The survey, undertaken in 1991, was of 109 young migrants who had left school in the Shannon area between 1986 and 1991. The survey collected data on the migration and labour-market experiences of these young people that can be used to evaluate the extent to which labour-market restructuring had its anticipated impact on youth migration. At the time of the survey all the young people for whom data were collected had left Shannon and, if necessary, contact was made through family or friends who were still resident in the locality. Because of these limitations the survey should not be considered as statistically representative of all young people in the area. Nevertheless, it can still be claimed that the results give an example of the experiences of young people from the Shannon area and some understanding of the structural forces that give rise to out-migration. Data were collected on standard explanatory variables such as age, gender, qualifications and family occupational background. These were then used to analyse migration and the relationships between migration, training, personal labour-market history and the reasons for leaving Shannon to give a reasonably comprehensive picture of the nature of young migrants from the areas.

Most of the sample were aged between 18 and 24, were male and came from backgrounds that were self-classified as semi-skilled/skilled manual. Some 30% migrated within Ireland with Dublin the most popular destination for these internal migrants. For those who left Ireland, London was the most common destination where 35% of the sample were resident at the time of the survey. In total about 75% of the migrants who left Ireland went to Britain, a proportion which accords well with what is known about Irish migration destinations from other sources (Garvey and Maguire 1989; Higher Education Authority 1990).

Table 7.1 profiles respondents' educational and training backgrounds. About one-third have no qualifications. A further third of the respondents have leaving certificate or apprenticeship qualifications. As training qualifications form one of the primary focuses of the chapter, their significance is explored below where three types of training are recognized in the survey results (apprenticeships, VPT basic training) are discussed in turn. Apprenticeships have long been considered the conventional route to acquiring skilled manual employment in Ireland. FAS operates apprenticeship training in association with the Department of Education in a number of 'designated trades' training schemes which last for four years. For the most able apprentices the course of training leads to the National Craft Certificate. The Vocational Preparation and Training (VPT) scheme operates in schools and is run by the Department of Education. it is aimed at young people aged 15 to 18 years who propose to enter the labour market but lack vocational experience. Basic training schemes cater for unskilled young people of low academic aptitude. They cover basic manual instruction and impart a knowledge of general work practices.

Table 7.2 presents employment and unemployment histories in terms of the

Table 7.1.   Education and training background of respondents (%)

Education	
No qualifications	39.4
Group/inter certificate	29.4
Leaving certificate	31.2
Training	
No training	34.9
Basic training	21.1
VPT	22.0
Apprenticeship	22.0

Source: Survey results, N=109

Table 7.2.   Employment and unemployment histories of survey respondents

Number of jobs held in Shannon		
	Frequency	%
0	24	22.0
1	28	25.7
2	15	13.8
3	13	11.9
4	17	15.6
6	11	10.1
8	1	0.9
Incidence of unemployment in Shannon		
	Frequency	%
0	34	31.2
1	44	40.4
2	10	9.2
4	9	8.3
6	6	5.5
7	1	0.8

Source: Survey results, N=109

number of spells of employment and unemployment experienced by respondents. The majority had been unemployed at least once when in Shannon and had also held at least one job in the area. The apparent availability of employment in Shannon is clouded by the likelihood that many of the jobs in the area, some 80%, are short term or unskilled. This impression of instability in the local labour market is reinforced by an analysis of these data in terms of educational qualification, which suggests that the labour market is polarized with skilled manual opportunities being eroded (O'Hehir and O'Mahoney 1993).

Over one-third of those with apprenticeships or other vocational qualifications had held no job in Shannon. In contrast, those with basic training had all been employed at some time in the locality. The same pattern is true for

educational qualifications. Young people who had left school with qualifications were more likely to have had no jobs in the areas than those with no
qualifications. Conversely, those with no qualifications were more likely than
those with qualifications to have had more jobs but also more periods of
unemployment. The types of opportunities offered by the Shannon local labour
market seem therefore to be unskilled and short term.

The interactions between gender, social background, education and training
complicate the relationship between training, education and migration. There
are important distinctions between males and females. First, no females received
apprenticeship training; this was the preserve of males, with the majority of
females receiving no training. Secondly, while there was no relationship between
gender and educational attainment, there was a strong relationship with
occupational background. Young people with better-off parents had higher
attainment and because of this ultimately had access to apprenticeships and
training schemes that were socially valued. However, this access to training,
together with relatively high educational attainment, did not lead directly to
success in the local labour market. The evidence reviewed suggests that there is
no direct and obvious relationship between qualifications and gaining a job in
the locality. If anything the situation was reversed, with the unqualified having
better chances of gaining a job in a labour market where it seems that most job
opportunities are short term and low skilled.

Migration from Shannon sharply altered this relationship. Before migration
only 10% of respondents had held a job with a regular contract, whereas after
migration the proportion rose to 50%. This was particularly noticeable for
those with apprenticeships who, on average, earned higher wages than thosew
with no qualifications or with just basic training. This is hardly surprising, with
all apprenticeship holders working, after migration, in jobs they considered
skilled. Respondents perceived economic pressure as the main reason for leaving
Shannon. Unemployment was the leading reason, given by 52% of respondents,
followed by 'unsatisfactory post' and 'better wages' cited by 23% and 17% of
respondents respectively. These economic motivations outweighed social and
cultural factors.

Migration from the Shannon area included both the unqualified and those
with apprenticeships and school qualifications. However, the migration of
skilled labour from the area indicates that vocational qualifications do not
necessarily lead to employment in the locality despite the explicit ideological
links made between training and the labour market. The economic causes of
migration from the area emphasize the lack of prospects for young people
regardless of training or education background in Shannon.

DISCUSSION

These results suggest that the socio-economic complexities of localities are of
major importance in determining migration experiences; local social class and

labour-market structures act to mediate trends that are apparent at the national level. Data at the national level show migration rates are closely related to the condition of the economic cycle (Walsh 1974) and that emigration from Ireland has been strongly correlated with cyclical economic change, particularly boom and bust in the south-east of England (Shuttleworth 1993).

Overlying these cyclical changes, it is probable that the composition of Irish migration flows has changed as a reflection of social and educational developments. Data on the migration of young people on leaving school, for example, also shows a cyclical pattern with long-term growth in the rates of out-migration for those with leaving certificates (equivalent to A levels or the French Baccalauréate) and lowest for those with no qualifications. The arguments advanced by Sexton (1987) with regard to the composition of migration flows at the national level are also well known, with an increasing share of white-collar occupations and third-level graduates.

Explanations of contemporary Irish migration have seized on these trends in the skill and educational composition of the population flows. Generally attention has been drawn to Ireland's subordinate position in the NIDL, the role of foreign employers in recruiting the most qualified abroad to work, the inequitable tax regime in Ireland, and the demographic pressures that have led Ireland to become the 'human resource warehouse of Europe' (King, Shuttleworth and Walsh 1996).

However, these explanations and experiences cannot necessarily be read as interpreting the experiences of localities within Ireland; national links between education, training and migration vary between different localities. At the national level it is often hypothesized that Ireland has been marginalized within the NIDL and that the consequent de-skilling of the labour force has destroyed opportunities for the highly qualified. Skilled emigration is therefore interpreted by some as a result of a crisis of neo-Fordism and as partly the result of the resumption of Ireland's traditional role as a supplier of labour, but this time in the changed context of a new world economic order.

The results of the survey, however, show the importance of locality and of local class conditions in responding to economic restructuring. Generalizations about neo-Fordism and the results of labour-market restructuring at the national level do not appear valid in the STLLM, as geography does matter in the explanation of migration flows. The results of labour-market restructuring and global economic forces are contingent on local histories and local class structures. For the STLLM the dominant local forces in the beginning were the creation of a working class in the area in the 1950s and the 1960s, the rise of union power on the crest of a world economic boom and comparative ease in attracting foreign inward investment. This was followed in the 1970s by economic crisis as TNCs struggled to come to terms with 'international economic disorder' (Thrift 1989). As a result of this crisis, measures were required to maintain the attractions of the area for foreign capital and to respond to the changed labour demands of TNCs. In some ways the power to influence events was outside the hands of the state as firms located in the STLLM substituted high-cost and possibly militant male labour for female workers. But another strategy, that of investment in technology, was followed simultaneously as part of the economic restructuring of the 1970s and 1980s. In many ways these forces were beyond the control of the state. However, it also intervened by the establishment of the avowedly technical University of Limerick. Its existence enabled employers to realize their aspirations to find locally available labour to cope with the increased application of technology to production. In summary, this put further pressures on the skilled manual segment of the STLLM.

The net result has been the destruction of traditional male employment and the former modes of entry by young people to the labour market in the STLLM. Economic restructuring has particularly weakened the position of males and young people seeking to enter traditional employment. Paradoxically, state intervention in the labour market has been contradictory. Policies such as training for skilled manual employment, associated with one round of accumulation, are contradictory in the light of changes in the labour market which have led to occupational polarization and the loss of this kind of work to female unskilled employment on one side and graduate employment on the other. Training for employment might be a dominant paradigm in the rest of the Ireland, but in the STLLM it is not the panacea that might have been imagined by the state nor the young people receiving it.

It is true that the provision of training allowed young people to remain in the locality for a short while. However, measures to increase the supply of trained labour did nothing to address the reduced demand for labour of this type. The training received, in effect, was for jobs elsewhere but not for employment in the STLLM. In essence, then, state training is training for emigration rather than training for local work.

CONCLUSION

The case study has illustrated the links between global economic forces, labour-market restructuring, education and training and migration. In this locality, economic restructuring has broken the ties between success in the labour market and training. Instead of training, as in the conventional view, being linked to the success in the labour market, it appears to overqualify young people for some jobs and underqualify them for others; young people who have completed state training and apprenticeships run the risk of competing for places in a non-existent middle ground in the labour market. At the national level, measures to increase certain types of 'human capital' might make sense, but in the STLLM investment in training hardly seems to be effective in the ways that would be envisaged by human capital theorists. For young people with second-level qualifications and an apprenticeship, the accumulation of 'human capital' does not offer a secure path to advancement in the local labour market. Instead, the jobs they would formerly have taken have become the preserve of either unskilled workers or graduates. This challenges conventional nostrums of the utility of training.

Training has no intrinsic value in peripheral localities such as Shannon because the worth of credentials is set by foreign capital. The value given to qualifications by foreign capital can just as easily be taken away. In a world with an ever-growing rate of economic restructuring, the value of supply-side policies for the labour market should therefore be questioned. At present, unskilled labour and graduate labour are in demand in the STLLM, but this need not always be the case. There is no way of forecasting what the results of changing patterns of investment will be and future labout demands may mean that present-day patterns will soon be superseded.

REFERENCES

Barry, F. and Bradley, J. (1991) On the causes of Ireland's unemployment, *The Economic and Social Review*, 22(4):253–86.

Breathnach, P. (1988) Uneven development and capitalist peripheralisation: the case of Ireland, *Antipode*, 20(2):122–41.

Breathnach, P. and Jackson, J. (1991) Ireland, emigration and the new international division of labour, in King, R. (ed.) *Contemporary Irish Migration*. Dublin: Geographical Society of Ireland Special Publication 6.

Breen, R. (1991) *Education, Employment and Training in the Youth Labour Market*. Dublin: ESRI.

Callanan, B. (1984) The work of SFADCO, *Administration*, 32:342–50.

Garvey, D and Maguire, M. (1989) *Structure of Gross Migration Flows*. 1988 Labour Force Survey Estimates. Dublin: Central Statistics Office.

Higher Education Authority (1990) *First Destinations of Award Recipients in Higher Education*. Dublin: Higher Education Authority.

ICTU (1993) *Trade Union Information Sheet 14*. Dublin: ICTU, November.

King, R., Shuttleworth, I. and Walsh, J. (1994) Ireland: the human resource warehouse of Europe, in Rees, P. Stillwell, J., Convey, A. and Kupiszewski, M. (eds) *Migration and the European Community*, Chichester: Wiley.

Limerick University (1990) *Graduate Employment Report 1950*. Limerick: University of Limerick.

MacLaughlin, J. (1991) Social characteristics and destinations of Irish emigrants from selected regions in the west of Ireland, *Geoforum*, 22(3):319–31.

McAuley, (1994) *The Politics of Identity*. Aldershot: Avebury.

Mjoset, L. (1993) *The Irish Economy in a Comparative Institutional Perspective*. Dublin: NESC.

Munck, R. (ed.) (1993) *The Irish Economy*. London: Pluto.

NESC (1988) *A Strategy for Development 1986–1990*. Dublin: NESC, report 83.

O'Hehir, J. and O'Mahoney, F. (1993) New forms of work: organization-strategic options for unions, Dublin: ICTU, unpublished paper.

Sexton, J. (1987) Recent changes in the Irish population and in the pattern of emigration, *Irish Banking Review*, Autumn: 31–44.

SFADCO (1992) *Annual Report 1992*. Limerick: SFADCO.

Sheehan, J. (1992) The economic relevance of Irish education: an emerging debate, *Irish Banking Review*, Autumn:27–42.

Shirlow, P. and Shuttleworth, I. (1994) Training, migration and the changing world order: a case study of foreign capital restructuring and training policy in the Republic of Ireland, in Gould, W. and Findlay, A. (eds), *Population Migration and the Changing World Order*, Chichester: Wiley, 91–111.

Shuttleworth, I. (1993) Irish graduate emigration: the mobility of qualified manpower in the context of peripherality, in King, R. (ed.) *Mass Migrations in Europe: the Legacy and the Future*. London: Belhaven, pp. 310–26.

Sklair, L. (1988) *Foreign Investment and Irish Development: a Study of the International Division of Labour in the Mid-west Region of Ireland*. Dublin: Pergamon Press.

Sweeney, P. (1995) Economic development: a trade union response, in Shirlow, P. (ed.), *Development Ireland: Contemporary Issues*, London: Pluto, 93–121.

Telesis Consultancy Group (1982) *A Review of Industrial Policy*. Dublin: NESC, Report 64.

Thrift, N. (1989) The geography of international economic disorder, in Johnston, R. and Taylor, P. (eds), *A World in Crisis: Geographical Perspectives*. Oxford: Blackwell, pp. 16–78.

Walsh, B. (1974) Expectations, information and human migration: specifying an econometric model of Irish migration to Britain, *Journal of Regional Science*, 14: 105–120.

8 Population Redistribution in the Sparsely Populated Periphery: The Nordic Case

JAN MØNNESLAND
Norwegian Institute for Urban and Regional Research, Norway

INTRODUCTION

Regional population redistribution has been a permanent aspect of human life. Both long-distance movements with a mass migration character, as well as more individual movements caused by uneven regional development, have been the rule more than the exception. As a consequence, settlement patterns have been influenced by different types of changing conditions, where some regions tend to lose and some tend to gain from ongoing migration streams. The scope of this chapter will be to present some aspects of the redistribution processes which are caused by uneven regional development.

The last decades have experienced a high rate of technological development. This will affect production structures, where productivity growth will reduce the demand for labour in traditional industries and new industries will take over the role as labour demanders. As the new industries often have different localization patterns to the old ones, this is in itself a factor generating regional redistribution. Technological development also creates better communications for goods, persons and information. Then, the competition between regions will sharpen as the shelter created by distance loses its importance. The result will often tend to be a polarization between winner and loser regions.

This growing inter-regional competition will take place both within and between nations. The strongest effect will in the first phases be within nations, as cultural and legal trade barriers will be weaker within than between nations. But as transport costs are reduced both absolutely and as share of the product price, and this share now will often be very low even for products which are transported over half the globe, international competition has become much more intense, especially during the last 10–20 years.

Growing international integration and a common trend (at least within Europe) to break down trade barriers will tend to bring the conditions of international trade closer to the conditions of inter-regional trade within

People, Jobs and Mobility in the New Europe. Edited by Hans H. Blotevogel and Anthony J. Fielding.
© 1997 European Science Foundation. Published in 1997 by John Wiley & Sons Ltd.

nations. The legal arrangements within the EU, between the EU and EFTA (EEA) and also between the EEA and central and eastern European countries will reduce formal and informal trade limitations on a rather large scale.

Both the general process as well as the new European trade regime, where all the Nordic countries are within EEA and Sweden and Finland are new EU members, will create a new situation where inter-regional competition will take place on a European as well as a national level. The regional effects of this development for the sparsely populated periphery is an important part of the ongoing debate in the Nordic countries.

As the effect on regional development of European integration is basically of the same character as the long-known effect of growing inter-regional competition, the experience from national-based regional research will be useful also in predicting some of the intergration effects. And as the Nordic countries (apart from Denmark) are located in the periphery of the EEA area, and have a rather low population density and weak home markets compared to the continental EU countries, the experience of the national peripheries in the past may give useful information also on possible national perspectives for the future in an integrated western European market.

Due to institutional differences (Denmark has been an EU member since 1973) and to the rather different regional structures, where Denmark has a population density at a continental European level while the other Nordic countries have small populations on great areas and a population structure based on very few metropolitan poles, the term 'Nordic' will mostly mean the other Nordic countries apart from Denmark.

CONTRASTING CONTINENTAL EUROPE

As mentioned, population density puts the Nordic countries in a situation quite different from most of the continent of Europe, as shown in Figure 8.1.

Numerically, the population density in the continent of Europe is usually ten times or more than of the Nordic countries (see Table 8.1 and Figure 8.1). Of course, this fact has important effects for regional structure and the regional effect of structural changes and market-intergration processes. For instance, the distances from the northernmost Nordic periphery to the nearest urban agglomeration with more than 100000 inhabitants can be on a level which is unknown in the rest of Europe except the northern Russian tundra. 'Travelling to town' will for many settlements mean journeys of up to half a day and even more, and air travel may have to be used. And even moderate distances to the nearest town will often need as much travelling time as would be needed to go from one capital to the next in more central parts of Europe.

Thus, even though the Nordic countries have a small population base, the area is of a size comparable to a rather big share of the EU+EFTA territory; see Figure 8.2. The Nordic countries excluding Denmark account for 32% of the area but only 5% of the population in the EU+EFTA countries; see Table 8.1.

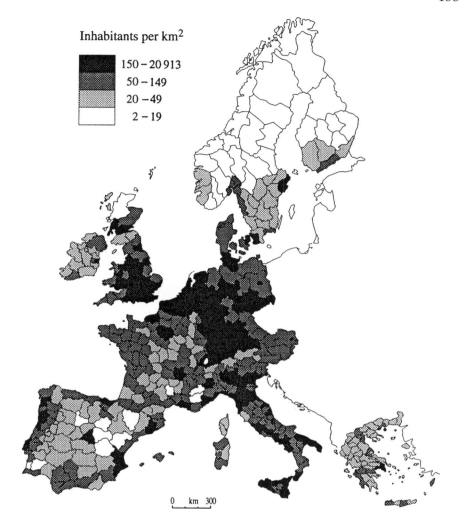

Figure 8.1. Western Europe: population density 1980 (Source: Basprojektet 1990/9)

This different regional structure of the Nordic countries has significant effects on how the integration process will affect internal regional balances. As mentioned, the population base is not strong enough to operate a number of metropoles with a variety of service and productive industries. Thus the capital regions will tend to be the dominating growth pole of these countries. Such a development is not accepted politically, and the aim of regional policy is to try to prevent or slow down this development, by efforts to stimulate the growth

Table 8.1.   Population and area in the EU and EFTA countries, 1992

Country	Population 1000	%	Area 1000 km²	%	Population density pop/km²
Iceland	260		103		2
Norway	4287		324		13
Sweden	8674		450		19
Finland	5042		338		15
EFTA-Norden	18263	5	1215	32	15
Denmark	5171		43		120
Belgium	10045		31		324
France	57372		552		104
Greece	10300		132		78
Ireland	3547		70	50	
Italy	56859		301		189
Luxembourg	390		3		130
Netherlands	15184		41		370
Portugal	9858		92		107
Spain	39085		505		77
U.Kingdom	57848		245	8	236
Germany	80569		357		226
EU 12	346228	91	2372	64	146
Liechtenstein	29		0		178
Switzerland	6875		41		168
Austria	7884		84		94
Central EFTA	14788	4	125	4	118
EU+EFTA	379279	100	3712	100	102

Source: Mønnesland (1994)
The terms EU and EFTA refer to countries enrolled as members in 1992

possibilities of regional centres and a general stimulation policy for activities in non-central areas.

In the EU, the regions which have the greatest priority in the regional policy transfers from the Structural Funds, the Objective 1 regions, have a rather high population density compared to the Nordic regions. Their problem is therefore not lack of people. On the contrary, they may be regarded as having too many people relative to their production potential. For these Objective 1 regions, the problem is partly connected to the production structure and partly to poverty (low income, high unemployment). Regional policy is also geared in this direction, the welfare indicators being the criteria for support and restructuring being the aim of the support. If these regions have net out-migration, this may be viewed as positive both for those who move and partly also for the region, since the welfare burden will ease. The demographic situation does not give rise to a fear of depopulation in these regions.

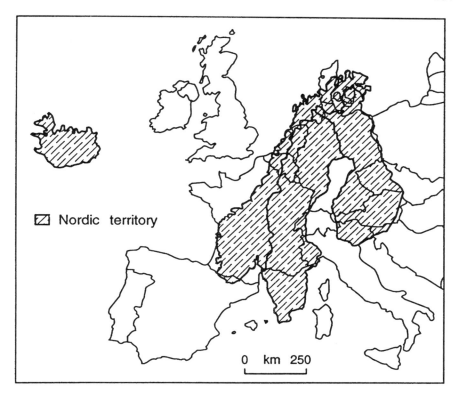

Figure 8.2. The Nordic territory superimposed on continental western Europe (Source: Oscarsson 1988)

Thus, the actions which may help some of the EU problem regions will not have the same effect in the Nordic regions. There are many projects directed towards modernizing existing industries which will have no chance when the population base is too weak. And as the Nordic countries have a strong tradition of favouring income redistribution policies, and also use industrial policy and public sector expansion as tools to reduce unemployment, the welfare indicators in the problem areas in the Nordic countries may often look quite good.

In the Nordic countries, we often get the situation where those living in the problem regions have a relatively good life and the industries may operate reasonably well, and still the regions are threatened by depopulation. This is partly because the low population base limits variability in business life and then the area will be attractive neither for new generations nor for entrepreneurs. The method for solving such problems will have to be directed towards business support as well as service supplies. 'More of the same' may be a more effective

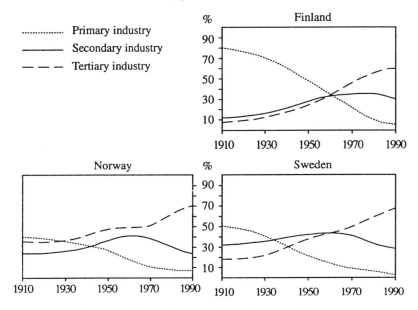

Figure 8.3. Employment shares of main industrial groups (Source: Basprojektet 1982; national statistics)

policy in regions where depopulating processes are the problem than in EU regions with severe structural problems.

This does not mean at all that the periphery problems are not connected to structural problems, as will be shown below. But it may give an explanation for regional policy in the Nordic countries being more directed towards operating support than most of EU policy, and for the traditional EU indicators of regional problem areas failing to fit the depopulation problems of the Nordic support areas.

CHANGING INDUSTRIAL STRUCTURES

Technological development will always imply that the same amount of production can be done with less labour. Then the surplus labour force must be used for some type of productive expansion. Historically, this type of expansion has often been of a territorial nature, where more marginal agricultural areas were settled and long-distance emigration took place for seeking new land.

In the past century, this extensive expansion has been replaced by internal expansion, where the development of services and above all of new manufacturing industries has created labour-demanding centres. These centres were partly in and near the older trade-based towns, and partly in new resource-based industrial towns (near mineral ores, waterpower etc). In the Nordic countries this development came somewhat later than in continental Europe, and it is not until the twentieth century that manufacturing industry reached the same employment level as the primary industries (see Figure 8.3). Later, manufacturing industry also reached a level where productivity growth caused reduced labour demand, and different types of services took over as the main labour-demanding industry (including public services).

Employment in primary industries has gradually been reduced in the last decades. Manufacturing industry had growing employment up to the mid-1970s, then a phase of stagnation set in, which after some years turned into employment reduction. The service industries have been expanding, but this is a rather heterogeneous group with big differences between branches.

This is more or less a common picture of industrial development in most countries. The countries differ in the timing of the different phases and the level of employment in the different groups. The point here is to show how this general development has influenced the regional production structure. The empirical base for the reasoning below will mostly be from Norway, and the other Nordic countries may have deviations from some of the features mentioned.

As the different industries have different localization patterns, structural changes between industries will impose significant effects on the regional structure. The primary industries have for natural reasons a widespread regional pattern, and as they reduce their employment the peripheral regions will be most strongly affected. For these reasons, actions to hamper the employment reduction in primary sectors, for example by support to small farmers and regulations to secure small-boat fishing, are an integral part of regional policy. For economic reasons, such policies will not be used on a level that stops the employment reduction totally. Therefore, the perspectives of the periphery depend on their ability to attract other industries to compensate for the reduction of primary employment.

Manufacturing industry had from the beginning of the twentieth century an urban-dominated locational pattern, due to the better transport and housing facilities around the old trade centres. Large industrial plants, however, were set up at remote places, being cornerstones in new industrial sites. And during the last few decades, small-scale industries have been located in many rural regions, a development which has been actively stimulated by the regional policy support schemes. At the beginning of the 1970s, the central regions were still the most dominant location for manufacturing employment. But the stagnation and reduction of manufacturing employment were also concentrated in the central regions, while in more remote regions manufacturing employment continued to grow. So it seemed as if the regional policy was rather successful, and that manufacturing industry could give a necessary employment stimulus to compensate for the reduction in primary industries.

After a while, however, the more remote manufacturing industry also started to stagnate and reduce its employment. It seemed that it was in fact the central

Table 8.2. Employment in newly created firms in manufacturing industry, by production segment, Norway, 1976–85 (%)

	The industrial concept based primarily on:				
	Raw material	Labour force	Customer adaptation	High tech-nology	Sum
Oslo region	3.4	41.6	46.8	8.2	100
Other big town regions	5.9	59.5	28.1	6.5	100
Smaller town regions	5.3	69.7	19.1	5.9	100
Rural regions	3.7	83.6	10.9	1.8	100

Source: Isaksen (1988)

firms who made the quickest adaption to the new technological and competitive climate, and also that it was the most labour-intensive industries which were located in the remote regions (see Table 8.2). This implies that those manufacturing firms which are best equipped to meet future challenges are centrally located, and those which are threatened by future employment reductions are located in the remote regions. Manufacturing industry has thus changed its position from being a likely employment provider to being a new source for future employment problems in the remote regions. And as manufacturing industries in the future will be more and more geared towards good network conditions and demanding highly competent more than routine labour power, the future locational patterns will probably be more and more oriented towards urban agglomerations of a size that only a few Nordic centres will achieve.

As it seems difficult to rely on manufacturing industry as a future employment source, both at the national level and especially at the regional level outside the larger centres (manufacturing will, of course, continue to be of importance as an income generator, even when the employment potential will be limited), then the service sector will be the crucial factor for regional development.

In general terms, service industries may be divided into two groups: firm oriented and household oriented. The first group will normally have a strongly centralized locational pattern, as they will be oriented mostly towards the R&D and administrative units of business life. The latter will more or less reproduce the existing settlement pattern, with a slight tendency to be somewhat ahead in the centralizing process.

Public economic policy will be of crucial importance. If the policy is geared towards stimulating personal purchasing power, personal-oriented services will expand, giving more even regional development. If the policy is geared towards stimulating the economy of firms (so-called competitive power policy), then the centralizing process will be speeded up. And since public activity constitutes a large share of personal-oriented services, the level and regional structure of public sector growth will be of great importance.

CHANGES IN PUBLIC POLICY

The post-war period up to the beginning of the 1970s was characterized by stable economic growth, and in the Nordic countries the social democratic parties were stable rulers. The common way of thinking was that business cycle problems were something of the past, due to better economic theories (Keynesianism) implying that the state did not stick to *laissez-faire* policies but used macro-economic planning. Then it should be possible to secure stable growth rates as long as the political decisions were carried out in a competent way. Growth should be used to build welfare, and the public sector should take its responsibility both to secure income redistribution and growth in collective welfare, by continuously expanding both the quantity and the quality of public services.

When economic business cycles weakened in the mid-1970s, this was looked on as something that the state could and should counteract. The growth rate of the public sector then continued at about the same speed as before. But, by the end of the decade, it was realized that the stagnation tendencies for manufacturing industry were structural more than cyclical. Actions were then taken to limit the growth in public expenditure and to tighten economic policy. In the 1980s, we returned to a better correlation between private and public growth rates. No wonder, then, that in the 1970s public employment took the lion's share of total employment growth, and that this decade became special, compared to both the 1960s and the 1980s.

Public expenditure was growing according to sector targets, where some predefined service levels should be reached within a certain time perspective. These service targets were most often set as maximum travelling time for each household to reach a school, a health station etc., minimum quality levels in each institution and so on. Those regions which originally were most below such targets got the highest growth rates of the services. Thus the public-sector growth rates were much stronger in the remoter than in the central regions.

These two factors – an unusually strong relative growth of public employment and a stronger growth in the remoter rather than the central regions – created a stabilizing development of the settlement pattern in the 1970s. As public-sector growth slowed down again in the 1980s, the centralizing mobility pattern from the 1960s reappeared. And as the causal description of the policy of the 1970s indicates, there are few reasons to believe that such a policy will be repeated. The specialities of the 1970s are not a Nordic phenomenon alone; we find the same changing pattern in both public employment growth and metropolitan growth in most other countries. But the strong welfare policy traditions in the Nordic countries may have made the pendulum effects stronger.

In the 1980s, international competition grew stronger and political attention was geared more towards the competitiveness of the country. This implied that redistributional policies received a lower priority on the political agenda. The result was tighter economic policy, with reduced growth of both public services

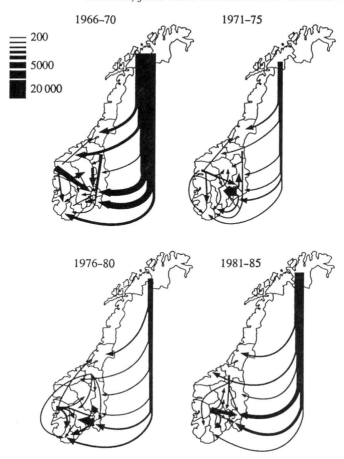

Figure 8.4. Annual net migration between groups of counties 1966–85 (Source: Byfuglien 1988)

and personal purchasing power. Both these factors tend to give more centralized development. As an effect of this reduced public-sector growth, more efforts were used to obtain better productivity in the public services. And as the regional targets were becoming less important compared to the overall competitiveness, the result was a more centre-oriented growth of the public sector. Both lower growth rates and a changed regional profile resulted in a serious weakening of the counter-centralizing effect of public activity.

CHANGING DEMOGRAPHIC STRUCTURES

Except for a temporary break during the 1970s, the net migration movements in the post-war years have followed a centralizing pattern. The migration pattern

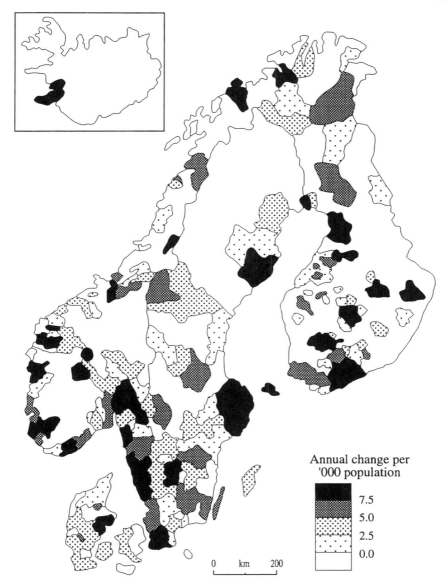

Annual change per
'000 population

7.5
5.0
2.5
0.0

0 km 200

Figure 8.5. Population change in the Nordic regions 1985–89 (Source: Nordic Council of Ministers 1991)

of the 1980s has strong similarities with the pattern of the 1960s (see Figure 8.4). Despite a declared consensus on the regional policy target of protecting the settlement pattern, these centralizing movements of the 1950s and 1960s were not regarded as violating that target. Even with high net out-migration, the

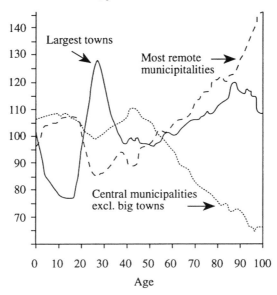

Figure 8.6. Norway: age structures for selected region groups in 1988. National mean=100 for all one-year age groups (Source: Sørlie 1990)

natural population growth of the remote regions were strong enough in those years to uphold and often even expand population levels.

Fertility rates were reduced during the 1970s. When the centralizing net migration pattern returned in the 1980s, there was no longer a natural population growth large enough to maintain the population levels in the remote regions. This time the centralizing migration pattern was no longer a redistribution of population growth, it was now a redistribution of the population itself as the nation approached a zero-sum population game. Thus the effects on the settlement pattern became more serious and, for many of the remote regions, a process of depopulation and ageing seemed to be a likely prospect. In the 1960s, nearly every municipality had population growth and it was sometimes formulated as a target that this should be granted! As shown in Figure 8.5, most of the peripheral regions now lose population. The exceptions are mostly centres with higher education institutions.

Even with net out-migration, there are in-migrating streams. The reinforced centralizing mobility pattern is more an effect of reduced in-migration and to a lesser extent of growing out-migration for the remote regions. A great part of this in-migration is return migration. One rather common life profile is for people to leave the remote regions when they have finished education, to spend some years in the larger towns. When they get older, many of them go back to where they have grown up and raise the next generation there. As the fertility level has traditionally been higher in the remoter than in the central regions, this implies that remote regions have been over-represented by children, under-

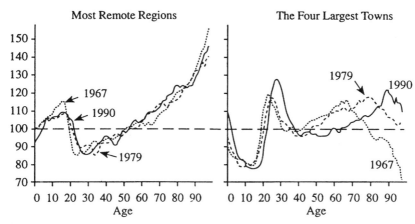

Figure 8.7. Norway: age structures for selected regional groups 1967–90 National mean=100 for all one-year age groups (Source: NIBR calculations)

represented by younger adults and then over-represented by parents aged around 30 and above (but under-represented by adults without children in the same age groups). At the same time, regions around the greater towns have also been over-represented by adults, and these adults have been somewhat younger than in the remote regions (see Figure 8.6). And as these regions often consist of housing areas build up in the last few decades, they are so far under-represented with old people.

Now the remote regions are gradually losing their role as raising areas for children. The new female generations are well educated and they often find that the labour market in the regions of origin mostly consist of male-dominated jobs in primary and secondary industries and low-qualified female service jobs. They therefore start to raise their children in the larger towns, and thus the family return migration is reduced. The full effect of this new trend is only visible at the margin, but the direction is clearly demonstrated in Figure 8.7. If this development continues, after a decade or so the remote regions will be under- instead of over-represented by children and parents, which will have a significant effect both on cultural life and on school employment. The accelerated ageing process will in turn make these regions still less attractive for new potential in-migrants.

PERSPECTIVES

Both from an industrial and a demographic viewpoint, there are reasons for expecting that the centralizing process will be strengthened in the future. As firms and households will consider both the perspectives and the actual state of a region before settling, and network conditions, service levels etc. will be important factors, we easily reach self-accelerating processes where the weaker regions will lose more and the strong regions will attract still more firms and households.

The driving force behind this development are partly structural. It therefore seems unlikely that the process will slow down without conscious interventions. It is always difficult to predict the future, and some of the remote regions of today may become attractive regions if their characteristics turn out to be more attractive tomorrow. Such factors may be environmental; bio-dynamic products from small-scale farming may be valued more highly in the future, fishing products may be strongly demanded and so on. But so far, we see few factors able to hamper the general conclusion that stronger inter-regional and international competition, combined with better mobility across regions and countries, will inevitably result in a centre-oriented regional redistribution. We also see a growing interest in regions lying close to the central towns. In addition to the main trend of centralization, there is a decentralizing trend within the short travel distances from the greater towns. The centralization process is a process between larger regions, where the tendency may be different within such larger regions.

The conclusion that stronger centralization seems to be the effect of stronger inter-regional competition and reduced geographical shelters may also be converted to the European level. Thus the European integration process should give the same effect for remote regions without strong metropoles. In fact, even when formal barriers are removed in the internal European market, a number of informal barriers will still be present. Different languages, traditions, environmental factors etc. keep international mobility on a much lower level than internal mobility. But through time, such barriers will also tend to weaken.

The experience from the 1970s shows that political activity, if strong enough, may have remarkable effects on migration streams. But as the underlying redistributive forces seem to be rather strong, regional policy will often be too weak to alter the direction of the process. The best policy advice may be to accept that a growing region needs to have central facilities within reach. If the old growth pole idea could be revitalized and on a more metropolitan level, then the decentralization tendency around the centres would give some opportunities for a relatively dispersed settlement pattern. For the Nordic countries, such a strategy will hardly be possible over the whole territory. For the more remote parts, the challenge will be to define separate factors which may keep the region attractive in spite of the long distances to other growth poles.

REFERENCES

Basprojektet *Regional utveckling i Norden. Årsrapport.* Yearly editions. Nordic Council of Ministers.
Byfuglien, J. (1988) Avfolkes distrikts-Norge? *Samfunnsspeilet nr. 1/1988.* Oslo: Central Bureau of Statistics.
Isaksen, A. (1988) *Næringsutvikling i sentrum og utkant.* ØF-rapport nr. 5:88.

Lillehammer: Østlandsforskning.

Nordic Council of Ministers (1991) *Nordic Regions and Transfrontier Cooperation.*

Oscarsson, G. (1989) Regional policies in the Nordic countries – origin, development and future. Speech at the NordREFO/OECD seminar Reykjavik 1988, reprinted in *The long-term future of regional policy – a Nordic view.* Borgå: OECD/NordREFO.

Sørlie, K. (1990) *Demografiske trender i fylkene.* NIBR-notat 122, Oslo: NIBR.

9 Unemployment in East-Central Europe and its Consequences for East–West Migration

HEINZ FASSMANN
Austrian Academy of Science, Austria

INTRODUCTION

Following the collapse of Communism and the end of the political division of Europe, euphoria reigned for a while in both the West and East. Mistaken ideas circulated envisaging a swift transformation of the planned economies into effective market economies. The idea of rapid convergence was very quickly superseded by other images. The East now appeared to be merely Europe's poorhouse which was being abandoned by the economic refugees streaming into western Europe. Both ideas are too simplistic and thus false. The former COMECON states did not sink into chaos but the enormous differences in living standards between East and West could not be levelled out within three years.

Academic research can also help to explain these very curious images of the changes in east-central Europe. It has increasingly addressed the subject of the social and economic transition after 1989–90.[1] It helped calm the situation when panic-striken images of the consequences of the fall of the Iron Curtain provoked overheated political discussion, but it also drew attention to the somewhat worrying breakdown of social structures.

This Chapter addresses the theme of the changes in the labour markets of east-central Europe and discusses the question of whether East–West migration represents a viable solution to the economic problems caused by the structural changes. East-central Europe comprises Hungary, Poland, the Czech Republic and Slovakia.

This chapter is in two parts. The first discusses the rise in unemployment and its causes, its spatial distribution and effects on society; the second considers East–West migration to Austria and its implications for the domestic labour market.

People, Jobs and Mobility in the New Europe. Edited by Hans H. Blotevogel and Anthony J. Fielding.
© 1997 European Science Foundation. Published in 1997 by John Wiley & Sons Ltd.

MASS UNEMPLOYMENT IN EAST-CENTRAL EUROPE

Privatization, restructuring and stabilization measures have led to far-reaching changes in national labour-market structures. The rise in unemployment, which is now a mass social phenomenon, is the visible proof of structural changes on the labour market. Unemployment figures not only signal the imbalance between jobs vacancies and job seekers but also illustrate impressively which social groups in which regions are the losers in the transformation process.

The developing gulf between jobs and job seekers is part of a growing social and spatial inequality in which unemployment and the impoverishment of wide sections of the population go hand in hand. They increase people's dissatisfaction with the pace of the reform measures and the measures themselves. The rebirth of post-Communist parties, social and ethnic unrest and signs of the breakdown of the state in the individual countries concerned are very closely tied up with the success or otherwise of the process of economic transformation.

The right to work, established both in law and practice, was one of the model arguments of practical socialism. Unemployment was dismissed as an inherent defect of capitalism. According to the official view, the planned economy was more efficient at directing the labour-market allocation process between supply and demand. This is now in contrast to the real situation and therefore part of the political problem.

The extent of unemployment

The rise in unemployment is impressively revealed in quantitative terms. At the beginning of 1990 the unemployment rates in all the east-central European countries were still zero or negligible. Unemployment rose first in Poland as a consequence of the early and radical reform programme. At the begining of 1990 the rate there had reached 6.5% – already above the average of all east and central European countries.

At the end of 1994 over 5.6 million people were registered as unemployed in the six east and central European countries: Bulgaria, the Czech Republic, Slovakia, Poland, Romania and Hungary. Poland lost its position as the country with the highest unemployment rate. One can observe a decline of national disparities. All countries now have unemployment rates higher than 10%, with the one exception of the Czech Republic. At the end of 1994 about 2.8 million people were jobless in Poland – an unemployment rate of 16%. In Slovakia 370000 people (14.6%) were registered as unemployed, in Bulgaria around 500000 (13%), in Romania more than 1.2 million (10.9%), in Hungary 520000 (10.4%), while in the Czech Republic the number of unemployed remained very low (170000 people; 3.2%).

Unemployment rates in east-central European countries have reached western European levels. Countries with high unemployment rates such as Ireland, Spain and Turkey have similar rates to those of Hungary, Poland and Slovakia. There

Table 9.1. Labour market data 1990–4

	Bulgaria	Czech Republic	Slovakia	Poland	Romania	Hungary
			Unemployed			
1990	65100	39379	39603	1126100	–	79521
1991	419100	221749	301951	2155600	337400	406124
1992	576900	134788	260274	2509300	929000	663027
1993	626100	185216	368095	2889600	164700	632050
1994	488400	166480	371481	2838000	1223900	519592
			Unemployment rate			
1990	1.7	0.7	1.6	6.5	–	1.7
1991	11.1	4.1	11.8	11.5	3.0	8.5
1992	15.2	2.6	10.4	13.6	8.4	12.3
1993	16.4	3.5	14.4	15.7	10.4	12.1
1994	12.8	3.2	14.6	16.0	10.9	10.4

Note: Preliminary data for Bulgaria 1994
Sources: Terplan; Slowakisches Statistisches Amt; Polish Academy of Sciences; Orszagos Munkaugyi Központ; Vienna Institute for Comparative Economic Studies (Monthly Report 1995/3 u. 4).

are differences, however, in the pace of the increases observed and expected. A quadrupling of the unemployment rate within two years is extraordinary and there is still no hope to the decline in sight.

Apart from the structural differences between the individual countries, it is noticeable that high rates are found at present in those countries (like Poland) where the reform process began comparatively early and was relatively radical; the converse is also true – namely that relatively low rates are found in those countries that have begun reforms very recently or are pursuing more gradual reforms (like Romania) or are very successful (like the Czech Republic). Thus unemployment rates do not exclusively reflect the functional efficiency of national labour markets but also show the stage of the transformation process at which individual countries are.

In the context of a quantitative interpretation of the unemployment phenomenon, attention should also be paid to the fact that the number of people who, although unemployed, have not registered as such, is probably considerably higher. People who are not eligible to receive unemployment benefits are prevented from registering. Especially in rural areas the proportion of unemployed people not registered as such probably still remains high. Agriculture – previously practised on a part-time basis – offers a basic, if often meagre, existence, and the poor chances of finding a new job outside agriculture deter many unemployed people from actually registering.

Another group of unemployed people, on the other hand, are accused of actually enjoying two sources of income: they register as unemployed, receive financial help accordingly, and begin an unofficial job on the side (Witkowski 1991, p. 3).

Groups affected by unemployment

With the increase in unemployment the demographic and socio-economic structure of the unemployed changes decisively. While in the socialist era unemployment was still a 'peripheral group phenomenon', today it also affects semi-skilled and skilled workers and white-collar workers. However, it is still the unqualified sectors of the occupational system that bear the main brunt. Unskilled workers are the group who most risk becoming unemployed and they also comprise the largest group of the long-term unemployed (those out of work for longer than one year). Skilled workers are in a better position since they are at low risk of becoming unemployed and have good chances of re-employment. Highly qualified groups are in a different position. A low risk of becoming unemployed goes together with a high probability of having to experience a long term of unemployment for some groups of them.

There is also a link between rising unemployment and a tendency to contracting labour markets. The groups particularly badly affected are the young and the old. With declining demand on the labour market, older people are ousted and younger people are kept out of employment relationships. The age distribution of the unemployed thus corresponds to a bimodal distribution. Very young people and older people approaching retirement become unemployed. In Poland two-thirds of the unemployed are under 35 and more than 36% are under 25. These figures also include school leavers who have not yet had a job. In Hungary about 53% of the unemployed are under 35 and some 22% are under 25.

The declining demand for manpower and the accompanying increased risk of unemployment for older workers leads in many cases to a forced exodus from the labour market. The high proportion, in relation to their age, of employed over-65s declines very noticeably. Being forced out of the labour market into deepndence on pensions results in substantial impoverishment for those concerned. However, some sort of income does remain – if a modest one – so that this declining demand for workers helps soften the blow dealt by structural adaptations, although the cushioning effect varies from one social group to another in line with national pension schemes.

The increased risk of unemployment also leads to an above-average number of women giving up employment. The decline in female employment thus has a compensatory effect on rising unemployment figures. The high numbers of employed females – for example 75.2% in Hungary and about 80% in ex-Czechoslovakia – form a kind of 'reserve army'. Part of the falling demand for manpower does not lead to higher unemployment but to women leaving the labour market in droves.

In the east-central European countries studied, women are now more affected than men. When unemployment first began rising sharply men were still disproportionately affected; now, however, women account for the majority of the unemployed and their proportion is continually rising. At the end of 1992

Table 9.2. Regional variations in unemployment, 1993

	Bulgaria	Czech Republic	Slovakia	Poland	Romania	Hungary
Mean	19.9	3.0	13.0	17.9	11.4	11.4
Std deviation	4.4	1.6	5.6	5.3	3.8	3.4
Variation coefficient	0.22	0.53	0.43	0.30	0.33	0.29
Number of regions	9	8	4	49	41	20
Regions with lowest rates	Sofija (11.4), Haskovo, Lovec (18.3)	Prague (0.3), West Bohemia (2.3)	Bratislava (5.0)	Warszawa (7.5), Krakow (8.5), Poznan (8.8)	Gorj (3.7), Bucuresti (5.6), Calarasi (6.2	Budapest (5.4), Győr (6.9), Pest (7.2)
Regions with highest rates	Montana (27.8), Burgas (23.2)	North Moravia (5.7), North Bohemia (4.4)	East Slovakia (18.1)	Slupsk (30.5), Suwalki (29.1), Olsztyn (28.2)	Vaslui (20.6), Bistrita (18.6), Iasi (18.5)	Szabolcs (18.5), Borsod (15.6), Nograd (15.5)

Note: Data for Bulgaria and Romania are from March 1995
Sources: Terplan; Slowakisches Statistisches Amt; Romanian Academy of Sciences; Polish Academy of Sciences; Orszagos Munkaugyi Központ; Österreichisches Ost- und Südosteuropa-Institut

women accounted for 50.7% of all unemployed people in Slovakia and even 57.9% in the Czech Republic (cf Holzgreve 1993, p. 27).

The social consequences of rising unemployment can thus be portrayed as: a contracting labour market, increased youth employment, the exclusion of women and older workers, the migration and impoverishment of whole population groups through falling wages, rising prices and the ending of dual occupations. The groups particularly affected are pensioners, young families and all those who previously had other jobs in the secondary economy (Hungary) or in the black economy (Poland). For with the disintegration of the state monopolies previous informal and private moonlighting jobs are forcibly changed into first jobs. Thus the chances of earning a dual income in the state and partly private sectors are continually declining.

Regional variations in unemployment

In east-central Europe there are very big regional variations in unemployment. Thus, in the Czech Republic, the relationship between the area with the lowest rate of unemployment to the one with the highest is 1 to 19, in Poland 1 to 4.1, Romania 1 to 5.6, in Slovakia 1 to 3.6 and in Hungary 1 to 3.4. The variation coefficient is particularly high in the Czech Republic and in Slovakia but lower in Poland, Romania, Hungary and Bulgaria, where unemployment is distributed more evenly throughout the regions.

These distinct regional disparities are typical of the early stages of the transition. In western European countries unemployment is more evenly distributed across national regions. But there, too, it is true that national unemployment rates often represent extenuating average figures which conceal the real seriousness of the problem.

In all the east-central European countries the following three types of region are particularly badly affected by unemployment (Figure 9.1):

(i) Underdeveloped rural areas in peripheral locations. In Poland this applies to Woiwodschaften in the north-east (Suwalki, Olszytn, Ciechanov and Koszalin); in Hungary it applies to the Komitat Szabolcz-Szatmar-Bereg and in ex-Czechoslovakia to Eastern Slovakia.

(ii) Old industries and mining areas. In Poland this applies to the Woiwodschaften, Lodz and Walbrzych; in Hungary to the Komitat Borsorg; in Slovakia to the districts around Kosice; and in the Czech Republic, once mass redundancies have been put into effect, to the Kladno district.

(iii) Mono-structured regions with 'local' employment disasters. Here it is a question of regions with one dominant industry or firm on whose prosperity a majority of employed people depend. In such tightly structured regions the collapse of companies means a decisive deterioration of the regional labour market. In Poland this was the case with Starachowice (with the closure of the truck-making factory), with Mielec (aircraft engines) and with Stalowa Wola

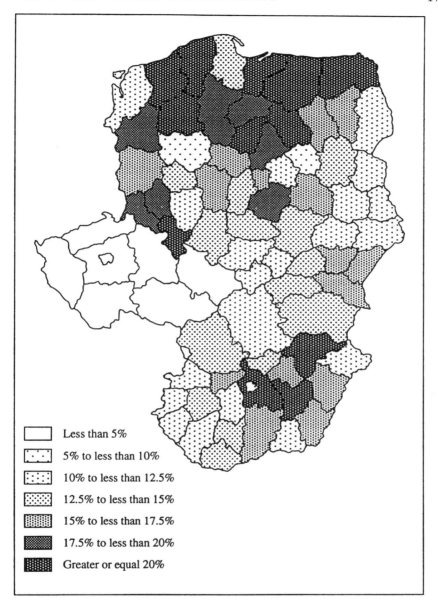

Figure 9.1. Unemployment rates in east-central Europe 1993

(metallurgy and building machinery); in Hungary the same applied to Odz (with the closure of the steelworks).

On the other hand, there are regions with low unemployment. These are often the big cities, which have a wide range of newly creative service-sector jobs. Budapest and the Komitat Pest in Hungary, Warsaw in Pland, Prague in the Czech Republic, Bratislava in Slovakia, Sofia in Bulagaria and Bucharest in Romania. In this case it must be remembered, however, that – as is also the case in western Europe – the unemployed are counted not at their place of work but where they live; thus big cities 'export' the problem of unemployment through commuting. Nevertheless, unlike in western Europe, the low level of unemployment in the cities is significant and thus marks out the metropoles as the rallying centres in the development of a new private-sector economy.

Causes of unemployment

The high and universally rising unemployment rates have numerous causes: more or less specific and more or less significant. One problem factor, however, is clearly of major importance: the change of political system implies similar structural changes in the economy from a planned to a market economy – i.e. a dissolution of the agricultural sector, a reduction in the industrial sector and an extension of the services sector. In western Europe both the development of a market-oriented type of economy and the economic structural changes occurred over a long period of time. What took over 100 years in the West is now supposed to be completed within a few years in east-central Europe. Frictions throughout the social and economic fields are the inevitable consequence.

Various other factors contributing directly to the high or rising level of unemployment can be listed:
(i)   Planned economies were characterized by an inbuilt lack of manpower because firms tended to stockpile workers. The origns of this lie in the nature of a scarcity economy. A sluggish, inefficient and centrally controlled distribution system was incapable of providing firms with the appropriate resources at the time they were needed for the production process. Thus, as soon as they became available, all goods and means or production, including human capital, were 'acquired' and 'stockpiled'. The principle of 'hoarding' personnel is now being abandoned and 'superfluous' manpower is being made redundant.

There was a second advantage in having a high employment rate. In the redistribution of firms' profits to cover their costs (salaries, development costs etc.) firms with a large number of workers were in a better negotiating position than small firms (cf Csefalvay and Rohn 1991). For most state enterprises in central and eastern Europe it was generally true that production goals could also be achieved with 80% of the workforce or less. The other side of this coin was a considerable underutilization of the workers employed. The lack of manpower constantly increased over the years. In 1980 the ratio of job vacancies to job seekers in Poland was 9 to 1 and by 1988 this had risen to 86 to 1.

(ii) Because of the strictly controlled employment market a considerable number of unemployed people preferred not to register. In several planned economies the non-acceptance of an allocated job or the continuation of unemployment was even punished by a prison sentence. 'A person who was fit to work, but not working, and with no other source of income, was liable to prosecution and imprisonment. In practice, there was a low rate of frictional unemployment which was officially recognized and went unreported in government statistics.' (Kapl et al. 1991, p. 199). After the change of regime this voluntary but hidden form of unemployment gives way to a more open one as soon as negative sanctions disappear or when the creation of unemployment benefits acts as a stimulus to register.

(iii) The transition from a planned to a market economy implies the retreat of the state as the employer and the institution which determines prices, incomes and production goals. Price deregulation is thus one of the first measures in all the east-central European countries. The removal of price controls itself leads to excessive increases in the cost of goods and services and strengthens inflationary tendencies, which must then be countered by extremely tight monetary and fiscal policies. This in turn leads, at least temporarily, to a decline in the total demand for consumer and investments goods. Through this kind of 'adaptation recession' the demand for manpower weakens further, thus also contributing to the growth in unemployment. This probably applies more to Poland than to ex-Czechoslovakia and Hungary.

(iv) As a result of the state allocating jobs and production goals and fixing prices and incomes, effective labour markets on the western model are non-existent. There are three major grounds why they are not emerging in the transition period. There are no mechanisms for fixing wages in line with productivity or institutions which distribute productivity improvements through annual wage negotiations. The low level of internal geographical mobility of the workforce in the countries concerned – which is also considerably aggravated by the lack of a housing market – prevents the distribution of jobs between regions with a surplus of labour and those with labour shortages. Finally, mention must be made of the continuing lack or malfunctioning of institutions to manage the labour market. Help is thus lacking in finding jobs and in supporting and retraining the unemployed.

There is yet another cause of rising unemployment which needs watching in future. In Poland, in Slovakia and in some parts of Hungary and the Czech Republic a growing stream of young people coming onto the labour market is to be expected. This demographically determined growth is a result of higher birth rates in the 1970s. The problems of integrating these numerically strong cohorts in the occupational structure are all too obvious.

The causes of unemployment make its further decrease unlikely. However, the question of how many people will be forced out of the occupational structure and of their chances of how many people will be forced out of the occupational structure and of their chances of returning to it is a fundamental one. After decades of state-guaranteed full employment, the post-socialist societies must first confront the new phenomenon and then develop institutional and social mechanisms to deal with it.

EAST–WEST MIGRATION AS A CONSEQUENCE OF UNEMPLOYMENT?

The rising unemployment and impoverishment of whole social groups in the East is giving rise in western Europe to fears of the threat of mass migration. In theory these fears are not difficult to substantiate. Push–pull models are based on the assumption that waves of migration inevitably occur between countries or regions where there are such wide income differentials and such obviously divergent opportunities on the labour market as in western Europe and east-central and eastern Europe at the moment. What is so surprising, therefore, is less the fact that after 40 years of a divided Europe migration from East to West has begun again, but that so far it has been quantitatively insignificant. About 1% of all non-self-employed workers in Austria are citizens of Hungary, Poland, the Czech Republic and Slovakia. East-central European immigrants account for only about 12% of all foreign workers. The question arises, therefore, as to why East–West migration has not yet materialized – despite steeply rising unemployment figures. Four hypotheses are offered as an explanation of this phenomenon:

(i)   The neoclassical labour market model, against the background of which the pull–push model was developed, assumes that individuals behave rationally and decide to migrate after weighing the costs and likely benefits. Neither the people of western Europe nor those of east-central Europe consider the costs and gains quite so rationally. Nevertheless, there is a lack of information and of well-established ethnic networks. The lack of networks makes migration more expensive and more risky. One can observe general cultural and historical links between Austria and its neighbouring countries, but there are no institutions that organize migration to Austria. Migration from the East to Austria is at an early stage where bridgeheads will be erected to help the following flows. Another consequence of the missing networks is the tendency of commuting on a daily, weekly or seasonal basis to avoid the risky permanent migration.

(ii)   A further factor for the people of east-central Europe is the fact that their geographical mobility was generally very slight and – because of the lack of an effective housing market – not part of the standard repertoire of individual behaviour. New behavioural norms, including a willingness to move home, must first become established.

(iii)   The neoclassical market model stresses the significance of unemployment and wage differentials. The unemployed and relatively low paid also move when no other opportunities exist within the framework of the regional labour market. Empirical findings, however, show that in fact this connection between migration and unemployment is much looser. Often the opposite case can also be observed: the unemployed stay at home while those who have a job and want to improve their income, career chances or working conditions migrate.[2] At the individual level the connection between unemployment in east-central Europe and the growth in East–West migration is much less close than assumed. Migration on the expectation of higher wages only take place, however, when it is based on the promise of a particular job. A precondition of this is an effective information network between country of destination and source country. While this may exist in certain individual cases, it has not yet become widely established.

(iv)   A fourth and very important reason why massive East–West migration has been prevented can, however, be found in the bureaucratic and political obstacles which have been set up in Austria and other western European countries. Tougher regulations for incoming travellers, an emphasis on the granting of asylum to certain core groups and upper limits on the employment of foreigners have contributed to keeping the stream of migrants from east-central Europe within bounds. The strong statistical growth of migration from east-central Europe – compared with a very low initial figure – contradicts this only superficially.

Immigration to Austria from east-central Europe

In the latter half of the 1980s Austria experienced a second take-off phase in the immigration of foreign workers. Positive economic growth and the growing demand for manpower linked with this led many employers to seek to recruit workers by the established route – i.e. abroad. Ex-Yugoslavia and Turkey were still the preferred areas for recruiting foreign workers. Towards the end of the 1980s a hesitant reorientation of the areas of origin began. East-central European countries came to the fore as recruitment areas for foreign labour. In 1981 about 4500 people from ex-Czechoslovakia, Hungary and Poland were in non-self-employed jobs in Austria. In 1990 their number had already reached 23000.

This amounts to a fivefold increase.[3] In 1991 the figure was around 35000 and for 1992 42000. Thus the number of east-central Europeans legally employed has risen by around 20% in one year. Since 1992 the number of officially registered foreign workers from east-central Europe stagnated. This is in contrast to all forecasts of a flood of Polish or Romanian workers coming to Austria. Workers from the five east-central European countries still, however, account for only around 15% of all foreign workers. Some of them are daily or weekly commuters and some are resident in Austria.[4]

The socio-demographic structure of the labour force

There is a dual perspective inherent in the transition of the socio-economic system in east-central Europe. The changes in east-central Europe are directly

Table 9.3. Origins of foreign labour in Austria

	Bulgaria	ex-Czechoslovakia	Poland	Romania	Hungary	Total
Foreign labour						
1981 (census)	–	811	2373	–	1378	171773
1990	–	6127	9983	–	6909	217610
1991	–	8534	11322	–	9234	266461
1992	1662	10715	11086	9241	10143	273884
1993	1516	11000	10952	9267	9976	277511
1994	1530	10860	11087	9501	9875	268843
% change						
(1992=100%)						
1981 (census)	–	7.6	21.4	–	13.6	62.7
1990	–	57.2	90.1	–	68.1	79.5
1991	–	79.6	102.1	–	91.0	97.3
1992	100.0	100.0	100.0	100.0	100.0	100.0
1993	91.2	102.7	98.8	100.3	98.4	101.3
1994	92.1	101.4	100.0	102.8	97.4	98.2

Source: Arbeitsmarktservice Österreich; 1990 data projected from a sample; 1991 data from June survey; since 1992 numbers are the annual average; 1981 census (total of persons in work)

and indirectly linked with changes in labour-market structures in Austria, Germany and Scandinavia. With the opening of borders and the geographical expansion of the labour market along the former Iron Curtain comes a massive growth in the labour supply. The term 'supply shock' attempts to express this sudden and quantitatively significant growth of a relatively cheap but well-qualified labour force.

Only limited comparisons are possible between the 'new' East–West migration and other historical worker migrations. The recruitment of foreign labour in ex-Yugoslavia and Turkey shows very clear differences. It was largely restricted to rural areas and involved people of low or average qualifications; it required organizational expenditure and took place over large geographical and cultural distances.

The foreign workers from east and central Europe have average to above-average qualifications; most of them did qualified work in their country of origin and most of them come from urban areas.[5]

Compared with the immigration of 'guest workers' in the 1960s and 1970s, the demographic structure of the 'new' immigrants from east-central Europe is less heterogeneous. Almost two-thirds of all officially registered workers are under 40 and a third are under 30. There were hardly any workers over the age of 50. The differences in the age structure by country of origin are not significant.

The phenomenon of the 'new' immigration from east-central Europe is still in its infancy. This is shown by the distinct age selectivity and disproportionately high percentage of men. Almost three-quarters of all foreign workers from east-central Europe are men. The balance between the sexes only evens out in a

Table 9.4. Socio-demographic structure of East–West immigrants to Austria, 1994

	Foreign workers from				
	Bulgaria %	ex-Czechoslovakia %	Poland %	Romania %	Hungary %
Age					
15–18	2.5	2.0	1.1	1.4	1.6
19–24	18.7	13.9	7.6	8.9	11.6
25–29	29.1	17.6	16.4	20.8	18.1
30–39	34.7	37.1	42.5	43.9	36.0
40–49	13.0	24.2	26.7	20.1	27.6
50–54	1.4	3.7	3.4	3.1	4.1
55–59	0.5	1.0	1.4	1.1	0.8
60+	0.2	0.5	1.0	0.6	0.3
	100.0	100.0	100.0	100.0	100.0
Gender					
Men	67.7	70.5	70.7	60.0	75.9
Women	32.3	29.5	29.3	40.0	24.1
	100.0	100.0	100.0	100.0	100.0
Total		10860	11087		9.875

Source: Arbeitsmarktservice Österreich

later, peak phase of immigration when the immigration of families replaces that of individuals.

The occupational differences between the 'new' immigration and the traditional immigration of guest workers are not so great. The large supply of workers who are employed for relatively low wages leads to structural changes on the urban labour market. A number of select branches experience a strong expansion. People-oriented service sectors, tourism, the building trade and the domestic sector make increasing use of east-central European manpower. The official statistics (cf Table 9.5) can only attempt to illustrate this expansion. Many of the occupations are practised without an official work permit.

The dense concentration of 'new' migrants in a few sectors is striking. Almost half the men are employed in industry and trade, a fifth in the building trade and a tenth in tourism. This pattern varies very greatly by gender. About a quarter of all women are employed in tourism, a fifth as domestic helps or cleaners, aother fifth in the health service and a tenth in industry and trade.

The fact that particular groups of immigrants only occupy certain positions in the labour market is a sign of 'ethnic segmentation'. Parts of the labour market are insulated by formal norms and informal mechanisms; the secondary labour market is still reserved for new immigrants. The differentiation among the east-central European migrants is also worthy of note. There are significant differences in job placement between migrants from Poland, Hungary, Romania and ex-Czechoslovakia. Two-thirds of the Romanians and more than half the

Poles are employed in industry and trade, compared with only one-third of Czechs and Slovaks. In contrast to this, Czechs and Slovaks are almost five times more represented in tourism. Of Polish women 26% work as domestic helps or cleaners compared with only 5.6% of Czech and Slovak women and 7.3% of Hungarians. In contrast, one-third of Czech and Slovak women work in the health sector, compared with only 18% of Polish women and 10% of Hungarian women and 6% of Romanian women.

Ethnic segmentation also seems to occur within the secondary market intended for immigrants. The accumulation of certain ethnic groups within particular occupations suggests that information about imminent job vacancies is only circulated within the ethnic group concerned. From this a self-reinforcing process arises. Because a group is quantitatively strong in a particular sector, it also has the best chance of obtaining and passing on information.

All in all there is a doubly competitive situation on the secondary labour market. It is not only a question of the members of lower Austrian classes competing with immigrants for jobs, but also of 'old' immigrants being ousted by 'new' ones. The rapid increase in the labour supply (called supply shock) following the fall of the Iron Curtain aggravated this competition, leading to older and thus relatively more expensive workers being pushed out. The large increase in unemployment among older workers is a reflection of this substitution process. The substitution occurs either directly through a personal exchange or indirectly, in that those firms that react quickly to the new situation and take on workers from neighbouring countries in east-central Europe gain competitive advantages.

For Austrian nationals the ethnic segmentation and 'supply shock' in the main bring only advantages. These phenomena assure for many of them a place in the privileged segment of the labour market and facilitate career promotion. For Austrian nationals are, on the whole, preferred to foreigners and thus have better chances. At the same time, the employment of foreign labour means that Austrian nationals need not go without many services which they themselves no longer provide. Within the 'cubbyhold economy' the economic activities of foreigners are even often seen to enrich daily life.

PROSPECTS

With the threat of the state the so far most important agent leaves the economic and social arena. It srole cannot be taken on by any other agent immediately. There remain massive deficits in many fields that are together termed 'new scarcity'. At first sight this seems to be a paradox, as planned economies are taken to suffer from shortages and market economies are considered to provide a surplus of goods and services.

This 'new scarcity' must not be mistaken for a transitory phenomenon that will disappear with time; it is a suddenly emerging but lasting consequence of capitalist conditions. On the one hand, state enterprises are being privatized,

Table 9.5. Occupational structure of East–West immigrants to Austria, 1994

	Bulgaria %	ex-Czechoslovakia %	Poland %	Romania %	Hungary %
Male					
Agriculture and forestry	1.5	6.5	6.2	2.2	3.0
Construction	10.2	18.0	22.6	13.9	19.3
Industry	40.3	36.2	52.4	66.0	44.5
Commerce, transport	11.4	5.1	5.0	5.4	9.6
Tourism	8.6	16.9	2.8	4.6	10.8
Domestic, cleaning	1.6	0.7	2.0	2.3	0.6
Technicians	10.7	8.2	3.5	2.7	4.7
Office work	8.1	2.5	1.9	0.8	2.5
Health service	1.7	1.9	1.2	0.8	0.5
Cultural, teaching work	5.8	3.7	1.7	1.0	1.8
Miscellaneous	0.5	0.3	0.7	0.3	0.4
Total	100.0	100.0	100.0	100.0	100.0
Female					
Agriculture and forestry	1.0	4.3	2.8	1.1	3.1
Construction	0.0	0.0	0.2	0.5	0.1
Industry	18.0	13.4	15.6	35.8	20.2
Commerce, transport	4.6	3.8	4.5	4.7	6.9
Tourism	22.5	25.1	19.3	25.5	31.7
Domestic, cleaning	10.9	5.6	26.0	16.5	7.3
Technicians	7.4	2.6	1.4	2.6	2.0
Office work	9.6	6.1	6.3	3.3	9.9
Health service	13.1	33.8	18.3	6.1	10.2
Cultural, teaching work	10.0	4.1	4.0	2.2	6.2
Miscellaneous	2.1	1.2	1.6	2.0	2.0
Total	100.0	100.0	100.0	100.0	100.0

Source: Arbeitsmarktservice Österreich

reduced in size or even closed down; on the other hand, demand impulses are lost due to budget restrictions and a lack of public commissions. This results in massive redundancies. Another problem is less obvious, but at least as harmful: employment as such has been reduced and many of the formerly employed have no chance of ever finding a job again. In this way, one of the long-term consequences of the 'velvet revolution' consists in the alarmingly rapid development of a 'post-socialist underclass'.

With resources becoming scarce in the labour markets, there emerges another general phenomenon: in response to the new problem of distribution the markets are closed. In the labour market the situation became precarious all of a sudden: young people, school leavers or university graduates have enormous difficulties in finding suitable jobs. In the civil service hardly any of the jobs seemingly becoming available through retirement are refilled. Therefore those looking for jobs have to rely on the expanding private labour market that cannot, however, provide openings for all of them. On the other hand, senior employees are strongly encouraged to retire. The retired formerly held jobs in order to supplement their meagre incomes, but they rarely have the chance to do so now. The employment rate of the over-60s keeps dropping dramatically. Moreover, women are increasingly being removed from the employment scene, not least because the social services formerly provided by firms no longer exist.

It is the contrast with conditions in the former political system that causes the problems to make themselves felt so drastically. Guaranteed jobs and cheap rents had met the basic demands of the bulk of the population – if meagrely, although more or less adequately. This appears not to be the case at present. Mass redundancies accompany the transition process and constitute a permanent massive threat to the social climate. The eager taking-up of nationalistic ideologies and a renaissance of post-Communist political parties is a problematic consequence to be understood against this background.

The reaction of the populations of east-central Europe countries has been one of dissatisfaction with and growing criticism of the political decision makers, of a return to the respective national ideologies but not one of international migration. The massive migration from east-central Europe has not yet begun. And migration will also remain the exception in the medium term. The medium- and long-term contraction of the workforce in Hungary and the Czech Republic supports this, as does the effectiveness of the measures taken by the West to insulate itself against a stream of immigrants from the East. However, new labour markets which extend beyond borders will develop. East–West migration will not be a mass migration of inconceivable proportions, but it will als not be an isolated phenomenon. New regional labour market structures are beginning to develop in a Europe without a hermetically sealed Iron Curtain.

With the expansion of their catchment areas, the labour markets in Austria and other countries of western Europe are in their turn experiencing far-reaching changes. The secondary labour market, which offers insecure, low-paid jobs without any real career opportunities, is expanding. All kinds of service-sector jobs are on the increase because their costs have fallen. The service economy is also developing into a service society.

The transition of the socio-economic systems of the former COMECON countries, the sharply rising unemployment figures and real and supposed threats posed by East–West migration once more underline the close links between societal events, even when they extend beyond national borders. The metaphor of the common European home has much in common with reality – even if many people refuse to accept this.

NOTES

1. Attention is drawn to the studies of the Vienna Institute for Comparative Economic Research, the Austrian Institute for East and South-East European Studies and the Institute for Urban and Regional Research of the Austrian Academy of Sciences.

2. A survey of 400 Polish workers in Vienna (carried out in May 1993 by students of the Institute of Geography of the University of Vienna in cooperation with the University of Krakow) showed that about 40% of the interviewees came to Vienna because they had lost their job; 50%, however, were attracted by the possibility of higher wages and 10% came for family, political or other reasons.

3. Unfortunately, for the years between the 1981 Census and 1991, when the labour market authorities began to keep statistics, no data are available on the countries of origin of foreign workers.

4. An example shows just how low the current level of migration to Austria from east-central European countries still is – despite the exceptional growth. With regard to the number of inhabitants and the distance from the dominant labour market regions, a good comparison can be made between Austria and Hungary and Austria and Bavaria. The population of Hungary is about 10 million – somewhat smaller than that of Bavaria. The distance between Vienna and Budapest is four to five hours by road, compared with five to six hours from Vienna to Munich. About 49000 Austrians work in Bavaria in non-self-employed jobs, either as commuters or as resident workers. That represents 1.1% of all non-self-employed workers in Bavaria. (To these must also be added about 11000 active self-employed Austrians in Bavaria.) This compares with a figure of 0.29% for Hungarians in Austria. Although the income disparities between Bavaria and Austria are considerably smaller than those between Austria and Hungary, the percentage of Hungarians in the total non-self-employed workforce is thus only a quarter of that represented by Austrians in Bavaria. On the basis of the 1% figure for Austrians in Bavaria, the corresponding figure for Hungarians in Austria would be 34000. They would not need to be immigrants because about a million Hungarians live in the three western Komitaten of Györ-Moson-Sopron, Vas and Zala alone. The Viennese labour market can be reached either daily or weekly from these Komitaten. Commuting can thus replace immigration.

5. The survey of Polish workers mentioned earlier offers appropriate if insufficient proof of this. About 95% of the 400 interviewees claimed to have completed at least one training course beyond compulsory schooling, while 11% had a university diploma.

REFERENCES AND BIBLIOGRAPHY

Altzinger, W. (1992) *Ost-West-Migration ohne Steuerungsmöglichkeiten?* Working Paper No. 15. Wien: Instituts für Volkswirtschaft der Wirtschaftsuniversität Wien.

Csefalvay, Z. and Rohn, W. (1991) . . .

Csefalvay, Z. Faßmann, H. and Rohn, W. (1994) *Regionalstruktur im Wandel – das Beispiel Ungarn.* Vienna: ISR-Researchreport Nr. 11.

Dövenyi, Z. (1995) Die strukturellen und territorialen Besonderheiten der Arbeitslosigkeit in Ungarn, in Meusburger, P. and Klinger, A. *Vom Plan zum Markt.* Heidelberg: pp. 114–29.

Faßmann, H. (1991) Ökonomische Voraussetzungen und Reormen, in Lichtenberer, E. (ed.) *Vom Plan zum Markt.* Wien: ISR-Forschungsberichte, Heft 3, pp. 9–15.

Faßmann, H. and Münz, R. (1994) *European Migration in the Late Twentieth Century. Historical Patterns, Actual Trends and Social Implications.* Aldershot: Brookfield.

Faßmann, H. and Lichtenberger, E. (eds) (1995) *Märkte in Bewegung. Metropolen und Regionen in Ostmitteleuropa.* Wien-Köln-Weimar.

Faßmann, H., Kohlbacher, J. and Reeger, U. (1995) *Polen in Österreich*. Vienna: ISR-Researchreport Nr. 14.

Fiejka, Z. and Jozefowicz, A. (1991) Human Resources Development in the 1990s: The Polish Dilemma. Paper presented at the International Conference *Human Resources in Europe at the Dawn of the 21st Century*. Luxembourg, 27–29 November.

Fischer, G. (1991) Labour Market and Social Development in Central and Eastern Europe: Impact on Western Europe. Paper presented at the *Conference on Medium Term Economic Assessment*. Wien, 14–16 October.

Gabrisch, H. (1992) The Economic in Central and Eastern Europe, Yugoslavia and the Soviet Union/CIS in 1991/92: Decline and Inflation, in WIIW (ed.) *Mitgliederinformation, Heft 3*, Wien: pp. 3–11.

Holzmann, R. (1991) Migrationspotential der postsozialistischen Reformländern Europas: Hintergründe, Daten und Einschätzungen, in Faßmann, H., Findle, P. and Münz, R. *Die Auswirkungen der internationalen Wanderungen auf Österreich. Szenarien zur regionalen Bevölkerungsentwicklung 1991–2031*. Schriftenreihe de ÖROK 89. Wien: pp. 18–31.

Holzgreve, M. (1993) *Der Prager Arbeitsmarkt. Eine empirische Untersuchung über die Arbeitskräftenachfrage unter besonderer Berücksichtigung ausländischer Stellenanbieter*. Wien: Diplomarbeit der Universität Wien.

Hönekopp, E. (1991) *Migratory Movements from Countries of Central and Eastern Europe: Causes and Characteristics, Present Situation and Possible Future Trends – the Case of Germany and Austria*. Strasbourg: Council of Europe.

Kapl, M., Milan, S. and Tepper, T. (1991) Unemployment and Market-Oriented Reform in Czechoslovakia. *International Labour Review*, 130:199–210.

Lado, M., Szalai, J. and Sziraczki, G. (1991) Recent Labour Market and Social Policy Developments in Hungary. Paper prepared for the OECD-CCEET/ILO Conference on *Labour Market and Social Policy Implications of Structural Change in Central and Eastern Europe*. Paris, September.

Meuburger, P. and Klinger, P. (eds) (1995) *Vom Plan zum Markt. Eine Untersuchung am Beispiel Ungarns*. Heidelberg:

Sziraczki, G. (1991) Labour Market Developments, in Lado, M., Szalai, J. and Sziraczki, G. Recent Labour Market and Social Policy Developments in Hungary. Paper prepared for the OECD-CCEET/ILO Conference on *Labour Market and Social Policy Implications of Structural Change in Central and Eastern Europe*. Paris, September.

Vintrova, R. (1991) Der Übergang der ehemaligen Ostblockländer zur Marktwirtschaft, *Wirtschaft und Gesellschaft*, 17(1):55–68.

Wiener Institut für internationale Wirtschaftsvergleiche (1991) Stabilisierung und Rezession. Die Wirtschaft der früheren RGW-Länder und Jugoslawiens 1990/91, *WIFO-Monatsberichte 5*:257–72.

Witkowski, J. (1991) Labour Market in Poland: Recent Changes and Prospects. Paper presented at the International Conference *Human Resources in Europe at the Dawn of the 21st Century*. Luxembourg, 27–29 November.

Part IV

PEOPLE, JOBS AND RESTRUCTURING IN EUROPEAN CORE REGIONS

10 Social and Economic Restructuring in Old Industrial Areas: A Comparison of North-East England and the Ruhr District in Germany

GERALD WOOD
University of Duisburg, Germany

INTRODUCTION

The two regions that will be discussed in this chapter, the North-east of England and the Ruhr district in Germany, are frequently referred to as 'old industrial areas' (OIAs).[1] Generally, this term is associated with two meanings. First, it refers to the face that the so-labelled areas have an 'old' economic history, which is characterized by a sharp break with past patterns of development occuring during the eighteenth and nineteenth centuries, the era of the (first) Industrial Revolution. Secondly, it implies that the commodities of the 'old industries' have reached the end of their life cycle[2] (Ache et al. 1989, p. 148), a fact which, according to some commentators, renders not only the 'old industries' but equally the areas concerned obsolete. One of the most outspoken advocates of the latter view is Hall, who claims that due to the economic changes that have taken place over the recent past OIAs, the 'yesterday regions' (Hall 1981) 'have little going for them. Determined policies, accompanied by liberal front-end government money, may succeed in creating some kind of work there: low-paid assembly industry of the Third World type; similarly low-paid work in service industries associated with recreational or tourist developments' (Hall 1988, p. 62). Is this long-wavist[3] scenario the inevitable development trajectory for OIAs? Will people, their skills and, in fact, entire areas need to remain or become 'redundant', as some observers seem to suggest? What could be an alternative route for such areas and what sort of public policy would have to go along with it? And, finally, what can be learned from the past in search of development options?

These questions are the most crucial and pressing issues associated with the

People, Jobs and Mobility in the New Europe. Edited by Hans H. Blotevogel and Anthony J. Fielding.
© 1997 European Science Foundation. Published in 1997 by John Wiley & Sons Ltd.

future of OIAs. However, it is neither possible nor the intention here to answer them exhaustively. What I wish to do is to give a brief account of some common patterns within the overall economic and social development of the two OIAs in question. It is hoped that outlining these shared characteristics will not only render a deeper understanding of the development history of the two regions, but will also hint at a future for OIAs beyond simplistic and deterministic assumptions.

One feature in particular will be looked at more closely: the formal educational and vocational qualifications of the population. There are mainly two reasons for doing so. First, if the assumption is correct that structural change is a necessary condition for a prosperous future of OIAs and if it is also true that such structural change will not come about merely by investing in the (material) infrastructure, by giving grants, tax incentives etc. but also by paying attention to other location factors, such as the socio-cultural fabric that supports the intended change, then the formal qualifications of the population will be of prominent importance.[4] Regarding the economic history and future of OIAs, it can be argued that the formal qualifications of the population were once an asset but have now become a serious bottleneck. This thesis or, rather, its verification, will be elaborated further on. Secondly, with regard to the central topic of this volume – the relationship between production systems and demographic and social change – the issue of formal qualifications is one of the few clear cases where this relationship is as much determined by the social as it is by the production system.

It needs to be pointed out here that the question of formal qualifications cannot and will not be discussed in isolation. The debate needs to be widened to take into account current economic and political trends occuring on a broader (inter)national level as well. This will be done in the last section of this Chapter. Taking such a broader view is crucial because current trends of massive economic restructuring and of departing from, if not dismantling, the welfare state in Germany and the UK are highly socially and spatially selective, affecting the people living in OIAs in so many ways and in such an acute manner (Martin 1989; Smith 1989; Lewis and Townsend 1989; Hudson and Williams 1989).[5]

THE REGIONAL BACKGROUND

One of the features that the North-east and the Ruhr district share is the fact that it is fairly difficult to use these names with any great ease once one has given them some consideration. To begin with, both names do not denote any administrative unit. As Byrne (1989, p. 40) observes, 'the significant "cultural" region is the North East coast, but this has no separate administrative existence'. Because of this the North-east is 'a difficult region to delineate in any realistic sense', as Warren (1972, p. 364) notes.

What, then, is the North-east and how can the Ruhr district be circumscribed? I would propose to choose a pragmatic approach, very much like Warren (1972,

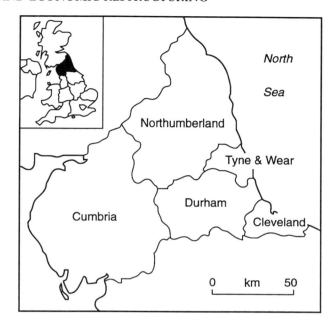

Figure 10.1. The counties of north-east England

p. 365) did when he defined the North-east for convenience as Northumberland, Durham and the whole North Riding of Yorkshire.[6] Because much of the data being used here is available at county level only (or at a higher level), the definition of the North-east in our case comprises the following 'new' counties: Cleveland, Durham, Northumberland and Tyne and Wear (see Figure 10.1). Together with Cumbria these counties make up the Northern Region which for some of the figures used here was the lowest level of aggregation.

It was stated earlier that neither of the regions forms an administrative unit. In fact, although both areas are important economic and social units, they are being governed from outside. In the case of the North-east, the UK Parliament or, rather, central government rules, and in the case of the Ruhr it is the *Land* government of North Rhine-Westphalia and the administrative tier between the *Land* government and the local authorities, the *Regierungsbezirke*, that administer the area. Interestingly enough, however, there is a tradition of quasi-autonomous organizations in both regions that has in a way served to fill the institutional vacuum that exists at the regional level. I contend that by their sheer existence these organizations have been instrumental in giving the two areas an identity. In the case of the North-east this tradition started in 1935 with the formation of the North East Development Board (Rowntree Research Unit 1974). Other organizations were to follow, the last being the Northern Development Company (NDC) which has been in existence since 1986. Typical

Figure 10.2. The Ruhr district

of all these groupings is the fact that they are a platform where capital and labour meet (Byrne 1989) in order to market the area for inward investment and to work out economic development plans (RRU 1974). Very similar to these is the *Kommunalverband Ruhrgebiet* (KVR; association of local authorities in the Ruhr district) which is the successor to the *Siedlungsverband Ruhrkohlenbezirk* (SVR), an organization that was founded in 1919–20 (Rommelspacher 1982, p. 16) and whose primary role was regional planning (Schnur 1970, p. 15). Due to the fact that this power was taken away from the SVR in the mid-1970s, the

KVR's principal task now is to act as a body through which the local authorities can 'speak with one voice' (to the potential investor and qualified staff that are being lured into the area). Mainly because of this, the KVR and the NDC are very similar and, in their respective national contexts, rather unusual establishments.

Because of the varied importance of the KVR (as a spatial frame of reference in much of the literature[7] and for many statistics, in providing a feeling of regional unity and an image of the Ruhr to the outside world etc.) our definition of the Ruhr district is congruous with the area that the KVR covers (see Figure 10.2).

THE HISTORY OF THE TWO REGIONS

With a high degree of justification it can be argued that the North-east and the Ruhr district both owe their existence as socio-spatial entities to the Industrial Revolution. This is why the following considerations will deal with the developments that have taken place since the late eighteenth century.

Industrial take-off and rapid growth

Since the early nineteenth century and right into the 1950s, the economies of the North-east and of the Ruhr district have revolved around the fuel coal which is found in the coalfields of the two areas. Although coal mining had been going on for centuries (Heineberg 1983; Schlieper 1986), the time of particular economic development, the industrial take-off, occurred during the second half of the nineteenth century.[8] The process of industrialization led to fundamental economic, demographic, social, cultural and political changes in both regions (McCord 1979; Schlieper 1986). Hitherto mainly rural areas[9] were transformed into industrial landscapes in less than 50 years, peasant cultures into 'industrialized and urbanized societies' (McCord 1979, p. 25).

The demographic and social transformation was brought about by high birth rates and, in particular, by immigration, and was especially pronounced during the second half of the nineteenth century. In Northumberland there was an increase in population from 304000 in 1851 to 603000 in 1901, and in Durham the population rose from 391000 to 1187000 during the same time (McCord 1979, p. 159). In the Ruhr district (SVR area) the population increased from 502100 in 1852 to 2867400 in 1905 (and continued to increase until it reached a peak in 1925 of 4132200) (Wiel 1970, p. 13).

Typical of the economies of both regions around the turn of the century were a high degree of specialization around a few products and the particular patterns of ownership. Byrne (1989, p. 42) calls the high levels of horizontal and vertical integration within the regional economy of the North-east 'organized capitalism'. In the Ruhr there was a process of syndicate formation (Weber 1990) in the late nineteenth century which was to shelter the regional economy from the hardships of recession and outside competition.[10] The large coal and steel companies formed trusts into which the banking sector was increasingly drawn

(Schlieper 1986, p. 90). For the North-east McCord (1979, p. 147) observes, 'In the later nineteenth and early twentieth centuries many of the key industrial and mining companies, the main mercantile and shipping houses, and the principal banks of the area, were under the direct control of a relatively small and coherent group of men'.

The economies of the North-east and the Ruhr district expanded to become pillars on which the national economies rested. As Weber (1990, p. 204) points out, during the time of the German Empire the Ruhr district became a region which produced well over 40% of the nation's pig iron and almost 60% of all steel and coal. The North-east had an added importance because it was, in contrast to the Ruhr, a major supplier of ships; at the beginning of the twentieth century more than a quarter of the world's new tonnage was built in North-east shipyards (McCord 1979, p. 128).

From boom to decline

The North-east and the Ruhr-district not only shared the experience of a phenomenal rise of an industrial complex around fuel coal, they also faced a very similar fate afterwards: that of continued or, rather, repeated industrial and social decline. This cyclical downturn of the two regional economies, that was to commence in the late 1910s in the North-east (McCord 1979, p. 215) and in the late 1920s in the Ruhr district (Schlieper 1986, p. 144), sometimes occurred simultaneously, sometimes after a time lag. However, the causes behind the problems of both areas were rather similar and they were of a structural nature. To begin with, as McCord (1979, p. 224) observes, the problems that the North-east faced after the First World War were 'not so much a national predicament of industrial decline but the very great regional disparities in the distribution of older industries in relative decline and newer industries set upon a course of rapid expansion'. According to Ache et al. (1989, p. 148) a similar trend can be observed in the case of the Ruhr and the agglomerations in the south of Germany, the latter being the growth centres of the newer (consumer durables) and newest (computing, telecommunications etc.) industries. Schlieper (1986, p. 202) claims that it was the inability of the Ruhr industry to diversify into electrical (light) engineering which laid the foundation stone for the structural problems that were to follow.

The problem besetting both areas after the end of the nineteenth-century boom era were momentarily halted when the goods of the regions were in great demand. This was particularly the case during and after the two World Wars (see Wood 1994; Schlieper 1986, p. 201). The prosperous period in the North-east and the Ruhr district after the Second World War lasted well into the 1960s.

But because the prosperity during that time was built on the traditional goods of the two areas and because the two regional economies hardly diversified at all as a consequence, it is, with hindsight, not surprising that in the 1960s problems commenced which are still not resolved today. Interestingly, there were strong interest groups in both regions that prevented economic diversification. As Ache et al. (1989) point out, lobbying for the old industries in the Ruhr was mainly pursued by a strong interest coalition of capital, labour and politics of the area.[11]

Another important aspect that helps to explain the predicament which both regions found themselves in from the 1960s onwards is the fact that the two regional economies were increasingly integrated into the wider economy mainly through amalgamation and nationalization (the latter in the UK). This resulted in the delocalization of industrial control in both areas (Byrne 1989, p. 42), a process by which – as I contend – the (perceived) market value and market position of the two regions became more and more precarious in an era of growing spatial flexibility of the production systems.[12]

State policies to combat decline

The slump conditions in the North-east and in the Ruhr forced the governments of both countries and that of the *Land* North Rhine-Westphalia to react. Regional policy in the UK was, after it had slumbered in the 1950s (Massey 1984), reanimated during the 1960s. With the help of massive state intervention the regional economy of the North-east modernized to become a branch plant economy (Buswell et al. 1987), a process which was to 'change the nature of the origins of the region's economic problems from overspecialization by industrial sector . . . into overspecialization by corporate function' (Byrne 1989, 43).

In the Ruhr district the deteriorating situation, first in the coal industry and, during the 1970s, also in the steel industry, prompted the governments of the Federal Republic and of North Rhine-Westphalia into action. They established a Keynesian instrument of national economic regulation: a tripartite 'concerted action' which was to 'socially carry out' the contraction of the mining industry. Apart from this, the *Land* government initiated a number of special programmes, some of which were intended to be integrated planning procedures for the development of the region with a temporal, spatial and financial coordination of the most important measures, i.e. the 'Ruhr Development Programme 1968–1973' ('Entwicklungsprogramm Ruhr 1968–1973') which was merged into the 'North Rhine-Westphalia Programme 1975' (Nordrhein-Westfalen-Programm 1975) in 1970.[13] These and other programmes had, however, only limited success. Most importantly, complex analyses of the Ruhr's 'capacity for structural change' make depressing reading because they clearly suggest that the region is lacking the capacity for coping with the inevitable contraction of the coal and steel industries in any future-oriented manner. This assumption has been verified with the help of indicators such as research, development and technology potentials (Butzin 1987, 1990).

The relative importance that the traditional industries retained in the Ruhr – despite worldwide restructuring processes and state modernization initiatives – can be illustrated by the fact that in 1991 the Ruhr produced 20.7 million tons of steel, whereas in the whole of the UK the output was 16.5 million tons (KVR 1992, p. 207). From the year 1970 to the year 1991 the drop in output amounted to 27% in the case of the Ruhr, but to well over 41% in the case of the UK.

RECENT DEVELOPMENTS IN THE NORTH-EAST AND THE RUHR DISTRICT

The economy

The structural weaknesses in the economies of the North-east and the Ruhr district that led to the described increase in state involvement in both areas first surfaced after the Second World War in the mid-1960s, when the coal industry was increasingly pressurized by competing fuels, foreign competitors and, in the case of the North-east, by the aim of the NCB to reduce coal output as well as unit costs of production (Hudson and Williams 1986, p. 69). As a consequence, both output and employment in coal mining fell sharply in both regions. In the North-east the output was reduced from 35.1 million tons in 1959 to 15.5 million tons in 1971–2 (–56%). During the same time the number of mines was cut back from 163 to 48, and the workforce from 130700 to 46300 (–65%).[14] Compared to this, the decline in the Ruhr was less dramatic. Output fell from 113.4 million tons in 1960 to 91.1 million tons in 1970 (–20%) (KVR 1992, p. 205), employment figures from 490200 to 252700 (–48%) (Petzina 1990, p. 523).

This decline continues to the present day. In the case of the Ruhr district, the most dramatic period for the coal industry after the Second World War coincided with the crisis of the steel industry which set in during the mid-1970s (Danielzyk and Wood 1993). As Petzina (1990, p. 537) observes, the steel crisis was a structural one as the old industrial countries came under increasing pressure from developing countries, such as Brasil, South Korea and China, and also from Japan. All of these countries either built up or expanded their own steel industries during this time so that the Ruhr and the North-east not only faced new or stronger competitors, they also lost these countries as customers.

Due to the global restructuring processes the steel industry, like coal mining, was confronted with a twin reduction in output and employment figures. At the zenith of its development, in 1974, the steel industry in the Ruhr produced 53.2 million tons of iron and 40.2 million tons of steel and employed 283000 people.[15] Ten years later, in 1984, these figures had dropped to 39.4 million tons of iron (–26%), 30.2 million tons of steel (–25%) and 184000 employees (–35%). Most disturbing was the fact that the loss of one job in the steel industry resulted in the loss of 2.7 further jobs in other industries (Petzina 1990, p. 539). In the Northern Region metal manufacturing faced a reduction of its workforce from 63000 to 47000 (–25%) between 1966 and 1976 and a further loss of 45% to 26000 in 1981 (Robinson n.d., p. 28). Coal output between 1971–2 and 1981–2 dropped by 14% to 13.3 million tons, employment in coal mining by

37% down to 29000 employees.[16] Added to the contraction of coal mining and metal manufacturing in the Northern Region was the decline in shipbuilding. Here the employment decreased from 58000 in 1966 to 48000 in 1976 (-17%).[17]

Problematic as these trends are, they need to be put into context. For instance, as Robinson (n.d., p. 14) notes, 'between 1966 and 1976, manufacturing employment declined by 5.2% in the North – but in Great Britain as a whole the loss was 15.6%'. Thus, the Northern Region was able to keep a large share of its industrial base during this time. What is more, because of an active regional policy in the 1960s the North-east managed to modernize its industrial base. This modernization, however, transformed a major part of the economy into a branch-plant economy, a process which led critics such as Firn (1975) to look on the transfer of 'screwdriver' jobs into development areas such as the North-east as a new dimension of the 'regional problem' rather than its solution.

Another development that helped to offset the drastic reductions in employment in the traditional industries in both regions was the rise in service-sector employment. In the North-east there was a growth of over 73000 jobs in this sector between 1966 and 1976 (+13%), many of which were in professional and scientific services (Robinson n.d., p. 15). This growth almost compensated for the losses in the primary and manufacturing sectors which stood at 88000.

In the Ruhr, employment in the service sector rose from 881100 in 1970 by 86900 to 968000 in 1980 (+10%), a figure which made up approximately 38% of the 226500 jobs that were shed in the primary and manufacturing sectors during this time. Compared with the rise in service-sector employment in North Rhine-Westphaia as a whole, however, which stood at 23%, the growth of the service sector in the Ruhr was only a modest one.[18]

The downward trend in the traditional industries of both regions continued throughout the 1970s and 1980s. At times it was more pronounced than at others. Added to the problems of the chimneystack industries were the difficulties that the branch-plants faced during and after the recession of the late 1970s and early 1980s. Table 10.1 and 10.2 give an overall impression of the economic development of the Ruhr and the Northern Region between 1981–2 and 1990–91. Both regions shed a large number of employees in the production and construction industries (SIC 1–5). The loss in the Ruhr between 1982 and 1991 amounted to 65300 jobs, or 6.4%. Both in absolute and in relative figures, the decline in the North was far greater; 86700 jobs were shed between 1981 and 1990, or 18.2% of the workforce in these sectors. However, the differential between regional economic developments and the national context displays a reverse pattern: whereas in the UK the trend was almost as negative as it was in the North (-16.7%), in the Federal Republic there was an increase in employment figures during the time in question, creating a differential of 9.3 percentage points between the KVR and the FRG.

Table 10.1. Employment:[1] *Kommunalverband Ruhrgebiet* (KVR)[2]

	SIC 0		SIC 1–5		SIC 6–7		SIC 8–9		SIC 0–9	
	('000)	%	('000)	%	('000)	%	('000)	%	('000)	%
1982										
KVR	27.3	1.3	1013.9	49.8	384.7	18.9	608.9	29.9	2034.8	100
NRW[3]	157.6	2.3	3191.3	46.4	1255.3	18.2	2279.4	33.1	6883.6	100
FR/W[4]	1346.0	5.0	11724.0	43.8	4728.0	17.7	8976.0	33.5	26774.0	100
1991										
KVR	28.6	1.3	948.6	44.0	406.3	18.8	774.8	35.9	2158.3	100
NRW	144.3	1.9	3182.2	42.5	1350.2	18.0	2805.8	37.5	7482.5	100
FR/W	1045.0	3.5	12065.0	40.6	5291.0	17.8	11283.0	38.0	29684.0	100
Change 1982–91										
KVR	1.3	4.8	−65.3	−6.4	21.6	5.6	165.9	27.3	123.5	6.1
NRW	−13.3	−8.4	−9.1	−0.3	94.9	7.6	526.4	23.1	598.9	8.7
FR/W	−301.0	−22.4	341.0	2.9	563.0	11.9	2307.0	25.7	2910.0	10.9

Source: KVR 1992, 198–9.

Notes:

[1] By Standard Industrial Classification (SIC 0: Agriculture, forestry and fishing; SIC 1: Energy and water supply; SIC 2–4: Manufacturing industries; SIC 5: Construction; SIC 6–7: Distribution, hotels and catering, repairs, transport and communication; SIC 8–9: Banking, finance, insurance, business services and leasing, public administration and other services).

[2] For a definition of KVR see text.

[3] North Rhine-Westphalia, including KVR.

[4] Federal Republic of Germany (West).

199

Table 10.2. Employment by Standard Industrial Classification: Northern Region

	SIC 0 ('000)	SIC 1-5 %	SIC 6-7 ('000)	SIC 8-9 %	SIC 0-9 ('000)	%	('000)	%	('000)	%
1981										
NR	13.7	1.2	476.5	42.5	270.7	24.2	360.0	32.1	1120.9	100
UK	369.7	1.7	8051.7	36.8	5599.9	25.6	7871.7	36.0	21893.0	100
1990										
NR	11.0	1.0	389.8	34.8	269.1	24.0	451.5	40.3	1121.4	100
UK	294.3	1.3	6706.7	28.9	6047.2	26.0	10184.0	43.8	23232.2	100
change 1981–90										
NR	-2.7	-19.1	-86.7	-18.2	-1.6	-0.6	91.5	25.4	0.5	0
UK	-75.4	-20.4	-1345.0	-16.7	447.3	8.0	2312.3	29.4	1339.2	6.1

Source: CSO 1991, Table 10.7

Another important point to make is the fact that, due to these employment losses and the coinciding employment growth in the service industries, the relative importance of the production and construction industries fell sharply in both regions. In 1982 employment in SIC 1–5 in the Ruhr made up almost 50% of the overall employment. By 1991 this figure had contracted to 44%. In the case of the North, the corresponding figures were 42.5% in 1981 and 34.8% in 1990 (see Tables 10.1 and 10.2). These figures, together with the different national trends in the production and construction industries, are a manifestation of the divergent development trajectories of both, the two national and the two regional economies during the time in question. In the case of the UK and the North, there was a process of deindustrialization underway which, according to Damesick (1987), was particularly pronounced in the northern regions of the UK, and which was a result of international restructuring processes of the production system (based on increased spatial flexibility) on the one hand and of the Thatcherite market-led approach in many policy areas and a simultaneous 'rolling-back' of the frontiers of the state during the 1980s on the other.

The less dramatic deteriorating position of the production and construction industries in the Ruhr and the growth of these sectors on the national level essentially show two things: first, the international position of the German production system was still continuing to gain in importance and, secondly, this importance shifted, albeit more slowly than in the case of the UK, continuously towards other areas in Germany. These areas, as Ache et al. (1990, p. 148) show, were essentially the south German agglomerations whose automobile, light electrical engineering and armament industries were the carriers of the positive development trends.

In stark contrast to the trends in the production and construction industries were the developments occuring in the service sector. The major growth took place in banking, finance, insurance and busines services as well as in public administration (SIC 8–9), whereas in distribution, transport and communication (SIC 6–7) there was only modest growth or slight decline (see Tables 10.1 and 10.2). In the Ruhr district service-sector employment in SIC 8–9 grew by 165 900, or 27.3% from 1982 to 1991. This increase even surpassed the national increase of 25.7%. The development of the other service industries was less striking. Employment in SIC 6–7 expanded by 21 600, or 5.6%, and amounted to only half the national increase which stood at 11.9%. Because of the distinct rise in service-sector employment the losses in other industries were more than offset. Therefore, the overall employment change was positive (+6.2%). However, compared with the development of the national economy (+10.9%) this gain was only moderate. This differential again highlights the different development trajectories of the Ruhr and of the prospering Southern agglomerations (Ache et al. 1990).

In the North the increase in service-sector employment between 1981 and 1990 was restricted to SIC 8–9. Here the net gain amounted to 91 500 jobs, or 25.4%. The other service industries (SIC 6–7), on the other hand, contracted by

1600 jobs, or 0.6%. This occurred against the background of a national growth of 8.0%, creating a differential between the North and the country as a whole of 8.6 percentage points. The positive trends in all of the service industries were far more modest than in the case of the Ruhr, and the overall employment situation hardly changed at all as a consequence. There was a net increase of only 500 jobs between 1981 and 1990 in the North (+0%), whereas in the UK this was well over 1.3 million (+6.1%). The main components of this relatively poor overall development in employment consisted in a decrease of full male employment (in the production and construction industries) on the one hand and a simultaneous increase of female part time employment (in the service sector) on the other. According to Damesick (1987, p. 37), the opposite developments taking place in the North and in the UK are the expression of a 'basic regional dualism' that 'can be identified within the UK between an area comprising much of South East England together with adjacent parts of East Anglia, the East Midlands, and the South West, on the one hand, and most of the rest of the country, on the other . . . This dualism essentially reflects the difference between "de-industrialization" and "post-industrial" development as alternative perspectives on the nature of structural change in the UK economy.'

Even though the Ruhr managed to retain much of its industrial base and to attract many new jobs in the service industries, it shared with the North-east a similar relative decline of its economic position within the national context. Therefore, the future prospects of both regions are quite precarious.

Labour market and social trends

Unemployment

Recent labour market and social developments in the North-east and the Ruhr district are in numerous ways mutually inter-related with the economic trends that were outlined above. For instance, mainly because of the sharp drop in employment in the production and construction industries there was a notice-able rise in unemployment figures in both regions. Between 1980 and 1985 unemployment rates more than doubled in the Ruhr district.[19] They rose from 5.5% to 14.1% and went up to 15% in 1988. Compared with those regions whose economies were faring much better (the agglomerations in the south) this increase was extraordinary. The highest increase in the unemployment rates of a south German agglomeration was recorded in Nürnberg: it amounted to 4.8 percentage points between 1980 and 1985. But the developments in the Ruhr even surpassed the national trends during this period. Particularly interesting is the fact that between the years 1985 and 1988 there was a reduction in unemployment in Germany as well as in some of the listed southern agglomer-ations, whereas in the Ruhr there was still an increase of almost 1 percentage point during this time.[20] The aggregate figures hide the great discrepancies that existed within the region. With a certain degree of simplification it can be said that those local authorities whose economies are still dominated by the traditional industries have the highest unemployment rates – such as Dortmund (11.2% in September 1991), Duisburg (11.3%), Gelsenkirchen (11.6%) and Herne (12.6%) – whereas other local authorities, because of their different economic and social structure, have (much) lower rates – (e.g. Hagen (7.7%), Unna (8.7%).)[21] The national average at the time was 6.0% (for West Germany only) and the NRW average (including the KVR) was 7.6%. Thus, in all of the local authorities of the 'Rhein-Ruhr-Nord' agglomeration, unemployment rates were above or well above the national and the *Land* averages.

In the North unemployment rates increased markedly from 11.7% to 15.3% between 1981 and 1986. This rise of 3.6 percentage points was well over the national increase of 3 percentage points. Only one English region, Yorkshire and Humberside, was confronted with a sharper rise (+3.7 percentage points), and only in Northern Ireland was the unemployment problem more austere than the North (in both years). Because unemployment rates fell in all regions between 1986 and 1989, the unemployment situation improved everywhere between 1981 and 1989, with the exception of Northern Ireland. In the case of the North unemployment rates decreased by 1.8 percentage points between 1981 and 1989 which was exactly the national average. However, it needs to be pointed out that, according to Robinson (1990, p. 19), the official unemployment figures are a statistical 'minefield' because the government changed the way of counting the unemployed over 24 times between 1979 and 1989; 23 of these changes resulted in a reduction of the officially stated unemployment rates.

Very much as in the case of the 'Rhein-Ruhr-Nord' agglomeration, there were considerable subregional variations in the unemployment figures of the North. Particularly high rates are to be found in the industrial core of the region, in the TTWAs of the North-east.[22] In July 1991, for instance, the unemployment rate for the UK was 8.3%, for the North it was 10.4%, but for the industrial North-east almost all the rates were well above these – Middlesbrough (12.5%), Hartlepool (14.0%), Sunderland (13.5%), South Tyneside (16.6%). In the countryside unemployment was either similar to or well below the national average – e.g. Berwick-on-Tweed (3.9%), Alnwick and Amble (8.6%), Hexham (4.7%), Cumbria (county level, 5.7%) – reflecting the stronger economic position of these areas *vis-à-vis* the industrial North-east.

Demographic trends

The negative developments occurring in the economy and the labour market were accompanied by, or rather resulted in, negative demographic trends in both regions. These population losses were mainly the result of a negative net migration which in some (subregional) areas was slightly offset by positive net natural changes.

Between 1980 and 1987 the population in the 'Rheim-Ruhr-Nord' agglomeration decreased by 3.9% to 6068000, whereas in the agglomerations in southern Germany there was a general trend of expansion which was particularly strong in the Munich area (+2.3%).[23] These contrasting developments of decline in the 'Rheim-Ruhr-Nord' agglomeration on the one hand and of growth in the south on the other resonate with the economic and labour market trends that were outlined above. However, there was a clear break with this pattern after 1989 (the year of unification). Between 1987 and 1991 the population in the KVR expanded to a considerable degree (+3.0%). This reversal of past trends was brought about mainly the large influx of people from the new German *Länder* in the former GDR. People primarily left for the 'old' *Länder* in the hope of better employment prospects. Another point worth mentioning is the fact that in the period between 1980 and 1987 it had been the big cities within the KVR that recorded a net loss of population (−4.0%), whereas the agglomeration fringe was slightly expanding during that time. There was a direct link between both developments because the expansion occuring in the agglomeration fringe was, to a certain degree, at the cost of the big cities, since there was a strong tendency for people to leave the cities for the more attractive urban fringe where the (rural) environment was intact and where it was much easier and cheaper to purchase a house.

In the North of England demographic trends reflected economic developments in a fairly similar way, as was observed in the case of the Ruhr district. Between 1981 and 1989, the North recorded a loss of 1.4% of its population, a figure which was surpassed only by Scotland where the population decreased by 1.7%. At the same time, and at the other end of the scale, the population in the South-west expanded by 6.2% to 4652400. In the South-east there was an incredible absolute increase of 374200 inhabitants, although the relative growth of around 2.2% was modest in comparison with that of the South-west. After 1989 there was a change in demographic trends in some of the British regions. Despite these, however, the relative position of the North remained virtually unaltered. In essence, the Northern Region lost a fair amount of its population in the periods between 1981 and 1989 (−43600; Regional Trends data) and between 1981 and 1991 (−68100; Census data). The developments in both cases were far worse than the national trends (difference in the 1981–9 period 3 percentage points, in the 1981–91 period 2.5 percentage points). As in the KVR, there were enormous subregional differences of demographic trends in the North. Interestingly, the direction of subregional developments is identical in both, the Regional Trends and the Census data. Hence, the only counties that recorded a positive overall demographic development were Cumbria (+1.2% between 1981 and 1991) and Northumberland (+0.4%), whereas all the other counties lost population. These latter counties, containing the largest share of the population in the North, make up the industrial North-east (Cleveland (−5.2%), Tyne and Wear (−5.6%), Durham (−3.6%).

Other patterns of inequality

In the preceding subsections a number of disparities between the North and the Ruhr district on the one hand and the prospering southern regions in the UK and Germany on the other have been elaborated. Apart from the economic, labour-market and demographic differences discussed, there were others that heightened the socio-spatial divide (the 'North–South divide'[24]) in both countries. These were:

— Lower household incomes. Robinson (1990, p. 38), for instance, shows that over 43% of all families in the North have a weekly income below £125, whereas the national average is 32.9% (South-east 25.2%).

— Lower per capita GNP. In the 'Rhein-Ruhr-Nord' agglomeration the per capita GNP amounted to DM26734 in 1984, which was below the national figure (DM27943) and well below the figures of the south German agglomerations (Rhein-Main DM36276; Rhein-Neckar DM32327; München DM39799) (all figures: BfLR 1987). In the North, the per capita GDP was only 90.9% of the national figure in 1979 and 86.6% in 1989 (CSO 1991, p. 178, Table 12.2). Thus, the poor position of the North continued to deteriorate within that decade. What is more, no other English region showed such a feeble economic performance.

— Higher and rising shares of people depending on supplementary benefit. Goddard and Thwaites (1990, p. 8) point out that the share of households receiving supplementary benefit in the North rose from 16.2% to 16.9% between 1980–81 and 1986–7, whereas on the UK level there was a slight decrease from 12.6% to 12.5% during this time. In the 'Rhein-Ruhr-Nord' agglomeration the proportion of people receiving supplementary benefit (*Sozialhilfe*) increased from 4.5% in 1980 to 6.2% in 1985, while in the south German agglomerations, both the rates of people receiving supplementary benefit and their rise were, with the exception of Nürnberg, far lower (Rhein-Main from 3.6% to 4.6%; Rhein-Neckar from 3% to 4.3%; Stuttgart from 2.2% to 2.9%; Nürnberg from 2% to 4.3%; München from 2.2% to 2.8%). The national figures rose from 3.3% to 4.5%.[25]

Formal qualifications

It can be argued that virtually all of the listed disparities were more or less the outcome or an expression of the deteriorating economic position of both regional economies *vis-à-vis* the national economy and the economies of those regions that were prospering while the OIAs were struggling with decline. Concerning the formal qualifications of the population, however, it would be difficult to assume such a unilateral dependent relationship between the production system and demographic and social phenomena, both with regard to the historical and the present situation. Historically speaking, it is, of course, legitimate to say that the formal qualifications of the people in the North-east

Table 10.3. Educational qualifications of the population,[1] KVR, and vocational qualifications of employees, Ruhr district and other selected agglomerations in Germany

| | Highest educational qualification (as of 1987)[2] | | |
| | Volks-Hauptschule[3] | Realschule[4] | Abitur[5] |
	% of persons who no longer attend school		
KVR[6]	57.6	14.1	9.0
KVR (ULAs)	57.1	13.9	9.0
KVR (TTLAs)	58.8	14.6	9.1
NRW[7]	54.5	15.9	10.7
	Employees with 'high' vocational qualifications[8]		
	1980	1985	June 1988
	% of employees		
Rhein-Ruhr-Nord	3.7	4.4	4.6
—Centre	no data	no data	5.6
—Fringe	no data	no data	3.3
Rhein-Main	6.1	7.3	8.2
Rhein-Neckar	5.2	6.3	6.9
Stuttgart	5.4	6.2	7.4
Nürnberg	4.8	6.1	6.9
München	8.0	9.4	10.8
NRW	3.9	4.6	5.2
FR/W[9]	3.9	4.7	5.4

Sources: KVR 1990, 30 (top section of table); Ache et al. 1989, p. 177, BfLR 1989 (bottom section of table).
Notes:
[1] Persons who no longer attend school.
[2] Census data.
[3] Certificate of education below O-level.
[4] Certificate of education similar to the British GCE O-level.
[5] Certificate of education similar to the British A-level.
[6] The KVR and NRW as a whole are not being compared with other *Länder* here. Doing so would be inappropriate because of data incompatibilities due to the different educational systems of the individual *Länder*.
[7] Including the KVR.
[8] The sources do not specify this indicator.
[9] The Federal Republic of Germany (West).

and the Ruhr district are an expression or a reflection of the economic history of the two regions. On the other hand, however, these qualifications, or rather their availability, was of crucial importance for the smooth operation of the traditional industries. At present, these former assets are not only becoming increasingly redundant, they are also a serious bottleneck because, due to the nature of the current restructuring processes, qualifications are now in demand which the OIAs do not have on offer in sufficient quantities. As Kilper (1992, p. 27) notes, the present situation of radical economic change in the Ruhr district is characterized by long-term unemployment on the one hand and by a coincident shortage of qualified staff on the other.

Table 10.4. Educational qualifications of the workforce[1] and 16-year-olds staying on at school,[2] UK regions

| | Highest educational qualification (as of 1990) | | | | | 16 year-olds staying on at school | |
	CSE below grade 1 %	GCE O-level or equivalent %	GCE A-level or equivalent %	Higher education below degree %	Degree or equivalent %	% of all 16 year-olds 1981/82	1989/90
Northern Region	7.0	17.8	19.0	4.0	6.5	51.5	60.0
Yorks. & Humberside	4.4	18.2	20.5	4.0	7.0	53.8	62.4
East Midlands	5.4	18.5	21.2	5.1	8.5	54.6	65.8
East Anglia	5.2	20.0	20.0	5.3	8.7	50.6	59.8
South East	4.6	20.1	18.4	8.4	13.4	60.8	59.8
—Greater London	3.7	18.1	15.0	9.7	16.8	–	–
—Rest of South East	5.2	21.4	20.5	7.5	11.4	–	–
South West	5.5	20.6	20.7	6.7	8.3	57.3	60.9
West Midlands	4.7	17.5	20.1	4.7	7.2	55.6	61.9
North West	4.8	18.8	20.9	5.4	8.2	56.7	64.7
England	5.0	19.2	19.7	6.3	9.9	56.9	61.6
Wales	5.5	19.4	20.9	5.0	7.2	58.1	63.1
Scotland	0.4	15.1	24.5	9.8	8.0	–	76.8
Northern Ireland	3.5	16.3	15.6	6.4	8.2	–	–
UK	4.6	18.8	20.1	6.6	9.5	–	–
GB	–	–	–	–	–	–	63.3

Source: CSO 1991, pp. 151, 139.
Notes:
[1] Economically active eprson aged 16–59/64.
[2] By region of residence.

What, then, is the current situation in both regions with regard to the formal qualifications of their populations? Tables 10.3 and 10.4 give an overview of the educational and vocational qualifications of the population in the Ruhr district and in the Northern Region, contrasted with other areas in Germany and the UK. Particularly striking about these tables is the fact that both regions show a poor relative performance with regard to the formal educational and vocational qualifications of their population. In the KVR, for instance, a far larger share than the NRW average has a Certificate of Education below O-level (57.6% opposed to 54.5%), whereas the share of people with A-levels (9.0%) is below the state figure of 10.7%. Really impressive, however, is the differential between the Ruhr district (in this case the 'Rhein-Ruhr-Nord' agglomeration) and other areas with regard to the indicator 'employees with "high" vocational qualifications' (see bottom section of Table 10.3). In 1980 the share of people in the 'Rhein-Ruhr-Nord' agglomeration who fitted into this category was 3.7%, while in the southern Germany agglomerations this was never below 4.8%, and in the case of München it was as high as 8%. Also, the share of the Ruhr was lower than the national and the NRW averages. Over the years these figures grew in all of the listed areas, but this growth was modest in the case of the Ruhr (0.9 percentage points) *vis-à-vis* the south German agglomerations. The indicator 'employees with "high" vocational qualifications', according to the BfLR (1987, p. 797, my translation), 'describes the relationship between job security and the quality of vocational qualifications. High vocational qualifications are more likely to warrant a crisis-proof job with above-average incomes. Thus, high figures of the indicator need to be seen as structurally positive.' With regard to the situation in the Ruhr district, then, the signs are not very encouraging.

This last observations also holds true for the North. Here, the educational qualifications of the workforce (as of 1990) are generally low, compared with most of the other UK regions, and the rate of 16-year-olds staying on at school, although rising, is still below national averages. For instance, the shares of those who have GCE O-levels or A-levels are both second lowest in England (17.8% and 19.0% respectively). Furthermore, only 4% of the workforce have participated in higher education without obtaining a degree, which is the bottom of the 'league table'; so is the share of people with a degree, standing at 6.5%. Even in Northern Ireland there is a larger share of the workforce with a degree (8.2%). With regard to the rates of 16-year-olds staying on at school in the North, a considerable increase can be noted between 1981–2 and 1989–90: from 51.5% to 60.0%. Although there were other regions in England with a stronger growth, the differential between the North and the England average narrowed from 5.4 percentage points in 1981–2 to 1.6 percentage points in 1989–90.

To summarize the discussion, it is obvious that with regard to the formal qualifications of their populations both regions, the Ruhr district and the North, are lagging behind national averages and, in particular, the growth areas in the South. This, I wish to stress, cannot be regarded as a sign of a general 'backwardness' of the two areas and their inhabitants. It is, however, a reflection of the specific internal structures of the space economies of the UK and of Germany: different regional economies demand different qualifications, thereby shaping the educational structure of the population in the respective areas. This essentially comprises two aspects. First, this process can be seen as causing the 'indigenous' population to acquire skills, degrees etc. which the production system requires. Secondly, it can be regarded as stimulating migration, because people will be attracted to those areas where their qualifications are in demand. In the cases of the North and the Ruhr district it can therefore be argued that the comparatively low qualification levels are due to the fact that the (traditional) production systems never required very high levels of formal qualifications on the one hand and that, on the other, a certain share of people with high qualifications left the area because they found more appropriate employment conditions elsewhere (preferably in the South).

CONCLUSION

I contend that, with the framework of the current global economic and political situation, the future development of the North-east and the Ruhr district alike will, on the one hand, depend very much on the readiness and the ability of the people in both areas not only to aquire more and more demanding (formal) qualifications but also to accept and adapt to change in general. This thesis is, of course, highly contentious and therefore needs to be elaborated. To begin with, people in both regions *are* used to change. But this change, such as new working practices effected by new technology etc., mainly took place within the traditional industries. What people are confronted with now, however, is the structural nature of change, causing the economic downturn of the traditional industries and thereby cutting back the livelihood of large sections of the population. What is more, the insight into this structural nature of change caused a collective shock that will take time to overcome (Schlieper 1986, 200).[26] However, there is a great danger of the shock and the feeling of powerlessness giving rise to a collective paralysis. Also, I would argue that because of the specific economic and socio-cultural traditions and structures of the North-east and the Ruhr district, there is a lower degree of acceptance of change than elsewhere. For instance, the predominance of large companies – often employing generations (of men) of one family – as well as the state in the labour market has led many to assume a certain continuity of affairs for which the economic framework and the scope for action of the state no longer exist. This socio-culturally embedded, 'taken-for-granted' view of the world is one of the most complex issues to tackle in the process of restructuring. It is an issue that, in particular, the individual has to come to grips with. But it is also a political challenge, forcing policy makers actively to support socio-cultural change. Because, according to the theoretical debate on regional economic trends, the future of OIAs depends greatly on changes in many social and socio-cultural areas, such as the formal qualifications of the workforce, (social) qualifications of employers, the attitudes towards work, technology, education etc., 'regional policy, which used to be geared to the re-distribution and expansion (of economic activities) must change to become a policy of regional change' (IBA 1991, p. 21). To conclude, I think it needs to be pointed out in this context that social and socio-cultural changes, negative as they or their causes may be, are also bearers of new opportunities, opening new and possibly (more) fruitful ways of social interaction.

On the other hand, as much as people need to and might try to adapt to changed conditions, there is an overwhelming case for intervention. If the feeling of being left alone that many people share is not to become or remain the reality, and if social and 'spatial' equality are still social goods with meaning in western European societies, then restructuring processes cannot be left to the chilly words of a 'free' market. I would like to take issue here with Champion (1988, p. 16) who argues that 'the time is therefore right to make a positive effort towards complementing economic development strategies based on the business sector with an approach geared to making the best use of individuals, one element of which is an explicit policy of encouraging migration and making it work for the region'. Although I do not believe that Champion has the industrial transference schemes of the late 1920s in mind, it is hard not to arrive at the conclusion that the unemployment problems of the OIAs could, and in fact should, be solved through the mobility of the workforce. The 'get-on-your-bike' climate of the Thatcher years is hardly an appropriate response to the serious issues raised by economic and social restructuring in OIAs.

With regard to the issue of formal qualifications, it must be pointed out in this context that the need for the people of OIAs to improve or add to their formal qualifications is a necessary condition for restructuring processes to take on (more) positive forms, but it is far from being a sufficient one. There is, at the same time, a strong case for state intervention to stop out-migration if the progress made in the OIAs is not be harvested by the 'escalator regions', like the South-east of England, which attract 'more than a proportional share of the potentially upwardly mobile young adults' (Fielding 1992, p. 1). Of course, in a market economy there will always be migration and this is not a negative phenomenon *per se*. However, I maintain that the material and human costs brought about by the current levels of migration are too high for all the regions involved to be economically sensible or socially acceptable.

It is interesting to note that, in the cases of the North-east and the Ruhr district, state intervention in the recent past was guided by an almost entirely different approach. Whereas, according to Thornley (1991, p. 35), the situation in the UK was characterized by an economic liberal strand on the one hand, 'which comprises monetarist policies, the facilitation of the free market and a desire to reduce state intervention, state enterprise and state expenditure', and a state authoritarianism which was to support the economic liberal position on the other (two of the three pillars on which 'Thatcherism' rested), in North Rhine-Westphalia the state government, which from the mid-1960s onwards has been formed by the Social Democrats (SPD), introduced a number of measures in order to devolve economic policy and spatial planning[27] and also to ensure that larger sections of the population could participate in the decision-making process than had been the case previously. Despite their inherent problems and contradictions,[28] the NRW initiatives can be seen as an important political innovation, an attempt to make the actions of the state more flexible and responsive and also to formally integrate a wide(r) spectrum of interests, thereby acknowledging the complexity of change and the increasing plurality in society. Thus, to my mind, this strategy is a sensitive and prudent way of handling structural change at a time of complex economic restructuring processes and of a diminishing role of individual (nation) states. In essence, this policy is a step forward, while the manner of dealing with structural change which the British government adopted in the 1980s primarily merits harsh criticism.[29]

However, even though this policy seems an appropriate way of handling structural change, the outcome is not at all clear. Neither the economic, the political nor the participatory effects can be judged at this stage. What is more, the future of OIAs is increasingly determined on an international level, which places limits on the scope for action even of national governments. A 'regional policy' for OIAs therefore also needs to be formulated on a higher political level, such as the EU. This issue, however, cannot be dealt with here.

With these last observations we have come full circle to the question posed at the beginning: what will the future of OIAs look like? I do not claim to have a definite or positive answer to this question, but two things, I believe, are quite clear. First, the development trajectories of OIAs will not be determined by any iron laws postulated by the supporters of long waves. As Marshall (1987, p. 228) points out, the 'evolving patterns of uneven regional development are not simply reflections or outcomes of the long waves in the national economy. They are the process of national economic change and development. The succession of leading industrial regions have provided the basis for regional social and political movements which have, at critical moments, contested and to varying degrees determined the ensuing course of national and sometimes international economic development.' Therefore, 'the precise course of these fluctuations is not pre-determined, but is the outcome of social and political conflicts' (Marshall 1987, 225). There is no pre-determined path of (economic) development that an OIA or, in fact, any region has to follow. What the alternatives to a long-wavist scenario, such as the one quoted at the beginning, might look like cannot be elaborated here. Yet I wish to point out that the complexity of current economic, social and political developments has given rise to very different theoretical conceptualizations of structural change[30] (such 'post-Fordism'). The plurality of these theoretical positions alone makes it virtually impossible to predict future development patterns with any accuracy. With regard to the future of OIAs, however, one thing seems to be quite certain: the importance that the traditional industries once held will never be restored.

Secondly, as Ache et al. (1989) and Martin (1989) point out, the positive economic and social trends in the prospering southern regions of Germany and the UK and the consequent growth of socio-spatial disparities in these countries did not just happen, they were actively supported, if not brought about, by the actions of the state(s). Therefore, there is room and scope for political action to benefit OIAs. How much attention will be paid to the 'underdogs' of today is highly dependent on the amount of pressure they exert on the government (see Marshall's argument above) and on the perceived usefulness of these areas for the central power. But state action on behalf of OIAs is not only possible, I maintain that there is also a need for political intervention if the challenge that the divisive nature of current economic, social and political trends constitutes for the legitimation of the state is to be met.

NOTES

1. For a discussion of the term see, for instance, ILS 1988, in which the regions around Pittsburgh (USA) and Glasgow (Scotland) are compared. Another comparative study analyses the situation in the Pittsburgh region, the West Midlands, the Nord-Pas-de-Calais region and the Ruhr (Hesse 1988).
2. For a critical discussion of this hypothesis (with regard to the Ruhr district) see Schlieper 1986.
3. For a concise, yet profound discussion of long-wave theory, the concept of lifecycles and other concepts of regional analysis, see IBA 1991.
4. At present, the importance of so-called soft factors in determining the future of OIAs is impressively demonstrated by the International Building Exhibition (IBA Emscher Park) staged ty the state government of North Rhine-Westphalia in the most problematic subregion of the Ruhr district, the Emscher subdistrict. The Building Exhibition can be seen as a comprehensive renewal strategy whose most interesting impulse, according to Kilper (1992, p. 145, my translation) 'must be seen in necessitating new marketing strategies for "soft" location factors, for the ecological and the visual quality of industrial development sites.'
5. It would, of course, be a rather biased view if the negative developments occurring in the prosperous areas (such as the strain on the infrastructure, the encroachment of 'developments' on green belts or the negative social trends in almost all of the 'inner cities') were left completely unmentioned. Since they are not the topic of this contribution, however, they cannot be dealt with here.
6. This was before local government reorganization.
7. This comes as no surprise because much of the literature on the Ruhr district is published by the KVR.
8. In other parts of the UK and Germany industrialization had already been well underway by this time: the North-west, South Wales, central Scotland (UK) and Oberschlesien (Germany) (Prestwich and Taylor 1990; Schlieper 1986).
9. With the exception of a few old urban centres.
10. In 1893 the *Rheinisch-Westfälische Kohlensyndikat* was established which controlled and marketed 87% of the Ruhr's coal output and which existed until 1945. In 1896 the *Roheisensyndikat* (pig iron syndicate) was to follow (Schlieper 1986, p. 90).
11. For the situation in the North-east, where the NCB successfully obstructed

modernization policies in the coalfield, see Hudson 1989.
12. See Massey 1984.
13. For a detailed discussion see Danielzyk and Wood 1993.
14. All figures taken from or based on Hudson 1989, pp. 171, 191.
15. All figures taken from or based on Petzina 1990, p. 523.
16. All figures taken from or based on Hudson 1989, pp. 171, 191.
17. All figures taken from or based on Robinson n.d., 28.
18. All figures taken from or based on KVR 1992, p. 198.
19. The figures for the Ruhr district used here do not refer to the KVR area, but to the 'agglomeration' named 'Rhein-Ruhr-Nord'. This area is not congruous with the KVR. It covers a larger (rural) hinterland to the south-east (Märkischer Kreis) and to the west (Kleve, Krefeld). Because this agglomeration together with others forms the basis of much of the BfLR's regional analyses, it is used here. In order to avoid confusion, instead of using the term 'Ruhr district', I will from now on either refer to 'Rhein-Ruhr-Nord' or to 'KVR', depending on the data used.
20. If not stated otherwise, data for the German regions in this subsection are taken from Ache et al. 1989, p. 172, and BfLR 1989; data for the UK regions taken from CSO 1991, p. 160.
21. All figures taken from KVR, 1992, p. 249.
22. All figures taken from *Employment Gazette*, September 1991, Tables 2.1, 2.3, 2.4, 2.9.
23. If not stated otherwise, data for the German regions in this subsection is taken from KVR 1992, p. 47 and Ache et al. 1989, p. 164, Table A 6; data for the UK regions taken from OPCS 1992 and CSO 1991, p. 44.
24. See Martin 1989; Smith 1989; Lewis and Townsend 1989; Hudson and Williams 1989.
25. All figures taken from or based on BfLR 1987.
26. The importance of the psychological effects of economic restructuring can be studied in the Ruhr district where the entire closure of the Krupp steelworks in Duisburg-Rheinhausen in August 1993, which made about 2500 people redundant, caused many protests and ensured an abundant media coverage, whereas the intention of the Thyssen management (also in Duisburg) to reduce the workforce by several thousand in 1993 alone almost passed unnoticed.
27. In 1987: *Zukunftsinitiative Montanregionen* ('Initiative for the Future of Coal and Steel Regions'), extra resources: DM1 billion (Kruse 1991, p. 331).
    In 1989: *Zukunftsinitiative für die Regionen Nordrhein-Westfalens*, phase one ('Initiative for the Future of the Regions in North Rhine-Westphalia'), no extra resources (Aring et al. 1989, p. 57ff). In 1990: *Zukunftsinitiative für die Regionen Nordrhein-Westfalens*, phase two, no extra resources (Aring et al. 1989, pp. 57ff).
28. Critics, for instance, contend that the partial devolution of economic policy to influential social groups ('stage-managed corporatism') is a clever way for the central power − in this case the *Land* government − to decentralize conflicts while at the same time retaining the power to set the guidelines for any regional initiative. For this and other points of criticism see Heinze and Voelzkow 1991; Danielzyk 1992.
29. For an extensive critique of economic structural and regional policies as well as 'central state localism', see Lawless 1988, 1989; Ambrose 1986; Thornley 1991; Prigge 1991; Damesick and Wood 1987; Heineberg 1991; Massey 1988; Wren 1990.

30. For a discussion with regard to the North-east see Wood 1991, and with regard to the Ruhr see Danielzyk 1992.

REFERENCES

Ache, P., Ingenmey, F.-J., Kunzmann, K., Bremm, H.-J., Claussen, M., Spiekermann, K., Thiele, A., Kiesslich, B. and Rummel, A. (1989) *Die regionale Entwicklung süddeutscher Verdichtungsräume: Parallelen zum Ruhrgebiet?* Essen: Kommunalverband Ruhrgebiet.

Ambrose, P. (1986) *Whatever Happened to Planning?* London: Methuen.

Aring, J., Butzin, B., Danielzyk, R. and Helbrecht, I. (1989) Krisenregion Ruhrgebiet? Alltag, Strukturwandel und Planung, *Wahrnehmungsgeographische Studien zur Regionalentwicklung*, Heft 8. Oldenburg: Bibliotheks- und Informationssystem der Universität Oldenburg.

Bundesforschungsantalt für Landeskunde und Raumordnung (BfLR) (1987) *Informationen zur Raumentwicklung. Heft 11/12: Aktuelle Daten und Prognosen zur räumlichen Entwicklung. Entwicklungstendenzen von Städten und Stadtregionen.* Bonn: BfLR.

Bundesforschungsanstalt für Landeskunde und Raumordnung (BfLR) (1989) *Informationen zur Raumentwicklung. Heft 11/12: Aktuelle Daten und Prognosen zur räumlichen Entwicklung. Städte und Stadtregionen im Vergleich.* Bonn: BfLR.

Buswell, R.J., Champion, A.G. and Townsend, P.R. (1987) The Northern Region, in Damesick, P.J. and Wood, P. (eds) *Regional Problems, Problem Regions, and Public Policy in the United Kingdom.* Oxford: Oxford University Press, pp. 167–90.

Butzin, B. (1987) Strukturwandel im Ruhrgebiet? Zum Entstehungs- und Wirkungszusammenhang der Krise, in Köhler, E. and Wein, N. (eds) *Natur- und Kulturräume. Ludwig Hempel zum 65. Geburtstag.* Münstersche Geographische Arbeiten Heft 27. Paderborn: Schöningh, pp. 301–14.

Butzin, B. (1990) Regionaler Entwicklungszyklus und Strukturwandel im Ruhrgebiet. Ansätze zur strukturellen Erneuerung? *Zeitschrift für Wirtschaftsgeographie*, 34:208–217.

Byrne, D. (1989) *Beyond the Inner City.* Milton Keynes: Open University Press.

Central Statistical Office (CSO) (ed.) (1991) *Regional Trends 26.* London: HMSO.

Champion, A. (1988) Migration from the North East: the need for a more positive approach, *Northern Economic Review*, 16:9–16.

Damesick, P.J. (1987) Regional economic change since the 1960s, in Damesick, P.J., and Wood, P. (eds) *Regional Problems, Problem Regions, and Public Policy in the United Kingdom.* Oxford: Oxford University Press, pp. 19–41.

Damesick, P.J. and Wood, P.A. (1987) Public policy for regional development: restoration or reformation? in Damesick, P.J. and Wood, P. (eds) *Regional Problems, Problem Regions, and Public Policy in the United Kingdom.* Oxford: Oxford University Press, pp. 260–66.

Danielzyk, R. (1992) Gibt es im Ruhrgebiet eine 'postfordistische Regionalpolitik'? *Geographische Zeitschrift*, 80(2):84–105.

Danielzyk, R. and Wood, G. (1993) Restructuring old industrial and inner urban areas: a contrastive analysis of state policies in Great Britain and Germany, *European Planning Studies*, 1(2):123–47.

Fielding, A.J. (1992) Migration and social mobility: South East England as an escalator region, *Regional Studies*, 26(1):1–15.

Firn, J. (1975) External control and regional development: the case of Scotland, *Environmental and Planning* A, 7(4): 393–414.

Goddard, J.B. and Thwaites, A.T. (1990) Regional economic development in the UK: the case of the Northern Region of England, paper presented to a National Economic Development Office conference on *Regional Policy*. Lumley Castle, Country Durham, March.

Hall, P. (1981) The geography of the Fifth Kondratieff, *New Society*, 535–7.

Hall, P. (1988) The geography of the fifth Kondratieff, in Massey, D. and Allen, J. (eds) *Uneven Re-Development. Cities and Region in Transition. A Reader*. London: Hodder and Stoughton, pp. 51–67.

Heineberg, H. (1983) *Großbritannien*. Stuttgart: Ernst Klett.

Heineberg, H. (1991) Großbritannien. Aspekte der Wirtschafts-, Regional- und Stadtentwicklung in der Thatcher-Ära. *Geographische Rundschau*, 43(1):4–13.

Heinze, R. and Voelzkow, H. (1991) Kommunalverbände und Verbände. Inszenierter Korporatismus auf lokaler und regionaler Ebene? in Heinelt, H. and Wollmann, H. (eds) *Brennpunkt Stadt: Stadtpolitik und lokale Politikforschung in der 80er und 90er Jahren*. Stadtforschung aktuell, Band 31. Basel: Birkhäuser, pp. 187–206.

Hesse, J.J. (1988) *Die Erneuerung alter Industrieregionen. Ökonomischer Strukturwandel und Regionalpolitik im Vergleich*. Baden-Baden: Nomos Verlagsgesellschaft.

Hudson, R. (1989) *Wrecking a Region. State Policies, Party Politics, and Regional Change in North East England*. Studies in Society and Space. London: Pion.

Hudson, R. and Williams, P.M. (1986) *Divided Britain*. London: Belhaven.

Hudson, R. and Williams, P. (1989) *The United Kingdom*. Western Europe Economic and Social Studies. London: Harper & Row.

Institut für Landes- und Stadtenwicklungsplanung des Landes Nordrhein-Westfalen (ILS) (1988) *Altindustrialisierte Gebiete*. Dortmund: ILS Schriften, 12.

Internationale Bauausstellung Emscher Park (IBA) (1991) *Strategien für alte Industrieregionen*. Emscher Park Tagungsberichte, 5. Gelsenkirchen: IBA.

Kilper, H. (1992) *Das Politikmodell IBA Emscher Park. Erfahrungen bei der Implementation der 'Arbeiten im Park'-Projekte*. Gelsenkirchen: Institut für Arbeit und Technik.

Kommunalverband Ruhrgebiet (KVR) (ed.) (1990) *Städte- und Kreisstatistik Ruhrgebiet. Volkszählung*. Essen: KVR.

Kommunalverband Ruhrgebiet (KVR) (ed.) (1992) *Städte- und Kreisstatistik Ruhrgebiet 1992*. Essen: KVR.

Kruse, H. (1991) Eigenständige Regionalentwicklungspolitik im gemeinsamen Binnenmarkt – das Beispiel Nordrhein-Westfalen, in Blotevogel, H.H. (ed.) *Europäische Regionen im Wandel – Strukturelle Erneuerung, Raumordnung und Regionalpolitik im Europa der Regionen*. Duisburger Geographische Arbeiten, Bd. 9. Dortmund: Dortmunder Vertrieb für Bau- und Planungsliteratur, pp. 323–44.

Lawless, P. (1988) British inner urban policy: a review, *Regional Studies* 22(6):531–40.

Lawless, P. (1989) *Britain's Inner Cities*. London: Paul Chapman.

Lewis, J. and Townsend, P. (eds) (1989) *The North–South Divide. Regional Change in Britain in the 1980s*. Liverpool: Paul Chapman.

Marshall, M. (1987) *Long Waves of Regional Development*. Critical Human Geography. Basingstoke: Macmillan.

Martin, R. (1989) The political economy of Britain's north–south divide, in Lewis, J. and Townsend, A. (eds) *The North–South Divide. Regional Change in Britain in the 1980s*. London: Paul Chapman, pp. 20–60.

Massey, D. (1984) *Spatial Divisions of Labour. Social Structures and the Geography of Production*. Critical Human Geography. Basingstoke: Macmillan.

Massey, D. (1988) What's happening to UK manufacturing? in Allen, J. and Massey, D. (eds) *The Economy in Question*. Restructuring Britain. London: Sage, pp. 45–90.

McCord, N. (1979) *North East England. The Region's Development 1760–1960. An economic and social history*. London: Batsford.

Northern Region Councils' Association (NRCA) (ed.) (1986) *The State of the Northern Region 1986*. Newcastle: NRCA.
Office of Population, Censuses and Surveys (1992) *1991 Census. Preliminary Report for England and Wales*. London: HMSO.
Petzina, D. (1990) Wirtschaft und Arbeit 1945–1985, in Köllmann, W., Korte, H., Petzina, P. and Weber, W. *Das Ruhrgebiet*. Düsseldorf: Schwann, pp. 491–567.
Prestwich, R. and Taylor, P. (1990) *Introduction to Regional and Urban Policy in the United Kingdom*. Key Issues in Economics. London: Longman.
Prigge, W.-U. (1991) Wirtschafts- und Sozialpolitik während der Regierung Thatcher. *Aus Politik und Zeitgeschichte* (Beilage zur Wochenzeitschrift Das Parlament) B 28/91: 27–36.
Robinson, F. (1990) *The Great North? A Special Report for BBC North East*. Newcastle: University of Newcastle upon Tyne, Centre for Urban and Regional Development Studies.
Robinson, F. (n.d.) *Economic Prospects for the North*. Newcastle: Centre for Urban and Regional Development Studies.
Rommelspacher, T. (1982) Staat, Montankapital und Ruhrgebiet, in Katalyse Technikergruppe (eds) *Ruhrgebiet – Krise als Konzept*. Bochum: Germinal, pp. 11–53.
Rowntree Research Unit (RRU), University of Durham (1974) Aspects of contradiction in regional policy: the case of North-East England, *Regional Studies* 8:133–44.
Schlieper, A. (1986) *150 Jahre Ruhrgebiet*. Düsseldorf: Schwann.
Schnur, R. (1970) Entwicklung der Rechtsgrundlagen und der Organisation des SVR, in SVR (ed.) *Siedlungsverband Ruhrkohlenbezirk 1920–1970*, Essen: SVR, pp. 9–32.
Smith, D. (1989) *North and South. Britain's Economic, Social and Political Divide*. Harmondsworth: Pelican.
Thornley, A. (1991) *Urban Planning under Thatcherism. The Challenge of the Market*. London: Routledge.
Warren, K. (1972) The North East, in Manners, G., Keeble, D., Rodgers, B. and Warren, K. (eds) *Regional Development in Britain*. London: John Wiley & Sons, pp. 361–86.
Weber, W. (1990) Entfaltung der Industriewirtschaft, in Köllmann, W., Korte, H., Petzina, D. and Weber, W. *Das Ruhrgebiet*. Düsseldorf: Schwann, pp. 199–306.
Wiel, P. (1970) *Wirtschaftsgeschichte des Ruhrgebietes*. Essen: Siedlungsverband Ruhrkohlenbezirk.
Wood, G. (1991) Nordost-England – Umstrukturierungsprozesse an der Peripherie, in Blotevogel, H.H. (ed.) *Europäische Regionen im Wandel – Strukturelle Erneuerung, Raumordnung und Regionalpolitik im Europa der Regionen*. Duisburger Geograpische Arbeiten, Bd.9. Dortmund: Dortmunder Vertrieb für Bau- und Planungsliteratur, pp. 149–68.
Wood, G. (1994) *Die Umstrukturierung Nordostenglands. Wirtschaftlicher Wandel, Alltag und Politik in einer Altindustrieregion*. Dortmund: Dortmunder Vertrieb für Bau- und Planungsliteratur.
Wren, C. (1990) Regional policy in the 1980s, *National Westminster Bank Quarterly Review*, pp. 52–64.

11 Population Mobility and New Industrial Districts: The Case of the 'Third Italy'

FRANCO SALVATORI
Societa Geografica Italiana, Italy

INTRODUCTION

The period of diffuse industrialization in Italy has, since the mid-1970s, been characterized by the creation of particular territorial formations. These have intrigued many researchers, who have been attracted by certain theoretical and practical aspects of the phenomenon (Brusco 1986; Goodman et al. 1989).

Indeed, the fact that in many instances industrial growth has been shown to be profoundly linked to town and country planning and settlement structure, and thereby clearly contradicting the presupposed organizational and dimensional characteristics of the hitherto accepted industrial model, has raised numerous questions about the spontaneous replication of the 'new' model and about the need to revise the theoretical framework, especially in relation to themes and problems of regional development (Stohr 1981; Sweeney 1985).

Having identified rapid rates of industrial growth in the regions of industrialization – especially compared with areas of traditional consolidated industrial development – the question whether, and to what extent, this constitutes an anomaly when compared to the models of geo-economic 'layering'. If it is not anomalous, then consistent elements of an analytical framework must be sought, capable of providing a coherent interpretation both of cyclical economic trends and – even more importantly – of the future structural transformation of the relationship between industry and territory, and more generally between productive and regional systems (Pyke et al. 1990).

Taking the Italian case as a point of departure, it is well known that conflicting schools of thought sustained by research into the basic tendencies governing changes in the creation of industrial areas, polarizing around Fordist and post-Fordist models of territorial organization, have found common ground when it comes to defining the conditions of local economic development. This tends to lean towards a multi-regional model. The key to interpreting the latter is

People, Jobs and Mobility in the New Europe. Edited by Hans H. Blotevogel and Anthony J. Fielding.
© 1997 European Science Foundation. Published in 1997 by John Wiley & Sons Ltd.

most simply expressed by the Marshallian concept of external economies. (Stohr 1981; Sweeney 1985).

Viewed in this light, Marshall's definition of the industrial district (1920), goes beyond its role as a concrete examination of the spatial organization of production; rather it is elevated to the status of a general model used to interpret the relationship between the organization of economic factors and environmental conditions. In fact, in the Italian case, territorial aspects of economic development are articulated in a complex set of local systems of which only a part may be clearly defined as industrial districts, but which, when taken together, display largely the same characteristics (Sforzi, 1989).

The organization of production based on the integration of a large number of businesses in any one area appears to be much more widespread than commonly thought and certainly does not apply exclusively to the regions of north-east and central Italy. Furthermore, the socio-economic territorial concept which underlies the notion of the industrial district and supports a model of local economic development has its negative counterpart in those parts of the country with regressive or non-dynamic rates of economic change.

In the Italian Mezzogiorno, it is this diffuse development which provides us with the frame of reference best suited to analyse the rocesses underway. The overall process of regional development in the Mezzogiorno, even taking into account the varying levels of scale at which economic development is expressed, is fundamentally connected to the mechanisms of spatial distribution of innovations in social attitudes and to the establishment of a new type of entrepreneurship, for the most part self-generating (Antonelli 1987; Zeitlin 1990).

With this in mind, it seems significant, even though contradictory signals abound, that in the Italian Mezzogiorno during the 1980s, in the manufacturing sectors of the metal and mechanical industries – where there is a higher incidence of innovation during the product cycle – the rate of expansion of businesses exceeds the Italian national average and is equalled only in some of the more dynamic regions of the 'Third Italy'.

Within the loose framework outlined above, the industrial districts become model expressions of the territorial restructuring which found its first and most significant origins in the Third Italy, but which now relates to a wider area and is also matched by analagous situations in different European regions.

THE INDUSTRIAL DISTRICTS

The phenomenon of industrial districts is most widespread in the regions of north-east Italy, although these same districts have been modified from their original form by an evolutionary process which will probably engender similar transformations elsewhere. For this reason it is worthwhile pausing to consider how these changes influence processes of population mobility.

In fact, the fundamental characteristics of this kind of industrial development remain intact, specifically their role as a geographically defined productive system composed of numerous organizational elements of production factors all concerned with different operational phases, but all contributing towards a uniform type of finished product. Also preserved is the method of system organization which generates a high degree of both interdependence and contrast between the elements. This process guarantees a sufficiently high degree of agglomeration and unusual synergy between the productive and the socio-cultural systems, so as to generate genuine initiatives in the locality. Finally, but not of least importance, a degree of flexibility operates both in the restricted environment of the productive apparatus and in the wider context of social organization. This flexibility has formed the basis for increased competition between different forms of territorial organization (Maruani 1989).

This said, however, the Marshallian industrial districts of north-east and central Italy, and more generally the industrialized areas within the same confines, are bound to break ranks and follow different evolutionary paths because of their intrinsically differentiated nature and their consequent reliance on their contextual environment.

On a global scale, the changes appear to revolve around the following specifications: (i) an extraordinary acceleration of innovatory processes in the production cycle and products; (ii) a marked increase in the integration of markets in relation to sectorial levels and types of product, and also to the spaces involved; (iii) a recentralization of the command functions in the larger cities and a decisive post-industrial requalification of the metropolitan areas; (iv) a resumtion of the strategic importance of territorial infrastructure. These specifications have all to a greater or lesser extent affected the Italian economic space (Camagni 1987).

On a local level, clearly, the range of tendencies in the modification of environmental conditions is as vast as the number of places where localized development is taking place within districts, and therefore each one must be dealt with separately. However, of the copious research carried out in this field, the recurrent theme consists of a three-pronged integration model (Balloni 1990; Bramanti 1991) based on: *territorial relations*, with a view to increasing the overall performance of the productive apparatus: *productive sectors*, aiming at restricting extreme forms of specialization and responding to economic crises by diversifying the supply; *relations between companies* in order to obtain management/worker synergy and improve political relations, commercialization, access to services etc. Generally present too, alongside persistent aspects of the informal economy, are signs of emergence from the submerged economy and a wish for representation on a managerial and institutional level.

The results are those already mentioned above. In general these may be summarized as the progressive formation of more stable and structured industrial districts, even in geographical contexts, for example those in the south of Italy, which are not generally associated with the phenomenon. And all this in the face of a complex division of developmental processes which – according to

CENSIS (1991) – consists of at least four types: areas of formation and development, of stabilization, of post-localism and of micro-systems.

With respect to the overall organization and individual sectors of micro-systems, there remains a fairly clear expression of territorial continuity with the wider regional context. However, for the other three types, a more strategic policy of inter-district integration may be defined which, while not altering the local nature of industrial development, lays the basis of interdependence on a supra-local and regional scale.

This is true for those districts (for example Prato) which have reached the final stage of post-localism and in which, beyond a tendency towards sectoral despecialization with an enrichment of the product mix, there is a growth in the average size of firm and a concentrated development of production services which reinstates localized schemes based on a hierarchical organization of the territory.

But the integrative element also applies to districts of more recent formation and development (for example the area of Casarano in the 'heel' of Italy or Salento) and to those in the stabilization phase (for example the area of Fermo in the Marche region), where a strong element of specialization persists alongside an expanding services sector with a market tendency towards territorial diffusion, which reinstates the localistic and localized model analagous to that already experienced in industry. On the whole the Italian experience of district-based industrialization displays a more complex and mature aspect than that of the pioneering days of diffuse industrialization in the 1970s and early 1980s. There also appears to be a higher degree of integration between sectors and areas than in the previous phase.

TERRITORIAL ORGANIZATION

Within the framework already described, above all in the initial phase, district-based industrial development implies a territorial organization founded on the tendency towards production innovation and the system of local values. Taken to its logical conclusion, this results in a continuity between, on the one hand, inherited systems of organization and their transformation and on the other, the maintenance of a dynamic equalibrium between vertical and horizontal structures which permeate the organization of territory.

In particular, it has been noted that, even where the industrial process has caused major restructuring and is firmly rooted, a degree of integration has been achieved between agriculture and industrial production. The two tend to complement each other, rather than industry subordinating agriculture as was the case with traditional forms of industrialization based on size and concentration. In the case of district-based industrialization as experienced in the Third Italy, there has never been a divorce between industrial areas and agricultural ones. In fact, one even talks about 'rural industrialization' (Fuà and Zacchia,

1983). In the same way, there has never been a real divorce between urban and rural areas, nor between towns and countryside.

The resulting territorial organization may be expressed as an equilibrium between residential and productive structures. This equilibrium also exists within the context of the respective settlement systems, with necessary repercussions concerning the relational system. Rural spaces have in fact been profoundly permeated by urban values, while the towns have been able to increase their efficiency without increasing in size, by relying on a solid network of economic, cultural and social relations with their hinterlands (Celant 1988).

The urban fabric on the other hand, due to the fact that it is based on a network of small and medium-sized centres, has been able to develop an organizational system capable of enhancing the productivity of the territory by means of the functional specialization of its constituent elements and the creation of polycentric urban-regional structures based on a super-local scale.

Consequently, the territorial organization, which was the basis of the transformation of productive structures in the Third Italy, has not needed to undergo restructuring except for a partial redistribution of the population settlement pattern in the area which was inherited from the evolutionary economic process of the pre-industrial concentration in the north-west of Italy, nor in the marginal areas of the Mezzogiorno, where the mechanisms of both inter- and intra-regional redistribution of the population has been a mass phenomenon.

This latter phenomenon does not affect the Third Italy even during the most intensive phase of industrial growth, above all because of the perfect correlation between the business initiatives and the local conditions of the labour market. Social, cultural and territorial integration between the entrepreneurial segment and the labour segment of the same human complex will be achieved, not just because of their complementary interests in the informal economy, nor because of their interchangeable nature, nor even in the spatial-temporal and sectorial flexibility of their relationship, but because of a real spatial formation which is closely identified with the local space.

For this reason, economic costs connected with restructuring of the settlement pattern were reduced. Also reduced were the social benefit costs incurred in the restructuring process. At the same time the endogenous competition of supply factors and subsequently of demand factors was maximized, with the increasing need for social adaptation in the face of the new production system (Maruani 1989).

DEMOGRAPHIC TRENDS

During the 1950s the main demographic features of the Third Italy (Trentino-Alto Adige, Veneto, Friuli-Venezia Giulia, Emilia-Romagna, Tuscany, Umbria and Marche) were strong inter-regional movements of the population. These were either for circumstantial reasons, for example the post-war redefinition of the eastern border or the catastrophic floods in the Po Delta; or they were for structural reasons, for example the elimination of pockets of unemployment or underemployment in the agricultural sector. By the 1960s, however, this phenomenon was already substantially modified, especially when compared with other spatial formations in Italy.

During the 1970s when the qualitative and quantitative trends of diffuse economic development in central Italy began to establish themselves, the demographic trend was determined in equal measure by its indigenous components (births and deaths) and also by migration, with the former bearing slightly more weight than the latter, usually producing population growth (Salvatori 1974).

The phenomeon was progressively reinforced during the 1970s, when the model of diffuse industrialization had ample opportunity to assert itself fully and to demonstrate its capacity to resist and react to the crisis which was hitting the industrial apparatus of the traditional core industrial regions and marginal areas. The crisis limited significantly inter-regional population mobility between core and marginal areas, to the point where it constituted a catalyst for structural inversion, unable however to stem the demograhic flux originating in the marginal areas (Berg et al. 1982; Dematteis and Petsimeris 1989). Demographic growth in the Mezzogiorno, in particular, in centres with more than 50000 inhabitants, tended to be higher than in the rest of Italy where centres of the same size showed negative growth (Salvatori 1983).

During the same period, furthermore, net natural population increase in the Third Italy declined in conformity with the general tendencies registered throughout the country, but in the case of Third Italy the decline seemed much faster, above all in relation to birth-rate statistics which were reduced both by the ageing population and fewer births. Compared to an annual natural population growth which in 1971 was 4 per thousand, just above that for the north-western regions (3.8) and 6.7 per thousand lower than that in the Mezzogiorno, by 1981 growth had fallen below zero to –1.7 per thousand: a figure slightly lower than that registered in the north-west (–1.6) and even further behind the figure for the Mezzogiorno compared to a decade previously, even though the latter had fallen to 5.4 (Tinacci Mossello 1986).

The demographic depression in the regions of the Third Italy sunk even lower during the 1980s, reaching –3.4 per thousand in 1991 and falling to 8.3 points behind the Mezzogiorno, which at the time stood at 4.9. The gap had also widened with the figures for the north-west (–2.4). Consequently during the last decade, in the face of expansion and stabilization of the industrial fabric and of the productive apparatus as a whole, the territorial structure of the Third Italy has had somehow to revise its relationship with the local population components, at least regarding the labour factor and the possibility of exhausting the local supply.

The consistent natural draining of the population (a drop of approximately 300000 between the inter-census years 1981–91) has been partially compensated for by a positive migratory balance (+260000) during the same period, which has reduced the population loss and which appears more significant when compared to the situation in the north-west where, in addition to a negative natural population growth of −345000, there is a negative migratory balance of −41000 units. In the Mezzogiorno the population gained 1220000 by natural increase while losing 855000 through migration.

The Third Italy is therefore changing from an area where immigration balances emigration to an area of net immigration; in fact into the only macro-region in Italy to have a positive migratory balance: a combination of inter-regional population flows and inward international migration (Cochrane and Vining 1988).

With this in mind, taking the index 100 to represent 8.8 foreigners officially resident in Italy per 1000 inhabitants registered in the 1991 census, the index for the Mezzogiorno is 67, that of the north-west is 99, but in Third Italy the index rises to 154. This index would probably have to be revised in the light of the substantial clandestine presence of immigrants, principally in the large metropolitan areas of the Mezzogiorno and north-west, but it nevertheless reveals a by no means negligible phenomenon of reduction of the self-adjusting characteristics of the territorial model in Third Italy.

CONCLUSION

So far this model appears to be conserving certain of its constituent elements, especially relating to the basic relationship between settlement and territory and therefore between residence, production and overall spatial organization. However, it is necessary to highlight the 1991 census results which revealed that in the settlement areas in Third Italy, the phenomenon of decentralization has been further accentuated. The quota of people resident in the provincial capitals diminished by 3 percentage points with respect to 1981, now standing at 27.9%. This variation was analagous to the north-west of Italy and not too much higher than that in the Mezzogiorno. This figure must nevertheless be analysed taking into account the following factors: the low figures given for those leaving the centres, a consistent overall increase in the population, and the already small to medium size of the centres.

The 1991 census shows that 23 centres in the Third Italy have between 50000 and 100000 inhabitants (that is 27% of the Italian total), with a population growth of over 7% compared to 1981, equal now to 28% of the national total. This latter figure is 2 points lower than that measured in centres of over 100000 inhabitants, whose overall population has reduced over the decade by almost 11%, that is of the same order as centres in the north-west (14%) and almost twice the figures in the Mezzogiorno.

At present, due to the increase in the size of small to medium centres (50–100000) and the reduction of those in the medium to large centres (100–250000), settlements of 50–250000 in the Third Italy house about 75% of the urban population, that is those who live in centres with over 50000 inhabitants. This figure is significantly different from those of north-west Italy (39%) and of the south (45%), and even more so since the values registered in 1981 were 69%, 38% and 42% respectively (Vitali 1992).

It seems possible, therefore, based on the preceding figures, to trace an evolutionary framework of population mobility in the Third Italy based on the central elements of the development model. Also relevant are the patterns of territorial transformation modelled on the phenomenon of diffuse industrialization, including the phenomenon of industrial districts in their role as the main driving factor behind the overall model.

The full entry of Third Italy into the final stage described by the demographic transition model (Chesnais 1986), characterized by the quantitative stability of the population with birth rates barely keeping abreast of the mortality rate, will feed and strengthen the previously demonstrated propensity to absorb immigrants.

The quantitative population level guaranteed by immigration appears in fact to serve to maintain the functionality of the productive system, which is organized around diffuse industrialization and industrial districts as an essential prerequisite for the vitality and flexibility of the labour market. Furthermore, the tightening of the labour supply would be much more limiting if, as well as a quantitative view, one also took a qualitative view of the population, derived from modifications in demographic structure, the rise in wage expectations, the changes in cultural attitudes relating to generational change and to the receding traditional values of the small city and its urbanized countryside.

Immigration serves to limit internal mobility and maintains a stable balance in settlement patterns, since it is the influx of foreign migrants which compensates for the lower natural increase of the indigenous population. Similarly, it ensures a high level of efficiency in the formation of economic and territorial spaces, globally considered, and an increased level of integration which, for all identifiable territorial typologies in the Third Italy, except for the case of micro-systems, represents the adaptational and evolutionary condition necessary for growth and change. This applies in particular to the districts in developmental and stabilization stages, where the small and medium size of the structures, the productive specialization and the diffuse nature of the fabric of services maintain intact a level of flexibility and integration of the demographic, productive and territorial systems.

On the other hand, in post-localist areas and in some cases in micro-systems, this flexibility is impaired (or is not particularly necessary, as in the case of micro-systems). In addition, centralization seems to assume a dominant role (starting with production services), and immigration from outside and also inter-regional flows seem to repeat the patterns of the centro–periphery model where rigidity and precariousness are two sides of the same coin.

The future challenge of Third Italy and its model of economic and special development hang on this possible bifurcation which both originates and terminates in the demographic field.

REFERENCES

Antonelli, C. (1980) *New Information Technologies and Industrial Organisation: Experiences and Trends in Italy.* Paris: OCDE.

Balloni, V. (1990) *Processi di aggiustamento delle industrie negli anni Ottanta.* Bologna: Il Mulino.

Berg (van den), L., Drewett, R., Klaassen, L.H., Rossi, A. and Vijverberg, C.H.T. (1982) *Urban Europe. A Study of Growth and Decline.* Oxford: Pergamon.

Bramanti, A. (1991) *Il modello dello sviluppo endogeno interrelato*, Rivista Economica del Mezzogiorno. Bologna: Il Mulino, pp. 291–315.

Brusco, S. (1986) Small firms and industrial districts: the experience of Italy, in Keeble, D. and Wever, E. (eds) *New Firms and Regional Development.* London: Croom Helm.

Camagni, R. (1987) *The Spatial Implications of Technological Diffusion and Economic Restructuring in Europe, with Special Reference to the Italian Case.* Paris: OCDE.

Celant, A. (ed.) (1988) *Nuova città e nuova campagna.* Bologna: Pàtron Editore.

CENSIS (1991) *Quale futuro per il localismo. Materiali per una rilettura dello sviluppo diffuso.* Roma: CENSIS.

Chesnbais, J.C. (1986) *La transition démographique.* Paris: PUF.

Cochrane, S.G. and Vining, D.R. (1988) *Recent trends in migration between core and peripheral regions in developed and advanced developing countries*, International Regional Science Review, 11(3), pp. 215–43.

Dematteis, G. and Petsimeris, P. (1989) *Counterurbanization as a transitional phase in settlement reorganization*, in Champion, A.G. (ed.) *Counterurbanization. The Changing Face and Nature of Population Deconcentration.* London: Edward Arnold.

Fuà, G. and Zacchia, C. (eds) (1983) *Industrializzazione senza fratture.* Bologna: Il Mulino.

Goodman, E., Bamford, J. and Saynor, P. (eds) (1989) *Small Firms and Industrial Districts in Italy.* London: Routledge.

Marshall, A. (1920) *Principles of Economics.* London: Macmillan.

Maruani, M. (ed.) (1989) *La flexibilité en Italie.* Paris: Syros.

Pyke, F., Becattini, G. and Sengenberger, W. (eds) (1990) *Industrial Districts and Inter-firm Co-operation in Italy.* Geneva: Institute for Labour Studies.

Salvatori, F. (1974) Movimento sociale e dinamica demografica nelle province italiane (1961–71), *Notiziario di Geografia Economica*, 3–4, pp. 32–7.

Salvatori, F. (1983) Recenti tendenze nel processo di crescita della rete urbana italiana: analisi allometrica, *XXIII Congresso Geografico Italiano*, Catania: AGeI.

Sforzi, F. (1989) The geography of Industrial districts in Italy, in Goodman, E. (ed.) *Small Firms and Industrial Districts in Italy.* London: Routledge.

Stohr, W. (1981) Development from above or below?, in Stohr, W. and Taylor, D.R.F. (eds) *The Dialectis of Regional Planning in Developing Countries.* Chichester: John Wiley & Sons.

Sweeney, G.P. (1985) *Innovation Entrepreneurs and Regional Development.* London: Francis Pinder.

Tinacci Mosello, M. (1986) La mobilità territoriale della popolazione in Italia: tendenze, prospettive, possibilità di intervento, *Rivista Geografica Italiana*, 3, pp. 285–98.

Vitali, O. (ed.) (1992) *Cambiamenti demografici e urbanizzazione.* Napoli: Edizioni Scientifiche Italiane.

Zeitlin, J. (1990) The Third Italy: inter-firm cooperation and technological innovation, in Murray, R. (ed.) *Technology Strategies and Local Economic Intervention.* Nottingham: Spokesman Books.

12 Internal Migration and the Business Cycle: The Example of West Germany

FRANZ-JOSEF KEMPER
Humboldt-Universität, Germany

INTRODUCTION

Since the early 1970s, the volume of internal migrations in West Germany has shown a declining trend which continued until the end of the 1980s, when the dramatic political changes in central and eastern Europe involved a striking increase in immigration to the FRG and indirectly, by redistribution within the country, a rise of internal migrants. However, this decline was by no means uniform; the rate of decline increased in the periods of economic recession in 1974–5 and 1981–2 and slowed down during the expansion phases of the trade cycle. The question therefore arises of whether and in which manner the business cycle has an influence on internal migration. This problem is the subject of the present chapter.

Theoretical arguments for and against close relationships between migration and cyclical fluctuations of business activities will be introduced, and the role of regional differences in reaction to these oscillations will be discussed. The second part of the chapter tries to give an overview of the literature concerning the relationships in question and of important results. Because the literature is rather fragmentary, there is a need for more empirical work and some results of such empirical analyses for West Germany will then be represented. After dealing with gross migration from a national perspective, the regional reactions to the business cycle are finally analysed in more detail by studying net migration.

NATIONAL AND REGIONAL RESPONSES OF MIGRATIONS TO THE BUSINESS CYCLE

One of the classical arguments for explaining the temporal variability of migrations in industrialized countries refers to the relationship between migration and the trade cycle. Cyclical fluctuations in the level of investment give rise to variations in business activities and in national income. This results in a

People, Jobs and Mobility in the New Europe. Edited by Hans H. Blotevogel and Anthony J. Fielding.
© 1997 European Science Foundation. Published in 1997 by John Wiley & Sons Ltd.

changing demand for labour and can effect wages. During the boom phases numerous new jobs are created. These vacancies on the labour market of a region can be filled by job-seeking people residing in the region or by immigrants, who can be separated into international and inter-regional migrants. If only the last-mentioned group of migrants is considered and if it is assumed that there are regional differences in economic growth, on the basis of neoclassical theory and on the premises of full employment it must be expected that the volume of inter-regional migrants should rise during an expansion period and that the migration flows will be oriented to the regions of economic growth, with vacancies on the labour market and high wages. On the contrary, in periods of recession the supply of jobs will decline, therefore the volume of migration will decrease and unemployment rise. Moreover, the migration directions preferred particularly during the boom will decline substantially and return migrations can be expected from the former regions of growth to regions with low costs of living.

Such relationships between the business cycle and migration volume as well as migration direction can be observed in Germany time and again. Thus it could be shown for the period of industrialization in the German Empire between 1880 and the First World War that the in-migrations to the cities as growth areas of that time regularly increased in phases of economic booms and declined during recessions (Langewiesche 1977). In the FRG particularly international migrations during the period of guestworker migrations clearly depended on economic fluctuations. At times of economic expansion foreign workers were recruited, whereas in recession periods many of the immigrants returned to their country of origin, partly provided for by financial incentives for their return.

If one turns to the internal migrations in West Germany during the last few decades, it must, however, be expected that the connections with the business cycle could be changed and obscured by intervening factors. To discuss such factors of influence we shall refer to some theoretical arguments and concepts which have been proposed in the literature for analysing recent internal developments in western industrialized countries.

First, effects of the housing market should be considered, especially concerning constraints on migration. For the UK it has been argued (Muellbauer 1990) that an upswing in the economy results in speculative investments in housing and an increase of house prices with distinct regional variations. Particular high increases are typical of affluent growth regions such as south-east England which embraces metropolitan London. The effects are constraints on in-migrations, just in the regions of economic growth. Therefore, the migration flows to these regions otherwise expected in boom periods cannot be realized, e.g. migration to south-east England in the 1980s. Even if stressing the housing market as the most important causal factor for the reduced volume of migration has been rightly criticized (see Fielding 1993), housing market developments can influence the possibilities for in-migration. In Germany the distribution of tenure is, indeed, different from the UK, as in the metropolitan areas privately rented dwellings dominate[1] and owner-occupation status falls behind, but the rents in some attractive agglomerations have been so high in the last two decades that they figure as barriers to in-migration. In the 1980s it has often been complained in the region of Munich that jobs in public services with lower qualifications could not be filled because the costs of housing were too high for family migrants. Since in phases of economic expansion the rents and housing costs often grow rapidly, the housing market may then cause special constraints for in-migrations to urban areas.

A second intervening and important factor is the restructuring of the economy and its effects on the job market. It is well known that, apart from the business cycles with a wavelength of about 8 to 10 years, further economic fluctuations exist with different wavelengths. Except for short-term cycles, these are long swings in building construction and in other infrastructure with 15–25 years (Kuznets cycle) and very long waves with a complete cycle length of about half a century (Kondratieff cycle). Such very long waves gave rise to the recent restructuring of the economy, the characteristics of which are the decline of the 'old industries', reindustrialization and the growth of parts of the tertiary sector. The transition to new forms of the economy is connected with a changing spatial division of labour, but also with high unemployment, especially of manual workers of the old industries. Since the early 1970s, the rate of unemployment in (West) Germany had strikingly increased in each recession phase, but could be reduced in the following expansion phases only in small amounts. This rise was high in the recessions of 1975 and 1982 and is again high in the current recession of 1993. Apparently, the new jobs which could be created during the recent upswings of the period of restructuring demand qualifications which can only partly be matched with the qualifications of the unemployed. On the other hand, many vacancies in the manufacturing sector or in the sector of personal services can be filled with job-seeking people from the region. This means for inter-regional migrations that in phases of economic upswing moves of manual workers should be strongly reduced in comparison with former expansion phases of the business cycle. Against that, the migrations of highly skilled employees should be numerous further on. The theory of search and transaction costs for migrations or other choice processes postulates a positive relationship between education and the information density for long-distance migrations which could often be approved empirically (Boersch-Supan 1989). Therefore, one can assume that inter-regional migrations of well-educated and qualified persons will still co-vary with the business cycle, whereas the mobility of the low qualified has slowed down.

However, a third factor comprising social and cultural attitudes and values should also have affected the mobility reduction of highly qualified segments of the population. Particularly relevant are attitudinal changes in the direction of a 'post-materialistic life style', for which the so far central position of work is reduced and ties to social networks, as well as regional and local affinities, become more important. Moreover, changing gender relations characterize this change of values which among others has brought about a rising female employment rate in (West) Germany. This should not be interpreted as sign of a rising dominance of work within the life course of women but as an attempt to reach a satisfying equilibrium between the different life domains (work, family, leisure). In any case, the increase of female employment has contributed to a decrease of inter-regional migrations of couples, since it is more difficult to get two new suitable jobs than just one.

The result of all these arguments is that the propensity of inter-regional migrations should have declined during the last decades and that possible relationships between migrations and the business cycle could weaken. Until now only developments within a whole country have been discussed, not regional differences of migration directions. Concerning these directions, it has often been argued that during the expansion phases people migrate to cities and urbanized areas with economic growth, whereas during economic downturns there is much return migration to the rural areas of origin with rather low costs of living. Recently, this thesis has been taken up in the context of discussing the causes of the process of counterurbanization which could be observed in many western industrialized countries in the 1970s. According to this 'recession theory', the migration turnaround from metropolitan to rural areas is a short-term phenomenon which is typical of a recession phase. After the economy recovers, the net migration flows will again turn their direction and the concentration process of urbanization will continue (see Kontuly and Bierens 1990). Therefore, it is postulated that the net migration of rural areas will show a countercyclical relationship to economic trends, while the net migration of urbanized areas will react pro-cyclically. This thesis has been rather controversially discussed within the extensive literature on the causes of counterurbanization, which cannot be presented here, and remains controversial even if during the 1980s in many countries a 'turnaround of the turnaround' could be observed. In any case, the influences of the above-mentioned processes of economic restructuring and value changes must be considered so that simple monocausal relationships between migration and recession should not be expected.

REVIEW OF THE LITERATURE

In this part of the chapter empirical results will be presented on the relationships between business cycle and migration propensity as well as migration flows. It may be surprising that there is a very limited amount of scientific work which has analysed systematically such relationships on an empirical basis, although corresponding hypotheses have often been formulated. So one of the leading experts in (economic) migration research, M.J. Greenwood, has recently noted, as an editor of several survey articles on migration, that 'perhaps in large part because little time-series have been available on internal migration, the relationship between national and regional business cycles and migration has almost never been explored' (Greenwood 1993, p. 296). Since Canada disposes of one of the world's best time-series data on internal migration, Milne (1993), in one of the survey articles, used inter-provincial migration data from Canada between 1962 and 1990 and analysed effects of the business cycle by correlating migration rates with real gross domestic product (GDP). The author could explore effects of the national trade cycle as well as influences of regional cycles on migration by taking the provincial GDP. In respect of migration data, net migration as well as in- and out-migration rates were analysed. Although no elaborate techniques for time-series were used, relationships between inter-provincial migration and the business cycle could be demonstrated for the selected Canadian provinces. It was shown, first, that the correlations between net migration rates and growth rates of national GDP were clearly lower (mostly about 0.20) than the coefficients with provincial GDP (between 0.3 and 0.5). Secondly, in-migration rates reacted pro-cyclically, whereas in some cases out-migration rates showed countercyclical effects, particularly in the economically dominating province of Ontario from which return migration flows could be observed to peripheral provinces during recessions. There were, thirdly, striking parallels between the long-term trends of growth rates of real GDP and of total migration rates. Therefore, the interpretation of this author is that the trend of declining migration can at least partly be reduced to the deceleration of economic growth.

Also for Germany there are only a few studies of the relationship between migration and the business cycle. An article by Ludaescher (1986) concentrates on the connections between GDP and international migrations, as well as the influence of the housing market on intra-regional mobility. Inter-regional migrations were not considered. The most detailed work on the influence of the trade cycle on internal migrations in (West) Germany was published by Birg et al. (1983). The authors studied the migrations between the federal states during the 1960s and 1970s. First of all, they could establish a clear relationship between gross migration and the growth rates of the national GDP. A simple linear regression model showed that a GDP change of 1% effected a stronger change of gross migration of 1.3%. Moreover, they analysed the migration flows between the states by means of measures of the intensity of interaction and compared the values in phases of upswing and downturn. Altogether there was a strong stability of spatial interactions, but the values of neighbouring states were often higher in recessions than in economic expansion phases. During an upswing, so the authors conclude, the regional distribution of job vacancies is wider than in recessions, therefore migrants have a better choice and may select more distant opportunities. Thus migration distances should react pro-cyclically to the business cycle.

The migrations between the states of the FRG were studied further by Haag et al. (1988) within the framework of a dynamic migration model. The time-series of 'global mobility' representing the volume of migration in the period 1960 to 1983 could statistically be explained by two cyclical variables and two

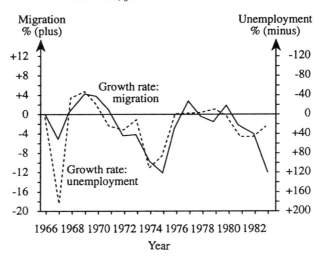

Figure 12.1. The relationship between rate of change in unemployment and in inter-regional migration 1966–83 (Source: Franz 1989)

non-cyclical ones. The conjunctural fluctuations were represented by the rate of vacancies in the labour market (with a time-lag of two years) and, more importantly, by an investment structure index which is an early indicator of the business cycle. With the two other variables the trend of decreasing mobility could be modelled. The first is the real income per capita as an indicator of living standard. It was argued that rising living standards result in a growing proportion of home owners and investments in the dwelling, both reducing mobility. The second variable of total employment was interpreted as an indicator of the growth of two-earner households. Because of the problem of finding two vacant jobs simultaneously, inter-regional migration of a household with two earners, mostly husband and wife, may be rather difficult. Since female employment rose considerably in the last decades, these problems must have grown during that period. Incidentally, a similar trend of decreasing migration rates can be observed since about 1970 in many industrialized countries (see Long 1991).

The trend of declining mobility since the early 1970s in West Germany is connected with a trend of rising unemployment. Particularly in the 1980s structural unemployment became more and more important alongside cyclical unemployment. Following the arguments of neoclassical theory, the unemployed should be mobile if they have the chance to get a job in another region. But what can be shown empirically is a negative relationship between the rates of change in unemployment and in inter-regional migration (Figure 12.1). With rising unemployment the mobility went down. By means of a refined time-series technique and causal tests, Franz (1989) could demonstrate that the migration rate reacts with a time lag of one year on the change of unemployment rate.

Therefore, a worsening employment situation seemingly effects a decrease in mobility.

However, in the 1980s many new vacancies in the labour market were created in connection with the restructuring of the economy. So it has been estimated that in 1986 West Germany had 2.1 million unemployed but 500000 vacancies. In recent times it has been very much discussed whether the reduced mobility resulted in a 'regional mismatch' between vacancies and unemployed workers. However, the hypothesis that a growing migration rate could reduce unemployment is not confirmed by recent analyses (Boersch-Supan 1990) because of the sectoral composition of the unemployed. Nevertheless, the relationship between unemployment and vacancies measured by the 'Beveridge curve' changed considerably in the 1980s (see Franz and Siebeck 1992).

Apart from such analyses on migration and unemployment,[2] there are very few studies which consider the regional differentiation of business cycle and migration in West Germany. Particularly in the 1970s several studies in the German-speaking countries showed that there were striking regional differences in the amplitudes of the business cycle (e.g. Eckey 1978, Nowotny 1976). While some regions showed only low cyclical fluctuations, in others strong ups and downs could be observed. This can be reduced, on the one hand, to the sectoral composition of the regional economy (structural effect), on the other hand to specific conditions of the location (locational effect). Whereas economic sectors such as agriculture, public services and administration show only weak reactions to the business cycle, capital goods and durable goods industries are often heavily dependent on economic oscillations. Because of their structural compositions, many urbanized areas with a relatively high proportion of manufacturing, but rural industrial areas also show strong cyclical reactions. This was strengthened in rural regions by the creation of industrial branch plants which have often been the first to dismiss their workers during a recession (see Gerlach and Liepmann 1972). Locational factors are particularly important in metropolitan areas with economic growth in expansion periods, when an ample supply of qualified workers and good infrastructure represent important pre-conditions for an economic upturn (Nowotny 1976). Such regional differences in cyclical reactiveness should have effects on migrations. This was studied by Koch (1977) using the example of the recession of 1974–5. Concerning inter-regional migrations, he could, however, observe only weak reactions to the business cycle. The disparities between the urbanized areas with in-migration and rural areas with preponderant out-migration seemed to be essentially preserved during the recession, even if the regional differences in net migration became lower and in some peripheral regions out-migrations declined. Yet this decrease was not brought about by improved labour-market conditions of the periphery, but by the lower opportunities to get jobs for unqualified workers in other regions.

The problem may be particularly interesting if such differences between urbanized and rural areas which were established during the 1970s are valid later, or if the tendencies of counterurbanization, which have been observed in the FRG especially since the late 1970s (Kontuly and Vogelsang 1988), changed the relationships. The chapter will now present some empirical results concerning these questions.

GROSS MIGRATION AND THE BUSINESS CYCLE

The presentation of our empirical results for West Germany begins with potential relationships between the volume of internal migrations and the economic cycle. For that purpose, the annual migrations between the 11 federal states were used for the period 1960–88. Most of these migrations are inter-regional and it can be assumed that many of the migrants have economic motives. For the cyclical fluctuations an indicator must be selected from a whole set of possible measures which have been proposed in the literature. Such indicators can be distinguished by their leads or lags with the cycle. 'Leading indicators' prematurely announce turns of the economic trend, 'coincidental indicators' take a parallel course to the cycle and 'lagging indicators' lag behind. The second group of coincidental indicators is built particularly by measures of the national income and of the labour market, which should also be important for migrations. As a first indicator, therefore, the real GDP was selected, followed by the number of the gainfully active and the rate of unemployment. For all these variables, including the number of migrations and excluding the rate of unemployment, annual growth rates were computed during the period 1961–88. The time-series were cut off after 1988, because migrations since 1989 are characterized by strong immigrations from East Germany, from ethnic Germans, asylum applicants etc. and their redistribution inside the country, and because these processes are politically determined, not influenced by economic cycles in West Germany.

At first the indicator GDP is used in accordance with the studies of Birg et al. (1983) and Milne (1993). If one compares the growth rates of migration with the GDP rates (Figure 12.2), a positive relationship is observed. This is confirmed by a simple correlation coefficient of 0.60, which is, nevertheless, clearly lower than the correponding coefficient of 0.72 for the period 1961–80 computed by Birg et al. A more detailed inspection of Figure 12.2 shows the following. First, the growth rates of gross migration are nearly always situated beyond the curve of GDP rates and they are mostly negative. This is affected by the negative trend of migration development. It seems, secondly, that during the 1960s and the early 1970s both growth curves are roughly parallel, whereas in the 1980s the migration curve lags one year behind the GDP curve. This impression can be confirmed by comutations, the results of which are collected in Table 12.1. The whole time span was divided into three overlapping periods of 13 years and for these time periods multiple regressions were analysed with the response variable migration growth rate and the predictor variables GDP growth rate of the same year, for which migration was measured, and GDP growth rate of the year

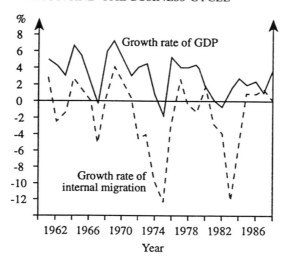

Figure 12.2. Growth rates for internal migration and GDP 1966–83

Table 12.1. Correlations and regressions of internal migration and GDP, dependent variable: growth rates of gross migration betwen the federal states

Time period	Simple correlation with GDP growth rate	Multiple correlation with GDP and lagged GDP	standardized regression coefficient for	
			GDP	lag GDP*
1961–88	0.600	0.659	0.48 (2.99)	0.32 (1.97)
1961–73	0.703	0.768	0.68 (3.15)	0.30 (1.38)
1969–81	0.622	0.689	0.52 (2.11)	0.37 (1.49)
1976–88	0.162	0.786	−0.09 (−0.40)	0.82 (3.63)

* t-values in brackets

before. The table shows for the first period with a multiple correlation of 0.77 a highly significant effect of the coincidental GDP and a much smaller, insignificant effect of the lagged GDP. On the contrary, in the third period there is only an effect of the lagged variable, with a nearly unchanged multiple correlation of 0.79. Therefore, gross internal migration not only shows a decreasing trend in course of time, but reacts with more inertia to the business cycle.

If the relationships are tested with the two labour-market indicators for the business cycle, the results for unemployment rates are worse than for GDP, but for gainfully occupied slightly better. The simple correlation coefficient with gross migration rates is −0.49 for the unemployment rate and 0.69 for the growth rates of the employment level. However, the quantitative improvement for the latter variable compared with the GDP is strongly reduced in a multi-variate perspective, because the effect of the lagged predictor is smaller than in the case of GDP variables. Yet it is remarkable that with the employment level predictors the migration rates are influenced also in the third period 1976–88 only by the coincidental growth rate of employment, not by the lagged predictor (with a multiple correlation of 0.72). It seems therefore that the delayed effect of GDP development on migration in recent years is caused for the most part by delays in the creation of new jobs. Thus the volume of inter-regional migrations in West Germany is clearly dependent on changes of the economic cycle also in the 1980s, in spite of the factors mentioned above, which could have effected a larger resistance of migration to fluctuations of the business cycle. These factors seem to be more responsible for the long-term trend of decreasing mobility, not for short-term variations of the business cycle.

NET MIGRATION OF REGIONS AND REGIONAL TYPES AND THE BUSINESS CYCLE

In this section regional differences in reaction on the business cycle are studied. To investigate such a question, it no longer makes sense to use migrations between states, rather a finer spatial detail is necessary. Therefore, migrations between the counties (*Kreise*) of the FRG are used. Unfortunately, this has the consequence that the time-series must be shortened because of the reorganiz- ation of administrative boundaries in the first half of the 1970s. Regionalized internal migration data are collected by the Federal Research Institute for Regional Studies and Regional Planning (BfLR). On the basis of the 75 planning regions (*Raumordnungsregionen*), which are functional regions comprising core cities together with their areas of influence, these data are available since 1978, and so only the relatively short time period 1978–88 could be used. But this period is particularly important in the context of the problems to be dealt with, because the process of counterurbanization began in 1979–80. Moreover, for selected planning regions it was possible to build longer time-series since 1973 by computing and converting migration data on the basis of counties that have been provided by the Federal Statistical Office.

At first a differentiation by regional types is considered, which are defined by the BfLR according to the degree of urbanization and agglomeration. Contrary to the last section, instead of gross migration the net migration rates (net migration per 1000 population) must be used. Figure 12.3 shows the develop- ments of the annual net migration rates for the four regional types. Apart from the urban agglomerations, regions with agglomerative tendencies are distin- guished. The rural regions are separated into peripheral areas of low density and areas of higher density.

As could be expected on account of the studies of counterurbanization in West Germany, the net migration rates of the agglomerations are slightly negative in 1978 and decline later. Yet some years later this trend changes and since 1985 migration gains can be observed in the urban agglomerations. Contrary to this

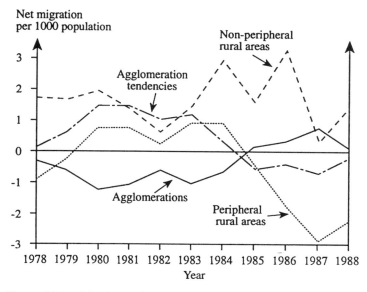

Figure 12.3. Net internal migration rates by regional type 1978–88

development are the net migration curves of the regions with weak agglomeration and the peripheral rural areas. Both regional types show migration gains during the first half of the 1980s, then migration losses, particularly in the rural regions. Very different is the development in the non-peripheral rural areas. They have a population increase by migration during the whole time span of investigation, with remarkable variations from year to year. This rural category of regions which mostly have a favourable economic structure could already benefit from migration gains before the general start of counterurbanization. However, the peripheral rural regions also experienced migration gains in the early 1980s, even during the recession of 1981–2. Therefore, the thesis stated in the literature of the 1970s can not be confirmed, that is, that the labour markets of rural regions are characterized by branches which react quickly to the business cycle and dismiss many workers in recessions leading to out-migrations.

If one correlates net internal migrations with growth rates of national GDP, positive coefficients can be found for the urban agglomerations (r=0.20) and the non-peripheral rural areas (r=0.46). Both regional categories thus show a slight tendency for migration gains during economic expansion. In comparison to that, during economic recessions a positive net migration is more typical of regions with agglomeration tendencies (r=−0.37) and of peripheral rural areas (r=−0.28). These relatively weak relationships are not strengthened by additional consideration of the lagged GDP.

These results are consistent with the recession theory of counterurbanization, but give rise to some important modifications. First, altogether the influence of the economic cycle on internal migrations is rather weak, particularly concerning urban agglomerations. Secondly, a differentiation of rural areas is necessary. Whereas the regions with agglomeration tendencies and the rural areas with low density react countercyclically as the recession theory predicts, the rural areas with higher density show pro-cyclical relationships.

To disclose such regional differentiations in more detail, the analysis should proceed from the aggregated regional types to individual regions. Certainly, the annual migration data on the basis of the regions depend on very special situations and random oscillations, thus an analysis of the development of all 75 planning regions is not recommendable. Instead, the changes of net migration during two years have been computed for selected phases of the business cycle. The first period extends from the high economic growth rates of 1978–9 to the recession of 1981–2 and can thus be interpreted as a period of downturn. The upswing embraces the change from 1981–2 to 1985–6. The net migration data are restricted to the working population being particularly dependent on economic fluctuations.

The detailed maps cannot be presented here, but the most important results should be summarized. The net migration changes in the period of downturn show that positive differences, which represent an enlargement of net migration until 1981–2, characterize many peripheral regions in the north and south Germany. Most rural areas could improve their net migration, even if this meant only a reduced out-migration. On the contrary, many big agglomerations like Munich, Stuttgart, Rhine-Main, Dusseldorf, Cologne, Bremen and Hamburg show negative values. Apart from this predominant group within the urban agglomerations, there are others with positive differences, particularly the regions of the Ruhr and the Saar district with old heavy industries. Here the strong migration losses diminished during the downswing. The same proves true for West Berlin which realized migration gains in the 1980s after decades of out-migration.

The spatial distribution of net migration changes during the upswing does not present a simple reflected image of the changes in recession, but shows quite another pattern. Even if some urban agglomerations like Stuttgart, Frankfurt and Dusseldorf have positive differences with migration gains, such developments according to the settlement structure are put in the shade by a prevailing North–South divide. While in most parts of south Germany the net migrations improved during the upswing, the North was characterized by declining values. Apparently, the internal migrations in this period strongly depend on the different success of economic restructuring. It is well known that in many regions of south Germany high-tech and other new industries could be established as well as modern subsections of the service sector, whereas the North was plagued by deindustrialization. These restructuring processes, as well as the economic changes in the heavy industry districts, are clearly of longer duration than the short-term ups and downs of the business cycle.

A last step in the analysis of net migration is dedicated to some selective

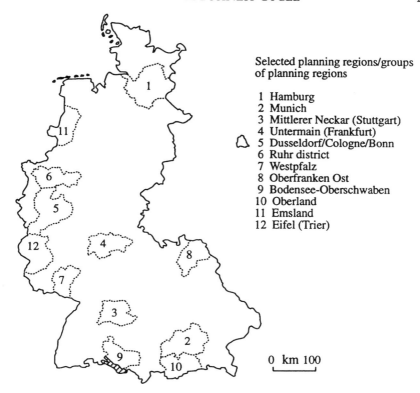

Figure 12.4. Selected planning regions/groups of planning regions

planning regions or groups of planning regions, for which internal migration data could be computed in the period 1973–88. Since the annual values are influenced by random fluctuations, the interpretation should be restricted to similar tendencies of groups of regions. Concerning the urban agglomerations, three groups were distinguished: the regional capitals Hamburg and Munich; the regions of Stuttgart, Frankfurt and Dusseldorf/Cologne/Bonn with relatively favourable economic structure; and the Ruhr district with its heavy manufacturing industries (for the localization of the regions see Figure 12.4). Many areas which are situated outside the agglomerations are characterized by manufacturing industries as well, particularly by light industries. We selected the planning regions of Westpfalz with old textile and shoe industries and Oberfranken-Ost (Fichtelgebirge) with old glass and stone industries. Within the rural areas the Bavarian Oberland and the region Bodensee-Oberschwaben represent areas with rather prosperous economic structure (tourism, but also 'new' industries), while Emsland and Eifel (Trier region) have been described for a long time as peripheral rural areas with unfavourable structure. It should be noted that this

Table 12.2. Migration efficiency of 1973–88 and relationships with growth rates of national GDP by selected planning regions

Region	Migration efficiency		Correlation with GDP rate	Multiple correlation GDP and lag GDP
	x̄	s		
Urban agglomerations				
Hamburg	15.8	11.8	−0.06	(−)0.23
Munich	54.4	20.3	−0.07	(−)0.15
Mittl. Neckar (Stuttgart)	12.9	25.3	0.16	(+)0.30
Untermain (Frankfurt)	6.3	20.9	0.17	(+)0.25
Dusseldorf/Cologne/ Bonn	20.0	23.2	0.29	(+)0.32
Ruhr district	−122.9	36.1	−0.42	(−)0.43
Other regions				
Westpfalz	−28.5	23.5	−0.07	(−)0.37
Oberfranken Ost	−19.8	25.1	−0.36	(−)0.56
Bodensee- Oberschwaben	23.3	18.0	0.24	(+)0.30
Oberland	60.7	31.8	0.38	0.40
Emsland	−44.2	53.9	0.02	0.18
Eifel (Trier)	−22.1	25.0	−0.18	(−)0.45

informal typology does not include regions outside the agglomerations with an average structure.

For each planning region the annual net migration figure was related to 1000s of gross migration leadig to the index of migration efficiency. As the average index values show (Table 12.2), the selected urban agglomerations with the exception of the Ruhr district experienced migration gains as did the rural regions with tourism, whereas the other regions outside the agglomerations recorded migration losses. However, the standard deviations show considerable annual variations which can be compared with the fluctuations of the business cycle. As a simple measure for these relationships, Table 12.2 contains the simple correlations between migration efficiency and the growth rate of the national GDP as well as the multiple correlations with the coincidental GDP and the lagged GDP rates. Although the multiple correlation coefficient is normally defined as a non-negative measure, it is provided with a plus or minus sign in brackets, if the effects of both predictors have the same direction. So it can be observed that the net internal migrations in the urban agglomerations with favourable structure and in the touristic rural areas react pro-cyclically, have relatively high migration gains during the upswings and lower gains or even losses in the periods of downturn. An example is the region of Stuttgart (Figure 12.5).

Counter-cyclical reactions are typical of the Ruhr district, the rural regions

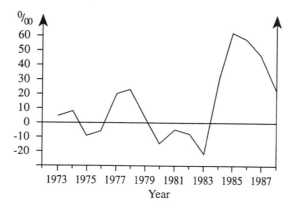

Figure 12.5. Migration efficiency in the Stuttgart region 1973–88: a case of pro-cyclical net migration rates

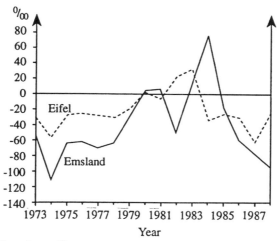

Figure 12.6. Migration efficiency in the planning regions of Eifel and Emsland 1973–88: examples of countercyclical net migration trends

with old light industries and the Eifel region. Here the migration losses diminish in periods of economic recession because of the decreasing chances of new jobs in other regions. But the regions with old light industries as well as the peripheral rural regions of Eifel and Emsland were able to realize migration gains during the early 1980s (see Figure 12.6). This was partly connected with employment growth. Further, it is remarkable that the regional capitals of Hamburg[3] and Munich differ from the other urban agglomerations. The migrations do not behave pro-cyclically, but show a slight tendency to an anti-cyclical reaction which is essentially smaller than that in the Ruhr district. Apparently, the labour

Table 12.3. Correlation of migration efficiency and of in- and out-migration rates with growth rates of GDP of federal states by selected planning regions, 1973–88

| Region | State | Migration efficiency | | Multiple correlation with GDP and lag GPD rates | |
		simple correlation with GDP	Multiple correlation with GDP, lag GDP	in-migration	out-migration
Hamburg	Hamburg	−0.23	(−)0.23	(+)0.51	(+)0.71
Munich	Bavaria	0.02	0.13	0.02	(+)0.20
Stuttgart	Baden-Wuerttemberg	0.30	(+)0.57	(+)0.74	(+)0.65
Frankfurt	Hesse	0.29	(+)0.29	(+)0.29	(+)0.48
Dusseldorf/Cologne/Bonn	NRW*	0.36	(+)0.38	(+)0.42	(+)0.58
Ruhr district	NRW*	−0.41	(−)0.47	(+)0.44	(+)0.54
Westpfalz	RhP*	−0.06	(−)0.28	(+)0.41	(+)0.40
Oberfranken Ost	Bavaria	−0.22	(−)0.31	(+)0.25	(+)0.46
Bodensee-Oberschwaben	Baden-Wuerttemberg	0.34	(+)0.48	(+)0.73	(+)0.50
Oberland	Bavaria	0.50	(+)0.56	0.20	0.32
Emsland	Lower Saxony	−0.04	(−)0.23	0.45	(+)0.14
Eifel (Trier)	RhP*	−0.15	(−)0.32	(+)0.30	(+)0.45

*NRW=Northrhine-Westphalia, RhP=Rhineland-Palatinate

market and other possibilities and attractions of the capitals are so manifold that influences of the short-term business cycles are surmounted.

The analyses documented in Table 12.2 are related to national GDP, but Milne (1993) has shown that for Canada better results could be obtained with provincial instead of national GDP growth rates. Therefore, it was tested whether regionalized GDP rates could also give substantial improvements for the FRG. For the 11 federal states the nominal and real GDP are regularly computed by the statistical offices. These time-series show considerable similarities with the national series, yet there are some significant deviations of the amplitudes of the business cycle and with regard to leads and lags. Therefore, for every selected planning region the GDP rates were taken from the state which includes the region. The results (Table 12.3) show that there are no changes in the direction of the correlations, but that the pro-cyclical relationships are now more important, particularly for the south German regions Stuttgart, Bodensee and Oberland. Against it, the counter-cyclical reactions of rural regions are mostly less clear.

Moreover, instead of net migration the growth rates of the inter-regional in-migrations and out-migrations[4] have been correlated with GDP rates to disclose different reactions which may be hidden in the net migration data. In Table 12.3 it can be observed, first, that according to the expectations pro-cyclical relationships are the rule, since the gross migration reacts in this way as could be shown above. Secondly, in most regions the out-migrations are more dependent on the business cycle than the in-migrations. This cannot be surprising for regions of predominant out-migration like the Ruhr district, Oberfranken Ost or the Eifel region, but is more so for the urban agglomerations of Hamburg, Frankfurt and Dusseldorf/Cologne/Bonn. Only in both of the regions in the economically prosperous state of Baden-Wuerttemberg, Stuttgart and Bodensee are the in-migrations more influenced by GDP growth rates than the out-migrations, if one disregards the north German Emsland. Here the multiple correlation coefficient could not be provided with a positive sign because, apart from the dominating positive effect of the coincidental GDP rates, a slightly negative effect of the lagged GDP rates was present.

Altogether, these results have clearly shown that the relationships between internal migrations and the business cycle differ considerably for the regional types. All the correlation coefficients demonstrate once more that these connections are not very strong. Apart from the short-term fluctuations of the business cycle longer trends are important. Such a trend seems to be responsible for the period of counterurbanization of the early 1980s, since similar turnarounds of migration flows could not or could barely be observed during the recessions of the 1960s and 1970s. Such long-term trends, which may be related to the economic restructuring process, can only be analysed on the basis of longer time-series than those that were available for this chapter.

NOTES

1. In 1987, 58.5% of total housing units in the FRG were rental. In large metropolitan areas the figure amounted to 62% in central cities, but also 55% in the inner suburban ring, 45% in the outer suburban areas (Gans 1991, p. 300).
2. The article by P. Riquet (1988) also studies only relationships between migration rate and unemployment in West German cities.
3. Particularly for the regional capitals the international migrations are also important. This can be seen for the city of Hamburg, where extraordinarily long time series of international and internal migrations, separated in mobility with the suburban ring and inter-regional migrations, are available. From the data published by Kamp (1993) it was computed that the international migrations during the time period 1961–1988 reacted pro-cyclically on changes in GDP (multiple correlation with coincidental GDP and lagged GDP growth rates: R=(+)0.57). On the contrary, the suburban mobility was counter-cyclical (R=(−) 0.55), because the flows to suburbia, and therefore the losses for the city, were especially high in expansion periods. The inter-regional migrations, however, corresponding to the results in Table 12.2, showed an essentially smaller counter-cyclical relationship (R=(−)0.33). Similar results with regard to the suburban flows can be found in Gans (1991).
4. It should be noticed that the in- and out-migration data are based on the migrations of the counties belonging to the planning regions. Therefore, also intraregional migrations are included. Moreover, the values of 1973 and 1974 for the regions of Northrhine-Westphalia, the values for Emsland before 1976, and the values of 1973 for the Frankfurt region must be used with caution, because of a change of county boundaries afterwards.

REFERENCES

Birg, H., Filip, D. and Hilge, K. (1983) Verflechtungsanalyse der Bevoelkerungsmobilitaet zwischen den Bundeslaendern von 1950 bis 1980. IBS-Materialien 8. Bielefeld.
Boersch-Supan, A. (1989) Mobilitaetshemmende und Mobilitaetsfoerdernde Qualifizierung, in Scherf, H. (ed.) Beschaeftigungsprobleme hochentwickelter Volkswirtschaften. Schriften Verein fuer Socialpolitik, Neue Folge 178, pp. 451–70.
Boersch-Supan, A. (1990) Regionale und sektorale Arbeitslosigkeit: Durch hoere Mobilitaet reduzierbar? Zeitschrift fuer Wirtschafts- und Sozialwissenschaften 110: 55–82.
Eckey, H.-F. (1978) Zur Bestimmung der Konjunkturreagibilitaet regionaler Arbeitsmaerkte, Raumforschung und Raumordnung 36:248–56.
Fielding, A.J. (1993) Migration and the metropolis: recent research on the causes of migration to southeast England, Progress in Human Geography 17:195–212.
Franz, W. (1989) Beschaeftigungsprobleme auf Grund von Inflexibilitaeten auf Arbeitsmaerkten? in Scherf, H. (ed.) Beschaeftigungsprobleme hochentwickelter Volkswirtschaften. Schriftenreihe Verein fuer Socialpolitik, Neue Folge 178, pp. 303–40.
Franz, W. and Siebeck, K. (1992) A theoretical and econometric analysis of structural unemployment in Germany. Reflections on the Beveridge curve, in Franz, W. (ed.) Structural Unemployment. Heidelberg: Physica, pp. 1–58.

Gans, P. (1991) Population change in the suburbanized areas of the Federal Republic of Germany with special reference to Hamburg (1970–1987), *Espaces, Populations, Sociétés* 2:293–307.

Gerlach, K. and Liepmann, P. (1972) Konjunkturelle Aspekte der Industrialisierung peripherer Regionen. Dargestellt am Beispiel des ostbayerischen Regierungsbezirks Oberpfalz, *Jahrbuecher fuer Nationaloekonomie und Statistik* 187:1–21.

Gordon, I.R. (1985) The cyclical sensitivity of regional employment and unemployment differentials, *Regional Studies* 19:95–110.

Greenwood, M.J. (1993) Migration: a review. Editorial, *Regional Studies* 27:295–6.

Haag, G., Munz, M., Reiner, R. and Weidlich, W. (1988) Federal Republic of Germany, in Weidlich, W. and Haag, G. (eds) *Inter-regional Migration. Dynamic Theory and Comparative Analysis*. Berlin: Springer, pp. 65–100.

Haurin, D.R. and Haurin, R.J. (1988) Net migration, unemployment, and the business cycle, *Journal of Regional Science* 28:239–54.

Kamp, K. (1993) Einige Aspekte zur Entwicklung der Wanderungen 1961 bis 1991, in *Hamburg in Zahlen*, Heft 2, pp. 44–7.

Koch, R. (1977) Wanderung und Rezession. Wanderungen in der Bundesrepublik Deutschland 1974 und 1975, *Informationen zur Raumentwicklung*, pp. 875–87.

Kontuly, T. and Bierens, H.J. (1990) Testing the recession theory as an explanation for the migration turnaround, *Environment and Planning A* 22:253–70.

Kontuly, T. and Vogelsang, R. (1988) Explanations for the intensification of counterurbanization in the Federal Republic of Germany, *Professional Geographer* 40:42–54.

Langewiesche, D. (1977) Wanderungsbewegungen in der Hochindustrialisierungsperiode. Regionale, interstaedtische und innerstaedtische Mobilitaet in Deutschland 1880–1914, *Vierteljahresschrift fuer Sozial- und Wirtschaftsgeschichte* 64:14–40.

Long, L. (1991) Residential mobility differences among developed countries, *International Regional Science Review* 14:133–47.

Ludaescher, P. (1986) Wanderungen und konjunkturelle Entwicklung in der Bundesrepublik Deutschland seit Anfang der sechziger Jahre, *Geographische Zeitschrift* 74:43–61.

Milne, W.J. (1993) Macroeconomic influences on migration, *Regional Studies* 27:365–73.

Muellbauer, J. (1990) The housing market and the UK economy, problems and opportunities, in Ermisch, J. (ed.) *Housing and the National Economy*. Aldershot: Avebury.

Nowotny, E. (1976) Zur regionalen Differenzierung des Konjunkturverlaufs, *Berichte zur Raumforschung und Raumplanung* 20:30–34.

Riquet, P. (1988) Mobilité résidentielle, marché immobilier et conjuncture dans les grandes villes allemandes, *Annales de Géographie* 97:1–39.

13 Greater London, the South-east Region and the Wider Britain: Metropolitan Polarization, Uneven Development and Inter-Regional Migration

MICK DUNFORD AND ANTHONY J. FIELDING
University of Sussex, UK

INTRODUCTION

In their conclusion to *Les régions qui gagnent*, Benko and Lipietz (1992) argue that the regions that are winning in countries that are winning are metropolises, whereas the regions that are winning in countries that are losing are mega-lopolises. A metropolis is a district of networks and the head of a few networks of districts (agglomerations of industries) that is human in scale and that corresponds with more organized and bargained solutions to the crisis of Fordism. A megalopolis, on the other hand, is a chaotic complex of networks agglomerated together because of their reliance on market modes of regulation. The evidence for this tentative conclusion is twofold. First, in Europe in the 1980s in the countries that 'won' the successful regions (southern Germany and northern Italy) were networks of districts and some medium-sized metropolitan districts of networks (Munich and Milan). Secondly, in the countries that failed (the UK and the US) megalopolises were the most successful regions.

Development might be expected to be more polarized in a megalopolis than in a metropolis, and there is also an important dialectical relation between polarization and the model of development. On the one hand, the existence of strong regional social blocs is a powerful obstacle and limit to centralization. On the other hand, centralized structures themselves can sap the vitality of other regions and deprive them of the scope for autonomous paths to development and can profoundly shape the trajectory of a society.

In Europe, according to Benko and Lipietz, there are two megalopolises (Greater London and – at least potentially – Paris). As recent EUROSTAT data on comparative economic performance shows, the UK did not do well. The

People, Jobs and Mobility in the New Europe. Edited by Hans H. Blotevogel and Anthony J. Fielding.
© 1997 European Science Foundation. Published in 1997 by John Wiley & Sons Ltd.

French case is, however, different. France is the second strongest economy in the European Union and, after the unification of Germany, its GDP per head is second only to Luxembourg, although as in other advanced capitalist countries there are profound crises associated in particular with the scale and intractability of unemployment, inequality and social exclusion. Nonetheless, since Paris dominates French growth, an assessment of the contemporary economic impact of metropolitanization needs to be more nuanced than the Benko and Lipietz hypothesis suggests. (Outside Europe, moreover, Tokyo polarizes Japan and Seoul polarizes Korea.)

This chapter attempts to explore these relationships between the London megalopolis and the rest of the UK during the recent period. It begins by setting out the main characteristics of the Greater London and South-east region economies. It then discusses the nature of recent developments in London and the South-east in the light of the relations between this region and the rest of the UK, focusing attention on three groups of relationships: those that have deep historical roots and reflect the underlying economic geography of the country; those that trace their origin to the post-war restructuring of the UK economy and to the transition from a Fordist to a post-Fordist productive and social order; and those that reflect the more conjunctural dynamics of the business cycle (closely related in the recent period to the performance of the housing market).

THE GREATER LONDON AND SOUTH-EAST ECONOMIES

In 1991 the South-east's share of the national population stood at 30.5% (16.8 million people, of whom 6.4 million lived in Greater London and 10.4 million in the rest of the South-east (ROSE) (see Figure 13.1). The dominance of Greater London and the South-east is expressed not just in demographic but also in economic terms. At the start of the 1990s Greater London accounted for 17.3% of national GDP, 15% of employment, and 11.8% of the population, while the comparable figures for the rest of the South-east (ROSE) were 18.4, 17.8 and 18.7%. As Figure 13.1 shows, the London and Heathrow 1984 travel to work areas (TTWA) are at the heart of a multi-polar megalopolis made up of a series of large TTWAs such as Watford and Luton, Southend, Hertford and Harlow, Medway and Maidstone, Crawley, Guildford and Aldershot, Slough, Aylesbury and High Wycombe near the capital, and the more distant Milton Keynes, Cambridge, Oxford, Southampton and Brighton.

In 1989 county gross domestic product (GDP) data, which includes commuters' incomes in the county where commuters work rather than in their county of residence, suggested that the GDP per head of Greater London was 48% above the national average (148). Berkshire (126), Surrey (111) and Buckinghamshire (110) were also well above the national average, as was Cambridgeshire (112) which lies in the Greater South-east but not in the South-east region. In the South-east region commuting plays an important role in shaping the map of output per head, as is clear if household income is analysed. The conceptual

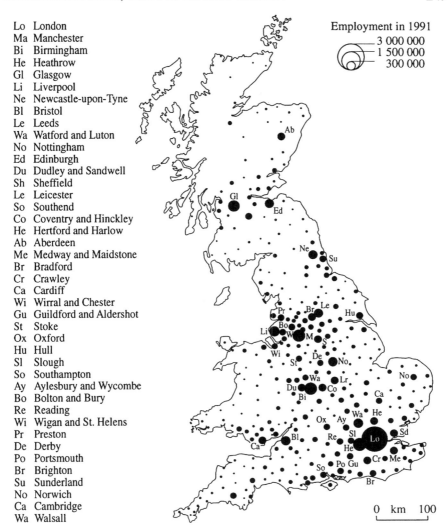

Lo London
Ma Manchester
Bi Birmingham
He Heathrow
Gl Glasgow
Li Liverpool
Ne Newcastle-upon-Tyne
Bl Bristol
Le Leeds
Wa Watford and Luton
No Nottingham
Ed Edinburgh
Du Dudley and Sandwell
Sh Sheffield
Le Leicester
So Southend
Co Coventry and Hinckley
He Hertford and Harlow
Ab Aberdeen
Me Medway and Maidstone
Br Bradford
Cr Crawley
Ca Cardiff
Wi Wirral and Chester
Gu Guildford and Aldershot
St Stoke
Ox Oxford
Hu Hull
Sl Slough
So Southampton
Ay Aylesbury and Wycombe
Bo Bolton and Bury
Re Reading
Wi Wigan and St. Helens
Pr Preston
De Derby
Po Portsmouth
Br Brighton
Su Sunderland
No Norwich
Ca Cambridge
Wa Walsall

Employment in 1991

— 3 000 000
— 1 500 000
— 300 000

0 km 100

Figure 13.1. UK: employment by travel-to-work area in 1991. Source: 1991 Census of Employment

difference between GDP and household income is that GDP measures the value of goods and services produced in an area, whereas income measures the income of residents. Differences in the two measures result in part, therefore, from commuting. The two indicators also differ because of the effect of incomes paid to economically inactive individuals such as pensioners and the unemployed on the one hand, and the differences that result from the inclusion of profits in GDP and investment income in household income on the other.

Table 13.1.   County Gross Domestic Product per head in the South East in 1989 (UK=100)

£ per head (UK=100)	GDP per head in 1989 (UK=100)	Average household disposable income in 1989 (UK=100)
Greater London	148.0	116.9
Berkshire	126.2	112.7
Surrey	111.3	133.8
Buckinghamshire	110.7	111.2
Hertfordshire	107.0	129.1
West Sussex	104.9	108.6
Bedfordshire	103.8	102.5
Oxfordshire	103.5	102.9
Hampshire	102.0	108.5
Kent	92.2	104.3
Essex	87.8	107.3
East Sussex	78.0	102.8
Isle of Wight	76.5	98.9

Source: CSO (1992)

As Table 13.1 shows, there are a number of counties in the South-east whose GDP per head expressed as a percentage of the national average is greater than household disposable income per head. The most important are Greater London and Berkshire. Other areas have higher household disposable incomes per head than GDP per head, and in some cases (Surrey, Hertfordshire and East Sussex) the differences are very great. Household income per head is relatively higher than GDP per head in counties with an above-average share of retired people (such as East Sussex, Isle of Wight and West Sussex), an above-average share of unemployed people and related income transfers, high levels of investment income but relatively low profits (such as Surrey and Kent) and a large share of residents who work outside the area. As is clear from the fact that almost all areas in the South-east have above-average per capita disposable household incomes, even though some fall well below the national average in the creation of wealth, commuting and transfers of value added play a very significant role in this region.

Differences in GDP per head are in part a reflection of differences in the industrial structure of different regions. An industrial analysis of GDP is presented in Table 13.2. (This data on regional GDP measures the income of residents. The income of commuters is included in the regions where they live and so the data differ from those in Table 13.1.) The striking characteristics of Greater London and the South-east are twofold. First, manufacturing and energy are under-represented (15.7 and 22.8% of output compared with 26.9% nationally). The divide is particularly pronounced in the case of Greater London and for the minerals, metals, chemicals, mechanical and electrical industries. Conversely, financial and business services are over-represented (35.5% of GDP

Table 13.2. Gross domestic product at factory cost by industry groups in 1989 (in current £ million and percentages)

	Greater London	Rest of South East	United Kingdom	
Distribution of GDP by sector (in percentages)				
Agriculture, forestry and fishing	0.1	1.1	1.6	
Energy and water supply	2.2	2.5	3.7	
Manufacturing	13.7	20.3	23.2	
Minerals, metals and chemicals	2.0	3.6	4.7	
Metal goods, engineering and vehicles	4.9	10.1	9.8	
Other manufacturing industries	6.7	6.7	8.7	
Construction	5.5	8.6	7.4	
Distribution, hotels and catering, repairs	14.8	15.2	14.5	
Transport and communication	9.8	7.6	7.2	
Financial and business services, etc.	35.4	22.5	18.5	
Ownership of dwellings	6.8	6.3	5.8	
Public administration and defence	5.8	6.7	6.6	
Education and health services	8.9	7.5	9.4	
Other services	9.0	6.9	6.7	
Total	100.0	100.0	100.0	
Total (£m)	64605	90879	436181	
Distribution of GDP by region (in percentages)				GDP (£m)
Agriculture, forestry and fishing	0.8	13.7	100.0	6967
Energy and water supply	8.9	14.0	100.0	15950
Manufacturing	8.8	18.2	100.0	101016
Minerals, metals and chemicals	6.5	15.8	100.0	20431
Metal goods, engineering and vehicles	7.5	21.5	100.0	42556
Other manufacturing industries	11.4	15.9	100.0	38026
Construction	11.0	24.0	100.0	32366
Distribution, hotels and catering repairs	15.0	21.7	100.0	63430
Transport and communication	20.4	22.0	100.0	31263
Financial and business services, etc.	28.4	25.4	100.0	80559
Ownership of dwellings	17.4	22.9	100.0	25155
Public administration and defence	13.2	21.4	100.0	28623
Education and health services	14.1	16.7	100.0	41094
Other services	19.9	21.3	100.0	29272
Total	14.8	20.8	100.0	436181

Source: CSO (1992), pp. 134–5

in Greater London and 22.5% in the rest of the South-east compared with 18.5% nationally). Over 28% of the output of financial and business services is produced in Greater London. This figure is equal to almost twice its share of national output. In the case of the South-east the corresponding figures are 25.4 and 20.8%. Also over-represented are the logistic functions of transport, storage and communications, and in the South-east the actual and imputed rental income associated with the ownership of dwellings and construction which themselves were connected with a wave of speculative development that ended in 1989.

Differences in industrial and economic structures are just one of the reasons for the dominance of Greater London and the South-east. Other contributory factors include high rates of labour-force participation and occupational and functional job profiles in which a range of well-paid jobs are over-represented due to the polarization of employment structures. Some indication of the polarization of employment structures. Some indication of the polarization of job structures can be derived from an analysis of industry and occupation tables. A 10% sample from the 1981 Census of Population was analysed to produce tables of industry by occupation. In the initial tables for Greater London, the rest of the South-east and Great Britain, 314 industries and 25 occupational categories were identified. At this point correspondence analysis was used to identify for Great Britain groups of industries with similar occupational profiles and groups of occupations with similar industrial profiles. After this step the occupations and industries were grouped if their industrial or occupational profiles were similar subject to the constraint that dissimilar occupations/industries should not be combined. In the case of energy and manufacturing industries, for example, four broad groups were identified: (i) industries with a high percentage of scientific and technical staff, (ii) industries with a high percentage of skilled manual workers, (iii) industries with a large share of craft workers and (iv) industries with a large share of unskilled workers. These groups fell in turn into subgroups depending on their occupational profiles. For example, the industries with a large share of scientists, engineers and technicians fell into four clusters with decreasing shares of the most qualified workers: oil, natural gas and nuclear fuels; office machines, data processing, electrical and electronic engineering and timing instruments; chemicals and man-made fibres; and aerospace and instrument engineering.

Figures 13.2–5 plot the overall occupational and industrial profiles for Greater London and the rest of the South-east. The width of each column is proortional to the corresponding location quotient. A quotient of more than one indicates that the industry/occupation accounts for a higher percentage of employment in the region than in Great Britain. The area of each rectangle is proportional to employment in the industry/occupation in the region as recorded in the 10% sample. (To derive estimates of employment absolute figures should be multiplied by 10.)

In the case of Greater London, manufacturing industries were in general under-represented. The only sectors in which Greater London's employment share matched the national share were in some of the energy and high-tech sectors (office machines and data-processing equipment) on the one hand and in a number of low-paid traditional industries (footwear, clothing and textiles) which serve the capital's markets and whose roots go back far into its economic history. There were strong specializations in (i) a number of distributional, communications, transport and logistic activities (wholesale distribution, leas-

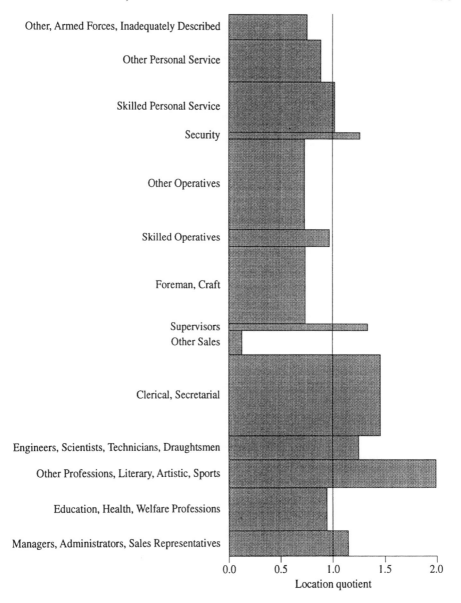

Figure 13.2. Occupational profile for Greater London in 1981 (Source: 1981 Census)

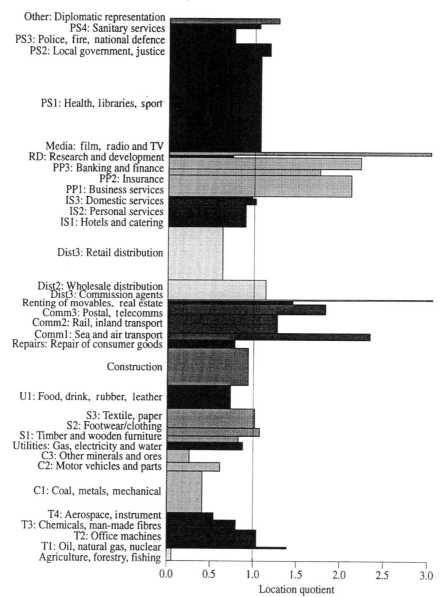

Figure 13.3. Industrial profile for Greater London in 1981 (Source: 1981 Census)

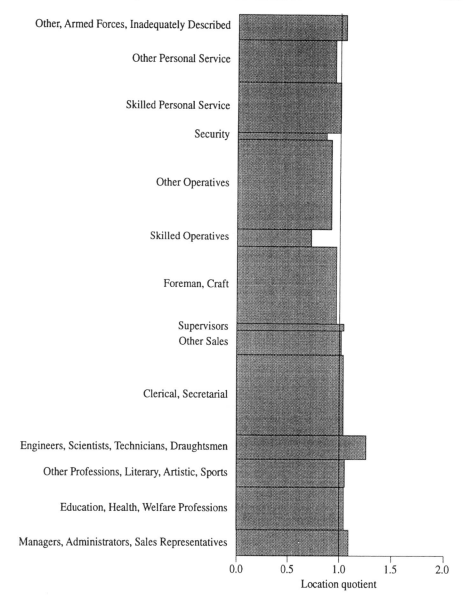

Figure 13.4. Occupational profile for rest of South-east in 1981 (Source: 1981 Census)

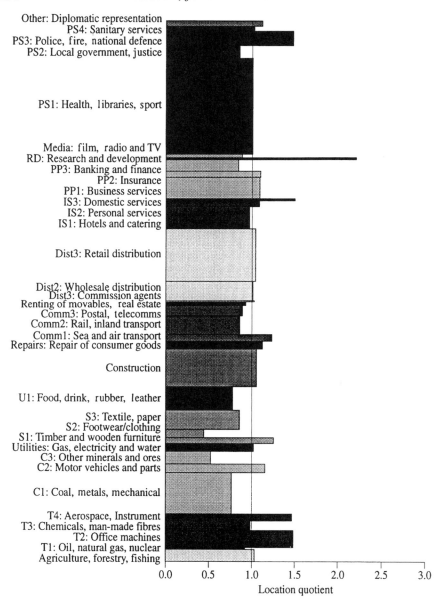

Figure 13.5. Industrial profile for rest of South-east in 1981 (Source: 1981 Census)

ing, postal services, telecommunications, and sea, air and rail transport), (ii) a cluster of producer services (banking, finance, insurance, consultancies and other services for firms) and (iii) the media. Of these activities the remunerative producer services played a crucial role in the creation of Greater London's wealth. At the same time there was a polarization of high-status white-collar occupations in the capital: (i) managers and administrators, (ii) accountants, lawyers, architects and other professionals along with literary and artistic occupations, and (iii) engineers, scientists and technicians. A corollary of the concentration of these skilled jobs was the strong representation of clerical and secretarial support staff on the one hand and a significant presence of skilled personal service occupations to meet the needs of the capital's affluent middle and upper classes. Manual industrial workers were conversely strongly under-represented.

In the rest of the South-east most industries were once again under-represented with the striking exception of some of the high-tech sectors (office machines, data processing, electrical and electronic engineering and timing instruments; aerospace and instrument engineering). Defence was another area of specialization, as were research and development, sea and air transport and domestic service, although in absolute terms employment in a number of these clusters was small. This industrial profile clearly shows the South-east's specialization in high-tech sectors, research and development and defence establishments. Secondly, it provides evidence of some over-representation of retail distribution and personal and domestic services, which reflect the high personal incomes of many of the inhabitants of the South-east. Thirdly, it is suggestive of certain complementarities between the rest of the South-east and Greater London, with shared specializations in transport and distribution on the one hand and a division of tasks in others. This occupational profile of the rest of the South-east creates a related image of an area with a strong representation of managers, engineers, scientists, technicians and other professionals, an under-representation of manual industrial workers and a significant presence of lower-status white-collar and personal service jobs.

To develop this account of polarization, Tables 13.3 and 13.4 provide data on the profiles of occupation by industry and industry by occupation. In these tables there is a row for each of the industries and a column for each of the occupations identified as a result of the correspondence analysis. The figure in each cell is the percentage of all jobs in Great Britain in the sector (row) and occupation (column) located in Greater London (Table 13.3) or ROSE (Table 13.4). The cells that are empty are cells whose absolute value accounts for a very small share of employment in the sector and/or occupation in Greater London or ROSE. As the bottom right-hand values indicate, Greater London accounted for 15% of GB employment in 1981 and ROSE for 17%. Cell values of greater than 15 or 17 suggest (as the data are for a 10% sample and not for the population) that employment in a particular sector and occupation is over-represented and polarized.

Table 13.3. Industrial, functional and occupational profile of Greater London in 1981 (percentage of employment in Great Britain located in Greater London by industry and occupation)

Greater London	1	2	3	4	5	6	7	8	9	10	11	12	13	14	Total
Agriculture, forestry, fishing										1					1
T1: Oil, mineral gas, nuclear			52	21	38										21
T2: Office machines, data processing, electrical	19		22	15	21			13		12				12	16
T3: Chemicals, man-made fibres	15		25	11	20			6		8					12
T4: Aerospace, instrument								7		7					8
C1: Coal, Metals, Mechanical	9		11	8	9			4		5					6
C2: Motor vehicles and parts					9			9		9				2	9
C3: Other minerals and ores	7				7			3		2					4
Utilities: Gas, electricity and water			20	12	37			16		12					13
S1: Timber and wooden furniture	15				13			12		10					13
S2: Footwear/clothing	28		29		17			23	13	11		24			16
S3: Textile, Paper	21		32	17	23	11		9	13	8		24		8	15
U1: Food, drink, Rubber, Leather	13		19	13	15			11	9	8		15	10	10	11
Construction	17		22	21	18			13		11			12	12	14
Repairs: Repair of consumer goods	11				11			11		14					12
Comm 1: Sea and air transport	34		53	29	40		44	38		22		39	14	38	36
Comm 2: Rail, inland transport	21		34	32	23			18		16			25	21	19
Comm 3: Postal, Telecoms			61	37	27		34	28	26	25		29	24		28
Renting of movables, Real estate			33		23			14		14		22	27		22
Dist1: Commission agents			53		52							55			47
Dist2: Wholesale distribution	15		27	27	20	12		12		12		19	11	14	17
Dist3: Retail distribution	14	15	25		17		15	15	13	13		15	13	20	10
IS1: Hotels and catering					24		16			19		13			14
IS2: Personal services				30	20					16		13			16
IS3: Domestic services											26		14		15
PP1: Business services	26		39	28	29		37	24		30		40	24	35	32
PP2: Insurance	16		41		26							33			27

	1	2	3	4	5	6	7	8	9	10	11	12	13	14
PP3: Banking and finance				58	31		31		58		32	21		34
RD: Research and development				11				39						11
Media: Film, Radio and TV			46	48	52				44		43			46
PS1: Health, Libraries, Sport	37	14	27	23	20		18	15		29	15	12	16	16
PS2: Local government, Justice	20	20	19	18	16			19	21	15		18		18
PS3: Police, Fire, National defence	16			11			15			17		11	6	12
PS4: Sanitary services									13			16	13	16
Other: Diplomatic representation					44								17	19
Total	18	14	30	19	22	2	20	11	15	19	16	14	12	15

I: The occupations are as follows:
1: Managers, Administrators, Sales Representatives, 2: Education Health, Welfare Professionals. 3: Other Professions, Literary, Aristic and Sports. 4: Engineers, Scientists, Technicians, Draughtsmen. 5: Clerical, Secretarial. 6: Other Sales. 7: Supervisors. 8: Foremen, Craft. 9: Skilled Operatives. 10: Other Operatives. 11: Security. 12: Skilled Personal Service. 13: Other Personal Service. 14: Other, Armed Forces, Inadequately Described.
Source: 1981 Census

Table 13.4. Industrial, functional and occupational profile of Rest of the South East (ROSE) in 1981 (percentage of employment in Great Britain located in ROSE by industry and occupation)

Rest of South East (ROSE)	1	2	3	4	5	6	7	8	9	10	11	12	13	14	Total
Agriculture, forestry, fishing					27			26		21					18
T1: Oil, natural gas				20				18		26		12			16
T2: Office machines, date processing, electrical	29		33	33	29			21		22			25	20	26
T3: Chemicals, man-made fibres	22		23	21	20			11		14					17
T4: Aerospace, instruments	30		32	28	25			23		22					26
C1: Coal, Metals, Mechanical	17		17	16	15			12		12			12	6	13
C2: Motor vehicles and parts	20		29	30	25			17		19					20
C3: Other minerals and ores	10				11			7		9				8	9
Utilities: Gas, electricity and water	21			17	17			18	17	18					18
S1: Timber and wooden furniture	21				23			22		21				19	22
S2: Footwear/clothing								8	6	7					8
S3: Textile, Paper	18		17	19	18			14	12	14		15		10	15
U1: Food, drink, Rubber, Leather	17		16	17	15	12		13	11	12			12	10	14
Construction	20		20	17	18			18	18	16				15	18
Repairs: Repair of consumer goods	23				21			19	18	19		18			20
Comm 1: Sea and air transport	21		17	21	19			21		23			33		21
Comm 2: Rail, inland transport	17			14	14			13		15			15	15	15
Comm 3: Postal, Telecoms					16		14	13	16	15		12			15
Renting of movables, Real estate			19		16			14		17		17			16
Dist 1: Commission agents			18		17	16	23					16			18
Dist 2: Wholesale distribution	17	17	18	24	18	18	20	17		16		18	16	15	18
Dist 3: Retail distribution	20		19		17	12	17	19	16	17	15	18	16	17	18
IS1: Hotels and catering					16					15		18			17
LS2: Personal services					20					19		24	25		19
LS3: Domestic services															26
PP1: Business services	21		17	22	19			18		17		18	16		19
PP2: Insurance	16		19	20	20							19			19

										Total
PP3: Banking and finance					9				15		15
RD: Research and development	38	43	40	36	38	39			15		15
Media: Film, Radio and TV	15	18	16	15	13	13		16	13		17
PS1: Health, Libraries, Sport	16	19	17	13	16	17	13	19	15	15	15
PS2: Local government, Justice	15	17	13	16	13	14	11	13	16	13	15
PS3: Police, Fire, National defence	17	38	27	28	25	25	17	32	26		26
PS4: Sanitary services			14			19		14	18		18
Other: Diplomatic representation								20			19
Total	19	22	16	17	18	18	18	18	15	13	17

Source: 1981 Census

Table 13.3 for Greater London shows clearly the relative absence of manual industrial jobs except in footwear and clothing. Outside of the traditional sectors and the electrical industries, the shares of national employment in Greater London were very low. There was, however, a strong concentration of professional and clerical jobs in the high-tech manufacturing industries and in the oil, gas and nuclear sectors in the capital.

In ROSE there was a stronger presence of production activities reflected in the scores for foremen and craft workers on the one hand and unskilled operatives on the other in motor vehicles and some of the high-tech sectors. Once again, there was a strong polarization of professional jobs, of related clerical and secretarial jobs and, in particular, of scientists, engineers and technicians (with one-third of all jobs in the office machines, data-processing equipment and electrical industries and 28% in aerospace and instrument engineering) and of managers in the high-tech sectors.

Within the industrial sectors and in particular some of the high-tech sectors, there was therefore substantial evidence of a selective concentration of command, control, research and professional functions in Greater London and ROSE which itself would contribute to the higher levels of value added per employee in these areas. Communications, leasing and distribution are other activities in which there was a strong polarization of jobs in Greater London and ROSE. Once again, the greatest over-representation was of professional, research, managerial and in some cases related clerical jobs – which reflects an underlying functional, spatial division of labour. In these sectors however there was also a strong polarization of some of the supervisory, manual and personal service jobs in Greater London. (ROSE accounted for a large share of manual jobs in sea and air transport reflecting the presence of seaports and airports and the role of the South-east as a logistic hub for Great Britain.)

There was a particularly marked polarization of the private producer services (PP3: banking and finance, PP1: business services and PP2: insurance) and the media in Greater London. Within these sectors there is a particularly strong polarization of professional jobs (39–58% of all the jobs in Great Britain) and to a lesser extent of skilled personal service and supervisory jobs in the capital. In ROSE private producer services were also over-represented but much less markedly, although there was a remarkable concentration of research and development and of scientists and technicians working in defence.

At the start of the 1980s, then, Greater London and the South-east were advantaged in so far as there was a selective concentration of critical white-collar occupations in high-tech industries and private producer services in the two regions. In some cases these two areas accounted for remarkable shares of all the jobs in Great Britain. Manual jobs were in general under-represented, although there were strong concentrations of low-grade service-sector jobs reflecting the comparatively high purchasing power of the middle and upper middle classes in the region. (As Table 13.4 shows, for example, 24–25% of personal service jobs in the domestic service sector were located in ROSE.)

The dominance of Greater London, the Home Counties and the wider South-east rested on their governmental, managerial, financial and logistic roles rather than on an industrial role. There was a significant concentration of scientists, engineers and technicians in ROSE; however these categories were not present in Greater London on a scale that one might expect of a service capital with a strong industrial vocation. The most striking fact was the extraordinary dominance of financial and rentier functions. In the rest of the 1980s its strength as the dominant metropolis of a deindustrialized economy would rest on a similar specialization: as Table 13.2 showed, in 1989 over one-third of the GDP of Greater London was accounted for by financial and business services. It was a model of development which was unsustainable even for Greater London and the South-east, as the recent dramatic recession has shown.

The characteristics of the London and South-east economies did not just appear in the recent period. They reflect long-term economic processes, some of which are so deeply rooted in the economic geography of the UK that they can be traced back to the earliest stages of modern capitalist development, if not earlier. In other cases the characteristics are the products of post-war restructuring and of the fundamental changes brought about by the transition from a Fordist social and productive order to the uncertain world sometimes conceived of as one of 'flexible accumulation'. The next two sections examine these connections.

SECULAR TRENDS

Metropolitan dominance can be traced far back into the past to the medieval and early modern periods and to the impact and character of successive phases of industrialization. In pre-industrial England the major focus of wealth and population was in Middlesex (the old county of London) and Surrey, where the wealth of London was concentrated. Outside London the major zones of population and wealth lay along the axes stretching north-eastwards to Norwich and westwards to Bristol. Moreover, during the eighteenth century, when the geographical distribution of wealth changed fundamentally, Middlesex remained by far the wealthiest county. In 1843 the five leading counties were situated along an axis stretching from Middlesex and Surrey through Warwickshire and Staffordshire to Lancashire in the north-west. In spite of the rise of ports and industries in the west and north, Middlesex continued to dominate Britain.

At the root of the economic strength and growth of the capital was the development of Britain, on the one hand as a major military power and a fiscal-military state with high levels of taxation and expenditure and a professional bureaucracy, and on the other as a centre of trade, commerce, insurance and finance. As a political and international trade and finance centre the metropolitan economy was at the forefront of the expansion of the international economy. At the same time it was also a centre of expenditure and investment for the landed classes and a focus for city and suburban infrastructural investment. As Lee (1986, p. 140) has argued, the growth of the South-east was centred on the twin pillars of accumulated wealth – trade and finance on the one hand and land on the other – and on a whole infrastructure of subordinate and often casualized and unskilled service and manufacturing activities required to meet the needs of urban professionals and the urban elite.

In the eighteenth, nineteenth and early twentieth centuries in Britain there were a series of fundamental dualisms which ran from economic affairs to social and political divisions. In the nineteenth century, British society was dominated by a city-based finance capital elite – along with associated civil servants and professionals – at the expense of northern industrialists from whom they were geographically, economically, socially and politically separated. Commerce and finance were the main sources of wealth, the commercial strata grew closer to the traditional landed aristocracy which itself became involved in city life, while the connections between them were reinforced by social distinctions. The south-eastern elite was Anglican in religion, public (i.e. private) school, 'Oxbridge' (i.e. educated at Oxford and Cambridge universities) and Conservative, while provincial industrialists were non-conformist, Liberal rather than Conservative and had attended church and charity schools. This economic, social and geographical division was of profound importance for subsequent British economic development, since it was a major factor in the chronic underinvestment in British industry.

As a result of the growth of the northern and western manufacturing districts in the first half of the nineteenth century, there was a shift in the distribution of output and wealth. Nineteenth-century data on income and wealth indicate that the highest income per head was in the South-east and especially in Middlesex. In 1812 – during the Napoleonic Wars when state military expenditure was high – this area accounted for 38.9% of all income assessed to tax: the gap between the Home Counties and almost all other regions was therefore enormous (Lee 1986, pp. 129–32). In the first 50 years or so of the nineteenth century there was, however, a rapid decline in the share of London incomes in the national total. But after 1860 there was an equally rapid increase. By the late nineteenth century the income of London – measured by county income-tax assessments – accounted for nearly half the total, just as it had a century earlier (Rubinstein 1988).

With the second Industrial Revolution the position of the South-east and Greater London was consolidated: consumer good industries and the new instrument and electrical engineering industries were concentrated in the South-east, as were the new service industries. After 1891 there was a dramatic growth of population in outer London and large cumulative increases in a number of the counties that surrounded the capital as the capital's workforce settled in suburban villages and overspill towns, and as investment and employment were decentralized into a hierarchical network of surrounding city regions. In the period 1891 to 1939 the South-east's share of the national population increased from 27.5 to 31.1%. In 1991 it still stood at

31% (16.8 million people – 30.5% – of whom 6.4 million lived in Greater London).

This concentration of wealth, employment and population in London and the South-east is reflected in the patterns of migration that link the region to the rest of the country. There is considerable evidence to show that the South-east has acted for a long time as a kind of social class 'escalator' region (Fielding 1992). It attracts able and ambitious men and women at the start of their working lives, provides many of them with accelerated promotion through the region's employment and housing markets, and then offers them the opportunity to make cost-of-living and asset-sale gains as they migrate away from the region in later stages of their careers or at retirement. Once again, reciprocal relationships are at work here. While on the one hand these migration patterns reflect the economic and social dominance of London and the South-east, this concentration of wealth and employment is on the other hand partly the product of, and is certainly sustained by, the migration exchanges between this region and the rest of Britain (see Figure 15.1).

LONG WAVE TRENDS AND THE RESTRUCTURING OF THE LONDON AND SOUTH-EAST ECONOMIES

The structure of Greater London and ROSE is in part a reflection of long-term secular trends in British development. Overlaid on these long-term trends and tendencies are, however, a succession of shorter-term cyclical and conjunctural movements. Among these cyclical movements is the golden age of Fordist expansion which lasted until the early 1970s and which was associated with historically unprecedented rates of growth in the UK, even if British economic performance was poor when compared with that of other advanced capitalist countries.

Although the underlying causes of the crisis of the Fordist model of development were rooted in a productivity slowdown and the increasing globalization of economic life, a critical turning point in the case of the UK was 1976, when monetarism emerged as the guiding principle of government economic policies. At that point a significant divergence in the economic performance of British cities and regions was set in motion, while the whole period from 1973 to the present was one of slower growth and growing mass unemployment. Figure 13.6 plots the cumulative annual growth of regional GDP per head for the regions of the South and East and the rest of the UK. (This graph is based on regional series which measure GDP by place of residence rather than place of work.) In 1976–90 there was an almost constant decline in the relative position of the rest of the UK, followed by a very small relative improvement in the recent recession. Greater London's overall position changed little up to 1991, although there were some sharp shifts of fortune: a significant strengthening of its position until 1979, level pegging for two years, a sharp drop in 1981–4, an upward phase in 1984–7 and a sharp drop in 1991–2. What was

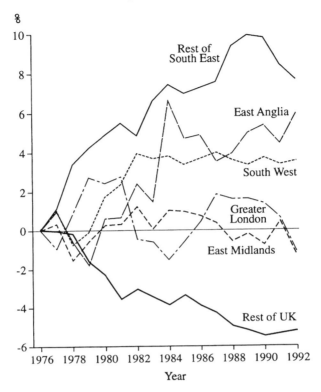

Figure 13.6. Cumulative growth of regional GDP per head relative to the UK in 1976–92. Source: CSO (1992)

particularly striking, however, was the improvement in the relative position of ROSE, whose cumulative growth in 1976–90 was almost 10 percentage points greater than the national average. There were also improvements in the relative position of East Anglia and the South-west, although these areas lay well behind ROSE.

Figure 13.7 plots the cumulative annual growth of GDP relative to the UK average. What this figure shows is that the redistribution of GDP was much greater than the redistribution of GDP per head. In 1979–92 the position of Greater London declined year in and year out, except in 1984–8. GDP per head did not decline as fast because of population loss. All the other regions experienced relative growth, although in all of these areas GDP per head increased less, relative to the UK, than GDP due to population growth.

These shifts in regional fortunes are in part an expression of trends in the distribution of employment. Figure 13.8 plots the cumulative growth in the civilian labour force in employment relative to the UK average. What it shows is that there was almost no increase in the South-east's share of employment –

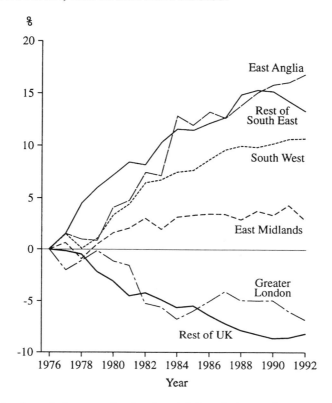

Figure 13.7. Cumulative growth of regional GDP relative to the UK in 1976–92.
Source: CSO (1992)

while Greater London suffered from a sharp drop in its share. The regions that gained relatively were East Anglia and the South-west. Figure 13.9, which plots the absolute change in employment by travel to work area (TTWA) in 1981–91, gives, however, a more detailed picture of the shifts in the location of employment that the aggregate data in Figure 13.8 conceal. These data cover a period which started with the end of the dramatic recession of 1979–81 in which there was a massive loss of industrial jobs and output. This period should be divided into at least two parts: the phase from 1981 to the end of a speculative service-led boom in 1989 and the subsequent recession. What is striking about this period as a whole is first the loss of jobs in the London and Heathrow TTWAs and in most of the large conurbations of the north and west. Secondly, there was very striking growth in a whole series of TTWAs in an arc that stretches around Greater London (with increases of 31 988 in Milton Keynes, 26 174 in Crawley, 24 713 in Bristol further to the west, 22 514 in Swindon, 21 522 in Guildford, 19 946 in Cambridge, 19 863 in Reading, 19 233 in Aylesbury and 16 293 in Basingstoke).

The growth in employment and output was to a large extent service sector led,

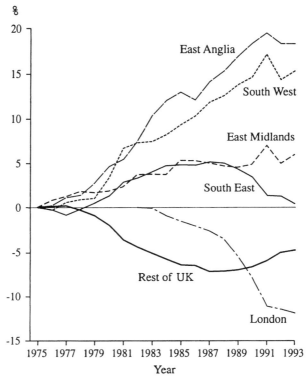

Figure 13.8. Cumulative growth in civilian workforce in employment relative to the UK in 1975–93. Source: CSO (1992)

but was also associated with a large wave of inward investment of which most was related to acquisitions. Many of the investments that occurred in the arc around Greater London were in logistic and marketing activities, whose growth was fuelled by a consumer-led boom, asset sales and a redistribution of wealth and income to the rich and affluent, although there was also a significant growth of white-collar jobs in industry and of producer services. At the same time the expansion of incomes led to substantial growth of a wide range of subordinate consumer service and low-level manufacturing activities, characterized by part-time employment, short-term contracts and informal work.

How has this economic restructuring with its associated changes in the nature and spatial distribution of work and employment affected patterns of migration? We can identify seven elements of post-Fordist economic restructuring: deindustrialization; privatization; flexible specialization; feminization; multiculturalism; social polarization; and globalization. Each of these can be expected, on *a priori* grounds, to have affected the size, socio-demographic composition and spatial distribution of the population of the London and South-east region.

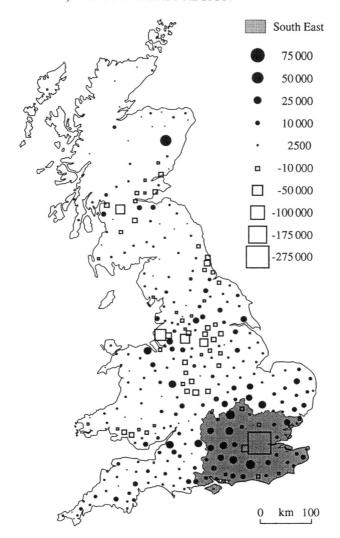

Figure 13.9. UK: employment change by travel-to-work area, 1981–91. Source: 1981 and 1991 Censuses of Employment

(i) *Deindustrialization:* By 1950 London had become the largest manufacturing city in the UK. But after the mid-1960s, first relatively then absolutely, London lost its industrial position. Industrial decline was reflected in manufacturing job loss, and in the decreasing share of UK manufacturing employment located in the London region. The effect of this manufacturing job loss was to reduce the attractiveness of the London region for both inter-regional and international manual worker migrations. Since such migrations had, in the past, contributed greatly to the population growth of the London region, their infrequency now propelled the region's population towards low growth or even decline.

(ii) *Privatization:* much of London's employment growth of the early post-war period had been supported by the expansion of the public sector. Increased state intervention in the economy and the growth of welfare services had boosted the London economy because each large public-sector corporation and each department of central government had developed large bureaucracies in their London headquarters. The privatization of state assets checked the growth of these bureaucracies. Thus the public sector service employment growth of the 1960s and early 1970s largely came to an end, to be partially replaced in the late 1970s and 1980s by private sector service employment growth. It is difficult to envisage what effects privatizations might have had on migration flows except, perhaps, to say that in so far as these changes encouraged the trend towards an 'embourgeoisement' of London's social structure, they further differentiated London socially and culturally from the other major cities of the UK, and thus were likely to have had the effect of reducing the migration flows between them.

(iii) *Flexible specialization:* the term 'flexible specialization' somewhat inadequately describes a number of potentially important changes in the labour process. Most of these changes, however, have been discussed largely in the context of manufacturing industry (for example, 'Japanization', 'lean production systems', etc.) and therefore might be expected to have less significance for a metropolitan city such as London which has come to be so heavily dependent on its role as a major centre for financial, property and business services. But there are at least two ways in which these changes in the organization of production might be expected to impinge on migration flows to and from the London region. The first is through the slimming down of corporate hierarchies, corporate decentralization and the fragmentation of production *filières*. This downsizing would imply a reduction in the importance of 'internal labour markets', leading to a reduction also in the likelihood of inter-regional or international intra-organizational transfers (London–provincial migrations). The second is the emphasis (found, for example, in the literature on high-tech industrial development and on 'new industrial districts') on the importance of local embeddedness. This process not only shuts others out, but ties those who are the participants in this process to the regions in which they presently reside. Both of these developments reinforce 'regional functional disconnection' and thereby reduce the levels of inter-regional migration. If you dispense with the 'mass collective worker', perhaps you also dispense with the 'mass migrations' in which such workers engaged (precisely the migrations which caused the rapid growth of London in the early post-war period).

(iv) *Feminization:* social and economic changes have resulted in greatly increased levels of employment of women in the formal labour market. In the UK much of this increase has been in the form of part-time employment (often in low-level white-collar jobs), but women have also entered the professions in large numbers in the recent period (for example, law, medicine, and account-ancy). This development has special significance for migration flows to and from London. It is not just that with more women working one inevitably finds more 'dual-income' or 'dual-career' households, with the likely result that migration will be reduced. (The reason migration might decline is because it is very much more difficult to satisfy two individual career aspirations in a single household migration than it is to satisfy one.) London is different from other UK labour markets in that it is uniquely large and uniquely diversified. Size and diversity allow both single people and working couples to make many more career moves without the need to migrate out of the region than would be the case in other parts of the country. London is, therefore, ideally placed for the development of dual careers. It is also uniquely favourable for the upward social promotion of 'career' women. The rate of movement of women into managerial jobs is particularly high in this region, when compared with other regions in the country (Fielding and Halford 1993).

(v)   *Multi-culturalism:* this is not just a social process. It involves the creation of ethnic subeconomies, and of ethnically specific patterns of occupational mobil-ity. London is the most culturally diverse city in Britain. This diversity increases its attractiveness to many international migrants, but reduces its attractiveness to many of those belonging to the dominant culture. The London region is far and away the most important destination for migrants from the Third World. This immigration not only affects population size directly, but also results in London becoming much more significant than previously in UK natural increase, because such immigrants tend to retain the family sizes of their countries of origin (at least initially).

(vi)   *Social polarization:* the dismantling of the welfare state and the substitu-tion of neoliberalism for the 'failed' social democratic compromise has exacer-bated income and wealth inequalities in Britain. London is where these inequalities are at their greatest. It is the site of the conspicuous consumption of press barons, property tycoons and pop stars, as well as of the abject poverty of the homeless and unemployed youngsters living in 'cardboard city'. How has social polarization affected migration? At the top end of the social scale it has appreciably enlarged the size of the socially and spatially mobile 'service class' of professional, technical and managerial employees. London is *par excellence* a service-class city. This is the city where middle-class careers are constructed. So a restructuring in favour of the middle classes is a restructuring in favour of the London region. The shift in wealth brought about by income tax cuts, privatisation of state assets, reduction in welfare payments was also a shift of wealth towards London which in the 1980s became the target for the able and the ambitious. But as the region became ever more dominated by the 'new middle classes' it became ever less hospitable as an environment for those on low incomes (due to high prices for housing, transport, etc.). There are some signs that such groups have been 'squeezed out' as a result of these changes, and pressed to migrate to low-cost regions in the north and west.

(vii) *Globalization:* the globalization of the British economy has expressed itself regionally in two main ways: the growth of direct foreign investment in manufacturing industry (notably Japanese car and consumer electronics investments in North-east England (Nissan) and South Wales (Hitachi), and the growth of the global financial and business service functions of London. This latter development has brought with it the sizable immigration of skilled manpower (especially in the early to mid-1980s) and has considerably added to the cosmopolitan character of the city and its region.

CYCLICAL AND CONJUNCTURAL TRENDS: DIVERGENCE AND INSTABILITY

The period since 1971 has witnessed not only structural changes but also severe cyclical volatility. A 'dash for growth' in the early 1970s, accompanied by a consumer boom and high house-price inflation, was followed by the deep recession associated with the 'oil crisis' of 1973–5. An upturn in 1978–9 was followed by an even longer and more severe recession in the early to mid-1980s when a significant part of British manufacturing industry located in the Midlands and North disappeared. This downturn was in turn followed by the consumer-led boom of the late 1980s.

At a national level, however, this late-1980s boom was part of a model of growth that was unsustainable. First, in 1973–89 real domestic expenditure on manufactures increased at about the same rate as expenditure on services and as domestic expenditure as a whole (30%). At the same time, there was little growth in manufacturing output. The inevitable consequence was a growing trade deficit in manufactures. As there was no equivalent shift towards greater net exports of internationally tradeable services or energy and raw materials, current account deficits grew, and there was a growing and ultimately unsustainable dependence on foreign savings, net capital inflows and increased international indebtedness.

Secondly, the growth of incomes was very dependent not on the creation of wealth but on a redistribution of wealth and especially on speculation. In particular, the growth of house prices was an active element in the boom and in the subsequent recession. In Britain the housing market is characterized by sharp cyclical movement in prices due in part to the fact that houses are bought not just as a dwelling but also as a means of accumulating wealth. A major determinant of house prices is the rate of house-price inflation: if house prices are increasing houses are bought in the expectation of capital gains and the upward movement of prices is reinforced; if house prices are falling the same mechanism reinforces their decline. In the years of rapid growth in the mid to late-1980s there was a major increase in house prices especially in the South-east, and many households sought first to use some of the increased value to finance consumer expenditure and second to use the increased value of their homes to secure loans. What resulted was first an increase in income and effective demand for goods and services not matched by an increase in supply, and second an increase in indebtedness. The increase in rentier and speculative incomes and increased indebtedness which were at the centre of Thatcherism and the increased territorial disequilibria to which they contributed were key factors in the subsequent crisis. These changes in the productive system were accompanied by a fundamental redefinition of the role of the state which itself reinforced the role of the South-east: reductions in direct and corporate taxation – allowed in part by privatization proceeds and North Sea oil revenues – and a clear transfer of government expenditures to the South-east.

Changes in the housing market and in general business confidence also had important effects on inter-regional migration to and from the South-east region, but the nature of the relationship is not that which might be expected on the basis of regional economic theory. Fist, at the peak in the cycle, even when it is the South-east economy which is central to national economic growth (as in the late 1980s), the South-east region experiences not net migration gain but net migration loss. Conversely, when the national economy is in recession, the South-east region experiences net migration balance or even a small net migration gain (as in the early 1980s). Figure 13.10 shows how these relationship come about. When the economy is booming, the number of people migrating to the South-east goes up significantly, but at the same time the number migrating from the South-east goes up even more significantly. As a result, a very much higher level of out-migration exceeds higher in-migration. At the subsequent trough, even though it may be the South-east economy which is instrumental in producing the downturn, the lower level of immigration coincides with an even lower level of out-migration. The result is the tendency towards net migration gain.

It can be argued that both housing and labour-market processes contribute to this situation. In downturns or recessions, job and housing moves (some of which will take the household out of the South-east region) are postponed, partly because of uncertainty about the near future, but mostly because of the difficulties experienced in disposing of property, land and housing. When turnover in both job and housing markets begins to increase as the economy improves and business confidence rises, these intended moves are actualized. As far as housing and land are concerned, this means that individuals can sell their homes and firms can sell their premises. In this way assets are realized in anticipation of new investments in other parts of the South-east or in other regions of southern Britain. Increasing turnover in housing and land encourages others to enter the market. This adds a further impetus to the South-east region's economy, which is heavily oriented towards employment in financial, property and legal services linked to property transactions. The regional economy also benefits from the fact that when people move house they tend to purchase consumer durables (carpets, furniture, white goods, etc.) and have building and decorating work done. A strong speculative element tends to contribute to the sharp rise in housing and land prices. However, when the ratio of house prices to

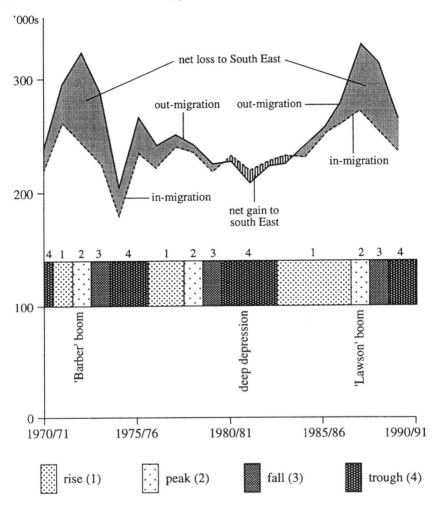

Figure 13.10. Inter-regional migration to and from the South-east region and stage in the business cycle, 1970–90

incomes becomes so great that entry into the market is essentially choked off, the process is thrown into reverse. The decline in transactions leads to a marked downturn in the regional economy, equity release dries up, house prices fall (in real, if not also in absolute terms), sellers withdraw their properties from the market and mobility is brought to a sudden halt by the inability of people and firms to dispose of their properties (even when, as often happens, they are desperate to do so). Mobility in the labour market is similarly checked by the risk-avoidance behaviour of individuals and firms. Because of this mechanism, the South-east region is prone to periodic bursts of out-migration and net migration loss followed by periods of low population turnover and net migration balance (see Fielding 1993).

CONCLUSION

These characteristics of the 1980s fitted well, first, with the secular role of Greater London and the South-east. Second, the neoliberal agenda of the cyclical, long-wave downturn that accelerated after 1976 is one that is very close to the interests of finance and of the rentier and thus in the interests of those activities which are particularly strongly concentrated in the South-east, although the area does also have real productive strength in research, high-tech activities and producer services. Third, the conjunctural movement of political and economic affairs, in particular with a government that was very active in reallocating resources towards its electoral supporters, further advantaged parts of the South-east. At the same time, however, its ideological opposition to any conception of strategic planning created a whole series of disequilibria which were significant additional contributors to the recession of the late 1980s and early 1990s and which have done much to start to reverse the fortunes of the UK's megalopolis.

The Greater London megalopolis – although ROSE rather than the capital itself – was clearly a region that won in the UK in the late 1970s and 1980s. As recent EU data on trends in GDP per head shows, the UK was a country that lost. The character of that development and its polarization in a south-eastern megalopolis may in future be seen as one of the key reasons for this failure.

REFERENCES

Benko, G. and Lipietz, A. (eds) (1992) *Les régions qui gagnent. District et réseaux: les nouveaux paradigmes de la géographie économique*. Paris: Presses Universitaires de France.

Buckatzsch, E.J. (1950–1) The geographical distribution of wealth in England, 1086–1843. An experimental study of certain tax assessments, *The Economic History Review*, Second Series, (1, 2 and 3):180–202.

Central Statistical Office (1992) *Regional Trends Vol 27*. London: HMSO.

Damette, F. and Scheibling, J. (1992) *Le Bassin Parisien*. Paris: DATAR.

Fielding, A.J. (1992) Migration and social mobility: South East England as an escalator region, *Regional Studies*: 1–15.

Fielding, A.J. (1993) Migration and the metropolis: inter-regional migration to and from South East England, 1971–1991, *Progress in Planning*: 71–166.

Fielding, A.J. and Halford, S. (1993) Geographies of opportunity: a regional analysis of gender-specific social and spatial mobilities in England and Wales, 1971–81, *Environment and Planning A* 25:1421–40.

Lee, C.H. (1986) *The British economy since 1700: a Macroeconomic Perspective.* Cambridge: Cambridge University Press.

Rubinstein, (1977) The Victorian middle classes: wealth, occupation and geography, *The Economic History Review*, 30.

Rubinstein, (1988) Wealth and the wealthy, in Langton, J. and Morris, R.J. (eds) *Atlas of Industrializing Britain 1780–1914*. London and New York: Methuen, pp. 156–9.

14 Jobs, Housing and Population Redistribution in Randstad Holland

FRANS DIELEMAN AND REIN JOBSE
University of Utrecht, The Netherlands

INTRODUCTION

This chapter discusses the migration flows between the western part of the Netherlands and the rest of the country. It also deals with the dramatic redistribution of population in the West, which is generally understood to consist of the provinces of North Holland, South Holland and Utrecht. The fundamental changes in migration rates and migration patterns during the past 25 years are largely determined by the overall migration flows to and from the four big cities (Amsterdam, Rotterdam, The Hague and Utrecht). Together with several medium-sized cities, planned growth centres and suburbs, these four cities constitute the large urban constellation in the western Netherlands commonly known as the 'Randstad' or 'Randstad Holland'. The urban places are arranged in a broad semi-circle surrounding the 'Green Heart', an area with less urban development that is still predominantly in agricultural and recreational use (Figure 14.1); hence the name, which translates literally as 'rim city'. But the concept of Randstad is also frequently used to indicate the entire western part of the Netherlands, not just the cities; this usage will be frequently encountered in the present chapter.

Amsterdam, Rotterdam, The Hague and Utrecht have functioned as the engine of the Dutch economy since the beginning of the Industrial Revolution. For 100 years, from 1860 to 1960, these cities were the major destination for a continuous flow of migrants from the economically less well-endowed peripheral parts of the country. Consequently, their share of the national population increased in that period from 14 to 21%.

During the 1960s, the economic engine of the Netherlands was stalling. This is reflected in a remarkable change in the century-old migration pattern. The population size of the four big cities declined; they lost population to areas outside the West, as well as to other parts of the Randstad. Their share of the national population declined to 13% by 1990. To some extent, this develop-

People, Jobs and Mobility in the New Europe. Edited by Hans H. Blotevogel and Anthony J. Fielding.
© 1997 European Science Foundation. Published in 1997 by John Wiley & Sons Ltd.

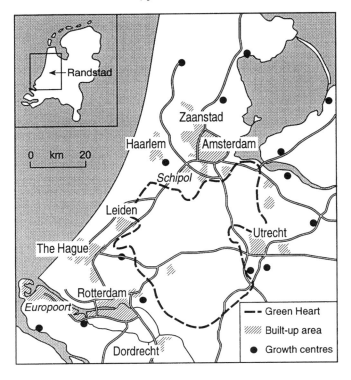

Figure 14.1.   Randstad Holland

ment took the form of a counterurbanization process. The regions that encircle the Randstad at some distance, such as parts of the provinces of Gelderland and Noord-Brabant, have particularly benefited from this development. Consequently their population increased rapidly.

Yet, just as in other countries, the counterurbanization trend was short lived. After 1973, urban development changed course again. The Randstad strengthened its position, and by 1985 domestic in-migration and out-migration were once more almost balanced.

In the first part of this chapter, the fluctuating migration flows between the Randstad and the rest of the country are discussed. They are related to the development of employment opportunities, especially those of the four big cities in the West.

The restructuring of the urban economy was only partly responsible for the population loss which the big cities have experienced since the 1960s. During the 1967–76 period, the Randstad underwent a surge of suburbanization. Apart from economic causes, demographic factors played a role. In addition, the government was deeply implicated, because of its manipulation of the locations of new residential construction. In the Netherlands, local authorities have an extraordinarily strong grip on land use. Municipalities control as much as 80% of land development, through ubiquitous land banking (Needham 1992). In addition, residential construction has been strongly regulated. The national government maintains a tight regime of building permits for new residential construction, which includes specifying where in the Netherlands, and thus also in the Randstad, residential construction is allowed to exceed local needs. The national urbanization policy thus played a decisive role in the selection of (major) development sites. Faludi and Van der Valk (1991) describe the 1960s and 1970s as the heyday of physical planning. As it turned out, growth management was very successful, and within the Randstad, an impressive half a million people migrated to where successive government policy documents indicated they ought to go.

The second half of this chapter focuses on this government-controlled process of population redistribution within the Randstad. It also highlights the (unintended) effects of this policy on the present structure of this urban region.

INDUSTRIAL RESTRUCTURING AND THE REVERSAL OF MIGRATION FLOWS

During the 1950s, the Randstad was still mainly the product of the industrial era. It was well adapted to the demands of the private sector typical of the times. The decade was dominated by the rapid growth of manufacturing and by declining employment in agriculture. The rural North of the country lost considerable numbers of people migrating to the East and the South, but above all to the Randstad (Figure 14.2).

Because of the primacy of the seaport function, the development of metropolitan activities of the Randstad had to take a back seat (de Smidt 1978, pp. 265ff). However, after the 1960s, the 'transactional economy', with its strong international orientation, became more clearly manifest and made new demands on the area: 'increasingly, the image of the city matters. Places compete with each other for mobile firms and mobile jobs on the basis of their attractiveness' (Hall 1990). But it was a long time before policy makers in the Randstad were aware of this.

During the 1970s and 1980s, the Randstad, like many other large metropolitan areas, had to confront the hard reality of economic restructuring and the problems this entails. Entire industries lost out to international competition and were either wiped out, decimated or forced to adapt their activities. The roots of these problems can be traced back to the 1950s and 1960s. But for a long time, few realized how vulnerable the Randstad was as a whole and how shaky were the economic foundations of the big cities in particular.

The virtual decimation of manufacturing has been the most obvious — and socially the most devastating — change in the economic structure to occur in the past three decades. In the big cities, this development caused both an economic revolution and a structural employment problem. The process is, of course, not unique to the Randstad; it has also affected locations elsewhere in the

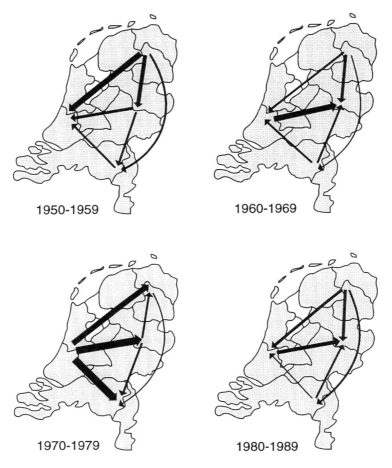

1950-1959

1960-1969

1970-1979

1980-1989

Figure 14.2. Inter-regional migration in the Netherlands 1950–89

Netherlands and abroad. Yet it was especially strong in the Randstad, and particularly in the big cities; these cities have lost the majority of their manufacturing employment over the past 30 years.

This development can be explained by a number of factors. Apart from the international competition and a prevailing negative attitude towards the private sector, the high wage level and the lack of quality of many older business areas played a role. The historic inner cities and the surrounding nineteenth-century neighbourhoods were important work locations, not only for services but also for manufacturing firms. Amsterdam clearly had the most pronounced profile in this respect; by 1965, almost two-thirds of all the manufacturing jobs were still concentrated in these predominantly derelict areas.

The proportion was generally lower in the other big cities of the Randstad, but they also showed a strong concentration of employment in the pre-war zones. These neighbourhoods may have been suitable as incubation areas for small start-up businesses. But they were much less suitable for large and expanding manufacturing firms because of their ageing plant, insufficient potential for expansion, poor accessibility and continual conflict with other forms of land use.

A number of the factors listed above also exerted their influence elsewhere in the Netherlands, but their effects were strongest in the Randstad. The overall industrial structure was not unfavourable, but many of the traditional manufacturing firms had to overcome many negative location factors. It therefore comes as no surprise that manufacturing employment in the northern wing of the Randstad – the region stretching from Haarlem to Utrecht, including Amsterdam – was already declining by the mid-1960s. In contrast, the south wing – The Hague, Rotterdam and adjacent cities to the east – initially managed to hold its own, thanks to the expansion of the (petro)chemical sector linked to the port of Rotterdam. But after 1973, this region also shared in the decline of manufacturing (de Smidt and Wever 1987). The big cities were hit hardest and Amsterdam suffered most. In 1950, its manufacturing firms still accounted for almost 40% of total employment (151 000 jobs). But by 1989, the sector employed no more than 43 000 people (14% of the active workforce).

The composition of manufacturing employment has also changed fundamentally during the past decades. The massive loss of blue-collar jobs is particularly noticeable. Consequently, this segment of manufacturing is now under-represented in the Randstad. Currently, the most important manufacturing activities are those basic industries tied to deep navigable water, producers of capital goods and a number of other highly qualified industries, such as the printing, tool and die making and until 1996 the aerospace industries. Also the high-quality end of the pharmaceutical (biotechnological) and electronics industries (Philips) are characteristic of the Randstad as a highly skilled metropolitan labour market. A further significant change in manufacturing is the shift from the factory floor to office jobs in administration and management (Stedelijke Netwerken 1988, p. 64).

The end of the manufacturing era of the cities of the Randstad caused a reversal of the migration flows between the western Netherlands and the rest of the country during the 1960s and 1970s (Figure 14.2). The migration balance of the Randstad with all other parts of the country turned negative. In the 1970s this even applied to the balance with the North, a peripheral region, where the labour-market structure was weak. Therefore, employment-related motives cannot be the only explanation of this change in migration pattern (Bartels and van Duijn 1981). The prevailing opinion at the time was that the most urbanized region of the Netherlands suffered from congestion and had therefore become less attractive.

Likewise, government policy for regional economic development and spatial development was based on the notion that the concentration of economic activities and population in the West had caused the problem of congestion. Consequently, a dispersal policy was adopted for the Randstad, which remained in force well into the 1980s. The most important elements of this policy were the improvement of infrastructure elsewhere and the availability of (re)location subsidies to firms that established themselves there (van Duyn et al. 1982). The policy discriminated against the West and continued to do so even when the huge unemployment problems in the big cities of the Randstad had become visible.

As stated above, the new out-migration from the Randstad in the 1960s and 1970s could be seen as a counterurbanization trend. This is revealed by the fact that the flow consisted predominantly of families (Jobse and Musterd 1989). Many of these families left the Randstad altogether for regions bordering the West of the country, because the supply of suitable new dwellings within the Randstad was insufficient (see below). But the picture changed again after 1973, the year of the oil crisis. Not only did the oil crisis have great economic effects, but it also had significant psychological consequences. The economic situation proved to be much more vulnerable than had long been assumed, and the future was much less secure than the rosy picture painted in the 1960s. Especially families seem to be sensitive to socio-economic developments (van der Erf 1984). Consequently, the number of mobile families dropped precipitously after 1973. Especially the number of families migrating to regions outside the Randstad declined sharply. After 1980, the increasing output of residential construction in the big cities also contributed to this decline.

This stark picture of the eroding economy of the Randstad should be qualified somewhat. While a large part of the manufacturing base of the Randstad collapsed, the service sectors underwent a healthy rate of expansion. In large parts of the Randstad, the employment in this sector has doubled since 1963. The rapid growth of the tertiary and quaternary sectors has bolstered the already strong position of the Randstad in these sectors. During the past few years, an ever increasing share of the new office space in the Netherlands was built in the Randstad – expecially in its northern wing. Its share of the larger offices even reached 90% (Lambooy 1988).

Comparing the different parts of the Randstad, the future perspectives of the northern wing seem to be relatively good. Entrepreneurs consider this region to be particularly favourable. Its assets are the proximity of Schiphol Airport, its traffic infrastructure and the international flavour of the city of Amsterdam, with its financial world and extensive networks of business services. Their presence creates a level of attraction that cannot be matched elsewhere in the Netherlands (Nederlands Economisch Instituut 1986, p. 99; Economische perspectieven 1986, p. 185). The number of jobs in the business-services sector in the larger Amsterdam region and the adjacent province of Utrecht expanded by no less than 30% in the 1987–91 period (Atzema et al. 1992).

The southern wing of the Randstad remains dominated by the large-scale production and distribution centres located in Rotterdam and by the govern-

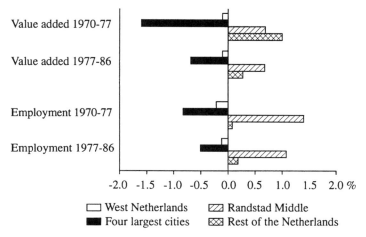

Figure 14.3. Netherlands: regional output and employment growth 1970–86.
Source: WRR 1990

ment centre of The Hague, which has suffered under austerity measures. Consequently, this region has shown a considerably slower expansion than the Randstad as a whole since 1984.

The combination of the developments in the two major parts of the Randstad has allowed its overall development to lag behind development in the rest of the country, both with respect to the total active population and value added (Functionele samenhang 1990). This relatively poor performance is mainly due to the employment trends in the big cities. In contrast, the suburban areas exhibited a healthy rate of growth (Figure 14.3). This is reflected in the migration balances between the West and the rest of the country, which declined to relatively small numbers during the 1980s (Figure 14.2). The flows between the West and the South were almost balanced. The North still loses population to the Randstad as well as to the East of the country. This latter flow and the outflow from the Randstad eastward reveal the expansion of the urban field of the Randstad in that direction. The province of Utrecht, comprising the easternmost part of the West of the country, and the adjacent province of Gelderland are the two Dutch regions that have shown consistent employment growth over the past 30 years. And judging from the net migration flows, they have also become the favoured destinations of migrants in the Netherlands. In this respect, these two centrally located provinces have taken over the role played by the four big cities in the West of the country for a century, between 1860 and 1960.

Recently, the net outflow from the Randstad to the rest of the country has been increasing somewhat. But the size of this net outflow is substantially smaller than in the first half of the 1970s (Figure 14.4). The conditions have fundamentally changed. Since 1983, the more vibrant economy has been exerting a positive effect on the migration role. However, this tendency is

Balance x 1000 persons

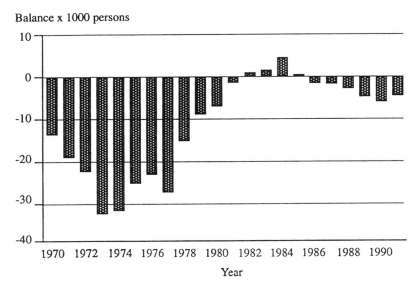

Figure 14.4. Balance of migration between the three western provinces and the rest of the Netherlands 1970–91. Source: Netherlands Central Bureau of Statistics

neutralized by the current policy to promote the position of the big cities of the Randstad. This provides a stark contrast to the situation in the 1960s and 1970s. At that time, the policy was distinctly anti-urban, which bolstered the tendencies of the marketplace.

RESIDENTIAL CONSTRUCTION AND SUBURBANIZATION

As recently as 1960, the population of the big cities was not markedly different from that of the surrounding municipalities. The city residents still comprised many families and households with a median and above-median income (Dieleman and Musterd 1991). But the four big cities lost more than half a million inhabitants between 1965 and 1985, which amounted to a quarter of their peak population. This was not only brought about by the same factors that were alluded to above as the causes of migration. There were also demographic and policy factors at play, resulting in the surge of suburbanization during this period.

The Netherlands underwent a rapid demographic transition after 1970; the birth rate declined precipitously, and singles and cohabiting couples became normal household types. This brought about the enormous growth in the number of households between 1970 and 1990: from 4 to 6.1 million. The big cities could simply not provide sufficient housing to meet this explosion of housing demand, and consequently, a wave of families moved to the suburbs (Figure 14.5).

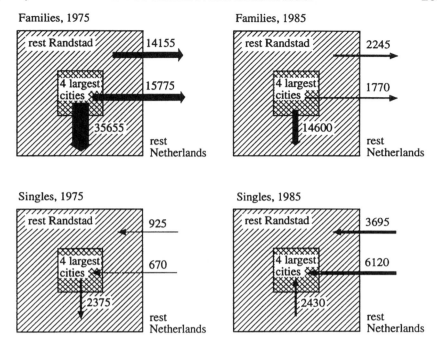

Figure 14.5.   Netherlands: internal migration by household type 1975 and 1985

In addition, policy-determined factors played a role and accounted for the unprecedented persistence of suburbanization for more than a decade (Jobse and Musterd 1992; Kruythoff et al. 1992). The competition between the various types of settlement in the Randstad was strongly influenced by the wide quantitative and qualitative variations in new construction. This largely affected their capacity to attract various population categories and to retain them. The big cities in particular distinguished themselves by a very specific though scarcely market-oriented policy. This was not the least important factor in the selective migration processes, which brought about the spatially segregated pattern of age groups and socio-economic categories.

The beginning of this development can be traced back to the end of the 1950s. The big cities then found themselves at a crossroads. On the one hand, they could choose a policy that could have helped them remain attractive to above-median income families. On the other hand, they could take the path towards becoming the residential area of non-family households and, in general, household types with a weak position on the market. In the first case, the policy should have aimed at improving the quality of the urban housing stock. The massive high-rise developments after 1965 can be seen as an attempt to embrace the first policy option. The high-rises were sited in a green, open environment and formed the urban response to the rapidly growing suburban areas at the periphery of the metropolitan region. The expectations and the actual developments, however, proved to deviate sharply from each other. The appeal of many of the new residential areas among the target groups was substantially less than had been anticipated. In a number of cases, the new housing complexes quickly deteriorated into problem areas.

The urban renewal programmes did little to enhance the attractiveness of the urban housing stock. The policy of the 1970s primarily sought to conserve and refurbish existing housing and to provide more social rental housing. It did yield great technical improvements, but hardly any betterment of the residential environment (de Kleijn 1985, pp. 172, 173, 195). Nor did the physical improvements offer solutions to the social problems (van den Beuken and Haest 1987, pp. 99–100). The widely used slogan 'building for the locals' meant in practice the continuation of the social problems in the urban renewal areas. Therefore, the renewal process often did not meet the expectations of the local residents (de Kleijn 1985, pp. 172, 173, 195). Neither new construction nor the urban renewal programmes contributed much to the task of substantially raising the quality of the urban environment. The supply was related more to the ideologies of politicians, urbanists and housing official than to market demand patterns.

While aspiration levels rose in the 1960s and 1970s, leading to a growing demand for larger, newer single-family homes for owner occupancy, the supply in the big cities remained dominated by small, older rental apartments. The newly constructed dwellings did not meet the demand of the above-median income families. Apartments in the social rental sector formed by far the largest share of new dwellings in the big cities. In most cities, single-family homes and owner-occupier dwellings accounted for no more than 10–20% of the supply of new dwellings. In Amsterdam, for instance, 87% of the total housing stock in 1991 consisted of affordable homes for below-median income households (VROM 1991).

The construction of only a token number of owner-occupier dwellings was first and foremost a political choice in Amsterdam and Rotterdam. Even the most attractive locations were sometimes deliberately not used for more expensive housing (Brunt et al. 1986, p. 197; van Eijkeren 1985, p. 23). The Rotterdam Master Plan of 1978 did propose raising the appeal of the Rotterdam housing stock for higher income groups, but eventually the priority was clearly given to the provision of housing for the lowest income groups (Rotterdams Structuurplan 1978). This was not entirely a free choice. It was at least partly forced on the big cities by the continued refusal of most of the suburban municipalities to provide housing for financially disadvantaged urban population groups (Ostendorf 1985, pp. 340ff).

The national government's urbanization policy also contributed substantially to the process of urbanization. During the 1960–80 period, it was assumed that the cities were overcrowded, and that large numbers of people in the Randstad would have to be accommodated outside the cities in growth centres (Figure

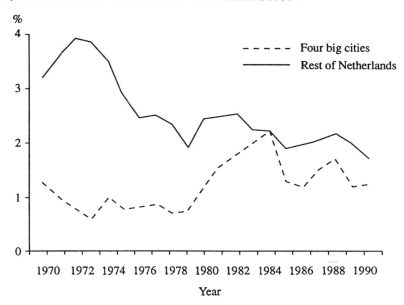

Figure 14.6. Netherlands: dwelling construction rates for the four big cities and the rest of the Netherlands, 1970–90

14.1). Therefore, the big cities built relatively few dwellings during that period. Consequently, the extremely negative migration balances caused a major decline in demand for urban services and facilities.

By the end of the 1970s, this deterioration of the urban structure triggered a complete policy reversal. The national government and the administrations of the big cities synchronized their actions. As many new dwellings as possible were henceforth built within the big cities. Abandoned industrial and commercial sites and buildings were converted to housing on a large scale (Brunt et al. 1986).

Consequently, new construction in the cities soared during the 1980s (Figure 14.6). But in spite of this rise in number of newly constructed dwellings, the evolution of the characteristics of the dwellings themselves remained limited. Initially, the specialization of the supply (predominantly social housing and apartments) even increased somewhat. Throughout the 1980s, the share of single-family houses remained very low. The proportion of very expensive dwellings even decreased substantially. On the one hand, this reflected the pervasiveness of the policy aimed at supporting deprived population groups with their typically weak housing market positions. But the tendency was also underlined by the stepped-up urban renewal activities. Furthermore, the collapse of the owner-occupier market continued to exert its effects throughout the first half of the 1980s. Only towards the end of the decade and at the beginning of the 1990s did the shares of single-family and owner-occupier housing clearly increase.

The position of the big cities has been strengthened considerably with respect to the other areas within the Randstad. During the 1975–85 period, the negative migration balance of the four big cities with the suburban areas decreased substantially (Figure 14.5). The slower outflow of people from the big cities has a strong statistical correlation with the diminished supply of new housing outside the big cities (Jobse and Musterd 1989).

In comparison with the migration patterns of the 1960s and 1970s, the contours of migration during the 1980s suggest a much more intricate pattern. The usual dominant flows of (young) singles towards the big cities and of families towards the suburbs and growth centres seems to have been supplemented by a number of variants. Today's flows are not easily described in terms of the old stereotypes. The migration flow towards the growth centres, for instance, has become much more varied over the past few years. Families are still dominant, but they are accompanied by other categories – the elderly, singles and probably also by ethnic minorities – to a much larger extent than in the 1970s.

This development partly results from the weakened competitive position of the growth centres with respect to the big cities. Because of the increased construction activity, far fewer families exchange the cities for the growth centres nowadays, which implies that other types of household can take their place. In addition, the decrease of families among the immigrants stimulates the growth centres to build more for other types of household than they used to do in the past.

But other factors seem to be influential as well. The current shifts in the migration flows towards the growth centres show some similarities to the processes that have been documented in US suburbs since the 1960s. These changes were described as the 'urbanization of the suburbs' (Masotti and Hadden 1973). One of the characteristics of this process was an increased heterogeneity of the groups that moved there. The suburb was no longer a 'green ghetto dedicated to the elite' (Mumford 1966, p. 561), not even 'just a family place' (Masotti 1973, p. 19). Many of the new residential areas in the periphery of the metropolitan areas of the big cities were initially very homogeneous in character and offered only limited opportunities for housing, employment and services. The larger peripheral settlements are obviously no longer only satellites of the central city but have developed into what Pahl (1965) called 'cities in their own right'.

As dwellings, jobs and services grow in number and variety, some of the larger suburban settlements and growth centres become more appealing to categories of residents that initially were hardly represented among the migrants to these places. The increasing urbanization of a part of the metropolitan periphery may tempt a larger share of the young adults leaving the parental home to set up their households in their current place of residence or in a similar suburb or growth centre. Such a development has already been observed in US suburbs by Masotti (1973), and seems to be a realistic perspective for the Netherlands as well. Not all young adults aspire to live in a large city environment. Especially among those with a limited formal education, many prefer the environment in which they have grown up. Beaujon and Wlötgens (1984) observed that three-quarters of the young adults in the population of suburban Purmerend and Uithoorn want to obtain a home of their own in their current place of residence. This preference is also independent of their degree of orientation toward the central city.

In addition, it seems questionable whether or not the big cities can maintain their current accessibility for young starters. The housing opportunities for this group are rapidly declining as the number of poor-quality, inexpensive dwellings diminishes due to urban renewal.

The effects of the changing migration flows are also manifest in the population structure of the big cities. They seemed to develop increasingly into areas for both the immobile elderly and the highly mobile younger generation. Households of the latter group tend to take their first steps in the housing and labour markets in the big cities before they settle down in a suburb. This has changed in recent years; the long-term trend seems to have shifted course. This can be inferred from at least two developments. On the one hand, the decline in population size of the cities, which set in by the mid-1960s, has been brought to a halt. On the other hand, the dual trend towards rejuvenation and greying of the population has turned into an expansion of the middle-aged population groups (Hoogvliet and Jobse 1989). But this population consists predominantly of singles and two-person households and single-parent families. In large parts of the big cities, singles have become the prevailing household type (Jobse 1991). The cornerstone of the metropolitan society is no longer the family but the single person (Brunt 1990, p. 21).

Notwithstanding the revived interest in urban living, traditional families – ethnic housholds excepted – still don't seem to be inclined to live in the big cities (Figure 14.5). Nor is there much evidence of an increase in higher-income groups among the cities' populations. In other words, the noted changes in the migration patterns do not provide unequivocal evidence of increased attractiveness of the big cities. The supply of attractive homes for population groups with a strong market position remains limited. And in spite of the recent shifts in residential construction policy, this situation is not about to change.

Parkinson et al. (1992) warn that the creation of high-quality residential environments should not be pursued at the expanse of 'socially balanced environments'. In other words, it would be shortsighted to resolve the one problem – the shortage of attractive high-quality residential areas – by creating another problem – social tensions. This obviously does not imply that a given structure in the housing stock should be retained at all costs. But it does mean that the social consequences of shifts between the sectors must be reasonable. For the big cities of the Netherlands, this means that a substantial expansion of the more expensive rental and owner-occupier sectors demands a long-term commitment.

CONCLUSION

The demise of the industrial era has wrought dramatic change in the positions of Amsterdam, Rotterdam, The Hague and Utrecht with reference to the pattern of migration flows in the Netherlands since 1960. During the preceding century, flows of migrants from elsewhere in the Netherlands were attracted by the expanding employment opportunities there. After 1960, these cities became the source of migration flows to the suburban areas in the West and to other parts of the country. This was brought about by the combination of overall economic restructuring and the huge output of residential construction outside the cities. During the past three decades, the suburban areas in the provinces of Utrecht and Gelderland were the dominant destinations; this signifies an eastward expansion of the urban field.

The increase of residential construction in the cities during the 1980s has resulted in more balanced migration flows between the cities, the suburban areas and the regions elsewhere in the Netherlands after 1985. Yet the increased housing production in the cities has not improved the labour-market position of the residents.

The population size of the cities declined faster than the number of jobs. This resulted in a more balanced ratio of people and jobs, but paradoxically the unemployment rate in the cities increased rapidly. The most important cause of this is the growing gap between the nature of the jobs and the characteristics of the local active population during the past two decades. Because of the selective nature of the migration, the categories of unskilled workers and of people with little specialized experience grew in a relative sense. But suitable jobs for them decreased rapidly in number.

The unskilled, including many ethnic-minority residents, were damaged not only by the disappearance of large parts of the manufacturing sector but also by shifts in the occupational structure. The upgrading of functions and the displacement of people with lower qualifications by people with higher ones, brought about by general labour-market developments, had an impact throughout the country. But these tendencies were felt most acutely in the big cities of the Randstad.

In absolute numbers, unemployment in the Randstad still compares favourably with the rest of the country. But in the big cities, the unemployment rate is much higher than the national average. In 1990, over 28% of all people registered as unemployed with the official employment agencies lived in one of the four big cities. This is a remarkably high proportion, considering that the number of jobs exceeds the population size by 30% in the big cities. The situation is especially unfavourable in Amsterdam and Rotterdam, with an unemployment rate one and a half times the national average.

The expansion of the tertiary and quarternary sectors was highly advantageous to the higher-qualified workforce living outside the big cities. The problems caused by the shrinkage of other sectors, on the other hand, had to be confronted by the central cities' residents. The restricted spatial horizon and limited mobility of many of the unemployed in the older parts of the cities prevent them from taking advantage of the growth in jobs outside the big cities. In other words, they are more easily victimized by the consequences of business displacements away from the cities (Atzema 1991; Kloosterman 1991).

The population loss of the big cities started to level off after 1985. But this does not mean that the job market has blossomed in the central cities of the Randstad. The suburbanization of jobs continues unabated, leaving many residents behind in the cities bereaved of their jobs and living in an environment where the chances to re-enter the labour market remain limited.

ACKNOWLEDGEMENT

Frans Dieleman acknowledges the support of the Netherlands Institute for Advanced Study (NIAS) of the Royal Netherlands Academy of Sciences, Wassenaar, The Netherlands.

REFERENCES

Atzema, O.A.L.C. (1991) Epiloog: Arbeidsmarkt en stedelijke vernieuwing: Een brede aanpak in beleid en onderzoek, in *De werkende stad: Aspecten van de grootstedelijke arbeidsmarkt*. Atzema, O.A.L.C., Hessels, M. and Zondag, H. (eds) Stedelijke Netwerken, Utrecht: pp. 167–79.

Atzema, O.A.L.C., Lensink, E. and Zondag, H. (1992), Economische dynamick en Werkgelegenheid in de Randstad, *Stedelijke Netwerken 47*. Utrecht: Stedelijke Netwerken.

Bartels, C.P.A. and Van Duijn, J.J. (1981) *Regionaal-economisch beleid in Nederland*. Assen: Van Gorcum.

Beaujon, E. and Wöltgens, E. (1984) *Raakt de suburb haar kinderen kwijt?* Amsterdam: Publicatiereeks ISG, Universiteit van Amsterdam.

Beuken, G.J. van den Haest, G. (1987) Integraal beleid en sociaal beheer van buurten: Leefklimaat, bewonersselectie en vormen van beheer, in Hortulanus, R.P. and van Kempen, E.T. (eds), *Sociaal beheer van buurten*. 's-Gravenhage: VUGA, pp. 97–112.

Brunt, H., Jobse, R.B. and Nichting, T. (1986) Transformatie van voormalige bedrijfs-terreinen: Een verkenning in middelgrote en grote Nederlandse steden. *Stedebouw en Volkshuisvesting* 67:195–201.

Brunt, L. (1990) Stedelijk wonen, in *Vernieuwde volkshuisvesting*. Zoetermeer: Raad voor de Volkshuisvesting, pp. 19–24.

Dieleman, F.M. (1993) Multicultural Holland, myth or reality? in King, R.J. (ed.), *Mass Migration in Europe: the Legacy and the Future*. London: Belhaven.

Dieleman, F.M. and Musterd, S. (1991) Maatschappelijke veranderingen en de herstruc-turering van de Randstad, *Geografisch Tijdschrift, themanummer Europese Steden* XXV(5):490–501.

Duyn, J.J. van, Lambooy, J.G. and Paelinck, J.H.P. (1982) *Rapport inzake het regionaal sociaal-economisch beleid en het ruimtelijk beleid*. Gravenhage: Sociaal-Economische Raad.

Economische perspectieven voor Amsterdam-Meerlanden (1986) Haarlem: Provincie Noord-Holland.

Engbersen, G. (1990) *Publieke bijstandsgeheimen: Het ontstaan van een onderklasse in Nederland*. Leiden: Stenfert Kroese.

Eijkeren, R. van (1985) Het ruimtelijk beleid in Rotterdam, in Burgers, J.P. and Stoppelenburg, P.A. (eds) *Het stedelijke woonerf*. Tilburg: IVA, Katholieke Hogeschool Tilburg.

Erf, R.F. van der (1984) Internal migration in the Netherlands: Measurement and main characteristics, in ter Heide, H. and Willekens, F.J. (eds) *Demographic research and Spatial Policy: the Dutch Experience*. London: Academic Press, pp. 47–68.

Faludi, A. and van der Valk, A.J. (1991) Half a million witnesses: The success (and failure?) of Dutch urbanisation strategy, *Built Environment* 17: 43–52

Functionele samenhang in de Noordvleugel van de Randstad (1990) *Economisch-Statistische Berichten* 75(3749):252–5.

Hall, P. (1990) *Reinventing the City*. Toronto: Centre for Urban and Community Studies, University of Toronto.

Hoogvliet, A. and Jobse, R.B. (1989) De veranderende woonfunctie van de vroeg-20ste-eeuwse wijken in de drie grote steden, in Dieleman, F.M., van Kempen, R. and van Weesep, J. (eds) *Wonen in de grote stad*. Meppel: Educatief.

Jobse, R.B. (1991) Eenpersoonshuishoudens in de drie grote steden: Een nieuw dominant huishoudenstype, in van Kempen, R., Musterd, S. and Ostendorf, W. (eds) *Maatschappelijke verandering en stedelijke dynamiek*. Volkshuisvesting in theorie en praktijk 30. Delft: Delftse Universitaire Pers, pp. 43–58.

Jobse, R.B. and Musterd, S. (1989) *Dynamiek in de Randstad, Een analyse van woningbouw- en migratiestatistieken voor de periode 1970–1986*. Stedelijke Netwerken, Werkstukken, 10. Utrecht: Stedelijke Netwerken.

Jobse, R.B. and Musterd, S. (1992) Changes in the residential function of the big city, in Dieleman, F.M. and Musterd, S. (eds), *The Randstad: A research and policy laboratory*. Dordrecht: Kluwer Academic Publishers, pp. 39–65.

Kleijn, G. de (1985) *De staat van de stadsvernieuwing*. Utrecht: Vakgroep Stadsstudies, Utrecht University.

Kloosterman, R.C. (1991) Stedelijke arbeidsmarktparadoxen: het Amsterdamse voorbeeld, in Atzema, O.A.L.C., Hessels, M. and Zondag, H. (eds) *De werkende stad: Aspecten van de grootstedelijke arbeidsmarkt*. Utrecht: Stedelijke Netwerken, pp. 25–41.

Kruythoff, H., Jobse, R.B. and Musterd, S. (1992) Migration and the socio-economic structure of the four big Randstad cities and their daily urban systems, *Tijdschrift voor Economische en Sociale Geografie* 83(3):180–96.

Lambooy, J.G. (1988) Technologische ontwikkeling en lokaal beleid, in Broekhuis, J.J. (ed.) *Technology Assessment in stad en regio*. Groningen: Wolters-Noordhoff, pp. 105–17.

Masotti, L.H. (1973) Prologue: Suburbia Reconsidered: Myth and Counter-Myth, in Masotti, L.H. and Hadden, J.K. (eds) *The Urbanization of the Suburbs*. Beverly Hills/London: Sage.

Masotti, L.K. and Hadden, J.K. (eds) (1973) *The Urbanization of the Suburbs*. Beverly Hills/London: Sage.

Mumford, L. (1966) *The City in History: its Origins, its Transformations and its Prospects*. Harmondsworth: Penguin.

Nederlands Economisch Institut (1986) *Randstad in economisch perspectief: Economische specialisatie, functionele samenhang en ontwikkelingstendenties*. Rotterdam: Nederlands Economisch Instituut.

Needham, B. (1992) A theory of landprices when land is supplied publicly: the case of the Netherlands, *Urban Studies* 29: 669–86

Nusselder, W.J., Schoorl, J.J. and Berkien, J.F.M. (1990) *Bevolkingsvooruitberekening allochtonen in Nederland naar nationaliteit, 1989–1999: Bevolkingsgroepen met de Turkse, Marokkaanse en EG or overige niet-Nederlandse nationaliteit.* Rapport nr. 16. 's-Gravenhage: NIDI.

Ontwerp Structuurplan 1990, Amsterdam: Deel II De Toelichting (1990) Amsterdam: Dienst Ruimtelijke Ordening.

Ostendorf, W. (1985) Gemeentelijk woningmarktbeleid in het stadsgewest Amsterdam. *Geografisch Tijdschrift* XIX(4):333–45.

Pahl, R.E. (1965) *Urbs in Rure: The Metropolitan Fringe in Hertfordshire.* London: London School of Economics and Political Science.

Parkinson, M., Bianchini, F., Dawson, J., Evans, R. and Harding, A. (1992) *Urbanisation and the Functions of Cities in the European Community.* European Institute of Urban Affairs. Liverpool: Johns Moores University.

Rotterdamse Structuurplan (1978) Rotterdam: Gemeente Rotterdam.

Smidt, M. de (1978) De Randstad: Problemen van stedelijke onevenwichtigheid en perspectieven van stedelijk vernieuwingsbeleid. *De Aardrijkskunde.* 2:263–91.

Smidt, M. de and Wever, E. (1987) *De Nederlandse industrie: Positie, spreiding en struktuur.* Assen/Maastricht: Van Gorcum.

Stedelijke Netwerken (1988) *Dynamiek van het bedrijfsleven in de Randstad.* Werkstukken nr. 7. Delft: Stedelijke Netwerken.

VROM (1991) *Volkshuisvesting in cijfers 1991.* Den Haag: Ministerie van VROM.

Part V

CONCLUSION

15 The Effects of Economic Restructuring on the Populations of Western Europe's Cities and Regions

ANTHONY J. FIELDING
University of Sussex, UK

INTRODUCTION

The purpose of this final chapter is to draw together some of the themes discussed in this collection of essays in order to address a key theoretical issue – to what extent and in what ways has the economic restructuring experienced in western Europe over the last 20 years served to shape the circumstances of people's lives, and in particular their choices about where to live and work. To do this the chapter moves from the conceptual to the empirical, and then attempts to bring the two together in a final synthesis. More specifically, the first section presents a simple conceptual framework designed to explore the effects of economic restructuring processes on inter-regional migration flows. It is based on research on South-east England, but the framework is very general and can probably be used for most large metropolitan city-regions in western Europe. The second section summarizes the main features of urban and regional population change, focusing on the changes since the eary 1970s. It is shown that one of the main characteristics of the urban and regional population system in the recent period has been its *quiescence* (stability). The third section examines the apparent contradiction between this quiescence of the population system and the radical nature of changes in the production system (brought about by western European economic integration, rapid technological change, the transition from a Fordist productive and social order to a post-Fordist one, the emergence of industrial districts, the rise of global cities etc.).

People, Jobs and Mobility in the New Europe. Edited by Hans H. Blotevogel and Anthony J. Fielding.
© 1997 European Science Foundation. Published in 1997 by John Wiley & Sons Ltd.

298

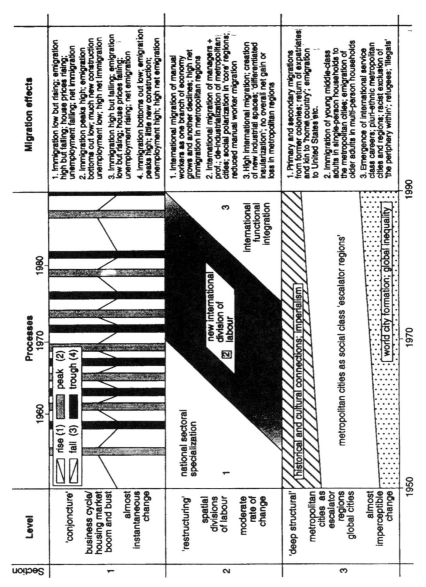

Figure 15.1. A conceptual framework for analysing the economic forces affecting inter-regional migration (applied to South-east England)

A SIMPLE CONCEPTUAL FRAMEWORK: THE EFFECTS OF ECONOMIC PROCESSES ON POPULATION REDISTRIBUTION

The emphasis in this section is on gross migration flows. Figure 15.1 represents an attempt to condense a number of important ideas about the way in which economic processes (including 'restructuring' in the strict sense of the term) affect the key mechanism for change in the population system – migration. Although designed to deal with inter-regional migration, this framework is appropriate also for conceptualizing international migration flows (Fielding 1993).

To summarize, inter-regional migrations to and from metropolitan city-regions (such as those containing London, Paris, Amsterdam, Milan, Frankfurt, Barcelona etc.) can be interpreted in the light of three sets of processes:

(i) *The housing market/business cycle.* People's decisions about where to live, where to move to and when to move are affected by the business cycle. As Kemper shows, there is a clear tendency in (West) Germany for inter-regional migration rates to increase in periods of economic growth and to decrease in recession. Or take the case of migration to and from the London metropolitan city-region. In the first stage of the cycle (rising output, falling unemployment) in-migration to the region tends to be low but rising slightly, out-migration is low but rising fast; at the height of the boom in-migration peaks moderately high, out-migration peaks very high and large net losses to the region result; in the third stage of the cycle (stagnant or falling output, rising unemployment) in-migration to the metropolitan region is moderately high but falling, out-migration is high but falling fast; and finally, at the bottom of the cycle in-migration bottoms out at a low level and out-migration bottoms out at an even lower level, leading to net migration balance or even a slight net migration gain to the region. It has been argued elsewhere (Fielding 1993a) that house and job turnover rates are the key mechanisms through which British inter-regional migration patterns are determined by stages in the business cycle (see Figure 13.10). In particular, decentralizing job and house relocations are far less frequent at the bottom of the cycle than at the top. It is interesting to note in this respect that Kemper also found that net migration balances showed a counter-cyclical trend for the three largest urban areas of (West) Germany (Ruhr, Hamburg and Munich).

(ii) *Labour market restructuring.* Changes in the production system redistribute employment opportunities and thereby influence urban and regional residential location decisions. Under regional sectoral specialization (which dominated in the 1950s and early 1960s), inter-regional migration of all kinds of workers occurred as one branch of the economy grew and another declined; the major metropolitan regions, with their highly favourable employment structures, experienced net migration gains at this time. In some countries the shift from a declining agricultural sector to growing manufacturing and service sectors had a totally dominant influence on inter-regional migration flows.

Under the hierarchical (or 'new') spatial division of labour (which became fully developed in the early 1970s) the inter-regional migration of professionals and managers became more important (particularly as a result of intra-organizational transfers) and the migration of manual workers became less important. As regions became increasingly differentiated, not on the basis of *what* they produced, but on the basis of their *role* in the production process (routine production, both unskilled and skilled; research and development; managerial control and strategic planning), a major deindustrialization of metropolitan city-regions occurred and this, combined with 'counterurban' shifts in both manufacturing and service-sector employment, led to net migration losses in these metropolitan regions and to net migration gains in regions with 'free-standing' cities and in rural and peripheral regions (see, for example, the discussion of the migration effects of the deindustrialization of the Randstad in Chapter 14). Both regional sectoral specialization and the new spatial divison of labour can be classified as 'Fordist' in character; they were associated with the mass production of standardized products for mass markets within a Keynesian welfare-state framework. Under regional functional disconnection (emerging since the mid-1970s), however, migration to and from the metropolitan city-regions is reduced by the increasingly divergent nature of regional housing and labour markets, resulting in barriers to inter-regional migration and to low levels of net gain or loss to those regions. Furthermore, the chance to co-presence of unrelated activities characteristic of regional functional disconnection leads to high leakages from local economies, and hence local multiplier effects remain low. This in turn means that the impacts of relocations of productive investment on local levels of employment and population are also limited. Regional funcational disconnection is 'post-Fordist' (and possibly also 'post-modern') in its associations. It connects with the globalization of economic relationships and with social and cultural fragmentation (see final section below).

(iii)   *The underlying and almost unchanging geography of the European space-economy.* In particular, metropolitan city-regions tend to dominate intra-national migration systems, and to act as locations of upward social mobility, that is as 'escalator regions'. As 'escalator' regions, these large metropolitan cities (especially when they possess 'global city' features) attract (from other regions in their national territories, and increasingly from other countries) many upwardly mobile young adults living in single-person households; they socially promote them and then encourage their out-migration in nuclear family or 'empty-nest' households to other regions in later middle age or at, or close to, retirement. In this way these households cash in many of the assets they have gained from their passage through the metropolitan city's housing and labour markets (see Fielding 1992 for evidence supporting the idea that South-east England is an 'escalator region').

The remainder of this chapter is concerned with processes of a 'restructuring' nature (that is, to level 2 in Figure 15.1); those of a more 'conjunctural' or 'deep structural' nature, although important for a full understanding of migration, will not be considered further, (i) because they are less closely connected to this book's main theme – the urban and regional restructuring of Europe; and (ii) because they largely affect the characteristics of gross migration flows rather than met migration balances.

URBAN AND REGIONAL POPULATION CHANGES

A major theme running through this volume has been the relative stability of the regional population and urban settlement systems during the economic restructuring of the recent period. This is probably most clearly expressed in the chapter by Champion where he writes: 'the general picture is one of remarkably low net migration values [in the 1980s] compared with the two previous decades'. Using Vandermotten's data, he shows that for the 557 level III regions of the EC there was a fall in the variance of net migration rates from 113.3 in the 1960s, to 42.2 in the 1970s, to just 15.2 in the 1980s! Vandermotten himself also says that employment and population disparities 'have not radically changed between 1960 and 1990'. And Salvatori speaks of 'the progressive formation of more stable and structured districts'.

The authors of these chapters also offer many reasons for this stability. Some of these reasons are specific to particular countries. Thus Fonseca and Cavaco talk about the industrial investment in Portugal by northern European firms which has reduced the need to emigrate to obtain manual employment, and they stress the 'pluri-activity' of farm households in central and northern Portugal which allows such households to survive by obtaining income from factory employment and tourism as well as from agriculture. Salvatori describes the 'continuity of town/country relations in the Third Italy', which allows economic growth to occur without 'territorial restructuring'. Similar, Dieleman and Jobse explain that one of the reasons for a stabilization of the population of the Randstad in the 1980s was the sudden change of government land-use planning policy, which now favoured urban renewal in the cities where previously it had favoured large-scale decentralization from the cities.

Part of the explanation for the stability of the population system seems to lie in the decrease in gross inter-regional migration rates. Kemper suggests that high rents and house prices in growth regions such as Munich act as a barrier to in-migration, and that such places have difficulty in recruiting lower-paid public-sector workers. He also reports other research which argues that a reduction in mobility is to be expected: (i) because unemployment rates have increased; (ii) because home-ownership rates (and their related lifestyles) have increased; and (iii) because inter-regional migration is adversely affected by the growth of female employment and hence the increase in dual-career households. And Öberg explains how inter-regional income disparities can, against expectations, help to keep inter-regional migration rates at a low level (by permitting the survival of low-productivity firms in low-income regions and restricting the growth of high-productivity firms in high-income regions).

But the main emphasis in these chapters has been on the general factors that have served to reduce the variability of population growth rates through the reduction of net migration balances. For example, in the chapters by Vander-motten, Mønnesland and Wood, fiscal and other forms of governmental transfers from high-income regions to low-income regions are given great emphasis. Mønnesland argues that the powerful redistribution mechanisms of Nordic welfare states have helped to maintain population levels in low-density peripheries such as northern Norway, and Wood tells us that 17% of the households in the depressed Northern region of England are dependent on social security support. Another common theme (found again in the chapter by Wood) is the way that population and employment stability was assisted by the counteracting force of service employment growth occurring in regions that were suffering from manufacturing employment decline. And Vandermotten suggests that after 1973 investments 'are more often defensive rationalization processes and thus modify less radically the spatial patterns [of population and employment]'. Finally, several authors join King in emphasizing the role that foreign workers and their families have played in counteracting the population and employment declines of certain cities and regions. In Salvatori's case it is the low birth rate of the Third Italy regions which is being compensated for. King points out that immigrants act as 'gap fillers', and that often they take over empty factories and start new businesses in run-down areas, thus maintaining levels of population and employment.

The impression must not be given that all the material contained in these chapters points in the same direction. In Shuttleworth and Shirlow's chapter, for example, it is shown that, while both highly qualified labour and part-time and unqualified female labour can find employment in their case-study are of western Ireland, those with apprenticeship skills cannot and must seek employment elsewhere (mostly in Dublin or in South-east England). And Mønnesland strongly believes in the importance of personal contacts for high-technology and high-information-content activities, and sees a trend towards a recentralization of production in metropolitan cities.

THE IMPACT OF CHANGES IN THE PRODUCTION SYSTEM ON URBAN AND REGIONAL POPULATION CHANGE

Notwithstanding these exceptions, it seems that the broad consensus of opinion is that fundamental shifts in the production system have not been matched by equivalent shifts in the geography of employment and population totals, or in the overall structure of the settlement system. This encourages us to ask two questions: (i) what are the processes which mediate the relationships between the production system and the urban and regional system, and why have these mediations been so important in the recent period? And (ii) is there something about the very nature of industrial change itself during the last 20 years which helps us explain this mismatch?

The results presented by the contributors to this volume conform to those that emerged from a review of recent literature on industrial change and regional development in western Europe (Fielding 1994). That review produced the following main conclusions:

(i)   The nature of the production system *has* changed in quite fundamental ways since the early 1970s. The main changes, of course, are to be found in how goods and services are produced. New technologies and new labour processes have revolutionized the factory and the office, and have altered the social relations of work in the process. But no less significant are the changes in what is produced, where production takes place and for whom these goods and services are produced. Put together, these changes have resulted in shifts in the sectoral distribution of employment, notably away from manufacturing and towards the producer services and private household services, large establishment workforces have given way to small ones, unemployment, self-employment, female and ethnic-minority employment have all increased, technological innovations have created new jobs for some while undermining the long-established jobs of others, many of the so-called rigidities which protected workers' rights and privileges have disappeared, production has been increasingly oriented towards international markets and towards luxury consumption, while much of the production for mass markets has been conceded to non-European producers.

(ii)   There are good reasons for these changes having failed, for the most part, to work their way through to the distribution of the population or the overall structure of the settlement system. For old industrial areas and marginal rural regions, much of the explanation seems to lie in the automatic fiscal transfer of resources through the state social services and welfare systems. This has maintained household incomes, jobs and services where in other circumstances a downward spiral of economic decline would have set in. For the regions containing new industrial spaces, growth has for the most part been without urbanization. New factories and new offices have been attached to an existing settlement system, typically consisting of an 'urbanized countryside' of small and medium-sized free-standing towns set in a largely rural environment. In part, the explanation for this lies in the socially embedded nature of the development of these industrial districts. This means that the special skills, mentalities and dispositions of the people living there have been major factors explaining the successful development of industries and services. Research on new industrial spaces repeatedly emphasizes the *endogenous* nature of this form of development – since the early 1970s investments related to locationally fixed *physical* resources such as raw materials or harbours (the important exception perhaps is North Sea oil) have had far less effect on the geography of production, while those related to locationally fixed *social* resources have come to have a far greater effect. Hence the population system is spatially stable in comparison with the dynamics of the production system. Finally, the population decline in the late 1960s and 1970s of the largest metropolitan cities has been either significantly arrested or, in many cases, reversed. The accretion of 'global city' financial service functions to these cities has led to an 'embourgeoisement' of their social structures and to a general social polarization, but it has also compensated, in many cases, for their deindustrialization.

This brings us nicely back to where we begin. In Blotevogel's opening chapter he outlines many of the theoretically possible links between the production system and the population system. He allows for the possibility that regional transfer payments might sustain livelihoods and settlements in regions adversely affected by economic restructuring, and he talks about the 'labour-oriented economic growth' which arises from the efforts by capital to seek out how labour costs on the one hand and highly qualified labour on the other. One of the main messages of this book seems to be that these population and employment-stabilizing forces have not just been theoretical possibilities in the recent period. They have been active forces shaping the economic geography of western Europe.

REFERENCES

Fielding, A.J. (1992) Migration and social mobility: South East England as an 'escalator' region, *Regional Studies* 26(1):1–15.
Fielding, A.J. (1993a) *Migration and the Metropolis: Patterns and Processes of Inter-Regional Migration to and from South England*. London: Department of the Environment.
Fielding, A.J. (1993b) Mass migration and economic restructuring, in King, R.L. (ed.), *Mass Migrations in Europe: the Legacy and the Future*. London: Belhaven, pp. 7–18.
Fielding. A.J. (1994) Industrial change and regional development in Western Europe, *Urban Studies*, 31(4/5):679–704.

Index